Foreign Footprints in Ajijic

Decades of Change in a Mexican Village

Burton, Tony, 1953-, author
 Foreign Footprints in Ajijic: Decades of Change in a Mexican Village
/ Tony Burton.

Includes maps, notes, bibliographical references and index.
ISBN 978-1-7770381-9-9 (paperback)

ISBN 978-1-7770381-9-9
First edition 2022
Text and cartography © 2022 by Tony Burton
Cover art by Peter Shandera

Sombrero Books, Box 4, Ladysmith B.C. V9G 1A1, Canada

Foreign Footprints in Ajijic

Decades of Change in a Mexican Village

Tony Burton

SB

SOMBRERO BOOKS, B.C., CANADA

Contents

Part D. 1960s: Free spirits

Part E. 1970s on: Modernizers

Tables

Maps

Introduction

Ajijic, on the northern shore of Lake Chapala, was a tiny, dusty village of farmers and fishermen until the 1940s. Today it is an international retirement haven and one of the most cosmopolitan villages in the world. Why and how did this happen? What and who were the driving forces behind this astonishing transformation?

Details of the founding of the village in the sixteenth century have been documented by several local artists and historians; several colorful public murals in Ajijic depict its early history. Researchers have also recorded the oral history, passed from one generation to the next, an equally important component of the village's cultural heritage.

My focus in *Foreign Footprints* is primarily on the period from 1940 to 1980, and on how foreigners have helped shape the Ajijic we know today. Of course, local residents have played at least as important a role in the village's development. But their story is better left to village historians who have a personal in-depth knowledge of the principal families and their tightly entwined social and political connections.

The first foreigners who settled in Ajijic did so with a mix of intentions. As they got to know the village, some set out to improve it, others wanted it to remain exactly as it was. Few of them had any inkling of just how dramatically their fishing village was about to change.

This book tells the stories of some of these new arrivals. The more colorful characters among them glossed over past indiscretions, rewrote their backstories, and successfully reinvented themselves.

In complete contrast to the town of Chapala—turned into an important tourist destination at the dawn of the twentieth century by enterprising entrepreneurs who added hotels, steamships, fine residences, a yacht club and even a railroad—development in Ajijic began fifty years later and was totally unplanned.

As recently as 1940, there were very few lakefront homes in Ajijic. Traditionally, most village homes were built a block or more back from the lake to avoid the risks of insect-borne diseases and floods. Foreigners, who loved the scenic shoreline, were able to snap up waterfront real estate at rock bottom prices.

Over the years, unregulated expansion filled in the gaps and crept north onto the lower slopes of the hills. Eventually Ajijic sprawled east and west to form an almost continuous amorphous urbanized mass stretching from La Canacinta to San Antonio Tlayacapan.

How fast has Ajijic grown?

Ajijic was only a small village in 1900, when its total population was recorded as 1355 (688 male, 677 female).[1] By way of comparison, San Antonio Tlayacapan then had 582 residents and the town of Chapala 1711, while Jocotepec was much larger, with 4074 inhabitants.

During the twentieth century these four settlements had very different rates of growth (Table 1). In the case of the two largest places, more than twice as many people lived in Jocotepec in 1900 as in Chapala. By the mid-1960s, the population of the two places was about the same. By 2020, Chapala's population had risen to 24,352, some 20% more than Jocotepec.

San Antonio Tlayacapan, the smallest of the four settlements, grew only very slowly until the 1960s. However, between 2000 and 2020 its population more than doubled, from about 3100 to 6616.

Ajijic grew only slowly during the first half of the twentieth century, especially during the uncertain decade of the Mexican Revolution (1910-1920), when its population increased by barely 3%. Since 1940, though, Ajijic has grown very rapidly. The fastest rate of growth was during the 1960s; in that decade its population rose by almost 65% to 5526. The 2020 census recorded Ajijic's population as 11,439.

Even though, during the twentieth century, Ajijic did not grow as rapidly as Chapala, it gradually replaced Chapala as the region's focal point for foreigners. This shift in foreign focus was reflected by the relocation of the Lake Chapala Society and the Lakeside Little Theatre, both originally founded in Chapala, to Ajijic and San Antonio Tlayacapan respectively.

How many foreigners live in Ajijic?

Assessing the number of non-Mexicans living in Ajijic is fraught with difficulty. At the time of the census of 15 May 1930, considered one of the most reliable ever carried out in Mexico, Ajijic had about a dozen different streets and 360 households. Only a single foreigner—Alex von Mauch—was recorded as living in Ajijic, and fewer than 20 villagers had been born outside the state of Jalisco.[2] No foreigners were reported in San Antonio Tlayacapan, which had six named streets and about 100 households.

Unfortunately, changes in census methodology, and the number of residents now holding more than one citizenship, make it impossible to derive comparable figures for more recent years. Even though modern censuses probably under-report the true number of non-Mexicans living in Ajijic, they do offer some clues about the trend in the number of foreign residents.

In 1940 the entire municipality of Chapala, including Ajijic, had 64 foreign-born residents. This number fell to 42 by 1950 before rising to 198 in 1960, when the foreign-born residents included 165 from the US,

	Chapala	San Antonio Tlayacapan	Ajijic	San Juan Cosalá	Jocotepec
1900	1753	582	1355	1178	4074
1910	2132	689	1689	907	4121
1921	3142	625	1741	962	4409
1930	2721	581	1882	778	3851
1940	4217	559	2041	1009	4950
1950	5249	672	2313	1204	6547
1960	7216	939	3357	1841	8017
1970	10520	1533	5526	2692	7736
1980	12626	1694	6857	3673	9173
1990	15664	1900	7572	4898	13143
2000	19311	*3100	*9900	6004	15639
2010	21596	4938	10509	6973	18852
2020	24352	6616	11439	8453	20286

Table 1. Mexican census data. Figures for main settlements, not municipalities. *Estimated figure, see endnote 1.

16 from Canada and 4 from Germany; the remainder came from the UK, France, Spain, Argentina and elsewhere.

By 1970, Chapala municipality had 594 residents born outside Mexico; almost 30% had lived there less than a year, 40% had been there from one to five years, 20% from six to nine years, and 12% a decade or more. Of these 600 or so residents, between 300 and 400 were probably living in Ajijic. In 1976 the number of Canadians resident in Ajijic was sufficient to warrant the "Mens Canadian Club" hosting an "annual mixed social fiesta."[3]

After the 1970s the number of foreign-born residents recorded in the municipality rose rapidly to reach 2492 by 2000 and 5384 by 2020. Of those recorded in 2020, 67% had been born in the US, and about 35% of those over the age of five had lived locally less than five years. Of these recent arrivals, 27% were younger than 60 years old, 40% were in their sixties, 26% in their seventies, and 7% in their eighties or older.

According to the 2020 census, the settlement of Ajijic had a population of 11,439, of whom 2198 had been born outside Mexico, and San Antonio Tlayacapan had a population of 6616, including 1977 born outside Mexico.[4]

Note on monetary values

Monetary values throughout this book are expressed in US dollars, unless otherwise indicated.

Part A

Pre-1940: Adventurers

"[In Chapala] our lone beach of soft sand is being invaded by houris from Guadalajara, society belles from Mexico City, scientists, geologists, mashers, victims of pulmonary complaints, poker sharps, clergymen, and bullfighters with malaria, who seek fresh air. We shall have to retire soon to Ajijic and publish our little paper where life is not so cosmopolitan and so nerve-wearying."
—*The Mexican Herald*, 24 April 1902

1

Ajijic before 1940

Ajijic was founded in 1531, and was the site of the second earliest friary (after Guadalajara) in New Galicia. The original inhabitants of the north shore of Lake Chapala belonged to an indigenous group known as the Coca. According to an early Franciscan account, Brother Martín de Jesús baptized Xitomatl, their local leader, as Andrés Carlos, in San Juan Cutzalán (San Juan Cosalá). They then "moved to a place called Axixique, where there was much water" to found a friary.[1]

Despite its long history, Ajijic entered the nineteenth century with only about 1000 inhabitants, including 35 Spaniards,[2] and this number had risen only slightly, to 1300, by the dawn of the twentieth century. Well into the 1880s, Ajijic was still very much an agricultural community:

> The land is mixed in kind and appearance. Rains are moderate from June to October. Frosts are rare. Corn and beans are cultivated; they are sown in May and harvested in October. Chickpeas, watermelon and cantaloupe are planted in December and harvested in March. Rarely are crops lost through a lack or an excess of water. The fruit trees grown, on a small scale, are: peaches, quince, pomegranates, oranges, mangos and tunas. The commonest wild plants are: chaste tree, morning-glory, guamúchil, mesquite, kidneywood, madrone and sunflower. Skimpy woodlands, comprised of oaks and tepehuaje. Water comes from the lake, and from a permanent spring of little importance.[3]

American novelist Charles Fleming Embree overestimated Ajijic's population when he penned this less-than-flattering description of the village in about 1899:

To this day Ajijic can claim no more than some two thousand souls. It has, even yet, no railroad, no stage; rarely has a vehicle been seen in that primitive place other than the awkward ox cart. Its low, unplastered adobe walls stand close together. The streets are alleys of extreme narrowness wherein there is mud when it rains, dust when it is dry, rocks and swine forever. Nigh every alley twists and turns, is for a block no more than a gutter, for another block a public stable for burros. Yet one may find some better quarters. The plaza, though it is only a bare, brown waste, is wide. The open court before the church, though it too is bare and dirty, with lonely, crumbling walls and pillars about it, yet has in its center a weather beaten cross that speaks of service to the Lord.[4]

Embree, honeymooning in Chapala, was writing at precisely the same time as an outbreak of smallpox was wreaking havoc in Ajijic:

Smallpox, according to an informed colleague, has struck Ajijic in a terrible way.... Despite being a very small village, it is recording three or four deaths each day.[5]

In 1929 screenplay writer Charles Kaufman (1904–1991) lived in Ajijic for several months. He later dedicated his first and only novel—*Fiesta in Manhattan*–to "the good people of Ajijic." In the novel, a wealthy American author takes a shine to Juan Pérez, a musician, and his wife, Elena, and pays for the couple to leave their lakeshore home and move to New York. Only as they adjust to life in a teeming Spanish-speaking section of Manhattan do Juan and Elena become acutely aware of what they have left behind. Kaufman's intimate knowledge of Lake Chapala and local folklore are evident throughout this searching examination of Juan and Elena's motives and thoughts.

Kaufman's trip to Ajijic had totally unexpected and positive longer-term consequences for the village. Four years after leaving Ajijic, Kaufman traveled to Spain with a business friend, Louis Stephens, and was so enthusiastic about Mexico in general—and Ajijic in particular—that Stephens stopped off in Mexico, settled in Mexico City, started a family and, in 1937, acquired holiday property in Ajijic.[6]

In the mid-1940s, Stephens and his wife offered the use of this property to their friend Helen Kirtland, who was looking for a suitable place to take her young children after leaving her husband, Read Goodridge, a rare books dealer in Mexico City. Kirtland took her three young children to Ajijic and never looked back. She employed weavers, founded Ajijic Hand Looms and, through enterprise, good fortune and hard work, built up a very successful business. Had it not been for Kaufman's powers of persuasion, none of this might have happened.

Also visiting Ajijic in the summer of 1929 was Indian yogi and guru Paramahansa Yogananda (1893–1952), founder of the Self-Realization Fellowship. He visited the "Russian" dancers Zara and Holger, then living in Chapala, and rode with them to their mine in Ajijic. This visit, and the beauty of Lake Chapala, led to the iconic photograph of Yogananda standing regally on a sail canoe in the middle of the lake, and inspired his heartfelt "Ode to Lake Chapala," which begins:

> O Chapala!
> Like the flickering flame of Indo-skies,
> Thy moods of limpid waters
> Boisterously play with fitful gleaming storm,
> Or rest on thy shining forehead
> without a ripply wrinkle![7]

Getting to Ajijic

Prior to 1940 it was not that easy to get to Ajijic, though there are occasional reports of day trips by boat from Chapala. For instance, on Saturday 8 November 1919, Juan Seimandi and his wife, Refugio Ramírez, arranged a day trip for several families from Chapala to Ajijic, where they danced and partied until sunset. The flotilla of small boats used for a similar day trip the following year included one for the accompanying orchestra.[8] These boats presumably landed on the beach.

Plans were announced in 1931 to build a pier or jetty in Ajijic.[9] Three years later, Ajijic formed a *Junta de Mejoras Materiales*, a group to oversee public works, with Manuel Urzúa, a schoolteacher, as president and Casimiro Ramírez (owner of the lakefront property later known as Posada Ajijic) as secretary. They immediately set out to build a pier and to rebuild the Chapala–Jocotepec road so that tourists could more easily visit Ajijic.[10]

By the following spring, the pier had been completed, a building had been restored for the use of the municipal comisario, and a large entertainment room had opened to cater to the needs of the many tourists whose arrival was anticipated that summer.[11] How successful these efforts were is unclear.

Improving the road was a much tougher challenge. It would be several years before anyone other than the most intrepid traveler could reach Ajijic. While there were regular hourly buses between Guadalajara and Chapala (1.50 pesos each way) in the 1930s, the earliest bus service connecting Chapala to Ajijic seems not to have begun until the following decade, mainly on account of the deplorable condition of the road. When Californian prison doctor Leo Stanley rode on horseback through Ajijic in October 1937, he commented that "The road, or trail, around the lake was very rough and narrow, and evidently was used only for burros and oxen. It certainly could not have been used for any vehicle." Stanley also noted the many groves of papaya, and mangoes, fields of corn, and small plots of beans and *garbanzas* (chickpeas) that he saw near Ajijic, and remarked on how campesinos were cultivating their plots with animal-drawn wooden ploughs.[12]

Over the years the names of almost all the streets in Ajijic have changed. In the 1930s the current highway had not yet been constructed. The main route through Ajijic ran along Calle Ocampo, called at that time Calle Camino Real, the name still in use today where it passes through La Floresta. Decades ago, different sections of Calle Independencia were known variously as Calle de la Posada, Calle de la Libertad or Calle Juárez. Its continuation east of Morelos (now 16 de Septiembre) was formerly known as Calle de los Placeres (Placers/Pleasures) or Calle Juárez.

North-south streets have also changed name. Colón–Morelos was Calle del Muelle (Pier Street). Going west, Niños Heroes was Calle Las Delicias, Libertad–Obregón was Calle Seis Esquinas (Six Corners), and Calle Río Lerma was Calle de la Ladrillera (Brick Factory). East of Colón-Morelos, Ramón Corona was known as Calle del Templo or Calle Porfirio Díaz.[13] Many of these new names were already in use by the time of the 1930 census, though the usage of the older, traditional names persisted in many quarters into the 1950s.

Ajijic in the 1930s

Guadalajara poet Idella Purnell, whose father had mining interests and owned a home in Ajijic, penned an excellent description of Ajijic in the 1930s to open her short story "The Idols Of San Juan Cosala":

The little Indian village of Ajijic in Mexico nestles between high green mountains and a thin strip of white beach along a lovely lake.

Its name is pronounced Aheeheec, and it sounds more like a hiccup than a name. Ajijic has one long main street, and a few other streets, a tiny town square, or plaza with trees and flowers, and a small high-steepled church, built in 1740.... Around the tiny church cluster the houses of the people, mud brick houses with red tiled roofs. Nearly every house has a patio, or flower garden in the center, and has behind it another garden, in which grow pomegranates, bananas, and trees bearing papayas.... Nearly everyone has birds in cages, and chickens and pigs. The pigs go into the streets and lie grunting in the mud puddles, rooting them up with their snouts.[14]

In Purnell's story a young boy wants to help his grandmother who is gradually losing her sight. He first tries a herbal remedy, with limited success. Then he searches for small carved idols in the lake that he can sell for a few pesos, so that he can take a bus to Guadalajara and buy his grandmother some reading glasses.

Purnell's description of Ajijic could scarcely be more different to the chaotic, eclectic Ajijic of today. But, even if the look and feel of the village have changed over the years, one aspect of Purnell's depiction of village life—a small store with its meager stock of essentials, run by the young boy and his grandmother—is timeless:

They had a grocery store so small and with so few groceries that we would wonder why they called it a store. A dozen paraffin candles, a few pounds of coffee, beans, corn, sugar, ropes, green peppers, soap, onions, ten bottles of soda pop, half a dozen cans of sardines and of hot green peppers, perhaps one egg or two, were for sale.

Twenty years on, a not dissimilar convenience store "sold candy, rock salt, flour, canned goods, rounds of cheese, pickled jalapeños, kerosene for house lamps, dried fish and, occasionally, pyramids of tomatoes, onions and potatoes,"[15] and, even today, Ajijic still has several small convenience stores.

Such local stores have long helped engender a sense of community, as have religion and the village's annual calendar of festivals. One early eye-witness to the celebrations for Día de Guadalupe (12 December) in Ajijic was pioneering feminist and anthropologist Elsie Clews Parsons. While staying in Chapala in 1932, she took a boat to Ajijic to see the performance of a dance called La Conquista (The Conquest). She was taken aback to discover that there were very few other spectators watching the procession and dances, and concluded that the events were held purely for the participants' own pleasure.[16]

A sense of community was also strengthened through marital ties, which were as much about the union of families as about uniting two individuals. An elaborate support system was involved, which extended from *pedidores de novia*—people of confidence, well respected in the community, who would help smooth the path for a formal proposal of marriage—all the way to the much more modest *leñeros,* who supplied all the firewood needed for the improvised kitchens where the wedding meal would be prepared.[17]

Serenading your loved one to express your feelings prior to any attempt to propose had its own rules and costs, as multilingual English diplomat and author Rodney Gallop reported after visiting Ajijic in about 1937. Gallop offered a brief summary of how fishing and farming sustained Ajijic, before reporting one particular courting custom that had made its way to the village:

> From Spain by way of Guadalajara, they have borrowed the custom of *el coloquio en la reja,* the lover's tryst at the barred window. The young man who wishes to honour both the custom and the lady of his choice is required to present himself at the Presidencia Municipal an hour before his tryst and at the cost of a peso to take out a license showing that he is sober. This does not mean that the Mayor thinks he must be drunk to wish to serenade any girl in Ajijic. On the contrary, it is a practical measure aimed at preventing brawls, and the high charge not only brings money into the municipal coffers but increases the value of the compliment to the lady.[18]

2

German land-grabber

One of the largest land owners in the Chapala-Ajijic area at the end of the nineteenth century was a young German businessman, Hans (Juan) Jaacks. Jaacks, who lived in Guadalajara and owned one of the city's largest pharmacies, amassed a massive property portfolio at Lake Chapala, including the Hacienda del Cuije, which extended as far west as Ajijic.

Hans Friedrich Thomas Jaacks was born in Rostok, Germany, on 29 July 1861 and died in Ajijic on 31 October 1896. By the 1890s he had become a prominent Guadalajara businessman and owner of Farmacia Alemana, a pharmacy in the heart of the city's downtown. The drug store supplied equipment and medicines to the Hospital Civil and placed regular front page advertisements in *Heraldo-Seminario*, the major regional newspaper of the time. In June 1895 the paper noted that Jaacks was providing supplies to a photographer contracted to take photos of the city for sale via his store.

Somehow, Jaacks amassed significant personal wealth. He must have been quite the wheeler-dealer since, in addition to the pharmacy, he owned shares in several mines and possessed numerous properties in Chapala, San Antonio Tlayacapan and Ajijic, including the Hacienda del Cuije. This hacienda, while not on the same scale as, for example, La Guaracha near the lake's southeastern corner, had its main buildings a short distance northwest of Chapala. From there it stretched westwards to a mescal mill on the lakeshore and to El Tejaban, Jaack's country home in Ajijic.

Jaacks may well have been the first to plant magueys and produce mescal commercially in Ajijic. It was traditional in those times for mescal mills, or *tabernas* as they were known, to provide refuge for the occasional travelers who found themselves stranded overnight in small villages. The Ajijic *taberna* was later transformed into the Posada Ajijic.

In some respects Jaacks was way ahead of his time. I was totally astounded to learn that he had the earliest telephone line installed between Chapala and Ajijic. An official municipal report in 1896 says that Jaacks had paid for the line, which had been installed but was "not yet in service."[6] Whether or not it ever functioned is unknown; it was to be several decades before Ajijic had any reliable public telephone service.

Relations between Jaacks and the townsfolk of Chapala and Ajijic were never very good. On one occasion, for instance, Jaacks lodged a complaint with the authorities in Chapala that someone had stolen 3000 mangos.[7] Ajijic villagers must have been less than impressed by his ambitious plans for the area, which led him to seek permission from the state governor to dam several local watercourses—including Lemitas, Vicente, Cristina, Canacinta, Cerro Colorado and Alseseca—in order to irrigate his farmland and provide water for his cattle.[8]

Seizing opportunities whenever they arose, Jaacks expanded his land holdings via invasion and encroachment onto neighboring properties, as well as by legitimate purchases from other families, such as the Sainz family. In August 1896 several Chapala agriculturalists complained that Jaacks had blocked long-established tracks they had used "since time immemorial" for moving their cattle to Corralito and Rosa Panal, and had confiscated sixteen cattle and five horses which he claimed were damaging his land. Jaacks was totally unmoved and started his own suit in state court accusing the Chapala mayor of arbitrary decision-making about matters beyond his competence.[9]

Shortly afterwards, Jaacks, still only 35 years of age, was brutally murdered in Ajijic. The murder occurred on the evening of Saturday 31 October 1896. Jaacks had arrived at about 5.00pm from Guadalajara with a small group of friends, including attorney Gregorio González Covarrubias and *Mexican Herald* correspondent Charles E Sponagle. After showing them round his "very beautiful Ajijic home," Jaacks went out briefly to turn on his irrigation system. This system raised water from the lake to a holding tank at the base of the hills, from where it was released on demand to flow between his coffee bushes, banana plants and orange trees back to the lake under gravity.[10]

When Jaacks answered a knock at the door at about 7.15pm, shortly after supper, he was shot dead by three assailants. His alleged last words were, "Gentlemen, they've killed me, I deserved it." The assailants fled, the authorities in Chapala were alerted, an armed posse arrived, and three suspects—José Orendain, Florencio Martínez (alias El Frentón) and Guillermo Zaragoza (aka Guadalajara)—were apprehended later that same evening.[11]

Various motives have been suggested for the murder. While it may have been the direct result of Jaack's disputes with the indigenous inhabitants of the area over land and rights of way, some have surmised that it involved a romantic entanglement. Testimony given by Ajijic resident Crisanto Sánchez to the judge in Guadalajara claimed that Orendain had ordered the assassination because Jaacks had abandoned one of his sisters and acquired her father's possessions. For his part, Martínez had a long list of priors and it was public knowledge that he had repeatedly threatened Jaacks, while Zaragoza was implicated because Orendain had been staying with him prior to the murder.

The drama did not end with Jaacks' murder. Jaacks' body was taken to Atequiza and put on a special train to Guadalajara, where members of the German colony paid their respects and a formal autopsy was performed.[12] Jaacks is best remembered today not because he was murdered but because his body was the first to be buried in Guadalajara's new municipal cemetery, the Panteón de Mezquitán. To celebrate its official inauguration on Day of the Dead (All Souls Day) 1896, city officials announced that the first burial in the cemetery would be free of charge. Legend has it that Jaacks' wake was interrupted by someone announcing this special offer. What followed was a mad scramble across the city. As competing undertakers raced to take advantage, Jaacks' body, in a funeral carriage, narrowly beat that of a more humble local being carried shoulder-high across the city to the cemetery gates.[13] Jaacks' body was interred on 2 November 1896; his tomb has become a somewhat macabre tourist attraction.

When all the dust had settled, ownership of his many properties appears to have passed in 1899 to his mother, Doris Vest de Jaacks (as she is known in Mexico).[14] This is somewhat surprising, given that there is no evidence that she ever visited Mexico or conducted any business there. Moreover, while Jaacks' death certificate described him as single, he actually had at least two sons: Juan and José, born to Rosario Covarrubias in about 1892 and 1895 respectively.[15] Rosario and her sons were seemingly deprived of any inheritance, perhaps because she and Jaacks had never married.

Doris Vest de Jaacks died in 1908, to be followed a year later by her husband. Their deaths came only months before the start of the Mexican Revolution, a decade-long period during which landowners' rights were often challenged and many formal documents were destroyed or went missing. The properties and parcels of land owned originally by Jaacks eventually found their way into the hands of various local families. Much of the agricultural land of the Hacienda del Cuije became the basis for the Ejido Chapala, which is still in place today.

According to local artist Dionicio Morales (whose account of Jaacks is based on local oral histories handed down through the generations), Jaacks' estate was eventually divided up by Olimpio Serna Castellanos, aided by document-fixer Leonardo González. González retained El Tejaban (Jaack's country house) for his own use, while Serna Castellanos appears to have taken over the Hacienda del Cuije.[16]

Among those who benefitted (by one means or another) from Jaacks' estate were Sebastian Sainz and his wife, María Dolores Stephenson Zambrano. They bought land in Chapala from Doris Vest de Jaacks in 1902, and may also have acquired some or all of Jaack's landholdings in Ajijic.[17]

The incredibly tangled web of real estate transactions in Ajijic in the early part of the twentieth century would make a worthy thesis topic for anyone with sufficient patience and persistence. Certain names keep reappearing in the land records. Besides Sebastian Sainz and his wife, they include José Efrén Casillas Tapia, Casimiro Ramírez, and the latter's wife, Josefina Jaime Abogado. In the case of the property later known as Casa Pepsi (chapter 12), Casillas Tapia partnered with Jaime Abogado to purchase it from Sebastián Sainz in 1926. Casillas Tapia also apparently gained control of Los Carrizales, an orchard, and other properties.[18] Born in Ajijic (but baptized in Jocotepec), Casillas Tapia (1874–1938) never married and lived his entire life in Ajijic.

Eventually, probably in the early 1920s, Jaacks' orchard in Tempisque and the *taberna* came into the hands of Casimiro Ramírez and his wife, who converted it into an inn, Hacienda El Tlacuache, the forerunner of the Posada Ajijic.

3

Ajijic gold rush

Silver was first reported in Ajijic in 1856 by Antonio Vallín, a resident of Chapala, and several small mines were being exploited by 1868.[1] Another ore vein was found by Lorenzo Gómez, in the presence of Marcelino Guzmán (the then comisario of Ajijic) and other witnesses, in 1875.[2] At least one of these mines belonged to Duncan Cameron (1827–1903), the Scotsman who had moved to Guadalajara in 1867 to oversee the operations of *Libertad*, the first paddle steamer on Lake Chapala. Cameron complained to the municipal authorities in 1878 that the villagers of Ajijic would not allow him access to grazing land to feed the horses he needed to work the mine.[3]

Gold and silver ores are often found in close association in the same mine and numerous new discoveries were reported over the next few decades; by 1885 there were already thirty silver and gold mines in Ajijic.[4] All the mines mentioned in this chapter are believed to have been in the hills above Ajijic, though their precise locations (and in some cases even their names) remain to be determined.

A letter to a newspaper in Guadalajara in 1887 announced that silver-rich placer deposits, thought to be even richer than those in the states of Guanajuato and Zacatecas, had been found near Ajijic. Each week 80–100 marks (640–800 ounces) of silver were being extracted and sold, mainly to a mint in Guadalajara.[5] This silver was probably from the (unnamed) Ajijic mine registered by Pascual García.

Table 2 (combining information from multiple sources)[6] shows the main gold and silver mines reported for the Ajijic area prior to the 1920s. On a massive map of Jalisco drawn up for the 1893 Chicago Exhibition, Ajijic was the only place in the Guadalajara district named for gold and silver.[7]

	Mine name / location	Associated person or company
1856	?	Antonio Vallín / Duncan Cameron?
1875	?	Lorenzo Gómez / Duncan Cameron?
1887	? (multiple)	Pascual García?
	Cerro Pochotoe (Pitayito)	Timoteo Aldana / Wenceslao Valadés
1888	La Trinidad	Feliciano Hernández
1895	?	Unknown
1898	?	Unknown (Querétaro)
1904	Refugio	Felix Vargas
1904	La Magdalena, Cerro Colorado	George P. Docker
1904	?	Compañia Chapala y Anexas S.A.
1905	La Esperanza	Feliciano Estrada
1906	?	Chapala Gold Company
1906	Tepehuaje silver mine	Compañia Mineria Quien Sabe
1906	La Trinidad (loma de Los Vueltos), Refugio (loma de San Miguel), Tempisque?	Compañia Mineria Quien Sabe
1907	Santa Lucía, Santa María	Toribio L. Arroya et al
1907	?	Butler's Chapala Mines
1907	Cerro Loma Ancha	Compañia Mineria Quien Sabe
1908	El Refugio, El Oro, Santo Domingo	Compañia Mineria Quien Sabe
1909	El Cacique, La Proveedora, San Carlos, Santo Domingo, Viola, El Refugio	Compañia Mineria Quien Sabe
1909	La Guadalupe	Timoteo Aldana et al
1909	Larig (aka Agirrag)	Francisco Giral y Franci
1909	El Señor de la Misericordia	José R. Benítez
1909	San Pedro	George A. Hutchins
1911	La Soledad?	Sabino Aguilar
1911	La Providencia	Salvador Brihuego
1911	Planeta, Estrella de Oro, La Guadalupe	Aurelio González Hermosillo / Victor Hunton
1925	El Señor de la Misericordia	Zara Alexeyewa

Table 2. Mining concessions in the Ajijic area.

New discoveries were coming all the time. In 1895, *The Daily Herald* of Brownsville, Texas, reported that "rich gold placer deposits have been discovered near Lake Chapala." *The Mexican Herald* reported in 1898 that "a Queretaro man" has a mine in Ajijic which yields silver ore and gold.

By 1904 the gold rush was attracting the attention of larger players, including Compañia Chapala y Anexas SA (Later called Compañia Minera de Ajijic), which sought the concession for copper and gold on 5 hectares in Ajijic. This is the earliest mention of a corporation in relation to Ajijic mines.

Among the others invested in mining at this time was the wealthy entrepreneur Arturo del Toro, owner of a luxurious mansion in Chapala, and the "principal owner in one of the abandoned Spanish gold mines of Jalisco."[8] Del Toro was an interesting character who subsequently helped establish (in Sonora) Mexico's first quickie divorce system for US citizens.[9]

In 1906 the Chapala Gold Company was incorporated by M Mc-Carty and G B Wright in Phoenix, Arizona, with a working capital of $100,000.[10]

The Quien Sabe Mining Company

However, by far the most prominent single company in the Ajijic gold rush was the Quien Sabe Mining Company (Compañia Mineria Quien Sabe), established in Guadalajara in 1906.[11] The principals of the company were two Texas businessmen—P E Blalack (president) and C H Maris (secretary)—and two Guadalajara residents: Leopold Walkup and Walter Wheeler (general manager), the son-in-law of English architect George E King, who designed Casa Braniff and Villa Tlalocan in Chapala.

The Quien Sabe Mining Company purchased the Tepehuaje silver mine in Ajijic from Aurelio Cosio for $10,000. The mine, once worked by the Orendain family of Guadalajara, was estimated by a Mexico City mining engineer to have at least 5000 tons of ore, expected to yield an average revenue of $35 a ton. The company planned to install a concentrating plant and had already claimed a further twenty concessions surrounding the mine. These included two existing gold and silver mines: La Trinidad (on the Los Vueltos hill) and La Refugio (on the San Miguel hill). The claims also appear to include the Tempisque mine. In 1907 the company asked for four additional concessions, all east of the Cantera arroyo on Cerro Loma Ancha.

When Italian traveler Adolfo Dollero passed through the area at about this time, he concluded that the gold and silver mines in Ajijic "judging by what has been discovered in them up to now... are not very rich."[12]

Initial plans to concentrate the ores were abandoned when the company decided in 1907 to treat its ores by direct cyaniding, following tests made by the Mexican Gold and Silver Recovery Company in Mexico City. The company had a ten-stamp mill,[13] and planned to use steel tanks in their cyanide annex.[14] Subsequent reports suggest it was several years before the annex was built.

Over the next twelve months the Quien Sabe Mining Company applied for numerous additional gold and silver concessions, including a 5-hectare area, a 15-hectare claim, a 9-hectare site called La Refugio, 8 hectares at Santo Domingo, a 6-hectare extension of La Trinidad, and a 2-hectare site known as El Oro. In 1909 it was awarded concessions for 4 hectares at El Cacique and a 5-hectare extension of La Proveedora (assumed to one of its existing properties).

The Quien Sabe Mining Company had its first big strike in 1909, when it struck a ninety-centimeter (three-foot) wide vein that yielded 212 grams of gold and 300 grams of silver a ton.[15] The company had already built a modern reduction plant to concentrate the ore, and planned to take the concentrates by boat from Ajijic to Ocotlán, and onward to smelters via the Mexican Central Railway.

The discovery prompted a rash of applications for further concessions, totaling 34 hectares, including properties known as San Carlos, Viola, El Refugio and Santo Domingo, as well as extensions of La Proveedora.

In August 1909 it was unexpectedly announced that the company's president, Patrick E Blalack, having made multi-million-dollar profits from land deals in Brownsville, had decided that the mines were not sufficiently profitable. *The Mexican Herald* reported that all work had ceased and that Blalack wanted to sell the mines and their modern reduction plant.[16]

Blalack and his partner, C H Maris, were bought out by two Guadalajara residents: Dr George E Purnell and Juan R Figueroa.[17] Purnell (1863–1961) had started a dental practice in the city in the 1890s, joined the Zapopan Gold Mining Company in 1904, and become President of the Guadalajara Banking Company in 1905. He owned a small house in Ajijic. His daughter—poet and novelist Idella Purnell—later became close friends with Zara (La Rusa).[18]

The new owners, it was reported, "will install a cyanide annex at the plant, which now consists of ten-stamp concentrators and amalgamating plates."[19] The use of cyanide on this scale may have been responsible for the bare red hillside scar near Rancho del Oro that is still so visible today. The company held 130 mining concessions at that time. The Tepehuana (Tepehuaje?) workings alone were estimated to hold more than 12 million tons of milling ore, expected to be worth, on average, 40 pesos ($20) a ton.[20]

This is the last we hear of the Quien Sabe Mining Company. The unrest of the Mexican Revolution presumably put paid to plans to develop the mines. After the Revolution, Purnell and his daughter became actively involved in mines elsewhere in Jalisco.

As shown in Table 2, several smaller operations and speculators also acquired mining concessions in Ajijic. Among them were Aurelio González Hermosillo, the owner of the Villa Montecarlo in Chapala, in partnership with his neighbor Victor Hunton, an English miner who lived in Villa Virginia.[21]

During the Revolution, many of the mining concessions expired, including Tepehuaje and Señor de la Misericordia, both in 1917.[22] Tepehuaje was the first mine that the Quien Sabe Mining Company had bought in 1906. The Señor de la Misericordia mine, formerly owned by José R. Benítez, was acquired in 1925 by Zara Alexeyewa (La Rusa).

One curiosity related to the Ajijic gold rush is that the earliest short story in English related to Ajijic is about the impacts of gold mining on the village inhabitants. The story is set in 1918, "the year of the plague," when "a group of Americans came to the Mexican village of Ajijic to mine gold in the mountains a bare two kilometers away." The protagonist is a young doctor who accompanied the miners and dedicated himself to treating, as best he could, the villagers who fell sick. As the epidemic raged around him, the doctor continued trying to help the local people before being gradually pulled into their world of intrigue, sorcery, and witchcraft.

The author, William Standish Stone, was a frequent traveler to Mexico. His connection to Ajijic was probably via meeting nine-fingered violinist John Langley in Tahiti in the 1930s. Langley later owned a lakefront home in Ajijic.

4

Zara "La Rusa"

Of all the extraordinary foreigners to make Ajijic their home in the past century, none can match the legendary Zara, or La Rusa as she was known in the village. From her precocious teenage years as a singer and actor to her brief career as an international ballet star, and from gold miner to strident environment activist and protector of the lake—it seems impossible that any one person could encompass so many varied lives. Yet La Rusa did all this and more. She first visited Chapala in 1924, moved to Ajijic—with her "brother" and mother—in about 1939, and died in the village fifty years later.

But just who was La Rusa? For starters, she was a biographer's worst nightmare because she used some twenty different names during her lifetime and regularly reinvented her past. Given her vivid imagination and love of fairy tales, interviews with her were akin to catching a fluttering whisper or a ray of sunlight. Even the autobiographical parts of her book, *Quilocho and the Dancing Stars*, are a mix of fact and fantasy.

The book claims that she was born in Russia as the daughter of Prince Alexei Pavlovitch. The truth is that Eleanore Saenger (her birth name) was born in Brooklyn, New York, on 11 August 1896, the only child of Oscar Saenger (1868–1929), a professional singer and voice coach, and Charlotte Welles Saenger (1865–1949), a prominent organist.[1]

Zara (her preferred name in Mexico) grew up with all the trappings of wealth. She was an entitled New Yorker, spoiled from childhood by a doting father who gave her whatever she wanted even though it eventually led to financial ruin.[2] After taking ballet, singing and acting lessons, she made her professional stage debut in 1915 using the name Khyva St Albans. A few months later, she played Juliet—to mixed reviews—in a production of *Romeo and Juliet* financed by her father at the 44th Street Theatre.[3]

The following April, Zara was on the cover of *The New York Dramatic Mirror* before touring with a repertory company which played in several US cities.[4] Newspapers were unsure what to make of her. While the *Buffalo Courier* sniped that "another thing you might do with a million is make your daughter a Broadway star without the necessity for long years of hard work in the chorus...", the *Owensboro Messenger* envied her lifestyle, describing how the actress "Travels with a maid and companion in attendance and two cars at her disposal. She has the most wonderful wardrobe... valued at $25,000."[5]

In 1918, Zara appeared on Broadway as the acting-dancing lead in *The Awakening,* a show bankrolled by Zara's father to the estimated tune of $43,000 (equivalent to about $750,000 today). Critics were merciless, with one calling Zara "a young actress whose ambitions are higher than her abilities seem to warrant." Even so, Zara bought her way back onto the cover of the *New York Dramatic Mirror* for the second time within a year.[6]

Two years later, Zara left New York to pursue her dreams in Europe and South America. This trip was to last more than three years, with her mother (now calling herself Nayan Saenger) accompanying her for much of the time. Zara rented the Garrick Theatre in London in November 1921 for several performances of *The Painted Laugh*, her adaptation of a play by Leonid Andreyev.[7] Following a critical drubbing, Zara and her mother skipped town, leaving a trail of debts in their wake. Scotland Yard looked for Zara but the paparazzi found her first, holed up at a fashionable hotel in Paris.[8] This was when Zara decided to end her acting career and reinvent herself as a ballet star.

Holger Mehnen

In this new life, Zara met Danish dancer Holger Karl Emil Mehnen, who was to become her dance partner, "brother," and life-long soul mate. Mehnen, born in Copenhagen in 1897, studied ballet at the Royal Danish ballet school, appeared in at least two films, and made his debut as a dancer at age 17 as Arlequin in the ballet *Carnival*. His performance was favorably compared in the press to the legendary Russian dancer Nijinsky.[9] In 1920, Mehnen joined the famous Ballets Suédois (Swedish Ballet), founded in Paris by Swedish millionaire Rolf de Maré, a friend of Michael Fokine, with whom Zara had taken ballet classes. Mehnen became one of the company's principal dancers and performed in numerous Ballets Suédois shows in cities across Europe.[10]

In *Quilocho*, Zara writes that Holger was in Vienna when an old friend, Ernst Walt, told him he had seen Zara perform and thought she would be the perfect dance partner for him. Holger met Zara for himself when the ballet troupe moved to Berlin. For her part, Zara later claimed that she met Holger shortly after a clairvoyant had predicted she would meet a young Russian dancer with whom she would become famous and cross the ocean many times.[11]

When the couple began performing as "Russian dancers," Mehnen helped fulfill the prophecy by Russianizing his name to Holger Alexeyev Mehner, the name later used on his Mexican death certificate.

Dancing through Europe and South America

Zara and Holger quickly realized they shared similar ideals. Their slight (two-inch) height difference made them ideal dancing partners and they proceeded to pirouette their way across Europe, performing two original ballets—*The Red Terror* and *The Black Swan and the Lily*—in Germany, Austria, Hungary, Bulgaria, Italy and Spain, before catching a steamer from Lisbon in Portugal to South America.[12]

After performing in Rio de Janeiro, Brazil, where *O Pais* billed them as "the most famous dancers in the world," they crossed the Andes to Chile, from where, in the words of *Quilocho*, "the young artists triumphed all up the coast, finally arriving at Bogota." In reality, as a letter from Zara reveals, the young couple was in a perilous financial situation:

> Owing to passport difficulties and unexpected expenses we are tortured with the possibility of not having sufficient funds to reach our destination. Indeed we have not enough unless the Consul in the next port helps us.[13]

From Bogotá the dancers traveled to Costa Rica, where Holger was temporarily laid low with cholera, and Cuba.[14] Zara finally set foot on US soil again, for the first time in three years, when the two young artists landed in New Orleans in March 1924.

Mexico City, Guadalajara and Chapala

The couple was on the move again within months, scheduled to perform in Mexico City in July. That show never happened; Zara lamented that people she trusted had failed to keep their word.[15] Even so, after visiting the pyramids of Teotihuacan, Zara realized that Mexico really appealed to her:

> There is a certain fascination in the surrounding hills, in the movements of the vanished Aztec splendor, and on arriving at the summit, after mounting the steep sides of the Pyramid to the Sun, my soul flung upward in an almost pagan worship of him.... Perhaps in this coming season when the Sun God smiles more steadily upon the land Fortune will prove less fleeting.[16]

From Mexico City the dancers (accompanied by Zara's mother) made their way to Guadalajara, with plans to perform at the Degollado Theater in January 1925. The local daily built up the excitement by describing their success in Europe and South America, and praising their dancing:

> The young Russian dancer [Zara] has a strong physical resemblance to Asta Nielsen, the popular movie star; she has great flexibility, a marvelous artistic intuition and great power of expression. Holger Mehner is an extraordinary interpreter of the most beautiful musical poems of the Russian masters by means of his artistic dancing.[17]

While they prepared for their performance, Zara and Holger lived at Villa Reynera, a delightful lakeshore villa in Chapala.[18] It was love at first sight when Zara saw Lake Chapala: she had found her forever home. The vacation they took at Villa Reynera after their Degollado ballet was a productive time for Zara. She recalled, much later in life, how one particular moonlit night at the villa in 1925 gave her the idea for a new ballet, *Princess of the Moon,* which she composed the following day. Not long afterwards, she wrote *Nauollin,* a second ballet inspired by Chapala. Neither ballet was performed in public until more than fifty years later.[19]

When American artist Everett Gee Jackson and his friend Lowelito Houser rented a house in Chapala in 1925, they thought the only other non-Mexicans in the village were "the two Russians who lived in the house with the bats." Jackson had a memorable encounter with Zara:

> I set up my easel at one end of that stretch of road because the place was for me mysterious and magical.... I heard a sound like thunder behind me. But it was not thunder. It was that Russian woman riding at full gallop on a dark horse, and she was coming right at me. For-

tunately she made her horse swerve just as she reached my position. She knocked my easel over but missed me.... She never slowed down, but kept galloping at full speed down the road.[20]

Early in 1925, following a tip from an American mentalist, Zara decided to invest in several local gold mines. Within months, she was writing dejectedly to friends that an unscrupulous individual had cheated Holger and her out of their rightful treasure.[21] She was, at least initially, philosophical about the loss: "Treasure hunting, as you know, is playing with life and death, but after all, life is a game."[22] Despite this initial setback, the dancers continued to own, and try to work, gold mines in Ajijic for several decades. These exploits are the subject of the next chapter.

Always looking for an opportunity to perform, but seeking near-total control, Zara thought a movie company might be interested in filming their search for treasure. She sketched out a possible storyline and enlisted the help of poet Idella Purnell to show their photos to:

> any good picture company... as they would naturally want to see what we look like, since we are going to take the principal parts. Also they would have to understand that the development of the story and choice of scenes is subject to our approval."[23]

The movie idea never came to anything.

Zara's mother, Nayan (as she called herself), was also enthralled by Mexico. She found Guadalajara "wondrously beautiful" and loved Chapala:

> I know of no place in the States where one gets that feeling of remoteness, away from the world and the stress and the turmoil. The water is very full of iron and agrees with me and I'm drinking about a quart of goat's milk each day, and eating quantities of mangoes for which I have conceived a great fondness. They are very plentiful.[24]

Even a bad fall, down the steps of Villa Reynera, which necessitated two weeks bed rest failed to dampen her enthusiasm:

> We have a charming villa, a very nice Indian maid, and a boy for the horses, to carry water [and] do all kinds of errands. It is ravishingly beautiful, always cool and quiet. The lake and mountains are magnificent and one never tires of watching the changing colors.... I have

never been anywhere else where the stars were so brilliant as they are here on a clear night—I'm deeply in love with the place.[25]

Zara and Holger also spent their time at Lake Chapala rehearsing for their American debut performance at the Metropolitan Opera House in New York on 16 February 1926. *The New York Times* review the next day, headlined "Two Foreign Dancers in American Debut," conveniently overlooked the minor detail that Zara was a native New Yorker.

The furore that broke out when Zara's identity was revealed did not stop the Philadelphia Grand Opera Company from asking "The Russian Dancers" to lead its corps de ballet. The dancers accepted a multi-year contract, and directed productions of *Otello* in March 1927 and *Carmen* the following month.

Their performance in Carmen was their last involvement with the Philadelphia Grand Opera Company. Between the second and third acts, Zara stormed on stage and launched into an impassioned tirade, railing against the startled audience that they were "inattentive, had failed to appreciate her hard and artistic efforts and were generally unworthy of their ancestors."[26]

Self-Realization

In the early 1920s, Zara's father, Oscar, had become a follower of the Indian yogi and guru Paramahansa Yogananda, who established the Self-Realization Fellowship, which taught that true self enlightenment came not from financial success but from meditation and internal happiness. Zara and Holger also joined the movement, and proclaimed that it "has been to us a fountain of life in the desert of modern materialistic civilization."[27]

The Saengers invited Swami Yogananda to use an apartment in their New York brownstone. When Oscar died of cancer in 1929, his estate barely covered his debts. After the Swami performed the funeral rites at the family home, Zara invited him to join them when they all left New York at the end of May to take a much-needed vacation in Chapala.

The Swami stopped off in Mexico City to meet President Emilio Portes Gil and then joined Holger, Zara and her mother in Chapala. Zara and Holger took him on a horseback ride along the lake and to their gold mine in Ajijic, and also arranged a boat trip to Tizapán el Alto on the lake's southern shore. This is when the iconic photograph of the Swami on a broad-sailed boat in the middle of the lake, was taken.[28]

In honor of their illustrious guest, Zara arranged two ballet performances in the Degollado Theater in June.[29] As in January 1925, the musical accompaniment was provided by the Guadalajara Symphony Orchestra, conducted on this occasion by J Trinidad Tovar. That November, Zara arranged another ballet presentation at the Degollado, stressing that it was the last chance to see the famous dancers in action before they left to perform again in Europe.[30]

Zara and Holger toured French provincial theaters in 1930–31 before being joined by Zara's mother in Italy in the spring of 1931. By this time, the Saenger family finances were a complete shambles. They tried, unsuccessfully, to persuade the Swami to repay a loan. Then, to make matters worse, the tenant renting their heavily mortgaged New York brownstone committed suicide leaving the rent unpaid.[31] Still in Italy, they could not even afford to ship their scenery and costumes back home.

As Holger descended into a world of cards, drink and hypnotism, Zara decided that they should put ballet to one side and return to Mexico to try their luck with the gold mine "which they had so strangely acquired on their first tour."[32] They returned to North America in July 1932, and probably returned to live at Villa Reynera while working the gold mine, the spoils of which may have funded their performances in Europe in 1934.

From Chapala to Ajijic

By 1936 they were again back in Chapala, preparing for another ballet performance at the Degollado. This performance, on Sunday 31 May, was well below their usual standard. What the audience had no way of knowing was that Holger had been injured only two days previously while getting into a car; the car had moved unexpectedly and trapped him against a lamp-post.[33] He chose to perform despite the injury, not knowing that it would be the last time he and Zara would ever dance together.

Holger's injuries were so severe that he gradually lost the use of his legs. He spent his final years having to be cared for by Zara, who (in 1940) bought the lakefront property in Ajijic formerly owned by Alex von Mauch. Both Zara and Holger lived the remainder of their lives there.[34] The property was later subdivided; Zara's former house is now numbered Independencia 26.

Holger, several years shy of his fiftieth birthday, died in a nursing home in Guadalajara on 10 August 1944 and was buried in Ajijic cemetery.[35]

After Holger's passing, Zara was grief-stricken but still had to look after her mother, who endured several years of dementia prior to dying in 1949.[36] She was interred next to Holger.

Following the loss of her soul-mate, Zara wrote *Quilocho and the Dancing Stars* to record their story for posterity. She financed its publication in the early 1970s after receiving an unexpected windfall from a land claim in Pennsylvania.[37]

Zara's adventures with gold mining, her positive contributions to Ajijic as an environmental activist, and the eccentricities which led to her becoming a beloved village character are described in later chapters.

5

Zara's gold mine

During her first visit to Guadalajara, Zara became friends with Idella Purnell, the daughter of George Purnell, the American dentist and mining investor. Idella was working at the Los Angeles Public Library in summer 1925, when she received a letter from Chapala in which Zara admitted that a disastrous mining venture had cost her financially.[1] Zara did not know, apparently, that Idella's father had previously owned several mines in Ajijic.

In a lengthy letter to a different friend, Zara explained the misadventures that had ruined her first attempt to purchase a mining concession.[2] Based on the visions of a mentalist,[3] Zara had somehow persuaded others to join her in investing in gold concessions, only to discover that the concessions had already expired, or were about to expire. Despite this initial setback, Zara persevered. Her mother reported to a friend in New York at the end of July 1925 that Zara was attending to various matters "in connection with the gold mine she has secured."[4]

According to one source, Zara and Holger accepted a one-third share in three mines—La Guadalupe, Buena Vista and La Misericordia, all believed to be located in the hills above Rancho del Oro (Gold Ranch) in Ajijic—in 1925 in exchange for their time and investigation. A further one-third share was acquired by Harold N May of New York City for an investment of $1000, and the final third was taken by Zara's parents for a similar amount.[5]

Several decades later, Zara told sociologist Francisco Talavera that she had first worked the mine in 1926, when it produced two kilos of gold a week, with general miners receiving 30 pesos ($14) a month, pickmen (*barreteros*) 45 pesos, mechanics 60 pesos and the administrator 150 pesos ($71) plus housing.[6] She and Holger showed their mine to Swami Paramahansa Yogananda when he visited in summer 1929. A photo of the Swami on horseback on "Ajijic Mine Mountain" appeared in *East–West*, the magazine of his Self-Realization movement.

In between European trips, Zara and Holger were still working their mine (or mines) in the mid-1930s, when there was another mini gold rush in Ajijic. Neill James, who first arrived in Ajijic a decade later, explained in *Dust on My Heart* that "Almost overnight practically everyone in the villages abandoned his work on his small farm and commenced to search for gold.... Corn mills were transformed into gold mills." This led to a shortage of female labor because all the housewives had to grind their own corn. Fishermen abandoned their nets and boats to look for gold. Food became scarce; murders and assassinations were rife.[7]

According to the account given in *Quilocho*, Zara and Holger arrived back in Guadalajara from one of their dancing trips to discover that their mine was being worked, without permission, by a shady lawyer and his accomplices, who claimed that their cooperative held the mining rights.[8]

In the 1930s, Zara and Holger again lived at Villa Reynera in Chapala, a lengthy ride from their mine in Ajijic. In addition to their mine, one of several in the hills above Rancho del Oro, Zara also owned a mill—located beside the lake at the foot of Flores Magón street—where the ore was crushed and concentrated.

In an unpublished manuscript, Neill James reported how she became accustomed to seeing:

> The two handsome dancers on horseback, the girl clad in red Bavarian riding costume, flowing sleeves, wearing ballet slippers and a sombrero astride Tony her black horse, were an exotic sight as they galloped down the Camino Real carrying gold dust in saddle bags to Chapala.[9]

The pages of *Quilocho* describe various nefarious characters and their multiple attempts to swindle Zara and Holger out of the mine, and to steal what little gold was produced. Zara regained control of the mine with the support of the American consulate in Guadalajara, the backing of the state government, and assistance from the local military chief, a General Mange. Mange told Zara that he had previously helped another "young foreign señorita" when her father had fallen ill and she had to manage the mine on his behalf, indicating (somewhat surprisingly) that Zara was not the first female mine operator in Jalisco.

Despite the General's help, Zara's success was short-lived. Her opponents infiltrated her workforce, disrupted production and threatened violent retaliation. Even her trusted mine manager—Enrique (Quilocho) Retolaza—who had sided with Zara from the start and become a family friend and confidante, was unable to prevent the inevitable. According to Zara's book, one fateful day, she was kidnapped and held to ransom by three local bandits: La Guayava; El Ferrel and El Tadallo.[10] Holger, Quilocho and the local federales managed to rescue Zara from the mountains above Ajijic, though she was injured in the escape. Contemporary newspapers offer no evidence for this kidnapping (though that is not unusual) and only the most tenuous support for any of the tale. If events unfolded as described, they probably did so in the early 1930s.

The only fragmentary references in *El Informador* to the mines in Ajijic date from this period. In 1934 the paper mentioned that mining cooperatives were being encouraged and that Ajijic had mining potential.[11] A few months later, it named the SCL Minera de Ajijic on a lengthy list of cooperatives that had been established in Jalisco. Within weeks, a judge in Guadalajara ruled that the file relating to a dispute between J Jesús Arévalo and others, and a lower court decision relating to their ownership of mining concessions in Ajijic, had to be referred to the federal Supreme Court.[12] In August that year, J Jesús Márquez was shot and wounded in Ajijic by Manuel del Río, an engineer working one of the local gold mines.[13] Whether or not any of these concessions included the mine or mines owned by Zara is yet to be determined.

For better or worse, the Ajijic gold and silver veins did not turn out to be anywhere near as rich as originally hoped, and few of the speculators made any return on their investment. Zara claimed to reporter Ruth Netherton in the 1970s that "the gold ran out. Low grade ore of about three grams is the usual find now with pockets up to 35 grams—not profitable mining."[14]

Correspondence between Zara and the federal Agriculture and Development Secretariat between 1938 and 1941 shows that Zara was still determined to make her mine pay. She requested permission to install two sedimentation tanks for water coming from an ore enrichment plant, in an orchard on land formerly owned by Alex von Mauch, and also built a house next to the gold mill she owned on the lakeshore at the foot of Calle Flores Magón.[15]

When Zara finally relinquished her mine is unknown. But Enrique Retolaza continued to pursue mining opportunities in Ajijic. In 1939, for example, he bought 770 square meters of property in Ajijic from a company called Minerales de Chapala, SA, which had, in turn, acquired it only three years earlier from Juventino Aceves. Retolaza bought another Ajijic mining concession—"La Sorpresa"—in 1941 and immediately asked for a federal water concession for an ore enrichment plant.[16] A map of La Sorpresa, located above Rancho del Oro, names the adjacent concessions as Cortés, Aurelia, Mi Lucha and El Oro.

Despite suggestions to the contrary, no evidence has surfaced that Retolaza bought these properties (or any others) on Zara's behalf. In fact, in 1955 he bought property from Zara herself. Zara sold Enrique Retolaza 1331.35 square meters of land on 15 March 1955.[17] This land was still held by Retolaza at the time of his death, along with several other properties he had acquired. After his death (in about 1966) and in accordance with his will, his estate was divided between Concepción Retolaza de Gómez (his sister) and Zara.

6

Austrian lakefront orchard

It was foretold in the cards. Alex von Mauch left his lakefront home in Ajijic, visited a local *brujo* (witch), paid a few cents for a potion and then caught the bus to Guadalajara where he checked in to a hotel, penned a note to Leonore, his wife of only a few months, and swallowed the witch's brew intent on passing quickly into the next world. He was only partially successful. Hotel staff found him and rushed him to the Hospital Civil, where the doctors expressed confidence that he would make a full recovery.

Hans Alexander von Mauch was one of the first foreigners to settle in Ajijic after the Mexican Revolution had started and the first world war had run its course. Born into an aristocratic family in Stuttgart, Germany, on 15 November 1879, von Mauch was an Austrian citizen, according to the registry of foreign persons in Guadalajara in 1932.[1] He was the second son of Eugenie de Bary and Baron Hugo Friedrich Wilhelm von Mauch. Alex became a highly proficient cellist before he eventually inherited the baronetcy, by then only a name, with no tangible assets to speak of.

The passenger manifest of the *SS Patricio de Satrústegui*, which sailed into New York harbor from Barcelona on 17 October 1920, lists Alex's last permanent residence as Mexico City, suggesting that he must have first settled in Mexico immediately after the first world war.

The earliest record of Alex in Guadalajara is when he performed in a chamber music concert at the city's Museo del Estado on 9 December 1922. The concert, organized by violinist Tula Meyer (who became a close friend), included works by Schumann, Haydn and Schubert.[2] Two months later, on 16 February 1923, Alex played in a concert at the

Degollado Theater in Guadalajara as a member of Tula Meyer's Henrique Meyer chamber music group (named after her father), which shared the stage with the Guadalajara Symphony Orchestra at a benefit event to aid the needy widows and orphans of the Ruhr region in Germany. Alex and Tula Meyer both played solos during this performance. A review lauded Alex as "indisputably a cellist of great merit." Alex and his piano accompanist were accorded four curtain calls.[3]

In July 1923, Alex left Mexico, with the intention of living permanently in the US. Alex sailed from Manzanillo on the *Newport* and told immigration officials in San Francisco that he was bringing $1000 into the country and planned to live in Los Angeles.

Despite his initial intention, Alex did not stay long in the US. Instead, he returned to Mexico and purchased a rural property in Tlaquepaque. He added to his property portfolio in January 1928 by buying two lakefront properties in Ajijic from American mining engineer William Carlstorm Strohbach junior. Strohbach had acquired them from Enrique Cuesta Gallardo only a few months earlier.[4] When Alex applied to the Secretaria de Agricultura y Fomento in Mexico City for a permit to use lake water to irrigate the land, his application was initially rejected for lack of proof of ownership.[5]

The two Ajijic properties totaled almost 9500 square meters in area. Bounded to the west by Calle Tempisque (renamed Calle Pedro Moreno in the 1940s), they extended from Calle Juárez (now Calle Independencia) to the lake. Two of Alex's fellow musicians in the Henrique Meyer group—viola-player Justino Camacho Vega and violinist Tula Meyer—later owned the lakefront property immediately to the west. Having acquired his Ajijic properties, Alex tried to rent out his Tlaquepaque orchard or exchange it for additional property in Ajijic.[6]

According to the 1930 census, taken on 15 May, Alex was the one and only foreigner then living in Ajijic. Despite the attractions of the village, Alex still had itchy feet, and later that year tried to sell his Ajijic land holdings so that he could return to Europe.[7] They either failed to sell, or Alex once again changed his mind. He took up beekeeping and placed numerous advertisements in 1931 and 1932 hoping to generate income by selling his own honey, which was for sale, among other places, in stores in Chapala, Colima and Guadalajara.

By 1932, Alex had made numerous improvements to his Ajijic property, including the addition of a three-room casita, two kitchens, and various additional rooms, as well as a well and irrigation pump. When registering the completion of the work, for tax purposes, Alex estimated that renting out the property might bring in between three and five pesos a month![8]

Alex next tried to boost his income by offering part of his Ajijic property for holiday lets or as a destination for day trips or honeymooning couples. When that enterprise failed, Alex (in 1934) put his Ajijic *huerta* (orchard)—complete with several homes, two kitchens, a garage and irrigation pumps—on the market again, claiming he wanted to return to Europe. He also listed a second property, planted with papayas, which had 130 meters of lakefront.[9]

Barely a year later, and seemingly out of nowhere, Alex got married. His bride was 40-year-old Leonore (Eleanor) Mason-Armstrong, a UK-born visual artist who had studied in France, Germany and Italy, prior to running an arts school in Pasadena, California. The couple married in Ajijic on 15 July 1935, with Olimpio Serna, Adrian Flores, Mateo Pineda and Esmenigildo Lázaro as witnesses. According to the marriage certificate, Leonore had been in Mexico less than six months. A prominent announcement in a Guadalajara daily told the world that they had married and would "receive visitors in their huerta in Ajijic."[10]

What little is known about Alex von Mauch's life prior to Mexico comes from US press reports of this marriage. Alex, whose mother came from French nobility, was born into an "old aristocratic Austrian family, whose members, holding large estates in Austria, Hungary and Bohemia, had served the state either as officers in the armed forces or in the diplomatic service."[11]

Alex had served in the Austrian army, and was a graduate of the Frankfurt Conservatory of Music and of the College of Agriculture in Stuttgart. He was "a cellist of note," who had performed as a guest artist in concerts with the Los Angeles Philharmonic orchestra. He had lived for several years in southern California and was "well known in Los Angeles, Hollywood, Pasadena, and San Diego society circles."

Alex had an additional family connection to Mexico. His sister (Elisabeth Johanna Leonie Julie Theodora Von Mauch) was the first wife of Baron Heinrich Rüdt von Collenberg, who was appointed German ambassador to Mexico in 1933. Two years later, the same year Alex married, Von Collenberg co-founded the "German national community in Mexico." He returned to Europe in 1942 when Mexico broke off diplomatic relations with the Greater German Reich.

American author Neill James, who never met Alex, later wrote that the gossip in the village when she arrived in the mid-1940s was that Alex von Mauch's marriage had been arranged by correspondence, because he was anxious to procure a rich wife and continue the family line. Each partner mistakenly believed they were marrying into money. Only after they were married did the truth emerge.[12]

Despite owning valuable property, Alex and his wife were clearly not well off. Within days of their marriage, they placed numerous adverts in *El Informador* offering honey and other items, including orange marmalade, for sale.[13]

Alex, frustrated in business and insecure in love, became increasingly desperate and despondent. In November, only four months after marrying Leonore, he attempted to take his own life in Room 503 of Hotel Fenix in Guadalajara. He was found, comatose, by hotel staff, who rushed him by Red Cross ambulance to the Hospital Civil. Alex left a final note, addressed to the German consul, indicating that he did not wish to live any longer, and that his wife had nothing to do with his actions. He then took a heavy dose of Veronal (barbital). Doctors expected him to recover, but Alex never regained consciousness, and his life slipped away four days later on 25 November 1935.[14] Alex died intestate; Eleanor, now widowed, inherited all his land and possessions in Ajijic. The following year she tried to rent out the main property—an orchard with buildings—and sell off the bee-keeping equipment.[15]

After losing her husband, Eleanor divided her time between Mexico and her old haunts in Pasadena. In 1937 she took part, costumed as a giant butterfly, on a Roses of Romance float in the Pasadena New Year's Day parade. Romance must certainly have been in the air, since later that year Eleanor remarried in Guadalajara; her new husband, Leif Clausen, was a Danish artist and writer based in New York.[16]

A few months later, Eleanor placed a series of small adverts in *El Informador* announcing that the Huerta Alex Mauch was for sale.[17] The property was eventually acquired, in 1940, by actress and ballerina Zara (La Rusa) Alexeyewa, whose home it would become for close to fifty years.

Part B

1940s: Trailblazers

"Many foreigners who come to Ajijic are misfits elsewhere, and there
is a tendency among them to lead unorthodox lives here."
—Neill James, 1946

7

Ajijic in the 1940s

Local community life in Ajijic in the 1940s continued to be centered on religious festivals associated with festival days and the eternal cycle of life. The village was divided into five barrios, a system of community spatial organization that engendered a spirit of neighborhood and of friendly competition and cooperation. The five barrios (see map) were Tecoluta (later known as Guadalupe), San Miguel, Santo Santiago, San Sebastián (also known as Barrio del Ojo del Agua de la Reina) and San Gaspar.[1] According to sociologist Francisco Talavera, the barrio system was already losing significance by the 1970s, though its use—with the addition of a sixth barrio, San José, for the much newer area east of Calle Revolución—persists to this day.

The first foreigners

By 1940 a handful of pioneering foreigners had found their way to Ajijic and made it their home. Those living in the village included Zara

Map 1. Barrios of Ajijic

(with her mother and Holger); British author Nigel Millett and his father; British engineer Herbert Johnson and his wife, Georgette; German siblings Paul and Liesel Heuer; and Dr Bernard Lytton-Bernard, an English doctor of dubious reputation, and his new wife, Muriel. Regular visitors to Ajijic included wealthy Mexico City businessman Louis Stephens, who visited occasionally with his wife, Annette Margolis, and their young children; and German-born artist Otto Butterlin, whose Mexican-born brother Ernesto lived year-round in Ajijic.

These pioneers had varied motives for being in Ajijic, but the outbreak of the second world war in Europe prompted many more to cross the Atlantic to Mexico, whether by personal choice or as political refugees displaced from their homelands. When the US entered the war in 1941, Mexico also saw an influx of draft dodgers. In addition, some spouses of serving military opted to live in Mexico, because it enabled their spousal allowances to stretch further than if they remained in the US. Their ranks included two young American artists—Sylvia Fein and Charmin Schlossman—who spent several years in Ajijic in the mid-1940s while their husbands served overseas.

The decision to move to Ajijic was sometimes, at least on the surface, for purely personal reasons. For example, Neill James was recovering from serious injuries when she arrived with companion Madeline Miedema in 1943. A few years later, American fashion designer Helen Kirtland left her husband in Mexico City and came to Ajijic, young children in tow, for a fresh start.

The wealthier incoming foreigners bought land, including lakefront property which was underappreciated by the local residents. Villagers saw the foreshore less as a place to live and more as a communal resource, valuable for drying and mending fishing nets, repairing boats, as a source of water, and as a place to bathe and do laundry. They had traditionally built their homes a block or so back from the beach, avoiding the worst of seasonal insect swarms, such as malarial mosquitos, and obviating the need to contend with the vagaries of changing lake levels and periodic floods.

Such potential drawbacks did not deter the newcomers from buying up the lakefront; they sprayed against the mosquitos and installed retaining walls to protect their property from the lake. The Heuers and Alex von Mauch had purchased rural estates west of the present pier in the 1930s. In about 1940, Herbert and Georgette Johnson bought an extensive swathe of lakefront east of the pier. Within a few years, they were selling building plots to the likes of recently arrived Neill James.

Getting to Ajijic in 1946

Compared to the "very rough and narrow" track reported by Leo Stanley in 1937,[2] the road between Chapala and Ajijic had been improved, at least somewhat, by 1946, when Canadian writer Ross Parmenter drove to Ajijic for a day trip. Parmenter, on the staff of *The New York Times*, was staying with friends in Chapala when they decided to visit Neill James. His account of visiting Ajijic on two consecutive days, first by car and then by boat, paints a fascinating picture of the challenges of traveling to Ajijic at the time, a few months before the publication of James' *Dust on my Heart*.[3]

On the morning of Thursday 21 March 1946, Parmenter and his friends borrowed a friend's 1932 Plymouth fourdoor sedan and set off. The road was smooth gravel until they had driven past the "villas of the wealthier residents" and left Chapala. Then it became much worse than Parmenter had anticipated: "It was dirt all the way and in very poor repair. To minimize the jolts it was necessary to go so slowly that most of the time I had to drive in second gear."

Much as he tried to enjoy the scenery and rural picturesqueness of goats, donkeys, cattle and peasant farmers carrying baskets, the road required his full concentration: "Lord, the going was bumpy! Trying to find the least broken surfaces occupied most of my attention."

A stream had washed out part of the "dirt tracks that comprised the road" at one point to form a narrow gully, four feet deep, "bridged only by two thick planks which were set a car's width apart." As they inched across the planks, Parmenter worried about what the return trip might be like if they had to cross them again at night.

In 1946 the present-day highway had not yet been built. The Camino Real that Parmenter drove along between Chapala and Ajijic traversed San Antonio Tlayacapan (along the street now called Ramón Corona) and entered Ajijic along what is now Calle Constitución. From San Antonio on, "the road had the appearance of a country lane, for it was shaded by gnarled trees that resembled mimosas.... Once in Ajijic the bumps came like bullets from a machine gun. The streets were cobbled."

Parmenter's worst fears about driving at night came true after they had problems starting the car for the return journey. The sun was already going down by the time they left Ajijic. The lights of the Plymouth sedan "dimmed and brightened according to our speed.... The trouble was that the road was so bad I had to go very slowly. It meant we had very little light." Driving through San Antonio proved to be particularly difficult, because "Not being electrified, there were no street lights and one turn looked very much like another."

Just as they made it safely back to Chapala, one of the passengers realized they had accidentally left their favorite hat at Neill James' home. To retrieve the hat, the group returned to Ajijic the following day (22 March), this time by hired boat. The *Colombina* was:

> hardly more than a large row boat with an outboard motor... The hull was trimmed with a broad red line under the gunwales, the interior was bright green, and it was shaded by a flat canvas awning.

The boatman produced some wooden steps and they all clambered aboard. With more time to appreciate his surroundings, Parmenter enjoyed this trip far more than the drive the previous day. The lake was calm and mirror-like.

After recovering the hat from Neill James, the group walked around the village before returning to the pier, which had been rebuilt a year earlier by engineer Ismael Retana.[4]

Parmenter's visit came at a time when more and more Americans (and to a lesser extent other foreigners) were exploring Mexico. Parmenter, though, was not your average tourist. He was an experienced writer with an artist's eye, acute powers of observation, and a near-obsessive attention to detail. He noted, for instance, that:

> nearly all the low houses had corrugated tile roofs. Because of the wide, overhanging eaves, the roofs seemed to slope towards each other as if they wanted to meet over the narrow, cobbled streets. Most of the houses were whitewashed, but some were cream-colored and others showed the brown adobes of which they were built.

He liked the magenta bougainvillea adorning high walls and the "fishing nets tacked for mending to the side of a house." Ajijic plaza, the source of so much civic pride today, was not in a very good state of repair:

> The bandstand, for instance, had railing posts, but no railing; and there was no sign of a roof. There were tiled walks radiating from the stand, but the more important outer walks were still unpaved.

There were cement lamp posts, but they were used only as supports for electric cord that was strung between them with a few exposed bulbs hanging at irregular intervals. And the fountain had a circular stone basin all right, but its source of water, instead of being an ornamental centrepiece, was an ordinary kitchen faucet on one side.

Most of the iron benches were broken and the flower beds were unkempt and forlorn, Indeed, the whole square would have been dusty and dreary had it not been for the trees. The jacarandas were a mass of blue blossoms. And among the pale green foliage of the flat-topped flamboyants were so many red-orange flowers that I could see why they are called "flame trees."

Parmenter found the church steeple impressive and noticed the date 1749 "cut in rough letters" above the main doors. In the interior he noted "a new entrance screen of highly varnished wood," as well as the "the floor of blue and white checked tile" and the ornamental wooden screen, painted white, behind the altar.

Having undertaken his trip to learn *about* Mexico, Parmenter admitted many years later that he had learned far more *from* Mexico, a sentiment still echoed by many visitors to this day.

How many foreigners lived in Ajijic in 1946?

In 1946, Rogelio M Chávez, who had just returned from Ajijic to Santa Fe, New Mexico, told journalist Brian Boru Dunne that the village was a colony of artists and writers with fourteen "white" people.[5] These included two "rich women with palaces or castles... a fascinating Russian ballerina... [and] an Englishman who wears a Persian robe, a hat and motorcycle goggles."

Dunne also reported that there were no door bells, that electricity was limited to three hours daily, starting at sunset, and that most people bathed "au naturel" in the lake. Ordinary mail was delivered occasionally "but air mail gets attention." For music, dancing and drinking, there was always a bus to Chapala. Dunne's article helped convince Santa Fe author John Sinclair to travel to Lake Chapala in December 1946 to write *Death in the Claimshack* (set in New Mexico).

Some idea of the social flavor of Ajijic at about this time comes from German-born artist Renée George, who stayed with a friend in the village in 1947. George, in her mid-twenties, was recovering from a bout of *turista* when she left Guadalajara in early August for Ajijic: "I still managed to drag myself out of Guadalajara and survive the jogging bus trip, flavored with chickens and pulque aroma." What she found on arrival was:

> [a] hideout for authors who have written books on Mexico... and those who are in the act of doing so. Without electric light and plumbing they get the feel of the primitive, and when they get tired of that they can always slosh through the mud to somebody's cocktail party.[6]

In another letter George wrote how "It has been raining quite steadily lately, and a knee-deep river is flowing in front of our door step," and that "A few robberies have been committed lately, and our neighbor was practically paralyzed when she saw a man in a black sarape jump over her wall."

Despite all these challenges, George loved the great sense of freedom she found in Ajijic:

> Don't ever tell anybody you are going to Ajijic, unless of course you are talking to an artist, because you will be classed as demented. Have found no cause here for such prejudiced classification. This is one of the most charming, uninhibited places, where man and beast run around loose, enjoying their life on the shores of the lake.

George's sentiment about a sense of easy-going freedom was echoed by writer and art collector MacKinley Helm when he visited Ajijic at about the same time:

> The small town of Ajijic, five miles up the lake, is the town described in *Village in the Sun*.... Life there is cheap and correspondingly rough; but it's heavenly quiet to loaf by the side of the lake, watch the fishing, take a dip on a warm afternoon, or paddle out in the twilight. You walk up and down the lake shore through the Indian pueblos, exchanging greetings with the friendly inhabitants. "Adios!" they say for both salutation and parting, and "Vaya bien!" to wish you Godspeed. If you don't mind the dust, the place is quite charming.[7]

The number of foreigners increased steadily. By the end of the decade, the transformation of Ajijic from an off-the-beaten-track fishing village to a community with a significant transient population of foreigners was well under way.

John Upton, writing in 1950, emphasized the significance of the annual summer art classes in bringing visitors to Ajijic, though he advised respectable young ladies to hold their parties in the hotel or in private homes:

> Townspeople frown on women who smoke or drink in public. The cantina has no 'table for ladies,' and discourages their attendance— mostly because the showpiece of the establishment is a large, white urinal installed just inside the door.[8]

Zoe Kernick, who helped organize social activities for these summer students, found Ajijic a fascinating, if sometimes infuriating, place to live, which different people saw in very different lights:

> For the pamphlet department, Ajijic is a quaint primitive village, full of fisherfolk; for Neill James... it possesses the placidity of Paradise; for the tourist, it can be sometimes drab, though, if he becomes acquainted with certain of the residents, it can become an exultant drunken town; for the clergy of Guadalajara, an evil village, a place that Sunday parishioners must be warned against in scarlet words; for lovers, flowers trumpet against the patina of night-pink walls, remnants of rainfall glitter in the darkness, and... stately stars travel in ancient and tranquil paths over the lake.[9]

At Kernick's favorite village fiesta, the Blessing of the Animals (Fiesta de San Antonio Abad), held on 17 January each year:

> Every animal in the village, from bulls to pet doves, from pigs to cats to burros, to goats, are bathed and sprayed with perfume. Some of the animals are lovingly painted with color and always they are bowed in great satin pink and red ribbons. The animals are then led under the wall of the church where the priest stands, reading to them an imposing text, and scattering over their sweet heads his liquid dispensation. Things often get a trifle out of hand, as bulls start bellowing, armadillos run away, and spoiled cats climb up the priest's robe.

8

Rustic German Inn

Chapala's transformation at the start of the twentieth century into a major tourist destination had little immediate impact on life in Ajijic. There is, for instance, no evidence that Ajijic had any formal hostelries for visitors until the 1930s. Before that the custom was for travelers who needed overnight accommodation to stay at the local *taberna*. The Ajijic *taberna* was later converted into Posada Ajijic.

The earliest accommodation for tourists in Ajijic was provided by a German brother and sister, Paul and Liesel Heuer. They owned, by 1933, an extensive lakefront property west of Pedro Moreno; Paul's home was at the north-west corner of the lot and Liesel's at the south-east corner. Over the years the siblings, both keen musicians, added several one-room guest cottages on this property, as well as a kitchen and communal dining room.[1] Soon after they first arrived in Ajijic, Paul advertised in *El Informador* that he wanted to buy a piano, provided it cost less than $200.[2]

Little is known about their back story. Paul (Pablo) Rudolf Heuer was born in Hagenohsen, Germany, on 21 September 1893, and his sister was born there the following year. According to Neill James, Liesel was already living in Mexico when Paul decided to leave Germany.[3] She was a writer who occasionally submitted pieces to German-language publications in the US.[4] And their possible motives for moving to Mexico? As German Jews the Hueurs may have decided to leave their homeland before Adolf Hitler gained power in 1933. Perhaps Paul, a rifleman in the first world war before he became a banker in Hamburg, had been caught up in the German banking crisis of 1931?[5] Or it may have been for personal reasons, following the collapse of Paul's marriage to Ilse Wolff Heuer, a classical dance teacher who later emigrated to Australia.

A good description of the Heuers and their humble inn Casa Heuer comes from Barbara Compton's autobiographical novel *To The Isthmus*, a veritable treasure trove of snippets about Ajijic in the first half of 1946. Compton describes Paul as "a tall emaciated figure," who wore a dressing gown most of the day, had huaraches on his feet, and smoked cigars. "By daylight his skin is like deeply tooled leather. He has a gaunt John the Baptist look about him, as if he lived on locusts. When he smiles, one notices several teeth are missing."[6] Liesel, by contrast, was aloof and distant.

The main building of Casa Heuer—built "like a long shack"—had a sunken kitchen. The dining room had "a refectory table running the length of it with a few hard chairs at either side." Bedrooms, with shuttered windows that lacked glass, were lit by hurricane lamps and candles; the bed was "tolerable, even if the pillow seems stuffed with cement."

Home comforts were still absent a few years later when Zoe Kernick described Casa Heuer as "a pension which continues its primitive existence as though electricity and showers had never come to the village."[7]

Over the years, many noteworthy individuals stayed at Casa Heuer, often referred to as Casa Particular (Private Home), presumably because it was an unregistered hostelry at the time. In 1937, Nigel Millett, coauthor of *Village in the Sun* and *House in the Sun*, and his father, Henry, stayed here when they first arrived.

Early in 1942 the multitalented American writer, composer and translator Paul Bowles spent several relaxing weeks at Casa Heuer to recover from jaundice. Bowles later composed the incidental music for the Broadway opening of Tennessee Williams' *The Glass Menagerie*. It was on the success of that show that Williams spent the summer of 1945 in Chapala to work on a new play: *The Poker Night*, later renamed *A Streetcar Named Desire*.

Neill James, when she first arrived in Ajijic in September 1943, also stayed at Casa Heuer for several weeks. At that time the daily rate was 3 pesos for room and board.[8] In *Dust on my Heart*, James describes Don Pablo as "a sparse, tall German whose sandy hair matched his leathery complexion." His sister, Doña Louisa, was "a rather buxom German woman with round face chiseled in a square head, twinkling brown eyes." James was especially taken with Don Pablo's tales of malaria and venomous snakes, black widow spiders and scorpions.[9]

Liesel Heuer was an avid hiker and liked James' company sufficiently to spend three weeks with her "tramping in the mountains looking for wild flowers," a year after James first arrived in Ajijic.[10] James was still far from fully recovered from her serious leg injuries, and the two women took a burro with them to carry James' knapsack (and occasionally James herself) so that she could keep pace with the fast-striding, all-conquering Liesel. Liesel also undertook the multi-day pilgrimage on foot, walking alone, across the mountains to Talpa. James incorporates a noteworthy version of this pilgrimage in *Dust on My Heart*.[11]

Laura Bateman, who arrived in 1952, knew the Heuers and their "tiny shacky inn on the lake's edge." She recalled how Liesel—topless, clad only in shorts—was accustomed to take a midday walk along the beach while local fishermen "hid in the rushes to watch her, convulsed."[12]

At the same time as Tennessee Williams was in Chapala, the remarkable German American psychoanalyst Karen Horney stayed at Casa Heuer for several weeks.[13] Horney, credited with establishing the field of feminist psychology, was editing her next book: *Are You Considering Psychoanalysis?*

The American surrealist painter Sylvia Fein, who lived in Ajijic in the mid-1940s, clearly recalls Rufino Tamayo, one of Mexico's greatest modern artists, lunching at Casa Heuer with a lady friend (presumably his wife, Olga) when passing through Ajijic.[14] The food at Casa Heuer was the best in town at the time. Katie Goodridge Ingram, for one, still hungers after its hearty, wholesome soups and somewhat plain food, with its "aroma of German dill and caraway."[15] She and her family ate there regularly, even if the menu and service were somewhat inconsistent. A brief note in a local newspaper in September 1945 reported that the American consul arrived by boat in Ajijic for a day trip and "improvised a simple banquet in the house of the Heuer siblings."[16]

Visiting attorney Kenesaw M Landis II, a nephew of baseball's first commissioner, thought he was escaping tourists when he stayed at the "isolated Indian fishing village" of Ajijic in April 1946. He was disappointed to find the best rooms already occupied when he arrived. But, after supper, he joined the other guests on the porch. Ajijic did not yet have any street lights and was "a spooky place at night."

Talk turned to the possibility of a revolution, and rumors that a truck carrying tomatoes had disguised a shipment of ammunition to the revolutionaries in Guadalajara. Landis suggested the revolution was imminent and might even begin before morning. Just before dawn the following morning, "bombs started exploding all over town, and tracers filled the sky. [The other guests] checked out early. No one told them it was a fiesta in honor of a local saint."[17] Landis was able to move to a better room.

Falling in love in Ajijic

Barbara Compton, quoted earlier, had left her husband at home in New York when she traveled to Ajijic. At Casa Heuer she met Richard Zdenko Moravec, a chemical engineer and filmmaker, whom she married several years after the death of her husband. The couple co-produced motion pictures together, including *The Story of A Volcano*, a short film about Paricutín Volcano (which first erupted in 1946).

Remarkably, only a few months after Compton and Moravec first met at Casa Heuer, two other guests—novelist Elaine Gottlieb and Elliot Chess—also fell in love there. Their precipitous romantic fling was the basis for Gottlieb's short story, "Passage Through Stars." Gottlieb was already in residence at Casa Heuer when the much older Chess, a playwright and wartime flying ace, arrived. The two hit it off immediately; Chess's magnetism and captivating storytelling held Gottlieb spellbound. Gottlieb returned to New York, and Chess promised to join her there two weeks later. He never made it, and the two never met again, but Gottlieb gave birth to their daughter, Nola, in July 1947.[18]

It was also in 1946 when the charismatic writer and artist Mortimer ("Mort") Carl, no doubt wearing his accustomed bandana, first arrived in Ajijic. During his stay with the Heuers,[19] he met Helen Kirtland, on vacation from Mexico City. When Carl returned the following year, he discovered that Kirtland and her three young children were now living full-time in the village. Kirtland's daughter, Katie Goodridge Ingram— then a young girl—vividly recalls one of Carl's early trips, when he drove down to Ajijic in a giant black Packard and "stayed at the Heuers where he said the mattresses were filled with softballs." Carl regularly invited the family to lunch at the Heuers.[20] Three years after they first met, Carl married Kirtland; together they established the first commercial weaving business in Ajijic.

Clearly, in 1946, there must have been both "writing in the air" and "love in the air" at Casa Heuer!

By the 1950s, two other establishments—the Posada Ajijic and Hotel del General—were out-competing Casa Heuer as the best place to stay in Ajijic. The Posada's restaurant and bar became the village's party central.

The Hotel del General (also known as Quinta Mi Retiro) was Ajijic's earliest spa retreat.

Casa Heuer limped on for a few more years. The lake level fell precipitously low in the mid-1950s, making the lake much less attractive to tourists. When the lake began to recover, following exceptionally heavy rains in 1956, the Heuers tried to woo former clients back, sending them a postcard of fishermen with their nets on the shore with this typewritten note on the back:

> - WONDERLAND: They have here for every trouble their special Gods, who do help them always! Now our dear Lake looks as on the other side! And we are happy and thankful about that: we bathe, swim, drive, row-, sail-, motor- & speed boat as before, eat fine fishyfish out of it, dream over it, let us sing out of it in our worriless sleep & dreams by the silvern waves! Maybe, you can share that once even in '56??[21]

Paul Heuer died in Ajijic on 19 December 1957. After his sister also died, it emerged that neither had left a will, though Paul had repeatedly told his village friends that they wanted their 4500-square-meter property to become a seniors' home for Mexico's German community. A Guadalajara lawyer, Fernando Gallo Lozano, was appointed executor of the estate. According to one account, the property remained vacant until 1969, when the municipal *delegado* for Ajijic, Timoteo Aldana, asked the state governor (Francisco Medina Ascencio) for permission to convert one of the buildings into a washing area, so that villagers could do their laundry there instead of on the beach. Gallo Lozano objected, claiming that the Heuers' descendants in Germany did not approve.[22] Given that neither of the Heuer siblings appear to have left any direct family—Paul's only son had been killed in the second world war—there is little doubt that Gallo Lozano had acted, as later alleged by Aldana, entirely on his own behalf, and had usurped the rights and interests of local villagers.

The property eventually passed into private hands, as did a second lakefront property once owned by Paul Heuer on the west side of Calle Donato Guerra. That property eventually reached the safe hands of the Eager family and is now La Nueva Posada, a particularly appropriate outcome for land that once belonged to Ajijic's first hotelier.

9

English squire's famous garden

A world-traveled and world-weary Englishman named H. B. Thompson built a beautiful home on the shores of Chapala. He is well satisfied with his way of life. He explains, 'no fog, no frost, no snow and it only rains at night.' He disdainfully pointed to a place across the lake known for its afternoon rains.[1]

Herbert and Georgette Johnson were almost certainly the earliest English couple to settle in Ajijic. They arrived in December 1939 and were fixtures of the local community for the next two decades. The Johnsons acquired an extensive lakefront property one block east of the current pier and built a roomy single-story home employing the local architecture style of adobe and tiles. Then, between their house and the lake, they created a stunning garden.

Herbert Braithwaite Johnson, the son of a Cambridge-educated clergyman, was born on 16 August 1877 in Lincolnshire, UK. He left school at 16 and became an electrical engineer.[2] He signed his Ajijic weather log "Dr. H. B. Johnson." Though nothing more is known about his education, the title is certainly not believed to be self-aggrandizement, given that it appears only in his private notebook.[3]

If Neill James is correct that Herbert Johnson had lived eleven years in France before moving to Mexico, then he moved to France, presumably for work, shortly after the death of his mother in 1928.[4] Following his marriage to Georgette Martin Wilkie in London on 2 January 1930, the couple, who had no offspring, made their home in Chinon, France.

In 1939, on the eve of the second world war, the Johnsons wisely decided to leave France and move to Mexico. Herbert (then 61) described himself as a retired engineer when he and Georgette (45) arrived, via the Panama Canal, in Los Angeles in June 1939.

The Johnsons visited Canada and took a trip to Alaska before heading south and crossing the border into Mexico on 5 December 1939. They returned briefly to the US eleven months later, perhaps to purchase items for the house they had built, given that many regular household items were difficult to find at that time in Mexico.

Everyone I've interviewed who knew the Johnsons has remarked that they were polar opposites in terms of their social graces. Herbert acted and spoke like the upper-class, well-educated Englishman that he was; his much younger wife was more brash, with a working-class accent. Gail Eiloart, who lived in Ajijic in 1949–50, believes that the much-respected Herbert Johnson had married beneath him.[5] Herbert and Georgette were the basis for the characters Richard Middleton and his much younger wife, Blanche, in the fictionalized travelogue *A Sudden View*, written by Sybille Bedford after she visited Mexico in 1946–47.

In an unpublished manuscript, Neill James describes Herbert Johnson as a feudal lord whose list of all the foreigners living in Ajijic was divided into two columns: the sane and the crazy. The only sane ones were Johnson himself, Georgette and a couple from Scotland. All the others—including La Rusa, Louisa Heuer, Neill James and Dane Chandos—were crazy. According to James, Herbert would blow a police whistle from the house to summon Georgette ("clad in slacks, a cowbell at her belt") from the beach where she was clearing any large stones. Georgette would answer by ringing her cowbell.[6]

Katie Goodridge Ingram, whose family moved to Ajijic in the mid-1940s, recalls how Georgette would walk onto the terrace at 4.00pm every day, blow a whistle, and call "You-hoo" to her husband, who was usually working in the garden, to come in for tea to the obvious amusement of their Mexican neighbors.[7] As a child, Milagros Sendis loved to visit the Johnsons at about 5.00pm to play with their dachshunds and help feed the fish.[8]

Quinta Johnson (known informally as Casa de los Johnson) had a garden and orchard covering 5000 square meters of prime lakefront. At the south-west corner of their property, Calle Ramón Corona met the lakeshore. From here, Herbert Johnson kept a close eye on activities on the lake, using his binoculars to check on the small boats bringing tourists or ferrying people and goods to and from Chapala.

The Johnsons' elaborate and colorful garden, with its formal lily pond, became famous and was pictured in *Gardens of the World*.[9] It was painted and photographed by prominent artists, and lavished with praise by visitors. A genealogical survey of Johnson's huge extended family lists him as "Keeper of the Sub Tropical Gardens at Ajijic," an engaging, if not entirely accurate, title for his role in Ajijic. Ross Parmenter, who visited in 1946, called the garden "one of the show spots of Ajijic":

> Its central feature was a long, rectangular lily pond that led the eye back to a wall of green vegetation... the pond was geometrically placed in the middle of the lowest level of the garden and its sharply ruled edges were paved with square red tiles.... The trees that rose above the walls outside were... eucalyptus and papayas. Those planted to flank the flower borders were palms. Papyrus grew at the far end of the lily-pond, and, though it was only March, the water flowers were blooming. And the superabundant big-leaved, vegetation within the garden was most un-English. It grew so thickly that the strips of green lawn could only have survived by constant vigilance and everlasting cutting back of encroaching plants. As a final contrast, instead of the usual ladylike colors of herbaceous borders, there was the hoydenish scarlet of masses of cannas.[10]

Herbert Johnson also showed Parmenter his kitchen garden:

> Here, too, we were awed by the abundance of growth. He raised asparagus, Brussels sprouts, carrots, egg plant, lettuce, potatoes, tomatoes, spinach, celery, cucumbers—almost all vegetables, in fact; in addition to melons, pineapples, limes, avocados, mangos, bananas and enormous poinsettias.

> Mr. Johnson said the basis of his success was the efficient irrigation system that he, as an engineer, had been able to install. He also praised the climate. He said it was the most perfect in the world and so equable that he could plant most things any day of the year and grow them with equal success, regardless of their seasons in other countries.

The Johnsons' irrigation system relied on raising water from Lake Chapala. In 1943, Georgette Johnson was granted a federal license to use up to 5760 cubic meters of water a year from Lake Chapala to irrigate their gardens and orchard.[11] A year earlier, she had requested the use of a section of the shoreline federal zone to expand what she called Balneario Ajijic.[12]

Before signing the guest book, Parmenter and his friends were given a tour of the house, with its lime plastered and whitewashed adobe walls. The tiled roof was supported by a framework of *carrizo*. Several separate rooms looked out onto the large verandah. The kitchen, at the back of the building, caught Parmenter's eye:

It was designed for the use of native cooks. In place of an American-type kitchen range, there were small pits sunk in tile shelves along one wall. The pits, Mr. Johnson explained; were filled with charcoal and the dishes were cooked on top of the little fires.

On the roof of the Johnson's sprawling one-story building, a tile-roofed mirador afforded shade while guests enjoyed the sweeping panoramic view across the immense lake to the shoreline beyond.

Ever the practical Englishman, Johnson, who feared being squashed into an undersized coffin when he died, had a local carpenter make him a wooden coffin years in advance of his death. Covered with a bright sarape, it was kept on his front porch.[13] Visitors had no idea they were sitting on his coffin! In actual fact, Johnson was no taller than the average villager: immigration forms record his height as 5'5", an inch taller than his wife.

Having completed his house and gardens, Herbert Johnson used his engineering skills to help others. He oversaw the construction in San Antonio Tlayacapan of a house which became the residence of Peter Lilley, one half of the Dane Chandos pen name responsible for *House in the Sun* and *Village in the Sun*. In addition, Johnson helped Neill James build Quinta Tzintzuntzan, now part of the Lake Chapala Society complex.

The Johnsons were also instrumental in fomenting the nascent artistic community in the village. In December 1944, for instance, they held an exhibition of work by area artists and authors on the terrace of their home. The show included paintings, drawings and watercolors, plus embroidery work by village women, "an art form revived by Ajijic resident Miss Neill James."[14] American artist Sylvia Fein made the original designs for this embroidery as her contribution to one of the first village enterprises that allowed local women and girls to earn some money at home during their spare time.[15]

A month before the art sale, Herbert and Georgette Johnson had attended one of the area's earliest formal art shows, an exhibition at the Villa Montecarlo in Chapala of recent paintings by Edythe Wallach. Other guests at the opening, most of them from Ajijic, included Nigel

Millett and his father, Henry Millett; Mr and Mrs Jack Bennett; Neill James; German-Mexican artist Otto Butterlin and his daughter, Rita; artist Charles Stigel; American poet Witter Bynner; Charlos Halmos and his wife; Pablo García Hernández; and Ann Medalie.[16] Medalie exhibited oil paintings of the garden at Quinta Johnson, and the view from the garden over the lake, in her 1945 solo show in Mexico City.

The Johnsons owned both a refrigerator and a generator, and would always store medicines for other people when needed.[17] Herbert was also the proud owner of one of the first Hi-Fi systems in the village and hosted mini-concerts (*musicales*) for friends to enjoy records from his extensive collection. Katie Goodridge Ingram recalls that he would play composers of a different letter (Bach, Chopin, Dvorak) each time, and that Georgette would serve everyone a glass of Orange Crush prior to the first record. There was a ten-minute conversation break before the second (and final) record of the evening.[18] Invitees to these soirees included Dr and Mrs Sendis, Helen Kirtland, Grace Wilcox, Tula Meyer, Justino Camacho and Giulia Cardinali.[19]

Herbert Johnson took a particular shine to Helen Kirtland and regularly visited her unannounced to share the latest fresh produce from his garden, be it asparagus, Brussel sprouts, avocados, grapefruit, lemons, limes or tangerines.[20]

Neill James and Herbert Johnson enjoyed a healthy rivalry as regards their prowess as gardeners. Johnson's formal gardens were a far cry from the somewhat unkempt tropical foliage that James preferred, but both had hundreds of rose bushes. In the aftermath of Johnson's death on 6 September 1960, James cut blooms from both their gardens "to fashion a blanket of three thousand roses to cover her friend's bier."[21]

With no compelling reason to stay in Ajijic, Georgette returned to the UK, where she died in 1975. Before she left Ajijic, Georgette was persuaded by James that, instead of selling Quinta Johnson and its garden to Helen Kirtland as she had long promised, she should subdivide Quinta Johnson into three distinct parts, each with a section of lakefront.

The western section, which had a guest cottage, was bought by Marian Powell Carpenter (1908–1985) and later owned by Georgette B Simons, and then by Michael Eager. The middle section, owned for many years by Canadians Ruth and Graham Darling, was acquired by the Lake Chapala Society in 2001. The eastern section (with the house, pond and main garden) was sold to Marc Perkins, who was in poor health;

Helen Kirtland helped him remodel the house to better accommodate his needs. When he decided to return to the US in about 1966, Kirtland bought the house, and later added a stable (eventually transformed into an apartment) and converted the garage into two studios.[22] Kirtland finally had her dream home.

The large metal cross on the lakeshore at the end of Calle Nicolas Bravo was originally erected by Herbert Johnson. It is one of the few remaining signs of the Johnsons' long period residing in, and presiding over, the foreign community in Ajijic.

The Johnsons' legacy

In 2019 a photograph album that once belonged to the Johnsons was found by chance at an estate sale in New York State. Among the album's 250 or so photographs are approximately one hundred images of Ajijic.[23] These document the construction of the Johnsons' own house and garden, and depict local scenery, streets, buildings, people and events. As an engineer, Herbert Johnson loved his gadgets, and the superb quality of these photographs, most of them from the 1940s, reflects his technical prowess with a camera. Apart from this album, very few photos are known of Ajijic in the 1940s or earlier.

Destination wedding / A love story

Quinta Johnson was the setting for the marriage in 1949 of a Canadian author and an English nurse. The story of how they met and fell in love is one of the most endearing tales to emerge from my research into the history of Ajijic.

The groom at the ceremony was Harold Walter Masson, a former Mountie who had served in the Royal Canadian Air Force before writing for *Maclean's* magazine. Masson headed south in 1947 looking for sunshine, and two years later landed in Ajijic where he rented the guest bungalow at Quinta Johnson. Meanwhile, on the other side of the Atlantic, Herbert Johnson's 29-year-old niece, nurse Helen Eunice Riggall, was on her way to visit her uncle in Mexico. Johnson drove down to the coast to meet her. But, on their way back to Ajijic, the car went off the road. Helen was badly injured and spent several weeks in a Guadalajara hospital. When Masson accompanied Johnson to visit her one day, he was instantly smitten. They quickly became good friends, and Masson proposed to Helen the day she was discharged.[24]

Guests at their wedding, held in the Quinta Johnson garden on 31 August 1949, included the Langley, Riggall, Masson, Butterlin, Johnson, Bauer and Stephens families, as well as Mrs Grace Wilcox, Miss Neill James and Miss Madeline Miedema.[25] The witnesses to their union were, for the bride, Johnson and Guillermo González Hermosillo (owner of the Villa Montecarlo in Chapala) and, for the groom, German businessman Kurt Weinmann and Peter Lilley, coauthor of the Dane Chandos books.

The Rigall-Masson wedding was not the first marriage between two foreign tourists in Ajijic, and certainly not the last. For example, David Holbrook Kennedy had married Sarah Shearer in Ajijic in 1941, though sadly that union ended in tragedy within months.

The stars were far better aligned for the union of Hal and Helen, who shared their lives together in happiness in Laguna Beach and Hawaii for more than 36 years. The romance of Lake Chapala and the love trap of Ajijic had struck again.

10

Posada Ajijic opens

The early history of the Posada Ajijic is, to put it mildly, murky. At the end of the nineteenth century the site was a mescal *taberna* on the Hacienda del Cuije, owned by Juan Jaacks. As such, it provided occasional refuge for travelers who had to spend the night in Ajijic.

Some of the hacienda land was under agaves and the *taberna* had a mill to grind the agave hearts for mescal. The mill was also used by villagers to grind their nixtamal (lime-soaked corn) for tortilla dough. The mill survived and became a feature of the Posada Ajijic many decades later.

After Jaacks' death, his many properties apparently passed to his mother, Doris Vest de Jaacks.[1] Jaacks' orchard in Tempisque and the *taberna* in Ajijic may then have been owned by Sebastián Sainz before they were acquired, probably in the early 1920s, by Casimiro Ramírez (1886–1971), born in Teocaltiche, and his wife, Josefina Jaime Abogado (1894–1986). Ramírez (aka El Huizachero) and Josefina married in October 1913 and had three children. The Ramírez family renamed the *taberna*, calling it Hacienda El Tlachuache (Opossum).

By all accounts Ramírez continued to produce coffee (for export to Germany) into the 1930s, perhaps in association with José Efren Casillas Tapia, who had taken control of several other properties formerly owned by Jaacks.[2] Casillas, born in Ajijic but baptized in Jocotepec, never married, lived all his life in Ajijic, and died at Ocampo 457 on 2 December 1938.

When English author Nigel Stansbury Millett first arrived in Ajijic in 1937 with his father, Henry, a retired civil servant, they lodged briefly at Casa Heuer before moving to Hacienda El Tlacuache, the lakefront property further east belonging to Casimiro and Josefina Ramírez. Precisely why the Milletts chose Ajijic is unknown, but they arrived in Los Angeles by ship on 29 March 1937 before crossing the border and heading south.

The Milletts fell in love with Hacienda El Tlacuache and persuaded their hosts to change its name to Posada Ajijic and allow them to run it as an inn. While proof is lacking, this may have been as early as 1938. Several rooms and a restaurant-bar were added during their tenure. In addition, according to Toby Smith, a few foreign visitors were allowed to build their own cottages on the property.[3]

The Posada's owners, Casimiro Ramírez and his wife, did not live there; they had their own home further along the same street.[4] They maintained good relations with foreign visitors, and their home was the venue for the wedding on 11 October 1941 of artist David Holbrook Kennedy (1919–1942), who had been commissioned to paint murals in the Chapala thermal baths, and Sarah Shearer, his "petite, blond, affable" girlfriend.[5] This was one of the first of numerous all-American marriages in Ajijic. The Ramírez family home was also where, six years later, one of their daughters, María Elena, married Eduardo X (surname illegible), a 38-year-old artist and writer.[6]

In the early 1940s, Josefina Ramírez and her husband encouraged José Mercado to construct several small handlooms and operate them at the inn. The looms were suitable for weaving table mats, serviettes and similar small items. After Mercado ran into problems and left Ajijic to live in Guadalajara, the looms languished unused in a corner of the inn. These looms were the catalyst for Ajijic Hand Looms (chapter 20), Ajijic's earliest large-scale weaving business, an enterprise later renamed Telares Ajijic.

By 1945 the Posada was proudly advertising a special Sunday lunch prepared by Chef de Cuisine Francisco Valdéz.[7] The multi-course menu consisted of "Hors Douvre Varié, Sopa Confiterola, Spaghetti Napolitano, Pescado Blanco con Salsa Tártara, Pierna de Cerdo en su Jugo, Ensalada, Crema de Chocolate." The cost, including coffee or tea, was just 4 pesos (slightly under a dollar).

Slowly but surely, the Posada Ajijic gained a reputation as the best place to stay or eat when visiting Ajijic. In August 1945, for example, a group of distinguished Tapatíos were all reported to be staying at the Posada. This was only a few days after Irene Halmos had brought a group from Chapala to the Posada for a day-trip.[8]

While managing the inn, Nigel Millett and his companion—fellow Englishman Peter Lilley (1913–1980)—used the nom de plume Dane Chandos to pen *Village in the Sun* (1945) about constructing a house in Mexico, and the vagaries of life in the village at the time. A follow-up book, *House in the Sun* (1949), recounted the adventures of running an inn, though Nigel Millett had died of tuberculosis several years previously, long before publication. Nigel's father, Henry Millett died (in the Posada Ajijic) on 7 June 1947; his death was duly reported by Casimiro Ramírez, with Paul Heuer and Herbert Johnson acting as witnesses.

After the Milletts, the inn was managed for a short time (albeit somewhat haphazardly) by Josefina Ramírez and her son, Dr Casimiro Ramírez Jaime (1921–2018). Neill James later recalled that the daily rate at about this time was five pesos, which was raised to eight pesos when Josefina began to cater for foreign guests.[9] According to author Katie Goodridge Ingram, who grew up in the house across the street from the Posada, the restaurant only survived because they employed a good cook, a local girl named Pilar.[10]

American anthropologist and travel writer Frances Toor summed up the Posada at this time, writing in her brief entry about Ajijic in a national guidebook that "One can also stay there in comfort at the Posada de Ajijic, a modernized hacienda house in a tropical setting."[11]

11

Dane Chandos books

The two entertainingly written Dane Chandos books—*Village in the Sun* and *House in the Sun*—introduced readers to life in Ajijic. Both remain perennial favorites. *Village in the Sun* was first published in the US in 1945. When it was released in the UK three years later, prospective readers were informed that:

> Mr Dane Chandos's European and US upbringing, followed by travels in many countries, left him with a desire to live again in the Mexico where he was born. He built himself a house at Ajijic amid orange, banana and mango trees, and came to love the people and the life.[1]

Several other reviews repeated this assertion that the author was an Englishman who had been born in Mexico. In reality, Dane Chandos was not a real person but a pen name used by two distinct writing duos. The early Dane Chandos books were written by Peter Lilley and Stansbury (Nigel) Millett; after Millett's death, Anthony Stansfeld partnered Lilley for later Dane Chandos works. All three men were English.

Stansbury Girtin Millett, via his mother a direct descendent of King Edward III, was born in London on 23 October 1904.[2] His father, Henry Stansbury Millett, was a barrister and district auditor. The younger Millett studied at Magdalen College, Oxford University, from 1922 to 1927,[3] traveled widely in Europe, and was fluent in several languages. He was teaching at Rugby School in 1929 when his debut avant-garde novel, *Frolic Wind*, sometimes classified as gay fiction, was published under the pseudonym Richard Oke, a name borrowed from an ancestor that Millett adopted for all his solo writing.[4]

Millett's mother died in June 1935. Eighteen months later, Millett and his father fled the UK for Mexico. A month of frantic activity prior to their move began in January 1937 when Millett formally changed his name by deed poll to Nigel Stansbury Girtin Stansbury Millett (sic).[5] The two men then got passports and left the UK, never to return. We will likely never know why they left the UK, or why they chose Ajijic. Did the younger Millett have a nervous breakdown following the death of his mother, or had his behavior or satirical writing been deemed offensive?

When the Milletts reached Ajijic, they lodged first at Casa Heuer before moving to the Hacienda El Tlacuache, the lakefront property belonging to Casimiro and Josefina Ramírez. Not long afterwards, the Milletts began to run the property as an inn and restaurant named Posada Ajijic.

As Neill James explained in a wonderful anecdote, his failing vision led to Mr Millett senior gaining an exalted status in Mexico as "Sir Henry":

> He received a letter addressed to Sr Henry. His eyesight was poor and for a fleeting moment the tall gracious old man thought he saw Sir Henry and was mightily pleased. The story went the rounds.... Later, when he died, the Guadalajara paper published a column about the English Nobleman dead in Ajijic.[6]

The second strand of the pen name Dane Chandos—and its originator—was Peter Lilley. Born James Gilbert Lilley on 25 July 1913 in Tendring, Essex, he was the only child of James Cecil Lilley and Madeline Clare Angus Thomas. Lilley's very wealthy father was a director of Lilley and Skinner, a famous London shoe brand. Lilley attended Stowe School from 1927 to 1932. He captained the school tennis team and remained an avid tennis player throughout his life.[7] He later built a grass court at his home in San Antonio Tlayacapan, one of the earliest tennis courts at Lake Chapala. Lilley, who had not published anything prior to the Dane Chandos books, conjured up the pen name by combining his school nickname—Dane, on account of his blond hair and square, Danish-looking jaw—with Chandos, the name of one of the school's boarding houses.

No evidence has surfaced that places Lilley in Ajijic prior to 1937. When British author Rodney Gallop reviewed *Village in the Sun* in 1948, he described having met two young Englishmen, one of whom was Millett, in Ajijic eleven years earlier.[8] If Gallop's memory is accurate, he visited in 1937, only a few months after Millett arrived, and at a time when Lilley (assuming he was the second young Englishman) would have been only 23 or 24 years old.[9] Unfortunately, Gallop neither described nor identified Millett's partner.

Regardless of precisely when Lilley arrived in Ajijic, the conventional story is that he then rented a boat and cruised the shoreline seeking the best spot to build his house. After choosing San Antonio Tlayacapan, he built a lakeshore home and lived there for 40 years, until shortly before his death in 1980. This story is, however, greatly oversimplified and not supported by the land records.

The land records for the 4261-square-meter property (now Calle de La Paz 69) show that it was originally purchased by Georgette Johnson (wife of Herbert Johnson) as two vacant lots. Johnson paid a total of 500 pesos in March 1944 to Francisco Cabrero García, who had purchased the land only a few months earlier from Casimiro Ramírez. She subsequently submitted a document (undated) showing that a two-bedroom house with studio, living room, bathroom and storeroom had been built there.[10] Her real estate purchase may have been prompted by the receipt of a small inheritance on the death of her father in England in 1942.

Herbert Johnson's meticulous weather records for the period show that he, and his personal rain gauge, moved from Quinta Johnson in Ajijic to San Antonio Tlayacapan in September 1944 and then back to Ajijic again precisely two years later.[11]

It is possible that Lilley contracted Johnson to build the house, and decided that the most expedient way to handle all the paperwork was to use Georgette Johnson (who already owned property in Ajijic) as a *prestanombre* to act on his behalf. Peter Lilley's occupancy of the property probably began in 1946. Not long afterwards, Lilley met English writer Sybille Bedford. In her fictionalized account of traveling in Mexico, Bedford describes how she visited "San Antonio Something" and "the place of el gringocito d'Inglaterra," where:

> Peter showed me over the house he had slowly built with, and sometimes against, the advice offered by Mr. Middleton [Herbert Johnson]. 'The worst thing of it is,' he said, 'that the old boy is generally right.'[12]

If Lilley was resident at Lake Chapala prior to 1945, it is surprising that he was not listed as attending the exhibition of paintings by Edythe Wallach, held at the Villa Montecarlo in Chapala in November 1944.

Nigel Millett and "Sir Harry Millet" (sic) were both there, as were Herbert and Georgette Johnson, Neill James, German-Mexican artist Otto Butterlin and American poet Witter Bynner.[13]

The following month, in a short piece for *El Informador* about the pre-Christmas show of art work at the Johnsons' house, Neill James listed the artists and writers resident in Ajijic at the time. She named Zara, Pablo and Louisa Heuer, Otto Butterlin and Nigel Millett. But the only reference to Peter Lilley is as Millett's collaborator, implying that Lilley was not yet considered a resident.[14] I think it likely that Lilley had only recently arrived in Mexico.

Village in the Sun, a fictionalized month-by-month description of building the house, was first released in the US in 1945. It is an interesting, keenly observed and reflective account of life in Ajijic in the 1940s, full of curious tidbits alongside anecdotes about local customs and superstitions. Advance copies reached Guadalajara at the end of August that year,[15] so clearly the writing must have had its final revision by spring 1945 at the latest, possibly even before the house had been finished.

House in the Sun—the second Dane Chandos book, and supposed sequel to *Village in the Sun*—was first published in 1949. It relates how the author has added extra rooms for guests and taken on the role of amateur hotelier, "held hostage by maddening servants and equally unpredictable and maddening guests."[16] *House in the Sun* became sufficiently popular that artist Frida Kahlo kept a copy in her personal library.[17]

Only a few months after *Village in the Sun* was published, Nigel Millett died of tuberculosis and was laid to rest in Guadalajara.[18] A year later, on 6 June 1947, his father also died and was buried in Ajijic. Josefina Ramirez later arranged for Nigel's remains to be reinterred next to his father's grave in Ajijic cemetery, close to his beloved lake. Nigel's other great love—his little Chihuahua dog, Motzin—was buried in the gardens of the Posada Ajijic; the dog's ghost is still said to haunt the grounds.[19]

Nigel Millett's death several years prior to *House in the Sun* being published has led some readers to insist—despite the strong similarities of style and language—that it must be the product of a different collaboration, where Anthony Stansfeld replaced Nigel Millett as Lilley's writing partner. Stansfeld himself, however, in a letter to the house's current owner, laid no claim to authorship of *House in the Sun*, writing only that he and Lilley had collaborated from 1950 onwards.[20]

American poet Witter Bynner, a long time resident of Chapala, knew all the parties concerned, and was completely convinced that both books were written by Millett and Lilley. Bynner wrote to friends that:

> Nigel's death was bitterly tough on old Sir Harry from whom I had a very sad note. Peter, on the other hand, seems to have borne up trimly and writes that another book is due for almost immediate publication. I judge that he and Nigel had finished it before the latter's death. I wonder if Peter will continue to do so well without his collaborator.[21]

In my view, the majority of *House in the Sun* was written before (not after) *Village in the Sun*. Its subject matter, running a small inn, was precisely what Millett had been doing for some years before his untimely death. Moreover, one short passage in *House in the Sun* refers to the other book as a work in progress:

> In October, it's true, I had contrived to finish *Village in the Sun*. But other work made very slow progress. In its own way running the posada was a full-time job, and, though I was enjoying the new experience, I regretted the days when I couldn't find time to write anything.[22]

One section of *House in the Sun*, however, relates to the activity of Paricutín Volcano in 1946, and must have been written after *Village in the Sun* had already been published.[23]

The two books share many of the same characters, including Candelaria (the cook) and other household help. Some of them stemmed from the authors' imaginations, others were based on real residents or visitors. The line near the start of *House in the Sun* that "An Englishman had built a long, low house fronted by a superb garden, which blazed with color the year round" was a public nod to the Johnsons, perhaps acknowledging their role in building the San Antonio Tlayacapan house. My favorite line in the book, though, comes in a letter written in broken English by Mr Humpel, an elderly German mining engineer who had lived in Mexico for more than 60 years: "I was climaxed to find your virgins reposing on my pumpernickel."[24]

In 1947, less than three weeks after Millett's father died, Anthony Stansfeld visited Peter Lilley in Mexico. While of similar age, it is unclear how or where the two men first met. This timing makes it perfectly conceivable that Stansfeld may have played a part in the final proofreading of *House in the Sun*.

Stansfeld (1913–1998) studied at Oxford University from 1932 to 1938, where he somehow met Millett, who had left the university a decade earlier,[25] before moving permanently to the US in 1950 to become professor of art history at Mercer University in Macon, Georgia. He traveled frequently to Mexico during the 1950s to collaborate with Lilley on later Dane Chandos works, including two travelogues—*Journey in the Sun* and *The Trade Wind Islands*—and a follow-up to *Abbie* (co-written by Lilley and Nigel Millett) titled *Abbie and Arthur*.[26] The two men also wrote two mystery books about the crime-solving exploits of a huarache-wearing Mexican detective—Don Pancho—for which they used the pen name (or more accurately pen name of a pen name) Bruce Buckingham.[27]

Lilley was a long-time resident of San Antonio Tlayacapan, where he was affectionately known as "Don Pedro, el inglés." Despite his poor Spanish, he gained a well-deserved reputation for being a social and community activist. Lilley made a substantial donation to enlarge the local reservoir, and was instrumental in getting street lights installed and bringing electricity into village homes. He also arranged annual Christmas posadas and parties for the village children. In the mid-1950s he helped launch a polio vaccination campaign, throwing his full support behind the annual vaccination program for village children.[28] Some of Lilley's efforts were less successful: when he gave land for a health clinic, the town caciques stole the property for themselves.[29]

Peter Lilley lived in his beautiful House in the Sun in San Antonio Tlayacapan well into the 1970s, before spending his final weeks in his native England, where he died at the London Clinic in Westminster on 17 April 1980. The executors of his estate included Leslie Chater, who, with his wife, Moreen, were long-time friends and subsequently became the new owners of the House in the Sun.[30]

After the Chaters moved in, a chance find in a desk drawer caused Moreen to revive the Dane Chandos brand, long after all three original authors had died. A "scruffy folder" contained a manuscript of recipes "faintly typed and badly eaten by mice."[31] They proved to be Candelaria's original recipes, with notes and anecdotes added by Lilley. Proceeds from *Candelaria's Cookbook*, compiled by Chater and published in 1997, help finance projects benefitting children in San Antonio Tlayacapan.

12

Violinist and the Pepsi House

Interviewed in Ajijic at the age of 96, concert violinist Tula Meyer went out of her way to distinguish herself from Neill James. Both women first settled in Ajijic in the 1940s. But:

> I am not like Neill James... drinking all that herb tea and not eating meat. I'd rather enjoy myself... a couple of glasses of wine now and then... and, maybe, not live as long.[1]

In the event, Meyer—who was born in Tepic, Nayarit, on 2 July 1888 and died in Ajijic in April 1988—lived just as long as James. Both women died only a few weeks shy of turning 100.

Gertrude (Tula) Henriette Meyer was raised in Guadalajara, where she attended the city's International College, became interested in music, and attended meetings of Ateneo Jalisciense, Guadalajara's leading artistic-intellectual society.[2]

Meyer then studied for more than a decade in music conservatories in Switzerland and Germany, before starting her career as a concert violinist. She married German musician Curt Hans Schroeder (known in Mexico as Kurt or Juan Schroeder) in Hamburg in 1920.

After the couple returned to Mexico, Meyer helped put Guadalajara on the classical music map. Meyer and her husband founded the Henrique Meyer chamber music group in 1922 and gave a series of performances in the city. Other members included Justino Camacho Vega (viola) and Salvador Villaseñor (cello), later replaced by Alex von Mauch. They were also wholehearted supporters of the Music Teachers School (Escuela Normal de Música).[3] In 1923, Meyer was appointed artistic director of the Guadalajara Symphony Orchestra, founded four years earlier. Despite her regular solos with this and other symphony orchestras, Mayer's first musical love always remained chamber music, where she could express her individual virtuosity and brilliance.

Over the next several years Meyer established herself as a concert violinist. She often played at fund raisers, including one for the needy widows and orphans of the Ruhr region in Germany (1923); for the widow of Amador Juárez, founding director of the Guadalajara Symphony, in July 1924; and, in 1926, for people in Nayarit who had lost their homes due to severe flooding.[4]

Having been born in Nayarit, this last cause must have been particularly dear to her heart, even though many people assumed Meyer was German, not Mexican.[5] In 1960 this misapprehension resulted in her being named as one of several undesirable foreigners then living in Ajijic. Village leaders and community groups rushed to her defense; their open letter testified not only to her good character but also proclaimed her to be "mexicana ciento por ciento."[6]

In order to further her career, Meyer moved to Mexico City in the 1930s to play first violin in the National Symphony Orchestra and teach at the National Music Conservatory. Being the only female in the symphony orchestra brought its own challenges. After concerts, Meyer's colleagues would repair to the nearest cantina. But cantinas were strictly male-only establishments. Since everyone was dressed alike in black, Meyer donned a wide-brimmed sombrero and pulled it down to hide her face and red hair and entered in the middle of the throng of fellow musicians.[7]

Meyer continued to live and perform in Mexico City well into the 1940s, with occasional trips back to Jalisco to play solos in Guadalajara, or rest and practice in Ajijic, where she owned an "orchard-ranch."[8] In 1951, Meyer bought land in Ajijic from fellow musician Justino Camacho to build a home.[9] The property (Pedro Moreno 75) included her private residence—spacious enough for a grand piano and good acoustics—and a guest cottage, used by Camacho whenever he visited.

Before living in Ajijic, Meyer had lived for a short time in Chapala. This must have been in the early 1930s, since she became accustomed to seeing Zara and Holger ride by each day on the way to their gold mine in Ajijic. (Holger suffered a serious accident in 1936 which paralyzed him from the waist down.) According to Meyer, even before that, "After the mine flooded out, they didn't ride there anymore," which offers an alternative explanation—flooding—to that normally given for why the mine ultimately failed.[10]

In later life Meyer loved to offer recitals for her circle of friends in Ajijic. Milagros Sendis recalls fondly how a loose-knit group of music aficionados would meet regularly to listen to live or recorded music, always dressing up for the occasion. The group included Grace Wilcox and her husband, Herbert and Georgette Johnson, Guilia Cardinali and Laura Bateman. The live concerts were in Meyer's house where Justino Camacho would play the piano to accompany the exquisite sound of Meyer's beloved seventeenth century Paolo Maggini violin.[11]

Sendis also remembers Meyer's impish sense of humor. On one occasion, the local priest bumped into her on the plaza and asked her, "Doña Tula why don't you go to church? I don't pinch!" Her instant response—"precisely because of that"—gave them both a good laugh.

More out of financial necessity than desire, Meyer eventually sold her lovely estate, accepting in part-payment a lot in Rancho del Oro, on the outskirts of Ajijic, where she built a new home and lived out the remainder of her life. According to Sendis, Meyer never really liked living in Rancho del Oro, especially because she did not drive and had to either walk or hitch a ride to run errands or visit friends.

After she moved to Rancho del Oro, Meyer continued to enjoy music and to care for her beloved dogs. Though utterly distraught when her rare and valuable violin was stolen, she never bothered to report the theft. However, when her "two adored pets, a handsome Dalmatian and his companion, a small white dog without a tail and only half a right ear" went missing, she immediately offered a substantial reward.[12]

Meyer's property at Pedro Moreno 75 in Ajijic subsequently became commonly known as the Pepsi House (Casa Pepsi). The 11,600-square-meter property, between Calle Independencia and the lakeshore, has an interesting and checkered history. Early owners (before Meyer) of the property included Sebastian Sainz (who perhaps bought it from the estate of Juan Jaacks), who sold it to José Casillas Tapia and Josefina Jaime de Ramírez. Several owners later, the various parts that make up the current property were pieced together in a series of transactions (between 1939 and 1961) by Aurora de Anda de Padilla and her husband, Salvador Padilla y Andrete. The final purchase was the part that belonged to Meyer. The Padillas, who already owned a house down the street, coveted this last piece and pressured Meyer into selling.[13]

Salvador Padilla held the Pepsi Cola concession for western Mexico. The family's wealth meant that money was no object. They tore down Meyer's former home to build a luxurious new residence, stables and a glass dome-covered swimming pool. Soon after completion, the Pepsi House appeared in *Guadalajara en Verano*, a popular cross-cultural romance movie.

When President Gustavo Díaz Ordaz and his wife were hosted by the Padillas at the Pepsi House for several days in May 1967, they enjoyed a relaxed stroll through Ajijic, visiting shops and chatting to villagers.[14]

The Padillas sold the property to Turistica Rivera de Ajijic SA de CV in August 1981.[15] It then passed through some less than reputable hands, including those of Flavio Romero de Velasco, the hardline Jalisco State governor from 1977 to 1983, who was arrested in 1998 for his alleged ties to drug cartels. Romero de Velasco sold the Pepsi House in the mid-1990s to Jorge Alejandro Abrego Reyna (aka Gabriel Pineda Castro) who remodeled it as the Hotel Rincón de Don Gustavo and passed it on to Rigoberto Gaxiola Medina. Abrego Reyna was subsequently convicted of money laundering for Gaxiola Medina, a convicted narcotrafficker of the Sinaloa cartel.[16]

The house (and stables) play more than a bit part in Jan Dunlap's novel *Dilemma*, a tale of international romance, drugs and intrigue loosely based on true events in Ajijic. Natalie, a beautiful young DEA agent, is sent to Mexico to investigate an alleged king-pin in the drugs world who lives in Casa Pepsi. Her life soon becomes far more complicated than she bargained for.

13

Neill James the writer

Author and world explorer Neill James (1895–1994), who lived in Ajijic for more than half a century, is revered today for her many positive contributions to the community that adopted her. James, the self-styled "Petticoat Vagabond," came to Ajijic in 1943—to recuperate from multiple surgeries—and never left.

Nellie Neill James was born in Gore Springs, Mississippi on 3 January 1895. Her family was far from wealthy; her father worked as a laborer in a saw mill. James was the sixth of nine children, and lost both parents before she was out of her teens.[1] She graduated as a stenographer from the Industrial Institute and College for the Education of White Girls (later Mississippi State College for Women, now Mississippi University for Women) in 1918 and then worked as a secretary at the US War Department.[2]

James traveled widely over the next few years, taking jobs in New Orleans and St. Petersburg, and writing for newspapers in Costa Rica and New Zealand, before working at the Institute of Pacific Relations in Hawaii. Her four months traveling around the world in 1934, from Shanghai to Manchuria and Vladivostok, and via the Trans-Siberian railroad to Moscow, Finland and Denmark, were the basis for her first travel book, *Petticoat Vagabond: Up and Down the World*, published in 1937. James then set off solo for Lapland; her adventures there provided the material for *Petticoat Vagabond: Among the Nomads* (1939) and for a successful juvenile fiction work titled *White Reindeer*. Her next book, *Petticoat Vagabond in Ainu Land: Up and Down Eastern Asia*, was published just as she set out to explore Mexico. These trips to far-flung places by a woman of limited means have led to speculation that James was undertaking espionage assignments for one or more US government agencies.[3]

James married Harold C Campbell (whose surname, coincidentally, was the same as her father's middle name) in New York in 1937.[4] After Harold was drafted into the US Army in February 1942, there was nothing to hold James back from her next adventure. Her early travels in Mexico and her time living with the indigenous Otomi people are entertainingly recounted, in rich detail in *Dust on my Heart*, a book completed only after two serious accidents and lengthy spells in a Mexico City hospital. First, she broke her collarbone and crushed her thighbone after slipping while descending from the summit of Popocatepetl Volcano. Then, in April 1943, still hobbling about on a cane, she visited Paricutín Volcano, where the hut she stayed in collapsed, smashing her hip and breaking a leg.

Finally discharged from hospital in August 1943, James traveled to Ajijic with a friend, Madeline Miedema.[5] A new chapter was about to begin; her multiple calamities had drawn her to Lake Chapala and her forever home.

The two women, James still on crutches, caught a train to Guadalajara in early September; they spent a few days in the city, and then took a bus to Chapala and a small boat to Ajijic.[6] They quickly realized that Ajijic was a very small village, with no electricity system and only a single telephone, located in the post office. The final two chapters of *Dust on My Heart* describe James' first impressions of Ajijic, of adjusting to life there, and of learning to appreciate all the idiosyncracies of living in a remote pueblo.

James and Miedema stayed initially at Casa Heuer, the informal lakefront posada run by German émigré siblings Paul (Pablo) and Liesel (Louisa) Heuer.[7] James was immediately taken with Don Pablo's tales of malaria, venomous snakes, black widow spiders and scorpions, and became good friends with Louisa, perhaps seeing in her some of the same rugged determination to prove that women were more than equal to men in any task of endurance. According to an account written many years after the fact,

> While still using a cane, Neill went on a walking tour with Louisa Heuer. They took a boat across the lake and wandered up valleys and hillsides for a month, sleeping wherever they could lay their blankets.[8]

This trip took the two women to Tamazula and Mazamitla. Louisa Heuer was always prepared to hike long distances; James' second-hand version of Heuer's pilgrimage to Talpa is among the more compelling passages in *Dust on My Heart*. James herself visited Talpa in March 1948.[9]

After four months at Casa Heuer, James rented a small village home near the plaza.[10] The owner, according to *Dust on My Heart*, was an elderly Mexican woman, "a very religious and rich old spinster."[11] Notes made by James in 1947 describe how she "made a garden, fenced it in, painted the house inside and outside, put in window boxes, wired it for electricity, at least extended the wiring, cemented down a tile floor laid on sand," only for her landlady to raise the rent from 20 to 25 and later 30 pesos.

Twenty years later, James offered a somewhat different account, in which the owner was a man:

> I felt experienced enough to accept the offer of an adobe casa whose occupant was forced to go to the city to replenish his exchequer. The rent was 20 pesos (about $4) a month. The casa was just off the plaza which was an excellent location... Shortly after I established myself in the adobe casa, our only millionaire (he had found a buried treasure) was kidnapped in broad daylight and held for ransom... For two years I lived happily in my simple adobe casa... added a brick floor, mended the roof, made a garden, learned to draw water from the well... All went well until the patron became homesick for Ajijic.[12]

She gave yet a third version in 1977, when interviewed about the cost of living in Ajijic in the 1940s, in which the owners of the house—rented for $5 a month (or about 27 pesos)—were a German couple who spent less than 2 pesos a day for food, supplies and maid.[13]

After a few years in Ajijic, and determined to avoid having any further unexpected rent increases, James decided to build her own house, an undertaking described in the next chapter.[14]

From the moment she set foot in Ajijic, James was keen to improve the welfare of the village children. The cook James hired, Apolonia Márquez de Flores, was a widow with three surviving children—Elpidia (aged 15), Josefina (11) and Xavier (9).[15] Tragically, she had lost an older son, Delfino, to malaria in April 1936, when he was only nine.[16] James took a shine to Apolonia's children, especially Josefina, and this prompted her to write a children's book about Mexico.[17]

James wrote excitedly to her sister, Jane, in September 1944:

> Have swell material for a dyed-in-the-wool Mexican background book for children, written about my village, with all the humor, color, strange customs and daily life packed in. I have my heroine selected. She is my little protégé, Josefina. When I first saw her she was clad in rags. She is bright as a new peso. I have bought her several dresses, and a pair of sandals.[18]

In the same letter, James described how she and other villagers had raised 8000 pesos ($1500) to buy a new clock for the church, though things did not work out quite as planned:

> No one in our village can afford a clock, so a village clock seemed a good idea. We had the Ceremony of the Priest blessing the clock, and started it hopefully. It ran one day, then was "discompuesto" [*descompuesto*, broken], and we went back to telling time by the shadows on the ground.

When she wrote that letter, James was still finalizing the manuscript of *Dust on My Heart*:

> Am about a third through with the second revision of my travel book and eager to get it finished and start my fiction.... If my project works out and produces enough to live on while I write, I will be happy. And if it makes profit enough for me to begin paying off my debts, Hurrah![19]

This reference to debts makes it abundantly clear that James had limited financial resources and was anxious to generate some income.

James garnered valuable advance publicity for *Dust on My Heart* by writing about Ajijic for *Modern Mexico*, the monthly magazine of the Mexican Chamber of Commerce in New York. Readers were informed that James had regained her health at Lake Chapala:

> I came to Ajijic to recuperate. When I landed I was so crippled I had to be helped out of the boat. Daily I worked to regain my health. I sunbathed, swam in Lake Chapala, and exercised. Now I walk upright and without crutch or cane.[20]

Life in Ajijic had its dangers: scorpions, snakes, spiders and mosquitos all play a part in the final chapters of *Dust on My Heart*. James' narrowest escape from death, though, came not at the hands of the local fauna but from arsenic poisoning, after Apolonia unwittingly stirred the frijoles cooking on the stove with a wooden spoon that James had used to mix a lead arsenic mixture for the garden.[21]

Despite the dangers, James had fallen in love with Mexico and with Ajijic. Within two years of arriving, she was quoted as saying:

> I love Mexico! It has all the old world culture of the Occident, the glamour, mystery, and color of the Orient and a very special brand of mañana of its own, more devastating than the legendary lotus in captivating the footloose stranger wandering in the realm.[22]

She based her book title, *Dust on My Heart*, on an old adage: "When once the dust of Mexico has settled upon your heart, you cannot then find peace in any other land."[23]

As she acclimatized to Ajijic, James became ever more determined to improve the lives of the villagers. While she wrote that "a man will instinctively better himself if given an opportunity," James focused on helping girls and women.[24] In March 1944, James attempted to interest them in knitting, a project which barely got off the ground because it took too long to produce finished items. In her rudimentary Spanish, James refers to this, in her notebooks, as her "panuoleta" project; *pañoleta* is Spanish for headscarf or shawl. She kept meticulous records (now in the Neill James archive) of all costs (wool, knitting needles, hoops, bus fare to Chapala), of who knitted what, in what colors, and whether or not it sold. A marginal note by one entry also lists recent household purchases: eggs, milk, *ocote* (torch pine, used for starting fires), *carbón* (charcoal), *frijol* (beans) and peaches.

After giving up on knitting, James purchased plain white cotton blouses and towels, and then paid local women to embroider them. Embroidered blouses were displayed with other art and handicrafts at the Johnsons' house in December 1944.[25] In her 1945 article in *Modern Mexico*, James hinted at the challenges of trying to write while simultaneously running a business:

> By way of diversion and to aid the women and girls of this village earn some money, I revived an old embroidery home industry, and put them to making beautifully embroidered but tailored blouses for women. They worked with such enthusiasm and the project grew

so rapidly that now it occupies my entire spare time and encroaches upon my writing time. My job is to direct the project, furnish raw materials and find a market for their produce! Tourists have made my little adobe house a Mecca, and few leave without one or a half-dozen handmade embroidered blouses 'Made in Ajijic.'[26]

The veracity of James' claim to have single-handedly "revived" the art of embroidery in Ajijic is unprovable in the absence of evidence that it was ever a traditional local craft. Many of James' embroidery designs were created by two American artists: Irma Rene Koen, who lived only briefly in Ajijic, and Sylvia Fein, who lived there from 1943–1946. Fein, who showed me photos of a big luau with hula dancing that James organized on the beach in Ajijic, helped market the finished blouses to Mexico City department stores.[27]

Dozens of women participated in the embroidery project, including members of the Campos, Flores, González, García, Ivon, López, Márquez, Pantoja, Pérez, Rochín, Saucedo and Navarro families. It was almost a full-time job to wash the finished blouses before sale. In January 1946, James' cook-housekeeper Apolonia Flores washed as many as 19 blouses a day; at 15 centavos each, this earned her $0.50 on a good day.

The challenge of marketing all this merchandise led James to open Ajijic's first gift shop. One early client, a Mrs Shloss from Des Moines, purchased a hand-embroidered blouse there in 1949.[28] The store sold items made in Ajijic, but its merchandise soon included select handicrafts from elsewhere.

Despite opening a shop, James had mixed feelings about tourism. She acknowledged the tourist potential of Mexico in general, and Ajijic in particular, and, even before the second world war ended, recognized the likelihood of a "surge of tourists southward over the Pan American Highway, by car, by train, boat and airplane." However, fearing that Mexico might be about to be overrun by tourists, James added that "come the end of the war, Mexico will have to erect strong barriers to protect her Paradise."[29]

What was it about Ajijic that James herself found so irresistible? After five years in the village, and shortly after building her own home there, she expressed its appeal:

Perhaps the real charm of the place lies in the people themselves who treat you in a friendly spirit and accept you as you are, or, as you've always imagined yourself, be it a Russian princess, titled Englishman, a baroness, famous psychiatrist, great painter or simple writer. No one checks your story.[30]

This rare insight into her psyche applies equally well to the many foreigners who have given themselves border promotions after choosing to move to Ajijic.

James' travel books were never best-sellers, her writing never made very much money, and *Dust on My Heart* proved to be her final full-length work. Her publishers rejected later submissions, even her children's book about Ajijic. The infrequent trickle of royalties was nowhere near sufficient to live on. One by one her books went out of print. To get copies of *Dust on My Heart* to sell in her store or give as gifts, James had to dip into her limited savings to personally fund small print runs. Given her lack of income, James moved on to other ventures. This short, undated note in her archives is quite revealing:

My books are now out of print. I got into the house building and became enchanted instead of writing another book. One has just so much energy. And I like to do what fascinates me at the time.

Despite not writing any more books, the Petticoat Vagabond certainly capitalized on her earlier life whenever the opportunity presented itself, using all her southern charm to captivate visiting journalists and tourists.

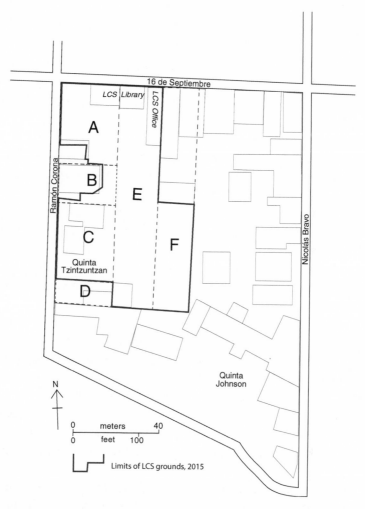

Map 2. Quinta Tzintzuntzan and adjoining properties

14

Neill James builds her dream home

Almost all the current grounds of the Lake Chapala Society once belonged to author Neill James. The foreign community in Ajijic reveres Neill James as a philanthropic woman who gifted her property to the Lake Chapala Society a few years before she died. For its part, the Mexican community remembers how James provided employment for many local women by starting embroidery and silk projects and how James created community libraries and donated buildings to the village for a library and a health clinic.

Mexican sociologist Francisco Talavera was far less complimentary about James. He saw her as someone who had generated wealth by exploiting the village and its residents before eventually trying to gain their trust and appreciation by becoming a benefactor. Both the capitalist and philanthropic sides of James' life are considered later. This chapter looks only at the challenges she overcame to build her own house.

James arrived in Ajijic in September 1943. Eight years later she owned four contiguous properties. Her house "Quinta Tzintzuntzan" on Calle Ramón Corona occupied the property marked C on the map, and was the entrance to extensive gardens (properties A, B, and E). She added an additional property, F, to the gardens in the mid-1950s.

How did all this come about? The hoops that Neill James needed to jump through in order to build her own house in Ajijic are a good illustration of the challenges and pitfalls of buying real estate in Ajijic in the 1940s.[1]

After renting for several years, James decided to purchase a plot of land and, with the help of retired engineer Herbert Johnson, build her own home. Acquiring a suitable building lot proved to be more of a challenge than expected. According to James, the price of land in Ajijic in the mid-1940s jumped from one peso to three and then five pesos (about one dollar) a square meter.[2] Moreover, in advance of any property purchase, foreigners needed federal government permission.

Prior to 1945, lots A, B, C and D were a single property, about 2700 square meters in area, with 28 meters of street front along Calle 16 de Septiembre (then known as Calle Juárez) and 99 meters along Calle Ramón Corona (then called Porfirio Díaz). When Jesús Ahumada Mercado (son of the owners of Quinta Mi Retiro) bought it for 2000 pesos (about $375) in September 1945, he immediately sold the southernmost 308 square meters (lot D) to Guadalajara-born artist Ernesto Butterlin, who still owned it into the 1950s.[3] The land (E) to the east had been inherited in 1942 by the family of Donato Rochín. The southern edge of lots D and E abutted Quinta Johnson.

In November 1945, Neill James wrote to the Foreign Relations Secretariat (Secretaría de Relaciones Exteriores) stating that she was a US *rentista* (i.e. independently wealthy individual) who had lived two years in Ajijic and wanted to purchase a small house, on a plot of about 10 by 30 meters, together with a piece of land about 25 by 25 meters for a vegetable garden. "I am an author," she wrote, "and hope to return here to write my books." She gave her name as Neill James Campbell and declared she was number 122000 on the National Registry of Foreigners.[4]

Within a month, James bought a 25.0 by 25.5 meter plot of land (boundaries unstated) from Ahumada Mercado. She paid him the curiously precise sum of 2902.76 pesos (about 540 dollars), and he agreed to keep it in his name while "legal difficulties [were] straightened out." When SRE asked her to send in her *rentista* papers, James hired a Chapala lawyer to act on her behalf. Three months later, James discovered that her papers were "still on [the] shelf of his closet," so she took them back and found a different lawyer, who "promised to fix everything and I was to pay $100 after I got the papers." Separately, James also requested permission to buy the house (Hidalgo 433) she had been living in for the past two years.

By February 1946 the land was still not legally hers, so she engaged another lawyer to write a letter requesting permission to buy. A month later, after this lawyer had still not done anything, James hired yet another lawyer. By May, after repeated excuses from this lawyer, who was busy building his own house, James was becoming increasingly anxious and annoyed.

Then, in September, Ahumada Mercado (and his wife, Susana Cárdenas) transferred lot B (504 square meters) to María Guzmán Canales, in exchange for a 480-square-meter lot adjoining land owned by his father on calle Juárez.

James hired another lawyer—this time one from Guadalajara—in October 1946 to draw up the transfer of ownership and new escritura (deed) for the property she had paid for the previous year. James' notes do not explain the long delay that ensued. But finally, in December 1947, she received unwelcome news. In her own words, she learned that her "rentista papers had been made out wrong, were not in order, and I possibly would have to leave the country at once." Following a "scene at immigration," a "bandit" arrived at her door to solicit a *multa* (fine). James noted that:

> Two immigration men had field day in Chapala collecting fines from foreigners... [who] were handing out 100 peso notes right and left, being under the impression that such a note would fix up everything. Didn't fix a thing.... Decided to hurry and get my property in name of a Mexican for safety.

James resorted to the legally dubious practice of borrowing someone else's name (a *prestanombre*) to sign the formal documents, keeping herself at arm's length from what would have been an illicit transaction if conducted in her own name. Despite the evident risks, using a *prestanombre* was quite common at the time. James clearly needed someone she considered trustworthy, and settled on the owner of lot D: Ernesto Butterlin. Part of James's confidence may have been due to the fact that Butterlin had befriended—and shared a house with—two visiting American artists, Charmin Schlossman and Sylvia Fein, without incident.

In January 1948, James, accompanied by Butterlin, took the papers to the home of Ahumada Mercado for everyone to sign, only to discover that her lawyer had made the papers out incorrectly and they needed to be redone. In her notes, James admitted that she wished she'd never heard of land! The deed for the property (C on the map) was finally signed a few days later; to satisfy legalities it stated that Ernesto Butterlin had paid 500 pesos for 841 square meters.

On the plus side, the successive delays had given James ample time to design her home, and she started construction almost immediately. She "drew house plans, figured dimensions in the metric system and supervised," while Herbert Johnson helped "figure out the stress and strain of wooden and steel beams" and oversaw digging a well. James was constantly changing the details:

> I added two more fireplaces, an extra bath, two bodegas, built a rock wall around my casa, made some lily ponds, a garage, and fenced in a mulberry patch and dug a second well.[5]

However, her bureaucratic nightmare was far from over. First, James was informed that back taxes were owed on the property, which prevented the formal registration of the sale. After numerous trips to Chapala, the taxes were finally paid in May. Then, when James hired a lawyer in Guadalajara to complete the registration, she found—though only after Madeline Miedema, her friend from California, had confronted the lawyer and "snatched the escrituras and flounced out of his office"—that the papers had not been properly notarized to the satisfaction of the Registro Público. It was almost back to square one. New documents had to be drawn up, and they all needed to be signed and correctly notarized. Meanwhile, Ernesto Butterlin was traveling in Chiapas, and the Ahumadas had a new baby....

Frustrated by the frequent delays, including one when her workmen took time off to build a wall near the church, James moved in even before construction was finished, naming her new house Quinta Tzintzuntzan, for the historic village Tzintzuntzan (Place of the Hummingbirds) on the shores of Lake Pátzcuaro in Michoacán.

On his return from Chiapas in May 1948, Butterlin submitted the paperwork showing that a modest two-story house (101 square meters of construction), with four rooms down and one up, had been completed. This was to be Neill James' home for more than forty years.

When James explained, several years later, why she had subsequently bought three adjoining properties, she claimed that the first was to guarantee peace and quiet, the second prevented its owner, a General, from building a barracks there, and the third saved her from having a two-story house overlook her garden.[6] Judging by the quick succession of land transactions (all completed before she had legal title to her own house), it is more likely that James had always planned to extend her property, but felt obliged to offer some justification after the fact. For the new purchases, James relied on another *prestanombre*, Irma Heinrich de Martínez, presumably a close and trusted friend. On 1 June 1950, Heinrich bought lot B, with its buildings, for 1000 pesos. Six weeks later, Heinrich paid 750 pesos to buy property E.[7] The following May, James and Heinrich took joint ownership of a rustic 1029-square-meter lot (location unstated), for $10 a square meter. The two women took immediate possession, agreeing to pay by instalments over the next six months.

Despite this flurry of activity, as 1950 came to a close Neill James still did not have any property registered in her name alone. She wrote to the Foreign Relations Secretariat in September 1951 seeking permission to buy a property extending from Calle 16 de Septiembre south to land owned by Ernesto Butterlin and Georgette Johnson, and west-east from Calle Ramón Corona to land belonging to Carlota Rochín and Sr Rochín. James also asked for permission to buy an additional 500 square meters of land on the west side of Calle Ramón Corona, where she wanted to plant mulberry bushes for the cultivation of silkworms.

Permission in hand, James then "purchased" lot C from Ernesto Butterlin on 28 November. Two weeks later, she purchased lot A from José de Jesús Ahumada Mercado and his wife, and lots B and E from Irma Heinrich de Martínez. James was finally the official owner of over 4200 square meters of prime Ajijic real estate, the perfect setting for an upgrade on her former "Adobe Hut in Heaven," the working title she had used for *Dust on My Heart*.[8] After she acquired lot F in 1956, the total area of her personal estate was well over 5000 square meters.[9]

James soon transformed her garden into a colorful tropical paradise with a luxuriant mix of vegetables, flowers, trees and ornamentals, perfect habitat for all kinds of animals—ranging from chickens, ducks and roosters to dogs, parrots and peacocks. The gardens and lily ponds were an animal refuge: James was both an animal lover and a committed vegetarian.[10]

To finance these land deals, James clearly had to supplement her meager writing income. The successful completion of her own home, and the realization that many other foreigners might also want to settle in Ajijic, prompted James to add to her money-making activities in the next decade by becoming an informal rental agent and land speculator.

15

Art community begins

So many visual artists have lived and worked in Ajijic and San Antonio Tlayacapan over the years that they merit their own encyclopedia. This chapter focuses on some of the earliest visual artists to depict local Ajijic scenes or people in their work, or form artistic groups in the village.

The first non-Mexican artists known to have lived and painted in Ajijic are Everett Gee Jackson and Lowell D Houser, who lived in the village for several months in 1925–26. Houser's paintings of Ajijic include "Maidens carrying water jars, Ajijic;" he subsequently became an expert on Mayan art. One of Jackson's paintings of Ajijic—a street scene near the church—appears on the cover of his memoir about their time at Lake Chapala. They were almost certainly, as he claims, the "first art students ever to live in Ajijic."[1]

The 1940s was a formative period for the nascent art scene at Lake Chapala. The contribution of the Butterlin family is noteworthy. German immigrants Hans (Juan) and Amelie Butterlin had settled in Guadalajara in 1910. Three of their sons became artists: Otto (1900–1956) and Friedrich (c 1905–?), both born in Germany, and their much younger brother Ernesto (1917–1964), born in Guadalajara.

The family had property in Ajijic and visited regularly. As early as 1930, Otto was painting local scenes including the family *huerta* (orchard). Otto lived in Mexico City and was close friends with many of Mexico's most famous artists, including Diego Rivera and Frida Kahlo; he moved to Ajijic with his wife and daughter in the 1940s. Middle brother Friedrich, a photographer, also spent time in Ajijic.

But the key to our story is Ernesto, who lived full-time in Ajijic from about 1940. "Lin," as he liked to be called, was tall, gay and more gregarious than his older siblings. He shared a house in Ajijic for several years in the mid-1940s with two young female American artists—Charmin Schlossman and Sylvia Fein—whose husbands were serving overseas in the US military.

Schlossman later exhibited her paintings of "the Indians of the remote Mexican village of Ajijic" in Brazos, Texas. She started a company making custom fabrics and was a co-founder of Houston Contemporary Arts Museum.

Sylvia Fein (born in 1919), now recognized as one of America's foremost female surrealist painters, whose work is comparable to that of Leonora Carrington and Frida Kahlo, has loved Mexico ever since. She was in Ajijic working on paintings for her first solo exhibition in New York City. Among her works from this time are "Muchacha de Ajijic" and "Insects that inhabit my studio in Ajijic." Fein gave paper, pencils and crayons to village children who brought her exotic insects to draw, and loved the children's spontaneity "and their meticulous observation, dexterity, humor and enjoyment."[2] She also prepared original embroidery designs for Neill James. On her return to the US, a friendly customs agent took one look at Fein's many paintings before declaring them "antiques" and therefore exempt from duty!

The Chapala Art Center

Fein exhibited with Otto and Ernesto Butterlin in a group show at the Villa Montecarlo in Chapala in December 1944 that was billed as the founding of the Chapala Art Center.[3] At least four other residents of Ajijic—Betty Binkley, Jaime López Bermudez, Ann Medalie and Muriel Lytton-Bernard—also took part.

Painter Betty Binkley became a close friend of poet Witter Bynner, then living in Chapala. She showed a selection of Lake Chapala paintings, including one titled "Sphinx of Chapala," in Santa Fe, New Mexico, in 1945.[4] She returned twenty years later to live for a year in Ajijic and Jocotepec,[5] before spending her final years in San Miguel de Allende.

Mexico City-born artist and architect Jaime López Bermúdez, recognized as one of Mexico's more important modernist architects, "occupied a *huertita* overlooking the lake and worked for several months with his charming wife, Virginia, and a Mexican cat for company."[6]

Latvian-born Ann Medalie assisted Diego Rivera in painting a mural in San Francisco in 1940, and became a confidante of Frida Kahlo, before spending six months in Ajijic in 1944. Her solo show in Mexico City the following year featured several oil paintings of Ajijic, including the garden at Quinta Johnson, and the view from the garden across the lake. Two of Medalie's other Ajijic paintings—of fishermen and women washing clothes—were used to illustrate an article about the village by Neill James.[7] Medalie, best known for her exquisitely detailed flower paintings, lived the latter part of her life in Israel.

Little is known about the artistic career of Muriel Lytton-Bernard, the wife of Dr Bernard Lytton-Bernard. The couple were both already living in Ajijic at the time of their marriage in June 1940.

Artists from near and far

Numerous other artists also lived and worked in Ajijic in the mid-1940s. Some were well known, others at the start of their careers; some were from overseas, others were foreigners already living in Mexico. They all sought inspiration from a quiet setting where they could benefit from Lake Chapala's beautiful scenery, reflections and perfect light.

After visiting Ajijic in 1944–45, Illinois-born Irma René Koen spent the rest of her life in Mexico. Koen had been labeled "America's leading woman artist" long before she visited Ajijic, where she helped design the blouses that Neill James had villagers embroider for sale.[8] Koen later donated a painting titled "Street in Ajijic" to the Rock Island YMCA in Illinois.[9]

Wisconsin-born photographer Dorothy Hosmer was one of the first female photographers to have work published by *National Geographic*. Hosmer visited Ajijic with her mother in 1945. Her photo essay about Ajijic, "Village in the Sun"—"an unspoiled spot that has become a paradise for Mexican and American artists and writers"—appeared in *Modern Mexico* the following year.

After visiting Ajijic in 1947, Renée George wrote and illustrated a short article about the village for *Modern Mexico*.[10] The title illustration is an Ajijic street scene. George was a founder member of the Martha's Vineyard Art Association.

Noted abstract expressionist painter Stanley Twardowicz lived in Ajijic in about 1948. An exhibition in New York of his stunning photographs of Ajijic fishermen and their nets from that visit won him instant acclaim.[11] Twardowicz was good friends with Jack Kerouac and Jackson Pollock, whose brother Charles painted in Ajijic a decade later.

Photographer Peter Smithers, a real-life James Bond, lived in Cuernavaca and was the British Acting naval attache for Mexico from 1942 to 1946. The several thousand transparencies (slides) of his now in Mexico's National Photo Library (Fototeca Nacional) include several interesting early color photos of Ajijic taken in about 1944, long before the village sprawled into the surrounding hills.

At the end of the 1940s the very accomplished print-maker Ruth Starr Rose spent two years in Ajijic and produced several striking lithographs of the village and Lake Chapala, including one titled "Fiesta in Ajijic."

Painter Violette Mège and her husband, violinist-turned-artist Michael Baxte, lived in Mexico City. When Baxte took up painting, Mège was his only teacher, and he was her only student. A decade later, Baxte won the Dudensing National Competition for American Painters. On visits to Ajijic in 1945 and 1946 they shared (with Helen Kirtland) a cottage owned by Louis Stephens, a mutual Mexico City friend. Mège's painting "Lavandera de Ajijic" was exhibited in Mexico City in 1954 and reproduced in *El Nacional*. Baxte's paintings featured frequently in *Mexican Life*.

The Ajijic art scene of today owes much to these small beginnings. As images of Ajijic made their way into the mainstream press, word spread, and more artists arrived.

The GI Bill

US servicemen returning from the second world war were offered incentives to complete their education via the various iterations of the GI Bill (1944–1956). Many former military opted to study art in Mexico, with schools in Mexico City, San Miguel de Allende and Guadalajara being popular choices. The proximity of Guadalajara to Lake Chapala meant that GIs enrolled at the University of Guadalajara often found it cheaper and equally convenient to live in Ajijic. Flexibility in this regard increased after 1952 when GI Bill tuition fees were no longer paid direct to institutions but given to veterans, who received a fixed monthly sum of $110 to cover tuition, fees, books and living expenses.

Mexican Art Workshop

By 1947, *Terry's Guide to Mexico* was making it clear that Chapala and Ajijic were blossoming as art centers: "In both places there has also grown up in recent years an extensive artists' colony comprised of painters, sculptors, and writers. Many are Americans."[12]

Art in Ajijic received a huge boost in 1947 when New York entrepreneur Irma Jonas arranged the first summer art school in the village. Why Jonas chose Ajijic is not clear, but she organized an annual workshop in the village from 1947 to 1949. The programs were many artists' first introduction to the creative opportunities at Lake Chapala.

Guest instructors included famous Guatemalan-born artist Carlos Mérida and North Carolina painter Gayle Jemison Hoskins. The three main resident teachers were Ernesto Butterlin, Nicolas Muzenic and Tobias Schneebaum. Butterlin was imposingly tall (6' 4"), blond, handsome, and effortlessly trilingual, fluent in Spanish, English and German. His abstract paintings were shown at major galleries in Mexico City and in the US. Muzenic, who had studied under Josef Albers at Black Mountain College, lived in Ajijic from 1948 to at least 1950, before later working as an interior designer for the WeltonBeckett architectural firm in Los Angeles. Schneebaum was a gay artist, author and activist, best known for his adventures in the Amazon and New Guinea. Two of his books—*Wild Man* (1979) and *Secret Places* (2000)—include recollections of his three years in Ajijic. Schneebaum first visited Mexico on the advice of Mexican muralist Rufino Tamayo. A neighbor in Mexico City, an elderly Romanian osteopath, asked Schneebaum to accompany her when she visited Lake Chapala to treat Zara Alexeyeva.[13]

A close friendship between the three young teachers was inevitable, but destined to end in heartbreak. An ill-fated love triangle developed between the three artists. Schneebaum fell in love with Muzenic, but Muzenic was in love with Lin.

In *Wild Man*, Schneebaum describes Ernesto (whom he calls Lynn) in glowing detail:

> A young blond painter, born in Guadalajara of German parents, also lived in Ajijic. He was twenty-seven, blue-eyed, four inches over six feet, and very handsome, and was subject to the attentions of both the men and the women who later passed through town... He was engaging and irresistible; he was slender and deeply tanned and had just the right amount of softness to his body and mind so that he threatened no one.... Lynn's casual ways bewitched and irritated Nicolas, just as Nicolas's arrogant, snobbish manner attracted and

mortified Lynn. Nicolas moved into Lynn's house and began a frenzied, volcanic affair that lasted two years.[14]

Matters became even more complicated when the "haughty and radiantly beautiful" Zoe Kernick arrived. Kernick had been living with Henry Miller in Big Sur, when she somehow heard about Lin and decided to visit Ajijic. She then became obsessed with Muzenik. When Kernick, who liked to call herself Party Planner, chronicled the Ajijic art workshop for *Mexican Life*, she explained how:

> For three years Mr Linares [Butterlin's art name] has conducted his summer school; not only teaching his students, he has had to be production chief, party giver, nose wiper and dancing partner.... A great deal of the spirit which guides the carnival gaiety of nightly fiestas is due to Mr. Linares, for his competent hands are as deft with bottles as with brushes.[15]

The Mexican Art Workshop grew in popularity. The first year (1947), when classes were held in the patio of Lin's Ajijic home, only eight students signed up.[16] The following year, with the sponsorship of a trio of renowned artists—Rufino Tamayo, I Rice Pereira and Max Weber—it attracted fifteen students: "several married couples, some university art instructors, a textile designer, a display artist, and two or three amateurs who wanted to paint for their own pleasure."[17] When twenty students signed up in 1949, it proved impossible to accommodate all of them at the Posada Ajijic, so the overflow became an extension art school in Taxco. Among the students in Ajijic that year was the famous African American playwright, artist and author Lorraine Hansberry.

After Irma Jonas moved the entire program to Taxco in 1950, art workshops in Ajijic were continued by an enterprising pair of Englishmen—Peter Elstob and Arnold Eiloart—who started the Peter Arnold Art Studio.

Crime scene became Ajijic's first art gallery

A year after the first summer school art workshop, Ajijic's first art gallery was established in El Tejaban, the nineteenth century building at Zaragoza 1, a block north of the plaza, where *hacendado* Juan Jaacks had been murdered in 1896. Conceived by Ernesto Butterlin, with help from his brother Otto, it started as a store named Ajijic Associates, which:

resembles a modern art gallery. It has chocolate walls, white walls, sells hand-painted materials, pottery, leather goods, and is hung with paintings by village artists, Nicolas Muzenic, Tobias Scheebaum, and of course, Ernesto Linares. All of this might be called a seed thrust of civilization; but Ajijic is not an art colony, and it is not a resort.[18]

It soon became known simply as La Galería, and remained an art gallery, off and on—sometimes in combination with a restaurant or boutique—for most of the next fifty years.

By the end of the 1940s all the pieces were in place for Ajijic to become an internationally recognized art destination.

Part C

1950s: Trendsetters

"During the last decade or so this somnolent village which lacks most of the amenities of life has become a sort of sun-drenched bohemia that somewhat bewilders its patient native citizens. An incredible number of American and Canadian artists and writers and would-be-somethings who have settled within Ajijic's adobe precincts do some creative work when they are not occupied with creative imbibing."
—James Norman, 1959

16

International tourists

Fortunately for the village, the twin issues of the near collapse of Posada Ajijic in the late 1940s, and the unexpected loss of the annual Art Workshop to Taxco, were resolved simultaneously following the arrival of two enterprising Englishmen—long-time friends and business partners Arnold "Bushy" Eiloart and Peter Elstob.

Eiloart arrived in Ajijic, in either late 1948 or early 1949, followed by Elstob in late 1949.[1] The two men combined their first names to establish Peter Arnold SA, a joint venture promoting Ajijic as a destination for art classes, vacations and retirement. The first Peter Arnold advertisements (considered more fully in chapter 18) appeared in US media in late 1949 and highlighted how inexpensive it was to live at Lake Chapala. Respondents were sent an information booklet giving more details about Ajijic and local prices. The many international visitors brought in by Peter Arnold were housed in the Posada Ajijic, with any overflow occupying other rental properties as needed. Elstob and Eiloart maintained a hands-on involvement in this venture until April 1952.

Particular emphasis was placed on trying to attract art students to the village, in order to build on the summer program begun by Irma Jonas. Local Ajijic modernist artist Ernesto Butterlin, who had helped Jonas, took over the organization of art classes after her departure. Butterlin must have had the confidence of Elstob and Eiloart since he signed the application in January 1951 to renew the Posada's business license as an inn. Two months later, in March, Peter Arnold Studios SA began operating the premises as a guesthouse with bar. The company claimed to have made total investments of about $35,000, presumably covering additions, improvements, rent, business fees and publicity. Later documents show that the name "Peter Arnold Studios SA"[2] was still being used as late as 1966, long after the two principal partners—Elstob and Eiloart—had returned to the UK.[3]

Quite how Eiloart and Elstob first heard of Ajijic remains a mystery. In association with actor Alec Clunes they had leased the Arts Theatre in London in 1946, and put on several plays, including the world premiere of *The Lady's Not For Burning* by Christopher Fry. Perhaps they learned about Ajijic from the London theater circle? The London theater and literary set at the time included friends of Nigel Millett, coauthor of *Village in the Sun*, first published in the UK in 1945. Perhaps Eiloart and Elstob knew this book and had met one, or even both, of its authors?

Both Eiloart and Elstob had interesting backstories prior to Ajijic. Arnold Beaupré Eiloart was born in Surrey. His parents were founder members of Whiteway, a socialist (Tolstoyan) experiment in Gloucester, which espoused money and property rights; they chose his middle name (French for beautiful meadow) on account of his place of conception. Eiloart's daughter, Gail, told me that her father "dreamed of being a writer but did not have Peter's flare." As a teenager, Gail visited her father in Ajijic from August 1949 to September 1950 and still remembers many of the characters she met there. Helping her father at the Posada Ajijic was Dorothy (Dolly) Whelan, the partner of the Black American artist Ernest Alexander.[4]

Peter Elstob (1915–2002), born in London, was educated in the US and retained a midAtlantic accent throughout his life. After failing his first year at the University of Michigan, he was sent to England. He was briefly in the Royal Air Force, before being summarily dismissed for trying to impress a girlfriend by flying unauthorized stunts over the Queen Mary on its maiden voyage. Elstob then volunteered with the Republican forces in Spain, where he was arrested and jailed on suspicion of being a spy. His release from prison, and expulsion to France, were due to the intervention of Medora LeighSmith, who became his first wife. Elstob's experiences were the subject matter for his first novel, *Spanish Prisoner* (1939).

The Elstobs and Eiloarts initially became business partners to market Yeast Pac, a beauty mask product they had jointly devised, which was so successful it brought financial security to both families.

When Elstob first came to Ajijic in 1949, Medora remained in the UK to look after the couple's four children and prepare for the arrival of their fifth. However, within a few months, her husband had fallen in love with a young American artist, Barbara Jean Zacheisz, who gave birth to their first child, Peter Mayo Elstob, in Mexico City in 1951.[5]

Life in Ajijic, with its high level of creativity and individualism, was not always smooth sailing. Eiloart and Elstob were still running the Posada Ajijic in 1951 when a scuffle broke out at a ticketed event one evening between José Ramos Pérez, the Ajijic *delegado*, and nine-fingered violinist John Langley. The argument centered on whether or not Langley had paid for a ticket. The following day, Langley's friends, fearing that the authorities might try to have him deported, rallied round to sign an open letter in the press, stating that they had witnessed the argument, and that Langley had NOT used any abusive language.[6] The signatories to the letter even included the now-mollified *delegado*.

In April 1952, Eiloart and Elstob (accompanied by Zacheisz and infant son) all left Ajijic and returned to the UK. According to Elstob's daughter, her father's decision to leave Mexico was partly due to the increasingly poor prognosis for the level of the lake in the early 1950s, and the difficulty he foresaw in attracting tourists.

The joint adventures of the two men did not end there. In 1958, Eiloart attempted a trans-Atlantic balloon flight from Tenerife to the West Indies, with ground support provided by Elstob. The attempt narrowly failed, but set a record for a gas-powered balloon flight that stood for decades.[7]

The publicity Eiloart and Elstob generated for Ajijic marked a turning point in the village's fortunes. The Posada Ajijic was no longer merely an inn serving local or passing traffic; it was fast becoming a port-of-call for international visitors from the US and elsewhere. The significant growth in the number of foreigners (many of them artists or authors) attracted to Ajijic over the next decade led to the provision of more (and better) accommodations in the village and a wider range of services for visitors.

Bob Thayer

The next manager of the Posada Ajijic, Bob Thayer, began the process of updating the inn to better serve the needs of the influx of new visitors. He also apparently acquired the rights to the business name Peter Arnold, which he continued to use in advertisements until at least 1956.

Robert (Bob) Henry Thayer was born in Montana on 19 October 1919, grew up in Long Beach, California, and died in Los Angeles on

4 May 1975. As a young man, Thayer worked for his father's auto sales agency prior to serving in the US military. He arrived in Ajijic in about 1951, claiming he wanted to escape high taxes and the pressure of living in the US.[8] At that time, it was possible to live in Ajijic, according to Thayer, on $150 a month, which covered renting a three-bedroom home, employing two servants, entertainment and some travel. $200 a month allowed you to live in luxury! A room in an ordinary inn, including meals and laundry, cost $24 a month, less than a dollar a day.

In 1953, Thayer, whose past included two relatively short-lived marriages, married Stella Mostert. The couple, who first met when Mostert stayed at the Posada Ajijic on vacation, married in Las Vegas on 4 October 1953 and then returned to Ajijic to run the Posada.

By 1955, Thayer had modernized several "little huts" on the Posada property into "units and cottages with modern facilities."[9] Earlier that year, the Posada Ajijic had joined the list of places where the Diners' Club card (the world's first independent credit card) was accepted.[10]

Los Angeles Times reporter Ted Hodges, who visited in 1955, wrote that "a filet mignon dinner complete from cocktail to coffee" in Ajijic then cost just $1, while a taxi from the airport to Ajijic was 50 pesos or about $4. He especially enjoyed the Posada's cantina where "a cocktail party for 18 of us cost the host a wad of pesos representing exactly $12."[11] Those were the days!

Another American visitor, Robert Hosmer, after several weeks in Ajijic in spring 1955, wrote to a New York newspaper to describe how the American colony in Ajijic "have converted many native houses into quite lovely places, and are building new ones." One of his friends was building a house in the village. With three bedrooms, "a servant's living and dining room," plumbing, well, pump and storage tank, the L-shaped building on a 5000-square-foot lot had a total cost of $2500. Hosmer reported that the Posada Ajijic had become quite cosmopolitan: "Last week there were cars parked in front from Massachusetts, Ohio, Minnesota, Maryland, Oklahoma, Maine, Illinois, Arizona, Texas, Canada, North Carolina, Oregon, California, Kansas, Nebraska, North Dakota and Tennessee."[12]

By 1957 the advertisements for the Posada Ajijic placed in the *Los Angeles Times* were no longer using the Peter Arnold identity but were headed "Thayer of Mexico." These adverts, which advised readers that they could retire to Lake Chapala on $150 a month, appeared regularly until September 1958.[13] By that time, a furnished two or three-bedroom house with modern kitchen and bath could be found in Ajijic for about $40 a month, and the monthly rate for staying at the Posada Ajijic, including three meals a day, was $130 for one person, $240 for a couple. The Posada bar and lounge were the "congenial social focal point of the entire region," the perfect place to make new friends, arrange groups for trips or find a golfing partner.[14]

Bob Thayer continued to run the Posada Ajijic until about 1959; two years later, like father like son, he opened a car dealership in Fullerton, California. After his departure the Posada was jointly managed for a short time by Enrique Rojas and Antonio Shafer. They later moved to the Chula Vista Holiday Inn, where they were appointed joint managers in 1964. They continued to run that establishment after it was renamed the Chula Vista motel.[15]

The Posada Ajijic in books

Journalist and novelist Bart Spicer stayed regularly at the Posada Ajijic in the 1950s and incorporated a scene set at Lake Chapala into his 1955 spy novel *The Day of the Dead*, a tale of international intrigue and betrayed friendships. The protagonist attended a lively party at an expat-owned house on the lakeshore, when the lake was fully "200 yards from its former shoreline." The lake reached its lowest level ever a few months after the book was published.

Novelist Kenneth Millar set several chapters of *The Zebra-Striped Hearse* (1962) in Ajijic. The book, written after Millar visited fellow author John Mersereau at Lake Chapala, won the Mystery Writers of America's Edgar Award for Best Novel. The novel's protagonist is shown by the night watchman to his room at the Posada Ajijic:

> He took me through a wet garden to my cottage. It was clean and roomy; a fire was laid in the fireplace. He left me with instructions to use the bottled water, even for cleaning my teeth.

17

Hotel health spa

The Posada Ajijic, and the more rustic Casa Heuer, were not the only places to stay in Ajijic in the 1950s. Quinta Mi Retiro, owned from the mid-1940s by retired Mexican general José de Jesús Ahumada Alatorre (c. 1893–1982) and his wife, Remigia, also had a limited number of rooms available. Located at Calle 16 de Septiembre 34, it was managed by their son, José de Jesús Ahumada Mercado. The extensive, walled lakefront property was often called simply La Quinta (not to be confused with the long-running hotel of that name in Jocotepec).

An eccentric Englishman, the self-styled Dr Bernard Lytton-Bernard (1890–1975), rented part of this estate in about 1950 to establish the first health spa at Lake Chapala; it operated here for about a decade.

The earliest mentions of Quinta Mi Retiro, which had horse stables, children's playground equipment, an orchard and a pool, come from 1945, when it was supporting both a local soccer team and a candidate for the Queen of the Fiestas Patrias in Ajijic.[1] These sponsorships were presumably at the general's behest and had no connection to Lytton-Bernard or his health spa.

The lack of any mention of Lytton-Bernard in most references to Quinta Mi Retiro leads me to believe that it was primarily a hotel run by the general and his family, and that Lytton-Barnard only ever rented part of it for his spa business. For example, in 1952, travel writer Mabel Knight told readers that "The General's House or Quinta Mi Retiro," had several elegant lakeview bungalows, which, given that the hotel did not offer any meals, were "designed for Mexican families with maids."[2] A Spanish-language article a few years later described the "Gran Hotel del General" as the most luxurious hotel in the village.[3]

Among those who stayed at Quinta Mi Retiro were Marcella Crump, a keen amateur photographer, and her six young children, when they first arrived in Ajijic in 1958, and Dr Everett Manwell (one of Kirtland's multiple husbands).[4]

As for English-born Lytton-Bernard, he had led an exceedingly colorful life prior to settling in Ajijic. Born Otto Bernhard Trappschuh, he had changed his name at least twice, and fought in the first world war. After winning a bronze medal for freestyle wrestling (featherweight) in the Antwerp Olympics in 1920, he married the following year and then lived for an extended period in the US, where his son, Peter, was born in 1928. His income in the US came from publishing a dozen or so popular books on topics such as diet, sex and marriage (somewhat ironic, given that his own marriage was in serious trouble). Lytton-Bernard, who stood barely five feet tall and had sparkling blue eyes, was subsequently convicted of mail fraud for a scheme promoting a height increasing apparatus.

Lytton-Bernard then returned to the UK and stood as a Labour party candidate in the 1935 general election. After he failed to win a seat in the new parliament, Lytton-Bernard immediately set sail for Australia with Peter and Miss Muriel Robinson, an artist who had been living with him in England. Some months later they returned Peter to his mother (then living in Sausalito, California) and settled briefly in Canada, in Windsor, Ontario, to run a correspondence school for stock market investors. When that scheme came unstuck, the couple moved to Mexico, where they married in Guadalajara in 1940 and established a home in Ajijic.[5]

Lytton-Bernard told reporter Roy Kelsey in 1968 that he had first arrived in Chapala looking for minerals. He claimed to have met several famous people while there, including poet Robert Penn Warren (who was there in 1941), Madame Lupesku and her boyfriend, the former King Carol of Rumania (who visited in 1943), and playwright Tennessee Williams (who wrote there in 1945).[6] These recollections may well be entirely accurate.

Lytton-Bernard was an ardent advocate of vegetarianism. During his time in Ajijic he came to recognize that papaya was the "king of fruit" and he may well deserve the credit for inventing the Papaya Diet that became so fashionable many years later. According to his promotional blurb, the papain enzyme could digest 300 times its volume of protein, which made it an effective cleansing agent, able to clean not only the alimentary canal but also reach all the tissues. Lytton-Bernard was so convinced that papaya was the key to a long and healthy life that he touted his famous diet, and expounded his medical philosophy, in a self-published eighteen-page promotional brochure, illustrated with numerous photographs, titled *Health Lover's Paradise in Old Mexico*. Lytton-Bernard and his wife presumably also publicized his dietary beliefs and attracted new clientele during the many cruises they took to various parts of the world.

In 1957, at the 15th World Vegetarian Congress in India, the lengthy vegetarian blessing used before meals at La Quinta Mi Retiro was shared with participants:

> Heavenly Father, in Thy Cosmic Presence, we ask Thee to bless this simple meal direct from the bosom and bounty of Mother Nature.... As no fellow-creature has suffered in any way in the procuring and preparation of the food, we know that Thine infinite Love will be with us and... that we shall be filled with thy Divine Spirit in health, a full life, and continuously close consciousness of our Oneness with Thee, Amen![7]

Lytton-Bernard was in India the following year to give "an interesting lecture on Vegetarian and Natural Hygiene movements in Mexico" to the Vegetarian World Forum in Bombay (now Mumbai).[8]

The spa at Quinta Mi Retiro closed in about 1960, the year when Lytton-Bernard opened the Rio Caliente health spa on land his son Peter had bought in the Primavera Forest, just west of Guadalajara. Rio Caliente became one of Mexico's premier spas, internationally renowned for its peaceful get-away-from-it-all location, thermal pools and healthy vegetarian meals. It had been in operation for fifty years by the time it closed in 2011.

Later owners of the General's Hotel, which was still going strong in January 1965, included the Aguilar Valencia family, responsible for developing the La Floresta subdivision in the 1970s.[9]

18

Advertising and marketing

Beginning in the 1950s, the touristic center of gravity at Lake Chapala moved steadily away from Chapala towards Ajijic. New hotels—some short-lived—sprang up in Chula Vista and Ajijic. Longer-established hostelries in Ajijic got a new lease of life. Rental properties became harder to find. The trickle of foreigners that had settled in the village in the 1940s became a rising stream in the 1950s and 1960s before becoming a torrent in the 1970s.

Many of the new incomers first heard about the charms of Ajijic from articles and advertisements in the foreign press. This chapter examines how mass media and adverts depicted Ajijic and how they emphasized different aspects of life in the village as it grew. The two common attractions in most accounts were the area's great climate and its inexpensive living costs.

The earliest prolonged English-language marketing campaign promoting Ajijic was launched in 1949 by Peter Arnold (Peter Elstob and Arnold Eiloart) and continued, albeit sporadically, until 1956. The advertisements appeared in a variety of US publications. Participants stayed at the Posada Ajijic or other rental properties as needed. The earliest advertisements claimed that it was more than possible to live in Ajijic on $80 a month:

> Mexico $80 a month per person includes food, liquor, cigarets, your own three bedroom furnished house and patio, maid, and 17 foot sloop on magnificent Lake Chapala. English American artist colony in fishing village. Winter temp. 75, summer 85. Write Peter Arnold, Chapala, Jalisco, Mexico.[1]

Advertisements like this certainly worked, as did one in the real estate pages of the *New York Times* for a much more expensive holiday—"Villa in Jalisco on Lake Chapala, Mexico.... Horses, five servants, launch and small boat, $150 a month, $500 the summer"—which drew Jack Bateman and his wife, Laura Woodruff Bateman, to Ajijic with their three young children in 1952. They settled in the village soon afterwards and quickly became pillars of the local community, making exemplary contributions to the local social, cultural and artistic scene.[2] Jack Bateman designed the Lakeside Little Theatre, and Laura ran one of the village's premier art galleries for many years. Several members of the family still live in the village.

Not everyone thought that Ajijic was ready to become a tourist destination. Mabel Knight, for instance, argued in 1952 that:

Ajijic is not a tourist resort and never will be for many years to come, but for those who want to see the real Mexico it is adorable. It is just a narrow strip of land between mountains and lake with more mountains across the lake and burros everywhere.[3]

By 1954 the Peter Arnold advertisements had revised the cost of living in, or retiring to, Mexico upwards to $90 a month.[4] Very similar advertisements, also quoting $90 a month, appeared in 1956:

RETIRE ON $90 A MONTH or less in a resort area, 365 days of sun a year, dry temp. 65-85°. Or maintain lux. villa, servants, ALL expenses $150–250 a mo. Am.Eng. colony on lake 60 mi. long. 50 min. to city of 1/2 million, medical center. Schools, arts, sports. Few hours by air. Train, bus, PAVED roads all the way. Fulltime servants, maids, cooks, $6 to $15 a mo., filet mignon 35¢ lb., coffee 40¢, gas 15¢ gal. Gin, rum, brandy 65¢-85¢ fifth, whiskey $1.50 qt. Houses $10 mo. up. No fog, smog, confusion, jitters. Serene living among world's most considerate people. For EXACTLY how Americans are living on $50—$90—$150—$250 a mo., Airmail $2.00 for 110 Pages current info., prices, roads, hotels, hunting, fishing and living conditions from Am. viewpoint (Personal check OK) to Peter Arnold, Box 12, Ajijic, Lake Chapala, Jal., Mexico.[5]

The reference to "paved roads" is interesting. If the road between Chapala and Ajijic was actually paved at that time, the surface did not last long. Five years later, James Norman wrote that "The road is unpaved, but good."[6]

Several distinct PO Box numbers were used in Peter Arnold advertisements, which enabled the advertiser to gauge the relative success of different media. The advertisements were also very well crafted. A Peter Arnold advertisement in *The Wall Street Journal* was praised for its excellence by John Caples in *Making Ads Pay: Timeless Tips for Successful Copywriting*.

Respondents to Peter Arnold adverts were sent an information package. A typical package (from 1956) included a 26-page mimeographed document with detailed information about climate, prices, immigration rules, roads, trains, servants ("what they lack in education they definitely make up for in loyalty, honesty, cheerfulness, and eagerness to please"), medical facilities, schools and banking. Monthly room rates (meals included) at the Posada Ajijic were $140 single occupancy, $260 double.

The success of this approach is evident from the fact that identically worded adverts (with updated prices) were placed, long after Elstob and Eiloart had left Mexico, by "Thayer of Mexico" in the *Los Angeles Times* from 1957 to 1958 and then by "Stone of Mexico" in 1959.[7] Murray Stone had taken over from Bob Thayer as manager of Posada Ajijic and his advertisements, including those in *Esquire* magazine in 1960, were headlined "Retire on $150 a month."[8]

This decade-long advertising campaign, begun in 1949, helped put Ajijic on the international tourist map. Ever since, a steady flow of advertisements, travel articles, television programs and books have extolled the virtues of visiting or retiring to Lake Chapala. Their collective message has always been that living cheaply (and in relative luxury) "in paradise" is easily attainable south of the border.

Unlike the Batemans, who secretly hoped their Shangri-La village would long remain a secret to the rest of the world, another New York couple—Haig and Regina Shekerjian—shared Ajijic's appeal as widely as possible. After their first visit in 1950–1951, Regina, a well-known illustrator and poet, wrote an article for *Design* that emphasized the attractiveness of Ajijic for artists seeking an inexpensive art-themed vacation: "Nine times out of ten, an artist pinches pennies. Nowhere in the world can a penny be pinched as hard as it can today in Mexico, a land intended for the artist."[9]

Her article highlighted the six-week summer art workshops and extolled the virtues of Ajijic to the art-loving public north of the border at a time when an American dollar was worth 8.65 pesos. She painted an enticing picture of why artists should visit Mexico and how affordable it was:

> Mexico is filled with color. Purples, pinks, red and orange. Color in a high key, layered through with dun-colored space and fingered with tall blue mountains. A checkerboard of tonal dissonance and silence. A strange land. Every era of civilization coexists, side by side, Aztec temples, pyramids and medieval cities, beautifully preserved. Pre-Columbian idols can be unearthed along the lake shore or mud edge. Its rural villages are much as they were before the Conquest. Ancient superstitions tangle with Catholicism, producing a pageantry that begs to be painted...
>
> We have discovered it is possible for two people to live comfortably in a five-room-with-patio-and-garden house; buy food, ice, kerosene for the stove, gas for the car, art and photographic supplies, postage, cigarettes, have lunch once a week in Guadalajara (forty miles way) and even indulge in a bit of entertaining for about $70 a month!

In Ajijic, rent for "big, cool, adobe houses with gardens [was] from six to twelve dollars a month," while "the standard wage" for domestic help was $5 a month. The mix of writers, artists and musicians reminded Shekerjian of Greenwich Village.

Articles like these, coupled with newspaper items about tourism and personal experiences spread by word-of-mouth, were more than sufficient to persuade many people to visit. During the 1950s, Ajijic's growing fame as an art center attracted all manner of excellent painters, sculptors, writers and photographers. Even the exceptionally low lake levels of the mid-1950s failed to deter visitors for long; optimism soon returned once the lake recovered.

Mainstream media published their own articles about Lake Chapala. The most important of these was a *Life* magazine article in 1957. *Life* commissioned photographer Leonard McCombe for a piece about the area's expatriates who "settle down to live and loaf in Mexico."[10] McCombe's striking images were the basis for a photo-essay which divided Americans at Lake Chapala into two categories: the bridge-playing "older upper crust" and the "younger crew of bohemians."

The most famous member of the former group was Neill James, who "writes books, builds and rents houses, runs a dress shop and organizes local charities," and was photographed overseeing a hunt for buried treasure with a metal detector. The expatriates in the younger set included Margaret North de Butterlin, a "rich and fashionable" American who had married into the Butterlin family and ran an art gallery; artist Lothar Wuerslin; author, educator and translator John Upton; dress-maker Colleen Wood and her Mexican partner Daniel Anaya; and former concert violinist John Langley. McCombe's wonderful image of Lothar Wuerslin and his wife, Ann, bathing in the lake amidst a mass of water hyacinths, perfectly encapsulates the spirit of the time.

Upton lived in Ajijic for over a decade, from 1949 to 1959, and returned to the village several times over the next thirty years. His masterful translations into English of works such as *La feria* (*The fair*), by Juan José Arreola, a book chock-full of local idioms and curses, will never be surpassed.

The "incorrigible John Langley," who arrived in Ajijic at about the same time as Upton, continued to play the violin but lived on insurance pay-outs following the "accidental" loss of his left index finger in a shooting mishap.[11] He was photographed lounging on a cot on his patio, chatting to British artist Jeanora Bartlet.

An article in *Esquire* the following year claimed it was possible to live in luxury in Ajijic on $200 a month.[12] In addition to 500 Americans living "in and around Ajijic and the village of Chapala," author Eleanor Morehead noted that the area also had "substantial British and French colonies."

In January 1960, "Ajijic is Fun," a double page in *Pemex Travel Club Bulletin*, a nationwide English-language monthly, mentioned two less desirable trends: drinking and nudity.[13] According to the author, the Alligator's Club was a drinking establishment with highly unusual rules: new members drank for free, and old members were billed monthly. If you didn't receive a bill, you were no longer welcome. The article also reported that an attempt by nudists to establish themselves in Ajijic, after being expelled from Acapulco, had been quickly thwarted by state officials.

Publicity articles and documentaries continued to heap attention on Ajijic. Throughout the 1960s. US journalist Irma McCall described Ajijic in 1962 as an "unspoiled paradise." She reported that staying at the Posada Ajijic cost $7.60 a day and included three meals.[14] For those who wanted to stay longer, Neill James rented out "comfortable Mexican-style homes with a gas stove, refrigerator, and fireplace for $65 a month." Maid service was $4 a week. Americans had regular bridge games; some were artists. Twenty philanthropic women met weekly as the Needle Pushers, making school uniforms for the needy. Another group had installed restrooms in the village's two schools. The religiously inclined could choose between Catholic mass in the Ajijic church and a Protestant service in a roadside chapel in Chula Vista. Sports included water skiing, hiking, riding, golf and hunting.

In 1964, after *Time* magazine publicized the low cost of living at Lake Chapala,[15] a "Mr. A. of Chapala" wrote an indignant letter to the editor that the Mexican government required expatriates to demonstrate a minimum income of $240 a month for the head of the family and $80 for each dependant. These figures, of course, applied to those who sought legal residency status in Mexico, not the many Americans who lived year-round in Mexico and made regular border runs to renew their tourist papers every six months.[16]

That year sports writer and publicist Ralph McGinnis sent his friends a detailed 21-page open letter titled "Lotus Land," extolling the virtues of living in Ajijic:

> This is Lotus Land, the land of the colonels and the afternoon cocktail, the land of the mozo and the extra maid and rum at a dollar a bottle. This is the Costa Brava of Mexico, where Mexicano and Americano meet and mix, like oil and water.[17]

Few have summed up Ajijic's post-1950 "progress" as eloquently as McGinnis:

> Discovered by a group of impecunious artists soon after World War II, it was then a sleepy Indian village given over to the pursuit of Lake Chapala sardines and the bucolic crafts of animal husbandry, maize cultivation, and wood cutting. The artists fell among the natives like a drop of water in a mill pond—there was a slight ripple and the two became one—frijoles, no bathrooms, tacos, no sewers and no barbers.
>
> Then the States-side newspapers and magazines, on a wave of nostalgia, began to thump the tub for the Shangri-la aspect of this Mexican paradise.... The adobe houses were bought and leased, white washed, a shower and bath added. The newcomers clamored for light and water, and the Mexican government, awakening after four hundred years of somnolence, tapped a mountain spring and brought the water into the pueblo.

The more affluent of the invaders built new homes or made elaborate changes in the old houses. They hired the women and girls as cooks and maids, the men as gardeners and handy men. Wages, from thirty pesos a week at the beginning, climbed to fifty, sixty, and on up to ninety and a hundred."

McGinnis also cautioned newcomers that some things were either expensive or had to be done without:

a can of corned beef costs $1.25 US. Cranberry sauce and canned asparagus are equally high.... There are no frozen foods, no TV dinners for the quick snack, and only a limited and inferior variety of canned fruits and vegetables. Residents who go to the border load up with US goodies to tide them through.

In similar vein, US veteran Garland Franklin Clifton, who lived in the Chapala area in the 1960s, published a booklet titled *American meccas in Mexico: Guadalajara, Chapala-Ajijic, Manzanillo, a comparison of the three vacation and retirement areas*.[18] This was the forerunner of several books which proclaimed the easy living at Lake Chapala on a limited budget, the most (in)famous of which was Thomas McLaughlin's *The Greatest Escape*, subtitled *How to Live in Paradise, in Luxury, for 250 Dollars Per Month*.

19

Radio, TV and Silver Screen

By the mid-1950s, Lake Chapala was also attracting the attention of TV documentary makers. The first TV travel documentary devoted to the area was "Valley of Spring," a 30-minute film in the popular *Vagabond* series hosted by Bill Burrud, which first aired in October 1957.[1] It mainly showcased Jocotepec and Chapala.

Burrud, producer of the series *American West* for KCOP-TV in Los Angeles, returned to Mexico a few months before the 1968 Summer Olympics to film an episode titled "Lake Chapala Paradise," written by Gerry Pearce.[2]

In 1958, Ajijic was the focus of a half-hour program titled "The Expatriates."[3] This was an episode in *Seven League Boots*, a wide-ranging series hosted by Jack Douglas. Douglas filmed several American expatriates living in Chapala and Ajijic, including "a modern American painter and his family" (it is unclear who this refers to) and "an American businesswoman whose interest is in the operation of hand looms" (Helen Kirtland).[4]

These travel documentaries were the harbingers of things to come. As more and more Americans settled at Lake Chapala, the number of English-language articles and film clips about the area, some making wildly inaccurate claims, increased exponentially.

In October 1964 executives and crew of Mexico City-based Filmex SA stayed at the Chula Vista motel to create and film explosions in the lake. The simulated explosions were made using compressed air which would reportedly not harm local wildlife. The special effects were for *In Harm's Way* (1965), which starred John Wayne, Kirk Douglas and Patricia Neal. A month later, a CBS film crew from Mexico City stayed at the motel while shooting footage of Guadalajara and Lake Chapala. Whether or not this footage ever aired is unknown.[5]

The earliest commercial film related to Ajijic is *Guadalajara en Verano* (1965), some scenes of which were filmed at the so-called Casa Pepsi.

The first short English-language movie known to have been filmed in Ajijic was *The Death of Antonio*, an experimental art film made by Geoffrey Goodridge, the younger son of Helen Kirtland, founder of Ajijic Hand Looms. Goodridge, born in Mexico City, grew up in Ajijic, studied cinematography at the University of California Los Angeles, and showed *The Death of Antonio* at Laura Bateman's Rincón del Arte gallery in June 1967.[6]

Many Spanish language news programs were also filmed at the lake. In 1974, for example, on the first anniversary of the state government's Conozco Jalisco campaign, Guadalajara TV Channel 6 interviewed five Ajijic residents: Jan and Manuel Urzúa (owners of the Tejaban restaurant-boutique), Antonio Cárdenas (La Canoa boutique), Gail Michel (El Angel store) and Zara (La Rusa), "owner of the old gold mine west of the village." Manuel Urzúa. who also owned an avocado orchard, told viewers about the different varieties of avocados grown in Ajijic.[7]

Cine Ajijic

Commercial movies have been screened in Ajijic since the late 1940s, when the Cine Tapatío, a form of traveling cinema, began making regular visits to Ajijic and other nearby towns. The Cine Tapatío bus bringing the equipment would drive slowly into the village advertising the latest movie offerings by loud-speaker: "The announcements blared maddeningly but enticingly."[8]

A generator was installed outside the venue (Morelos 5) to power the projector. A whitewashed wall initially served as the screen. Following its partial collapse, films were projected onto a large white sheet, strung between two posts in the then-unroofed, dirt-floored patio, and sometimes onto the backs of the clucking chickens and squealing pigs who shared the experience.[9]

The weekly schedule included *cine tapatío* (Guadalajara films) on Tuesdays, *cine fronterizo* (border films) on Wednesdays and *cine hungaro* (Hungarian films) at weekends.[10] Cinema-goers could either bring their own chair or rent one for 20 centavos; children usually sat on the ground. Audience involvement was part of the fun:

When there was a love scene or a scene that required some reaction, those who were seated on the ground would flick their cigarettes to explode in red embers on the black and white images on the wall.[11]

Going to the cinema was not only about the films or enjoying a romantic evening: there were palm readers to tell your fortune, and tasty food available at the impromptu *fonda* (snack stand) set up in the street outside. In late 1966, Roberto Mosqueda Serna and his American-born wife, Carol Ann Melendy, returned to Ajijic from Los Angeles, bringing with them professional projectors.[12] They took over the showings while they helped build a purpose-built cinema, Cine Ajijic, on the north-east corner of the plaza.

Cine Ajijic opened in May 1969 on a property—belonging to Roberto's father, Florentino Mosqueda—which had previously been used as an animal jail, where stray animals were kept until their owners paid a small fine to recover them.[13] Roberto and his wife later bought out Florentino and operated the cinema jointly until 1975 when Carol Ann returned to the US with five of the couple's six children, including the two youngest, both born in Ajijic. Roberto continued to run Cine Ajijic after Carol Ann left.[14]

Ricardo Mosqueda, one of Roberto's sons, still lives in Ajijic and recalls that Cine Ajijic had two levels with seating for 850 people. Films for children were shown at weekend matinees; hungry youngsters could buy candy bars for 50 centavos and refried bean *lonches* for a peso.[15] Young boys were recruited to distribute promotional flyers throughout Ajijic, San Antonio Tlayacapan and San Juan Cosalá. While most films were in Spanish, English-language movies were also screened, usually on Wednesdays and Thursdays.

Carol Ann ran a *lonchería* outside the cine serving *aguas frescas*, hot dogs and other foods. For the English-speaking clientele, she baked home-made pies, relying on whatever fresh ingredients were in season. Old-timers still drool when they recall her apple, lemon meringue and banana cream pies.

As 8-tracks and home movies became more common, cinema-going diminished, and Cine Ajijic dimmed its lights for the final time in 1994. A succession of restaurants then rented the space. The Serratos family bought the property in 2006, and the Café Jardín opened the following year.[16]

International Film Festival

The standout cinematographic event in Ajijic in later years (and admittedly stretching the time frame of this book) was the Ajijic International Film Festival (Ajijic Festival Internacional de Cine), first organized in 1999. Founded by Jim Lloyd and Robin Lawrason, it was held annually for almost a decade. An army of volunteers helped raise funds, coordinate publicity and organize showings. Awards were given in various categories for films, shorts and screenplays. In the first year, 120 entries were received. By 2002 this number had doubled to 240 entries from 30 countries. In 2001 a special award was given to *Me Llaman Vida* (*I am Called Life*) for the best film drawing attention to the ecological plight of Lake Chapala.

Screenplays set in Ajijic

Eileen Bassing and her second husband, Robert (Bob) Bassing, both writers of some distinction, lived in Ajijic with her two sons between 1950 and 1954. Despite renting a home in the village for a paltry $5 a month, the family struggled to survive financially and eventually resorted to selling homemade fudge and operating a small fee-based lending library. Eileen later recalled that:

> [the library] was an amazing success even though most of our books were texts on psychiatry and philosophy. We were only open three hours a day but out of our returns we supported our family, a maid, a cook, a laundress and a gardener. We rented everything—even the *New York Times*, section by section, at 15 centavos per section. And those who borrowed the crossword puzzle had to promise to erase it when the page was returned.[17]

Besides being active in local theater productions, Bob, a former story editor at Colombia Pictures in Hollywood, was one of only two foreigners on Ajijic's "Junta de Mejoramiento Moral, Cívico y Material" (Council for Moral, Civic and Material Improvement), alongside Charles Moore.[18]

While in Ajijic, Eileen Bassing completed her first novel, *Home Before Dark*, later made into a Warner brothers movie. After returning to California, she wrote *Where's Annie?* (1963). Plans for a movie version of this novel, set entirely in Ajijic, were never realized.[19] In the book, a middle-aged female novelist seeking inspiration for her next novel gets to know a success-hungry young painter, a Black American bar-owner and a group of young men addicted to jazz and drugs. A rich *extranjero* newcomer buys up properties, evicts impoverished renters, and tries to get some of them deported. Money lending, shady real estate deals, betrayal, mayhem and even murder—nothing is beyond this motley crew of foreigners trying to escape their pasts.[20] The book explores the underlying tensions between local villagers and foreign incomers, tensions as true today as they were then.

The Bassings were already living in Ajijic when Glendon Swarthout, twice nominated for the Pulitzer Prize for fiction, spent six months there in 1951 with his wife and young son. Swarthout's short story "Ixion" is "the semi-autobiographical story of a young advertising man attempting to write his first novel in the little artist's colony of Ajijic."[21] His son, Miles, later turned it into a screenplay called *Convictions of the Heart*:

> Johnson [the main character] slowly realizes that his writing career is drying up faster than Lake Chapala, and this tale's poignant climax is a warning to impressionable young artists about getting sexually involved with their neighbors, to the detriment of their art and their life.[22]

If this movie were ever to be produced, surely it would strike a chord among the many Americans who have experienced romantic challenges as they tried to reinvent their lives in Mexico. Perhaps it is time for a crowdfunding campaign.

Hollywood writers

In addition to the many former stars of stage and film associated with the Lakeside Little Theatre (described in a later chapter), a long list of Hollywood celebrities have visited, lived in, or retired to Ajijic.

Famed Hollywood writer Lorenzo Semple Jr., best-known for creating the big-screen and TV character Batman, lived in Ajijic in the 1950s and returned several times. While at Lake Chapala, Semple wrote *The Golden Fleecing*, and *The Honeymoon Machine*, starring Steve McQueen.[23] He also worked on *Papillon* (1973), *King Kong* (1976), *Flash Gordon* (1980) and the James Bond film *Never Say Never Again* (1983).

Martin M Goldsmith and his wife—Estela Quinn-Oaxaca, the younger sister of movie star Anthony Quinn—lived in Ajijic in 1964, while Goldsmith worked on scripts for *The Twilight Zone*.[24] Goldsmith wrote more than a dozen screenplays including *Detour* (1945) and *The Narrow Margin* (1952), which earned him an Academy Award nomination.

English novelist and playwright Raymond "Ray" Rigby (my personal mentor) turned his back on a successful Hollywood career in 1972 to move to Mexico. After renting initially in Jocotepec, where he had numerous run-ins with the local postmaster who allegedly checked all incoming mail personally for cash and valuables, Rigby moved to San Antonio Tlayacapan for two years. Rigby's screenplay of his novel *The Hill,* starring Sean Connery, became a famous anti-war movie. Rigby subsequently married and moved to Guadalajara.[25]

Directors and producers

Film director and screenplay writer Alfredo Bolongaro-Crevenna visited Ajijic in about 1944 with Francisco Cabrera.[26] Both men were important figures in the golden age of Mexican cinema. Bolongaro-Crevenna, who had worked at the UFA film studios in Berlin, married his high school sweetheart Renate Horney, the youngest daughter of German American psychoanalyst Karen Horney (who spent several months in Ajijic in 1945).

Sherman Harris retired from Hollywood and moved to Ajijic with his second wife, Jane, to run the Posada Ajijic. Harris, a film editor and TV producer, was best known for the *Lone Ranger* movies and TV shows, and for the long-running TV series *Lassie.*[27]

Author and screenwriter Alejandro Grattan-Domínguez, born in El Paso, moved to Lake Chapala in 1987. He worked for 25 years in the film industry and has credits—as writer, director or producer—for *No Return Address* (1961), *The Undertaker and His Pals* (1966) and *Only Once in a Lifetime* (1979), which was the first major movie about the Mexican-American experience. Grattan-Domínguez, author of several novels and a long-time editor of the English-language monthly *El Ojo del Lago,* founded the very active Ajijic Writers' Group in 1988.

Set designers, artists and cinematographers

Allen Wadsworth, born in about 1939, exhibited his paintings in Ajijic in the mid-1970s, and honed his carpentry and painting skills in the village prior to embarking on a long and distinguished career in Hollywood as a scenic artist and set painter.[28] His Hollywood projects included *A Star is Born* (1976), *Arthur* (1981), and *Men in Black* (1997), as well as TV shows such as *The Love Boat, The Dukes of Hazzard* and *Falcon Crest.*

Orville Charles Goldner spent the 1970–71 winter in Ajijic with his wife, Dorothy. Goldner was an art director, puppeteer and special effects artist who worked for RKO Studios in the early 1930s on such films as *The Most Dangerous Game* (1932) and *King Kong* (1933).

William Colfax Miller and his third wife, Virginia Downs Miller, lived in Ajijic from the 1980s. After a stint in Hollywood in the 1930s, Miller fought in the Spanish Civil War before moving to Mexico to continue his career. He later claimed to have worked as an actor, director and film technician on more than 150 films, including *The Forgotten Village* (1941), Luis Buñuel's *Subida al Cielo* (1951), and the award-winning documentary *Walls of Fire* (1971).[29] Mexican-born Virginia Miller wrote dozens of columns for local papers and was a regular contributor to *El Ojo del Lago.*

The final paragraph belongs to the incomparable Elizabeth Taylor. This great American actress visited Chula Vista and Ajijic several times following her engagement in August 1983 to wealthy Guadalajara lawyer Victor González Luna, who so nearly became her eighth husband.

20

Ajijic Hand Looms (Telares Ajijic)

Several stores in Ajijic stock locally made handloomed textile items. The basic techniques of weaving in Mexico date back centuries, and the earliest *National Geographic* photos related to Lake Chapala, published in 1904, portray "Indian" women spinning and weaving in a domestic setting.[1] They were taken by hotelier-photographer Winfield Scott in the vicinity of his shoreline estate at Las Tortugas, near Ocotlán. Domestic spinning and weaving may be centuries old, but the earliest hand looms business in Ajijic dates back only as far as the 1940s.

That was when the Posada Ajijic's owner, Josefina Ramírez, hired José Mercado to construct several small hand looms and operate them at her inn. The looms were suitable for weaving small tablecloths, napkins and similar items. That business was short-lived; when Mercado and his family left Ajijic to live in Guadalajara, the looms languished unused in a corner of the inn.

These looms became the catalyst for Ajijic's earliest large-scale weaving business, an enterprise later known as Telares Ajijic, when their potential was recognized by an American couple living in the village: Helen Kirtland and her artist-writer husband, Mortimer (Mort) Carl. Carl arrived in Ajijic in 1946 to work on a book.[2] This is when he first met Michigan-born Kirtland who was enjoying a summer vacation with her three young children. Kirtland and her youngsters moved permanently to Ajijic the following year. Owing to the move, Kirtland never received notice that she owed 10 pesos (less than $2) for a minor infringement of the maritime trade law, and her name appeared on a list of tax debtors![3]

In 1950, shortly after Mort and Helen married, they came across four small dusty hand looms sitting, forgotten, at the Posada Ajijic and purchased them from Sra Ramírez for 500 pesos (about $40).[4] The creative genius behind the project was Helen, who had studied fashion and worked as a dress designer in New York.

Kirtland later tracked down José Mercado, who had made and operated the looms, and persuaded him to move back to Ajijic from Guadalajara, to teach apprentices the art of weaving, and make her some much larger foot-operated looms, suitable for producing dresses, larger tablecloths and yardage. While Mercado did not work full-time with Kirtland, he remained her master weaver for many years.[5]

Kirtland started by making placemats and belts but soon focussed on weaving enough fabric in original patterns to make clothes of her own design. She used plain cotton from Mexico and sourced threads dyed with colorfast aniline dyes from Germany. Wool came from New Zealand.[6]

Production rapidly outgrew the limited space available at the back of the Kirtland family home (at the intersection of Morelos and 16 de Septiembre) so Kirtland rented the next-door property and moved the business there. This property (16 de Septiembre 1) was immediately opposite the entrance to the Posada Ajijic, the perfect location to attract passing traffic.

In the early days Kirtland employed women weavers on the small looms for making belts and placemats, and men on the larger fabric looms. At its peak, Ajijic Hand Looms had 25 weavers, mainly men and boys. The largest loom was 2.5 meters (more than 8 feet) wide. Kirtland also employed many female workers to cut cloth and make, sew and embroider items of clothing.

Her designs, variants of which have been made in Ajijic ever since, were sympathetic to the different textiles used. The designs were often unusual and combined flair with a sound sense of fashion. Her judicious choice of colors and textures always worked perfectly. Kirtland's daughter, Katie Goodridge Ingram, explained that her mother's original designs often had colored stripes of different widths—where the precise tone and width of each stripe determined their visual and artistic impact—whereas most modern imitations used stripes of identical width and lacked such balance.[7]

Perhaps inevitably, the success of an outsider—and a woman—in establishing the looms business created a degree of envy and resentment in the village. Some Ajijitecos thought that Mercado deserved all the credit;

after all, he built the looms, taught the apprentices, and was the master weaver. For her part, Kirtland went out of her way to support Mercado and his family. She arranged a home for them when they first moved back to Ajijic, and intervened, despite the risks, when she saw him "being beaten for drunkenness by two soldiers" during a brief period when Ajijic was effectively under martial law.[8] Kirtland might not have succeeded without Mercado's considerable help, but Mercado had previously failed to succeed when lacking sufficient support.

The Ajijic looms business quickly became a success story, so much so that many of Kirtland's original designs were much imitated. The couple continued to innovate and paid a brief visit to Woodstock, New York, in 1952 (where Carl had lived prior to Mexico) to research that village's weaving industry.[9]

In addition to his writing and art, Mort Carl enjoyed golf and tennis. In the late 1940s he built his own clay court (probably the first court in Ajijic) on an empty lot rented for the purpose behind the family home (now the store Mi México). Kirtland made the white lines for the court out of bleached canvas; they were stapled (later nailed) into the ground and re-whitewashed every week. The net was an old fishing net, complete with weights, bought from a local fisherman and adapted for its new purpose with the addition of a double-stitched canvas band, precisely matching the sport's official regulations. Carl hosted regular tennis parties for friends from Guadalajara.[10]

By 1955, the looms in Ajijic were sufficiently well-known to be recommended in a US newspaper as a tourist sidetrip from Guadalajara:

> For handloomed fabrics you can drive to quaint little Ajijic (Ahhee-hic) on the edge of Lake Chapala, pick your own cloth from the looms of Helen and Mort Carl and then drive on to Jocotepec for the best selection of handwoven serapes in Western Mexico.[11]

Veteran travel writer James Norman, writing in 1959, complimented the weavers at Ajijic Hand Looms for turning out "fine-loomed woolens that are interesting in texture and shade." In the adjoining display store, Norman found "a variety of made-up men's tweed sport jackets, raw silk and linen shirts, linen bush-jackets, hand-loomed cotton shirts, skirts and blouses."[12]

By then, Ajijic Hand Looms already faced competition in Ajijic, mostly from former employees setting up their own shops. Norman, for instance, commented that Alfredo Villaseñor, who ran the Casa Mexicana (only a few doors further along 16 de Septiembre at number 353), had "a nice collection of locally embroidered blouses, quexquemetls, finely woven serapes and an interesting, featherlight woolen rebozo," all with prices "among the most reasonable in the village."

Weavers who had apprenticed at Ajijic Hand Looms were quick to emulate Kirtland's designs, colors and styles. Some former workers set up makeshift displays of their work alongside the main highway; another took his skills and made items for sale in Puerto Vallarta and other coastal towns.[13]

After Kirtland and Carl separated in about 1960, Kirtland remained in Ajijic; she continued to run Ajijic Hand Looms, aka Helen Kirtland Hand Looms, until 1973. Carl moved to Mexico City, where he established a similar hand loom weaving business.

Much as Kirtland loved her home at Morelos 8, where she raised her three children, and where Ajijic Hand Looms was first conceived, she coveted the wonderful garden property developed by her good friends Herbert and Georgette Johnson. After Herbert's death in 1960, Georgette returned to the UK. A few years later, Kirtland bought the eastern section of the property (Nicolas Bravo 35), complete with the main house, lily pond and famous garden.

All three of Kirtland's children grew up in Ajijic. John Goodridge, her elder son, was an international pharmaceuticals consultant. After he and his wife, Ingrid, bought the looms business, they settled in Ajijic, and were active in Amigos del Lago and the Lakeside Little Theatre. Together with his sister, Katie, and two other families, he founded Open School, a small pre-school; they also helped ensure the success of Oak Hill School.

Kirtland's younger son, Geoffrey Goodridge, studied cinematography at the University of California Los Angeles, and made *The Death of Antonio*, the first English-language movie shot in Ajijic, before changing his name to Azul and becoming a professional flamenco guitarist in Europe.

Katie Goodridge Ingram, Kirtland's daughter, is a prize-winning poet and writer who studied in California and taught in Africa. In the 1970s she returned to Ajijic, where she ran two successful art galleries—Galería del Lago and Mi México—for many years. She was also the Lake Chapala correspondent for the *Mexico City News*. She is the author of *According to Soledad: memories of a Mexican childhood*, a fascinating fictionalized memoir of growing up in Ajijic.

In addition to raising a family and starting a weaving business, Kirtland also found time for photography. When a baby died in the village, Kirtland was sometimes asked by the mother to take a portrait of their child prior to burial.[14] This practice, though sounding somewhat macabre, was common throughout Mexico, since very few families had a camera or could afford to have photographs taken of their offspring. Female photographers, seen as having greater empathy with the mother, were especially in demand on these sad occasions. From quite a young age, Kirtland's daughter, Katie, sometimes stepped in for her mother as photographer.

Prior to moving to Lake Chapala, Kirtland's home, in the Coyoacán district of Mexico City, was abuzz with the upper echelons of Mexican intelligentsia and highly educated refugees from Europe. Her neighbors and close friends included visual artists Diego Rivera, Frida Kahlo, Juan O'Gorman and his wife, Helen; Violette Mège and her husband, Michael Baxte; sculptor Armando Quesada, and Otto Butterlin, as well as writers and poets such as Anita Brenner, Gustav Regler and architect Alexander von Wutenau. Many of these illustrious friends subsequently visited Kirtland and her children in Ajijic; some took a cottage in the village to paint or complete their next book.

In the mid-1950s, Kirtland convinced Erik Erikson and his wife, Joan, to take advantage of the peace and quiet of Ajijic to write *Young Man Luther*. In the preface, Erikson thanks Larry Hartmus (who later married Kirtland) for reading "some of the medieval Latin with me in Ajijic." Hartmus was a Classics Professor at Reed College in Portland, Oregon.

In retirement, Kirtland bought herself a Swedish loom, and started hand-weaving her own tapestry designs, each a work of fine art in its own right.[15]

Telares Ajijic

When Helen Kirtland retired she sold the hand looms company to her son John and his wife, Ingrid, who ran the business, rebranded as Telares Ajijic, for the next twenty years. Telares Ajijic became "internationally famous for its cloth of bright and subtle colors, unusual textures and engaging designs" and developed an extensive line of wool, cotton and acrylic dresses, blouses, tablecloths, napkins and other items.[16] It was a perennial draw for tourists: a "big part of the charm in nosing around" was to watch the weavers "operate the ancient looms with their hands and feet to turn out huge rolls of brightly colored cloths."[17]

Telares Ajijic gradually moved away from the more artistic Helen Kirtland designs and adopted a more pragmatic approach to fabrics and clothes. It produced both the woven cloth and original fashion designs on the same premises and displayed its products at international trade fairs in the US, Switzerland and Germany. As times changed, wool gave way to cotton, and mass-produced competition from countries such as China and India adversely impacted the bottom line.

When Ingrid Goodridge retired in 1993, Telares Ajijic closed its doors, and the looms were sold to the weavers, several of whom started their own weaving studios. One former employee, Isidro Reyes, later moved back to the exact same premises opposite the former Posada Ajijic that Helen Kirtland had first occupied almost seventy years earlier. Visiting any of the village *talleres* offers visitors a rare opportunity to witness a weaving process largely unchanged since the introduction of the foot-operated loom into Mexico in the sixteenth century.[18] Little can Kirtland have imagined that her entrepreneurial efforts and passion would yield such long-term fruit.

Restaurant Los Telares (next door to Mí Mexico where John Goodridge grew up and named in honor of Ajijic Hand Looms) was formerly the residence of Esther Merrill, one of Helen Kirtland's best friends. So far as the foreign community in Ajijic understood, Merrill, a New Yorker, had been married to a very wealthy man connected to the Pepsi-Cola company. She lived on her own in the village, and it was widely assumed that she had an independent income from her ex-husband or his estate. She used a third party (*prestanombre*) to buy the house, a dubious procedure used by many foreigners in the early days to circumvent what they perceived as stringent regulations governing property ownership by non-Mexicans. Merrill completely renovated and updated the property, significantly increasing its value. Within days of her death, the *prestanombre* showed up, took immediate possession of the house, and flipped it for a massive windfall.[19]

21

Neill James the businesswoman

Even if her original motivation had primarily been to provide gainful employment for local women, Neill James was not a woman of independent wealth and needed to generate some income. During the 1950s she continued to run the shop, but also began a weaving business, had a short-lived venture keeping honey bees, and started to build and rent out village homes. She even found time, as described in later chapters, to organize a children's library and art program.

Embroidery, weaving and gift store

James expanded her embroidery and weaving business in the 1950s, working initially with cotton and wool, and then introducing her locally produced silk. By 1952, when the village population was about 2500, James employed up to eighty women doing piecework embroidery and making blouses.[1] With James' dog, Pluto, and her parrot, Paco, looking on, the women lined up every Thursday in James' tropical garden to exchange their work for much-needed pesos. The finished items were sold mainly via the gift store.

Katie Goodridge Ingram, who grew up in Ajijic in the 1950s and bought all her blouses from the store, explained that James "bought fabric and chose some simple cross-stitch patterns and had a series of shirt-blouses made with little men and women embroidered up and down the front."[2] The gift shop labels proudly proclaimed "Neill James: Cottage Industry Handwork for Women, Men, Children. Tropical Gardens. Open Daily" below a sketch of the arched entranceway to the shop.

Veteran guidebook writer James Norman liked Ajijic and admired the locally embroidered blouses at Casa Mexicana, run by weaver Alfredo

Villaseñor. He was, though, less than flattering about James' own gift shop:

> Quinta Tzintzuntzan is a larger, louder, Jones Beach kind of shop run by ex-author Neill James. I was not particularly stirred by the haphazard abundance of embroidery, the informal earring apparel and similar items. A block away in the tiny Casa Ajijic on Marcos Castellanos 235, I found much more appealing embroidery on table linens, blouses and skirts.[3]

The short-term promise of James' self-proclaimed revival of embroidered blouses fizzled out as the difficulties of marketing them became more apparent. She was envious of the almost immediate success of Helen Kirtland and her husband, Mort Carl, who had started their commercial looms business in 1950, and were selling enough items to make a decent living. While James could never hope to compete directly with their venture, she began, in 1952, to teach local women how to use smaller hand looms to weave small cotton and wool items such as women's blouses and scarves.[4] Whereas Kirtland employed mainly men as weavers (very much the tradition in this part of Mexico), James's weavers were almost all female, in line with indigenous practice in southern Mexico.

It had long occurred to James that it might be much more profitable to weave move valuable fibers than wool or cotton; items made of silk would fetch premium prices. But how could she get a steady supply of silk? James hatched a plan to produce her own. Having seen, and written about, silk production in Japan, James knew that starting sericulture in Ajijic required her to source silkworm eggs, as well as lots of mulberry leaves to feed the silkworm caterpillars.

According to her notes, James believed that she was introducing silk to Ajijic, apparently unaware that the Lake Chapala area, like many other parts of Mexico, once had native silkworms. The native silkworms in the Chapala area died out in the nineteenth century, according to this response (from Guadalajara) in 1885 to a nationwide appeal for silkworms: "in Chapala there are no longer any wild silkworms because they lived on the guayaba trees that have been cut down."[5]

In December 1950, James acquired 25 mulberry trees from Dr Varton Osigian, a world-renowned silk expert living in Mexico City, and planted them in her garden as a trial.[6] Each tree could yield, in just eight months, 8.5 kilograms (19 pounds) of leaves. She planted a further 80 trees the following April. Then she tried to hatch some silkworm eggs brought from Mexico City. Later that year Dr Osigian visited Ajijic, bringing with him some silkworms that were about to make cocoons. On 22 November 1951 the "first cocoon ever spun in Ajijic appeared on a piece of dry asparagus stick in a jar."[7] The good doctor held an open meeting in the plaza two evenings later to explain the industry's potential for helping the village.

James wrote excitedly to a friend in Wyoming in December 1951 that "My silk caterpillars grow apace. If this silk project is a success, ours will be the richest village in Mexico in five years. Can't wait to see!! I have unwound one silk and it is very fine."[8]

The following February, James hired Consuela Flores as her first "silk employee," with an initial monthly salary of 65 pesos ($7.70), raised to 90 pesos a year later. Working alongside Flores with the silkworms and silk spinning in October 1952 were Digna Padilla, Anita Padilla, Antonio Ramos and Venancio Cárdenas.[9] At that time, James was also employing two brick masons, three weavers and a girl to spin the delicate silk thread, in addition to her domestic staff of two women doing the washing, two gardeners, a maid and a housekeeper.

James acquired more mulberry trees and continued to experiment. Among the cocoons harvested in November 1952 were some Golden Chinese that "produce a most beautiful rich golden thread." James eventually brought in hundreds of white mulberry trees (mora blanca) from Uruapan in Michoacán, and planted as many as she could in her own garden, offering others free to families around the village.

And, whereas she had purchased her first silkworm eggs, she now developed a self-sustaining system to retain and hatch eggs laid by her own adult silk moths each season.

In December 1953, James was justly proud to be invited to take part in the Primera Gran Feria de Jalisco. James' well-decorated booth attracted lots of interest from the viewing public and earned her a thank-you letter signed by the event's organizer, businessman Jorge Dipp Murad.[10]

Scaling up silk production was not without its challenges. James built a specialist silk farm in the mid-1950s to house up to 60,000 silkworms at a time; they all needed to be fed fresh mulberry leaves for about 40 days before making cocoons, with silk moths hatching out eighteen days later. To preserve the cycle, James collected the eggs laid by adult silk moths and stored them in her refrigerator for up to a year until it was time for the next batch of worms.[11]

Some batches were trouble-free. In April 1954, for instance, James reported that she had harvested 1292 cocoons weighing 1.57 kg. However, most of the August batch of silk worms had a "horrible death" when they were fed mulberry leaves that proved to be toxic. The leaves had been contaminated when nearby olive trees had been sprayed with a mix of chlordane and nicotine (widely used at the time but now banned) as protection against a plague. Several weeks of rain since the spraying had done nothing to diminish the potency of the pesticides.[12]

Despite the obstacles, James still retained high hopes for her silk business as it entered the 1960s.

Beehives and honey

Alex von Mauch had tried keeping bees and selling honey in Ajijic back in the 1930s. Neil James tried again in the late 1950s and kept a dozen colonies of honey bees for close to a decade.[13] A series of postcard images of Ajijic taken in about 1957 by Dutch-Hawaiian photographer Jacques Van Belle included an image of a beekeeper (not James) attending her hives. This postcard was one of several taken by Van Belle, presumably on commission, to promote her store and other assorted businesses. Honey production proved to be more of a hobby than a business and was never very profitable.

Building a property portfolio

During the 1950s, in addition to the final transactions needed to consolidate ownership of her own home and gardens, James entered the murky world of property speculation. James' nemesis in this enterprise— as it was for her weaving venture—was Helen Kirtland, who had lived in Ajijic since 1947 after many years in Mexico City. The two women could hardly have been more different. East coast sophisticate met Dixie. Kirtland was fluent in Spanish and had close friends among the artistic and literary elite in Mexico City; despite her world travels, James had limited language skills and no real connections in Mexico. Kirtland was never long out of a relationship with a man and was married half-a-dozen times; James, allegedly lesbian, had few serious relationships and preferred her own company.

James completed a dizzying succession of real estate transactions in the 1950s, as she snapped up inexpensive land or properties and then remodeled any existing buildings or built small, modern cottages suitable for rentals. The first was in April 1953, when James agreed to pay 2500 pesos (in instalments) to Mariano Medeles Arreola for an undeveloped lot near the La Reina spring (Ojo de agua La Reina). The following year, Laurance Williams wrote to the tax authorities in Chapala from overseas saying that James had just bought his house in Ajijic and he wanted them to assist her with the transfer.

In February 1955, James received permission to buy four more pieces of land: a 400-square-meter lot planted with fruit trees further along Calle 16 de Septiembre; an undeveloped 2200-square-meter lakefront parcel called El Ahuacate; an undeveloped lot—La Ruina—of 2835 square meters adjacent to El Ojo de Agua; and a small 312-square-meter lot with a building on Calle Guadalupe, adjacent to the church. She sold this central Ajijic property to Italo Brandi the following year for 286,250 pesos (about $22,900).

James bought a large 3727-square-meter rustic property at Seis Esquinas on the western side of Ajijic in August 1955. This land, intended (at least originally) for growing mulberry trees, was the southeast corner lot, bounded to the north by Calle Ocampo and to the west by Calle Libertad (formerly Calle Colmena). James added an adjoining 420-square-meter property the following year, when she also acquired a nearby small finca of 133 square meters on the west side of Calle Libertad.

When Canadian photographer Leonard McCombe arrived in Ajijic in 1957 to document the somewhat indolent lifestyle of expatriate Americans at Lake Chapala for *Life*, he photographed Neill James using a metal detector to look for gold on a recently acquired property.[14] Searching for buried treasure was one of her more offbeat pastimes. Like Zara, James was completely convinced of the veracity of local legends about hidden treasure dating back to the Revolution. Every time a village home passed through her hands, James and her then workman, Marcos Guzmán, never failed to check for treasure before moving on.[15]

In October 1957, James paid Juan Ibon Villanueva and Juana González viuda de Rivera a mere 500 pesos between them, according to the relevant deed, for 1100 square meters at number 304 on the north side of Calle 16 de Septiembre. By May 1960, James had built a 108-square-meter (1160-square-foot) house there with boveda ceilings, dining room, bathroom, living room and kitchen. When she registered the work as complete, the property was assessed for taxation purposes as having a value of 9000 pesos and a rental value of 70 pesos a month.

During the 1950s land prices had risen rapidly. Whereas James had paid only a few pesos (at most) a square meter for properties she bought in the early 1950s, she had to pay 75 pesos a square meter by September 1960, when she bought another 512 square meters on Calle 16 de Septiembre (numbers 359 and 360) from José Perales and his mother, Aniset Antolin. At that time she also bought a 325-square-meter property in west Ajijic.

James was by no means the first property speculator in Ajijic. Not long before her arrival in Ajijic, Ernesto Butterlin had purchased several undeveloped plots of land (with a combined area of 10,998 square meters) on Calle Juárez (now Calle 16 de Septiembre) in April 1943 from Esther Rivera Casillas. Their eventual sale must have netted Butterlin a tidy sum. Herbert and Georgette Johnson also undoubtedly made a handsome profit by selling some of the land they had acquired in the early 1940s.

By the end of the 1950s, James had amassed a considerable land reserve, which she would expand even further in later years.

22

Save the Lake

The pioneering foreign residents of Ajijic had been attracted to the lake more by its climate, scenery, small villages and rural life style than by its amenities, infrastructure or living costs. Many saw it as a small slice of paradise. Little did they know that the lake—so central to their decision to live in Ajijic—would by the mid-1950s be on the very brink of extinction.

Villagers had always lived with the vagaries of the lake. It was a reliable source of water and fish, its beaches were used for washing clothes and drying nets. It could also, though, generate waves that overturned fishing boats, and winds that spawned fearsome water spouts. Based on a visit to Ajijic in the 1940s, novelist Barbara Compton wrote:

> I gathered that what they most dread is a waterspout that can sweep everything, houses, people, cattle into the lake. Apparently this thing forms itself out over the lake from among the clouds, and slowly winds itself into the form of a snake overhead. When this happens, all the women go out from the village in a solid phalanx to pray that the snake remain in the cloud above and not point its head down to strike.[1]

This is an accurate depiction of the local oral tradition that, when a waterspout (*culebra*) is seen, women should rush out of the house and hold a child aloft. They pray as the child wields a knife to make a cross slashing the waterspout (not the safest behavior in an electrical storm), thereby diminishing the fury of the storm.

Way back in time, in June 1588, it literally "rained little white fish" on Ajijic.[2] Three centuries later, in August 1880, two waterspouts struck

Ajijic on the same day. They wrecked crops, washed rocks and trees into the lake, and destroyed three houses, fortunately without any loss of life.[3] In September 1988 a severe storm with waterspouts caused massive damage to several houses on Calle Tempisque, with localized flooding in Las Salvias, Rancho del Oro and La Floresta.[4] In recent years similarly severe storms in Ajijic, such as that of October 2021, have caused even greater damage, serving to expose a lack of oversight as regards urban planning regulations and enforcement.

Soon after Neill James arrived in the village in 1943, several years of unusually poor rainfall caused the lake level to start to drop. It fell by more than 5 meters (16 feet) to reach an all-time low in 1955. Fishermen had to cross a wide expanse of dried-up lakebed just to reach their boats. Dust storms during the dry season were worse than ever. Had the level of the lake, which is far shallower than its size would suggest, dropped even one more meter, it would have disappeared completely.

One of the first foreign residents to become aware that the lake level was falling was English engineer Herbert Johnson. Johnson had installed a rain gauge and began keeping meticulous weather records in August 1940.[5] In the middle of that month he witnessed his first *culebra*, on a day when more than 8 centimeters (3 inches) of rain fell in a 24-hour period.

The following year, Johnson also started to record the level of the lake, by reference to where it lapped against specific trees, rocks and marks on the pier. Serious concern for the lake's future emerges from the additional notes he made in his log. One page, titled "Climatic Changes," summarized a 1949 article about the dramatic shrinking of the Caspian Sea over the previous decade;[6] Johnson was clearly worried that Lake Chapala might do the same.

Johnson's data show that 1941 was an exceptionally wet year in Ajijic, with 196 centimeters (77 inches) of rain. Rainfall the following year totaled 113 centimeters (44 inches), close to the probable long-term average for the village. However, the average rainfall for the next twelve years (1943–1954 inclusive) was only 88 centimeters (35 inches). This low rainfall (echoed throughout the Lerma-Chapala basin) was the direct cause of the precipitous fall in the level of the lake in the mid-1950s.

Johnson clearly recognized the impacts of the falling level of the lake. For example, his entry for 31 July 1943 noted that, "Owing to lack of rain, the *huerta* [orchard] was irrigated from the pump." Things only got worse. In June 1946, he wrote "The lake level has sunk so low that the intake pipe was at, or [above] water level, so that pumping was restricted or entirely suspended. The *huerta* suffered much." He added, in pencil: "It would seem that the change in currents and 'wash' of the beach, wrought by the construction of the *muelle* [pier] has altered the contours of the little bays on either side of the muelle."

Thankfully, once normal rainfall patterns were reestablished, the lake recovered. The average rainfall for 1955–59, the final five years of Johnson's records—he died in 1960—was 116 centimeters (46 inches).

In the early 1950s, Johnson was certainly not the only one to realize that the lake was falling. The drought affected much of western Mexico, and farmers throughout the region were suffering. River and lake levels were dropping, wells were drying up, animals perished, and crops were lost.

What could be done to reverse the crisis? One of the more harebrained proposals was to reduce the amount of water the lake was losing from evaporation each year by reducing its area. Lopping off the easternmost 180 square kilometers of the lake, by building an embankment across the lake from Petatán to El Fuerte (midway between Ocotlán and Jamay), would—argued some engineers—save the lake for future generations.[7]

The federal government made plans in 1953 to carry out this scheme. Not surprisingly, it met fierce resistance from Lake Chapala residents, and was one of the catalysts for the formation the following year of the Comité Pro-Defensa del Lago de Chapala, a citizens' group to protect the lake. José Guadalupe Zuno was the group's first president and Ricardo Delgado Román its founding secretary. Zara (La Rusa) was at the forefront of this fight to save the lake.

As the drought worsened, the continuing extraction of water from the lake to power the hydro-electricity plant at El Salto was seen as wasteful and potentially the final nail in the lake's coffin. Already, the water was so low that the electricity supply to Guadalajara had become increasingly erratic. A huge swathe of lakebed was exposed and it was almost possible to wade to the nearby islands.

In May 1955, at the height of the crisis, Zara made a direct appeal on behalf of concerned American residents to US President Eisenhower for mobile electricity generators, asking him to enact the good neighbor policy and send help immediately to save the dying lake. A month later, the US consul announced that a 10,000-kilowatt, self-contained, diesel-fueled power-train had been placed at the service of the Jalisco state government.[8] Zara headed the list of more than twenty Americans who signed an open letter publicly thanking Mexico for its warm hospitality and the US government for its positive response.[9]

Zara had no doubts about gender equality and was never one to shirk a challenge or take "No" for an answer. If she decided to fight for something, she used a combination of reason, strongly expressed opinions, and theatrics to take on anyone, regardless of their social or political status. Nowhere was this better exemplified than in Zara's role in the Save the Lake campaign of the 1950s.

The level of the lake was still alarmingly low when *Life* magazine photographer Leonard McCombe visited in 1957.[10] McCombe took a striking image of Zara, dressed all in white, astride her chestnut horse in the garden of Quinta Tzintzuntzan. The "US-born ex-ballerina who wears Hungarian riding costume" was visiting Neill James to "discuss how the American colony can help save the local lake which is drying up." Fortunately for all local residents, by the end of the decade, several years of plentiful rainfall had returned the lake to its normal level.

There is no question that Zara was one of the earliest female environmental activists in the region. In 1959, for instance, she wrote on behalf of the American community in Jalisco to the United Nations in New York, requesting urgent humanitarian help to supply gloves and masks to the young men who were spraying DDT across Jalisco in the government's efforts to eradicate malarial mosquitos.[11]

In the 1960s and 1970s the level of the lake was actually higher than its long term average, and in 1967 the lake reached its highest level for decades, so high that it submerged the pier in Chapala and flooded parts of Chapala, Ajijic and other lakeside communities.

23

Violent crime

One of the most jaw-dropping moments I've had in recent years was in 2017 while watching a CGTN America video in which correspondent Mike Kirsch somehow kept a straight face while claiming that "not one foreigner" had been the "victim of violent crime in Ajijic since the 1940s."[1]

If only that were true! Ajijic is no more dangerous than most places—and a lot less dangerous than many—but there have been many violent crimes against foreigners in the village over the years, some more eye-popping than others, starting with the infamous murder of German pharmacist Juan Jaacks in 1896.

Back in those days, the security apparatus was very different to today. A small number of paid "police" were based in each major center to oversee law and order. For instance, in 1898 the security detail in the municipality of Chapala consisted of one inspector, one leader (*cabo*) and four gendarmes. Whenever extra manpower was needed, the gendarmes would call on the volunteers in the local *acordada* (which functioned somewhat like a posse) to ride their own horses, and carry their own weapons, in pursuit of bandits. The Ajijic *acordada* in 1898 had twenty members.[2]

A similar system of social defense groups was still in operation in Ajijic in 1935. After armed bandits made a series of assaults on Ajijic that year, the federal forces who chased after them were assisted by the social defense groups of Ajijic, Potrerillos and several other places. The resulting five-hour gun battle east of Chapala left five men dead. The Ajijic contingent of twenty men was led by Arnulfo Rosas.[3]

The earliest recorded murder related to Ajijic where both victim and perpetrator were foreign resulted in a body washing ashore in the village in

1922.[4] The corpse was found without any clothes and missing some gold teeth. The murdered man was eventually identified as an Italian man, S Revel, who had come from Canada to Guadalajara to buy property and was said to have brought a valise containing around $10,000 in gold with him.[5] He met two Spaniards, who suggested he purchase land at Lake Chapala. Posing as a friend of theirs, an Italian man took Revel out to the lake, where he robbed and murdered him.

As we move forward, Mike Kirsch, please take note: here are brief details of selected noteworthy violent crimes in Ajijic involving foreigners since the 1940s.

In 1956, German-born artist Otto Butterlin, who had become a naturalized Mexican citizen in 1935, died in suspicious circumstances in Ajijic from a gunshot wound to the head. Did he take his own life or was he murdered? The German Embassy in Mexico City reported to one of his friends in Germany that Otto had died by his own hand.[6] However, Otto's brother Friedrich claimed that, even if the weapon used was Otto's, the trajectory and path of the fatal bullet was not consistent with someone trying to shoot himself. According to Friedrich, the local police had carried out only a lax and half-hearted investigation before closing the case as quickly as possible.[7] If Otto was murdered, who was responsible? According to journalist Kenneth McCaleb, some people said that Otto had been "killed by his mistress." Otto's daughter, Rita, later told her own daughter that "Otto was murdered by Mr Green."[8]

The motel in Chula Vista was the scene of a barroom brawl and murder in July 1968. Harold W Tobin, a prominent San Francisco attorney who had been living in San Juan Cosalá, was arrested by police after he shot Michael Rodriguez of San Jose, California, to death during an argument.[9]

On 21 June 1975 an elderly Canadian woman, Agnes Bresner, was assaulted and killed in her Ajijic home. The police arrested several young men for burglary and murder. Under questioning it emerged that members of the gang were also responsible for the previously unsolved homicide two years earlier of Manuel Venegas (El Memin), a local bricklayer.[10]

Residents of Ajijic were sufficiently concerned about the high level of crime in the village following this murder that they called for a meeting with government officials.[11] Such meetings have occurred with increasing frequency since then. A year after the murder, Zara wrote to a friend explaining that she thought the situation had improved:

After the shocking murder of the Canadian lady most of the really wealthy left and with them most of the thieves. We have had no more major robberies. Perhaps getting out the Federales if only for two days and a patrol at night over a period of time made them see what they were in for. I hope so.[12]

Things did not remain quiet for long. A spate of brazen carjackings occurred in 1977–78, including one immediately outside the Posada Ajijic at 8.00pm on a Monday evening. Anyone who resisted was badly beaten and thrown to the sidewalk.[13]

Getting away with murder

Joe Kovach's horrific slaying of Donna McCready in January 1987 is one of the most scandalous ever in Ajijic, not least because Kovach fled first to the US and then to his native Hungary (where he died in 2011), without ever being apprehended or charged. Between 1983 and 1986 both Kovach and McCready had directed several shows at the Lakeside Little Theatre. The titles of the three plays she directed now seem prescient of impending doom: *An Almost Perfect Person* (1984), followed by *Send Me No Flowers* (1985) and *Duet for One* (1986), in which Kovach played a psychiatrist.

McCready was a cold, calculating lesbian who was looking for fun, money and revenge, and found all three, to paraphrase the words of the late Jan Dunlap, who knew her better than most. McCready had arrived in Ajijic a decade earlier with a much older woman, Lois Schaefer. When that relationship broke down, McCready embarked on a series of affairs with married women, including one with Kovach's wife, Barbara. With his wife watching on, the enraged Kovach stabbed McCready to death with a hunting knife in her home on Calle del Roble in Chula Vista.[14]

What made this crime particularly heinous is that McCready had allegedly killed at least two husbands of former lovers, according to local gossip and her own unguarded claims when inebriated. Her alleged victims included Stephen Harris Harrington (whose wife watched from a closet) and Albert Taylor. In Dunlap's fictional version of events, McCready also murdered two female victims.[15]

Apart from expressing sadness and revulsion in the aftermath of Kovach killing McCready, the Mexican community was, according to the *Guadalajara Reporter,* "asking a probing question: If the murderer had been a Mexican citizen, what would the US press be doing at this moment?"[16]

Three years later, in June 1990, the Ajijic community was appalled by the murder during a home invasion of Betty Mathews, a long-time resident of the village, who had been extremely active in the community for more than two decades, raising funds and working tirelessly for various non-profits, including the Lakeside School for the Deaf. Betty, a nationally known US tennis star, and her husband, Ralph, a pioneering radio engineer and co-founder of Zenith Radio Corporation, had retired to Ajijic in the 1960s.[17]

In 1999 amateur archeologist Robert Koll and his partner, Melba Wasey, both in their nineties, were murdered in their own living room, in the home they rented within a block of the Lake Chapala Society. Koll had retired with his wife, Peggy, to Ajijic in 1968 and indulged a passion for archeology, including field trips to Easter Island. After an amicable separation from his wife, some years later Koll met Wasey, a former Broadway singer and dancer, who volunteered in the Lake Chapala Society library. An assailant, who was never caught, cut Koll's throat and strangled Wasey.[18] None of their valuables was taken, so this was a targeted killing, reportedly because the rental's owner wanted to regain possession.

The following year, Norris Price, aged 67, and his wife, Nancy, 62, both very prominent in community activities, were shot to death at their home in Ajijic, allegedly over a land dispute. A brief report of the incident in *The Seattle Times* added that "Four Americans have been slain in Ajijic in the last 2½ years."[19]

In 2011, Chris Kahr, a US citizen, was helping his wife unload groceries from their car when a thief tried to steal his wallet. Kahr was fatally shot in the chest when he turned to confront his attacker, who fled empty-handed. Kahr was the third American from the communities bordering Lake Chapala to have been murdered that year.[20]

During a home invasion in February 2014, Canadian writer Linda (Nina) Discombe and her long-time partner, Edward Kular, were both killed. They had been regular winter visitors to Ajijic for years.[21]

Hiding out in Ajijic?

One stand-out among the many dubious characters who have lived in Ajijic over the years is Mitch Marr junior, an amateur artist who moved to Villa Nova with his wife, Ermajean, in the mid-1970s.[22] Marr was the notorious CIA handler for Terry Reed, who played an active role in the Iran-Contra affair when he established a machine-tool business in Guadalajara as a front for the "guns-in, drugs-out" operation in Central America. Reed and his wife, Janis (who taught at Oak Hill School), lived in Ajijic from 1986 to 1988. Reed coauthored *Compromised: Clinton, Bush and the CIA*, an international best seller.[23]

In recent decades, a number of known, wanted or former criminals have tried to avoid justice by hiding out in Ajijic. Every few years, it seems, another fugitive is hauled out of Ajijic in handcuffs. In 2005 it was Perry March, a Nashville lawyer on the lam after killing his wife. In 2010 it was Rebecca Parrett, who fled before her sentencing in a multi-billion-dollar corporate fraud case in Columbus, Ohio.

In an entirely different category—since she had already served her time—songwriter and artist Gail Delta Collins lived the last years of her life in Ajijic. Tall and glamorous Collins moved to Ajijic in 1985, having served a short sentence for killing her rock star husband, Felix Pappalardi. Collins, who died in Ajijic in 2013, wrote the lyrics for dozens of tracks performed by the bands Cream and Mountain, and created artwork for numerous album covers.

24

The Lake Chapala Society

On 15 January 1955 a diverse band of foreign residents then living in Chapala met to form The American Society. Twenty-one people signed up, elections were held for officers, and two committees established: Mosquito Control and Information Service. General John Ratay was elected president, with Colonel Louis Lippincott as vice president and Alan Campbell as treasurer.[1]

In February 1955 the members changed the name to The Chapala Society. In its first year this group opened a children's reading room (*biblioteca*) with English and art classes, a lending library for society members and an information office, all operating out of a leased building at Lopez Cotilla 282 in Chapala. It also started the process to have a section of the Chapala municipal cemetery set aside for foreign residents.

The society's information officer prepared a summary of living expenses to mail out to anyone seeking such information. In June 1955 rents ranged from 200 to 1200 pesos ($15 to $96) a month. Rentals were usually unfurnished; low rent homes usually required "from 2000 to 5000 pesos or more to make the house or apartment habitable." Wages for housemaids were 80 to 120 pesos a month, with the employer either furnishing at least two meals a day or an additional 2-3 pesos a day food allowance. Cooks earned 100-200 pesos a month, with a similar food allowance. Daily rates were 7-8 pesos for a gardener-handymen, 10-14 pesos for a mason, 12-30 pesos for a carpenter and about 15 for a plumber.[2]

A list, probably compiled by the society, of 34 foreign families (50 individuals) residing in Chapala in June 1955 reveals that many of them had not joined; some non-members at that time were undoubtedly opposed to the whole idea.

The Chapala Society was renamed the Lake Chapala Society (LCS) on 1 July 1964, in an effort to increase its appeal to other communities around the lake such as Jocotepec and the villages on the southern shore.[3]

Almost all the society's early members lived in Chapala. By 1971, however, a growing proportion lived in Ajijic. The 1971 Membership Roster listed about 550 members, with approximately 230 living in Chapala, 110 in Chula Vista and 160 in Ajijic.[4] The remaining members were scattered between San Juan Cosalá, Jocotepec, the south shore, and a handful had addresses further afield.

In the 1970s the LCS began setting aside funds for the education of students in need. Its scholarship program to assist students, particularly those in tertiary education, has continued to grow, and the society now provides funding support for a large number of children and young adults.

A newsletter hand-dated October 1973, when the society offices were still in Chapala, explained that it was sponsoring a Spanish language *biblioteca* in Chapala for local children and offering free lessons in English, painting and flower making. However, the completed artwork and flowers would be exhibited and sold at the Galería del Lago in Ajijic, with the young artists receiving 50% of the sale price.[5]

The earliest mention of the LCS talking books program, a literary lifeline for those with limited sight, comes from 1976, when Gertrude Ratay (the wife of the society's first president) received talking books from the Library of Congress.[6] The program was later formalized (for members who were US citizens and visually impaired) by Helen Horder and an assistant into the LCS Talking Books Library; it was the only library of its kind in Mexico. Modern technology has reduced its significance today, though LCS continues to organize a varied menu of medical services and life-long learning opportunities.

By 1979, LCS had almost 1000 members, with a much higher proportion living in Ajijic than previously, following the completion of a succession of new subdivisions. The society's growing links to Ajijic led it to relocate its administrative offices there in about 1980, not long after seeking legal non-profit status as a Civil Association (Asociación Civil). Following an unusually lengthy process, which took more than a decade, LCS finally acquired this status in 1989, more than thirty years after the soceity's initial foundation.

The society moved to its current location in Ajijic, on Calle 16 de Septiembre, in October 1983, when Neill James offered it the use of part of her Quinta Tzintzuntzan property rent-free for five years, provided it took over the management of the Ajijic children's library located there.[7] Despite rarely having been an LCS member, it was James' generosity that enabled the organization to move from Chapala to Ajijic at a time when it was struggling financially and desperately needed new premises. And she made this offer despite always having been far more interested in helping her Mexican neighbors than in helping the foreign community. As the late Tom Faloon succinctly put it, in fact "Neill James was not very interested in the foreign colony at all."[8]

About a year after the LCS moved to Quinta Tzintzuntzan, James suffered a severe stroke that impaired her memory and faculties. In October 1986, with her sister Jane's help, she made a will leaving everything to her surviving nieces and nephews, except for the library building which was bequeathed, with the ground beneath it and all its books, to the LCS, provided it maintained the children's library in perpetuity.

This was apparently not generous enough for the society, whose membership and services had grown rapidly during the 1980s. Perhaps not surprisingly, one faction within the society had long coveted all 5000 square meters of James' property with its two brick houses, fish ponds and gardens.

Shortly after Jane, now legally responsible for James' financial affairs, was widowed in 1989, she was contacted by the newly elected LCS President Arthur Melby, a former FBI undercover intelligence officer, who proposed that the society take care of all James' future day-to-day needs, and provide whatever support she needed to remain in her own home, in exchange for ownership of the entire property. For a mix of motives, Jane, who had always declared she had no interest whatsoever in owning any property in Mexico, agreed.

Melby's own version of how this agreement came about is refreshingly blunt:

> At our first board meeting, I announced that we should convince Neill James to gift her entire property to the LCS in exchange for lifelong elder care. Miss Neill, now well into her 90's, was having a difficult time managing her own affairs and I felt that we could create a win-win situation for both her and us. Both Miss Neill and the board eagerly agreed and 34 years after its founding, the LCS had its own home.[9]

Though none of her close friends believed that Neill James was in any fit state to sign any such agreement, the legal title was transferred in January 1990[10] and the LCS orchestrated a campaign to ensure that James was recognized as a major benefactress of the village. James was named Woman of the Century and was the subject of numerous adulatory newspaper pieces. She was, quite rightly, awarded a Lifetime Achievement Award by *El Ojo del Lago* in 1990. Homage was also paid to James by Ajijic's homegrown artistic community.

Yet, despite their stated love for James, the LCS board apparently rejected an offer from Jane to purchase and install a television with satellite channels to give her sister some contact to the outside world in her final years.[11]

James died on Saturday 8 October 1994, and her ashes were interred at the base of a favorite tree in her beloved garden. Some twenty years later, a thoughtless remodeling of the garden disturbed her remains, causing offence to all who still remember her. The plaque commemorating James in the LCS does not even have her date of birth correct. The gardens today are beautiful and well-kept, but a pale shadow of what they were like when James was tending them, or how they looked after Alejandro Treviño's tasteful restoration in the early 1990s.

Shortly after her death, the LCS disposed of most of James' memorabilia, photographs and small personal library, with little or no thought as to their true monetary or historic value. What is most saddening about this unfortunate loss of a significant part of Ajijic's cultural heritage is that, only five years earlier, the LCS itself—and its then president Cody Summers—had appealed publicly for donations of similar materials:

> It has been brought to our attention that private libraries and memorabilia of Ajijican residents are winding up in Guadalajara. It is urgently requested that consideration be made to keeping those libraries in Ajijic. The Lake Chapala Society would welcome all such donations to the Neill James Biblioteca. Plans are now on the drawing board for an addition to our present library... a research room.[12]

Thankfully, at least one interesting volume, signed by James, found its way from the discard stack outside the LCS Library to my own bookshelves, and some exceptionally important early photos of Ajijic were rescued from the trash by a concerned individual and are now in safekeeping elsewhere in the village.

The society does still store and maintain a small archive of documents and photographs related to James, an archive which was of immense help in the research for this book. In 1997, barely three years after her death, the LCS published (and copyrighted) a re-issue of *Dust on My Heart*, possibly not realizing that James had renewed the copyright of the book in 1973, a renewal that remains in effect under US law until 2041.[13]

In addition to its main property, the LCS also owns the Wilkes Education Center, which provides learning materials and support for Mexican students and their families. The building, at Galeana 18, was bequeathed to the society by long-time member Ed Wilkes. Its four classrooms, kitchen, covered patio, and Spanish-language library were dedicated in March 1999 and provide an invaluable link with the local Mexican community. In 2016 the LCS added to its main property by buying the two-story lakefront home formerly owned by Ruth Darling. Its most recent acquisition (in 2021) is the former home (Ramón Corona 14) of Doris and John Molinari, a property adjacent to Quinta Tzintzuntzan.

Of particular value to anyone interested in Ajijic's history is the LCS Oral History Project, in which old-timers (Mexican and foreign) and former art students were interviewed on camera about their memories of the LCS, Neill James and life in Ajijic in past decades. Many of these worthwhile and interesting recordings are available online. One common thread that emerges from watching them is just how much more socially cohesive Ajijic was thirty or forty years ago than today.

The annual LCS membership directories for 2016-2019 offer strong support for claiming that Ajijic is one of the most cosmopolitan villages in the world. While acknowledging that only most (not all) of its 2500-plus members live in Ajijic, the non-Mexican LCS members during that period came from at least 38 different countries.[14]

The Lake Chapala Society is easily the largest single organization of its kind in the area and an invaluable resource for the foreign community. But it has a mixed history in terms of its engagement with the local Mexican community. Despite its many laudable efforts to expand its educational and other services for children, which have been a huge benefit to local families for decades, the society's efforts to reach the adult Mexican community have, to date, been far less successful.

25

Educational initiatives

From its early days the foreign community, including those who opted for one reason or another to homeschool their children or send them away to school, got firmly behind (and in some cases led) efforts to improve the provision and quality of public education and health care in the region. This chapter considers education, a later chapter looks at the provision of health care.

Public schools

As long ago as 1896, Ajijic had both a boys' school, directed by Apolonio Arellano, with 128 students, and a girls' school, directed by Maria Gallardo, with 164 students. San Antonio Tlayacapan had classes for 100 boys and 27 girls. We don't know for sure what subjects were taught in these schools. However, at that time a small school in San Nicolás (east of Chapala) offered geometry, physical education, writing, reading, arithmetic and grammar, while a larger school in Jocotepec also offered instruction in morals, politeness, human rights, Mexican history, natural history and singing.[1]

A US journalist who visited the Ajijic schools in 1898 found that they were well attended and that "enthusiasm for learning abounded."[2] The children were especially good at geometry. The teachers "showed zeal and a genuine love of their work." The visitor also reported that fifty adult males assembled nightly to study in an evening school, and had learned to read newspapers and discuss current events. Evening classes, disrupted during the Mexican Revolution, resumed in 1923, when Domingo Flores Baeza, the director of the Economic School for Children of Ajijic-Chapala (Escuela Económica para Niños de Ajijic-Chapala), received permission to start an Evening School for Workers (Escuela Nocturna para Obreros) in the village.[3]

The good reputation of teachers was further enhanced in 1932 when Ajijic schoolteacher Manuel Urzúa was hailed as a hero after he pulled three young children out of a house fire on Calle Ocampo; sadly two of them died shortly afterwards. The six-year-old girl who survived still lives at the same address and, at the time of writing, is still going strong at 95 years of age.[4]

A new primary school was built in 1933–1934 on part of the former graveyard which had extended from the church to the plaza. The new school was named in honor of Father Marcos Castellanos, one of the leaders of the insurgents defending Mezcala Island during the War of Independence. Castellanos died in Ajijic in 1826.[5] The movers and shakers behind the new school included then delegado Arnulfo Rojas Morales, and the local priest, Father Eligió, aided by contributions from Antonio Pantoja and Roberto Mosqueda; villagers provided the labor.[6]

When Jalisco began a state-wide program in the 1950s to build additional schools, the entire Ajijic community supported a proposal to build one of them in the village. On 14 July 1951 a dinner and thanksgiving program were organized for state officials, local teachers and dozens of invited guests at a property belonging to Casimiro Ramírez.[7] Cocktails, *atole* and tamales helped everyone enjoy the occasion. The village already had a site for a school; the state undertook to build as many as seven classrooms, provided the village raised $8000 towards construction. Organizers were already more than half-way there, thanks mainly to a fundraiser organized by the foreign community that netted $3000. A second fundraiser on 21 July (admission 50 centavos, free for under 12s) was held on the main plaza. Billed as Fandango Tapatía, it featured live music, booths, singers, raffles, auctions and fireworks.

Even as villagers raised funds for a new school, the existing primary school was in desperate need of maintenance. Neill James stepped up and organized for all the broken benches to be taken to a local carpenter and repaired at her own expense. James thanked a supporter in December 1951 for a contribution towards the kids' Christmas party. She wrote that 21 of the benches had been fixed, "but they still don't have chairs for the teachers to sit on." James arranged a Christmas cocktail party for the teachers that year and gave each of them a blouse. She expressed her hope that the new school would open in the new year.[8]

The Saúl Rodiles Piña primary school opened at Calle Hidalgo 45 in 1952.[9] By 1960 it had five classrooms and an office. The school welcomed some distinguished visitors in October 1963: President Adolfo López Mateos and his wife, Eva Sámano, President Tito of Yugoslavia (on a two-week state visit), Jalisco governor Juan Gil Preciado, and US vice-president Lyndon B Johnson.[10] The following summer, two more classrooms were added to the school, as well as a breakfast room and stage.[11]

Vocational secondary school

In May 1965 a successful fundraiser with folkloric dancing at the Posada Ajijic raised money for a Federal Free Secondary School in Ajijic.[12] The following month, Chapala mayor Luis Cuevas traveled to Mexico City to present the proposal for the school to Agustín Yañez, the federal Secretary of Education. Following a dinner featuring Lake Chapala whitefish, flown to the city specially for the occasion, Yañez gave his approval.[13] Fund raising continued and, on 1 July 1966, President Gustavo Díaz Ordáz visited Ajijic for the formal opening. Classes for 600 students began later that year.[14] This was Ajijic's first secondary school.

The school, initially called a School of Arts and Crafts (Escuela de Artes y Oficios), was subsequently renamed a Regional Handicrafts School (Escuela Regional de Artesanias), managed by the Jalisco Handicrafts Institute (Instituto de la Artesanía Jalisciense), which also opened a handicrafts store in Ajijic. At one time or another the six-classroom school, located on the highway immediately west of where the Lakeside Auditorium (Auditorio de la Ribera) was later built, offered classes in weaving, painting, carpentry, piñata making, papel maché, and other handicrafts, as well as professional pastry making and basic English. Among the many teachers were local artists Julian Pulido and Dionicio Morales.

In 2016 the Jalisco Handicrafts Institute donated the buildings and all the facilities, including the handicrafts store, to the Chapala municipality, which plans to use them for its own arts and culture school.[15]

Regular secondary school

The first regular secondary school in Ajijic opened in 1976, a decade after the secondary school specializing in arts and crafts. The Secundaria por Cooperación was an evening school, and shared the premises used during the day for the Escuela Marcos Castellanos girls' primary. Well-wishers in Studio City, California, a sister city of Ajijic, threw their support behind the new secondary. In 1977 the aptly named Ms Teecher-Rhodes coordinated several fundraisers for the new school.[16] When the secondary school in Escuela Marcos Castellanos closed in 1982, some of the students continued classes for a year in the Tejaban building, while others traveled daily to Secundaria Foránea #1, in Chapala. The purpose-built secondary school opened in upper Ajijic in 1983; initially with two classrooms, a science lab, bathrooms and an office.[17]

Oak Hill School

The founding of Oak Hill School, the first bilingual school in the area, owes everything to the tenacity of Wayne Palfrey, a native of Virginia and graduate of Wake Forest University, who arrived in Guadalajara in 1974 at the age of 23 to teach at a small school in the city run by Lourdes Garduño M. The following year, they co-founded a branch of the school on a vacant lot in Chapala.

While building got underway, Palfrey took charge of 32 students (kindergarten to second grade) at a temporary location in La Floresta. Plans for the Chapala location were derailed by Garduño's untimely death in 1976. Palfrey managed to keep the school afloat and grow student numbers, but only at the cost of successive changes of location within Chapala. By September 1977 the school had 70 students and 6 teachers. A larger rental property on Niños Heroes finally enabled the school to put down roots for six years.[18] The school expanded to offer secondary grades in about 1984 and later also offered *preparatoria*.

In September 1986 the school moved to a permanent new site near San Antonio Tlayacapan. Several prominent local business people—including Ricardo O'Rourke and his wife, Delia, Richard Tingen, Alejandro González, Roberto Luquín and John Goodridge—chipped in to build a purpose-built bilingual school. Prior to the 1990s, Oak Hill School was the area's only bilingual grade school. Palfrey, who died in 2018, was its director for more than a quarter of a century. The school closed at the end of the 2003 academic year and the campus was subsequently used by Instituto Loyola Chapala.

Lake Chapala Society of Natural Sciences

Several well-qualified professionals established the Lake Chapala Society of Natural Sciences (Sociedad de Ciencias Naturales del Lago de Chapala) in 1964. The first president was Howard E Smith, a chemical engineer from Arizona who had moved to Ajijic three years earlier. Other members included Robert Whipple (owner of Hotel La Quinta in Jocotepec), Walter Connor (a professional cartographer from Pittsburgh), artist Robert (Bob) Snodgrass, George W Mitchell (a retired mining engineer who published articles about local geology), and a Mr Stever, a professional science photographer.[19]

The group studied the environs of Lake Chapala, and was one of only five scientific societies allowed to work with the University of Guadalajara on investigations in the Atotonilco-Zacoalco-Sayula basin. Members of the group were thrilled when bones and man-made artifacts they unearthed at San Marcos were confirmed to be at least 37,000 years old and a major archaeological find. They were, at the time, "the oldest evidence of man's presence on the continent by some 10,000 years."[20]

West Mexico Society for Advanced Study

For a few years in the 1970s, Ajijic had a higher education institution specializing in archaeology, anthropology and history. Two Ajijic residents who lived at Calle Colón 36—geographer Dr William W. Winnie junior and his wife, archaeologist Dr Betty Bell—were the driving force behind the creation in 1971 of the West Mexico Society for Advanced Study (Sociedad de Estudios Avanzados del Occidente de Mexico).[21]

Winnie, who taught at the University of Guadalajara, wrote numerous papers and a book about Mexico and migration from western Mexico. He also produced a map of Lake Chapala towns and helped plan the Lakeside Auditorium (now Estación Cultural Chapala). Bell had been on the staff at Colorado State University before coming to Ajijic, where she gave lectures and undertook several pioneering archaeological excavations.

The state government offered the society the use of buildings belonging to the Regional Handicrafts School, and the Ajijic Museum of Anthropology was inaugurated on 9 October 1972 in a building adjacent to where the Estación Cultural Chapala is today. The museum was closed in July 1974, following a revised federal law pertaining to archaeological investigations which reflected the nationalistic change of direction being taken by the National Institute for Anthropology and History (INAH).

The West Mexico Society for Advanced Study was disbanded in 1974, but not before holding a successful summer school for 25 students from Angelo State University in Texas. Students were housed in the Hotel Chula Vista, and spent three weeks taking college-level classes for credit in the summer of 1974. The program was well received by local residents, and the Chapala mayor hosted a special dinner to celebrate the program, the first of its kind in the area.[22]

During its short lifetime, the society helped with several archaeological projects in western Mexico, including research in the Marismas Nacionales (Nayarit), and in Ahualulco, Teocaltiche and El Grillo, all in Jalisco. As pointed out by University of Guadalajara researchers, the society, despite its entirely laudable aims, was perceived as "an American institution in Mexico."[23] Mexican archaeologists had played only a minor role in most of its activities, though several contributed chapters to *The Archaeology of West Mexico*, a collection edited by Betty Bell and published by the society in 1974.[24]

26

Children's libraries and art

The idea of providing a library for children was suggested to Neill James by George B Smith in April 1952, when he wrote to her from California:

> I used to send books to the Goodridge children who are now at school in New Jersey.... I have some nice books on hand, mostly children, a few good adult volumes - I thought that it might be a good idea to establish a little library of some sort, especially for children - if you or some one would be able to take charge of it. I will send books from time to time in both English (mostly) and some in Spanish.[1]

Smith had apparently not realized that the books he mailed to the Goodridges were already in use as an informal library. As Katie Goodridge Ingram, one of those children, recalls with gratitude, her mother (Helen Kirtland) "created a small library across the street from our house and a variety of visiting children took books home and brought them back."[2]

Neill James clearly liked Smith's idea and organized the first public library for children in Ajijic. It opened in about 1953 in a room donated for the purpose at Calle Ocampo 6, near Serna's grocery store. James persuaded the municipio to part with funds for books, and hired María de los Angeles (Angelita) Aldana Padilla to oversee its activities. As a reward for reading and studying, students using the library were offered the incentive of free art supplies and classes. This humble beginning led, after many twists and turns, to the justly praised Children's Art Program.

A decade later, in about 1965, and to better serve children who lived on the western outskirts of the village, James opened a second library for children in a building she owned known as La Colmena (The Beehive) at Seis Esquinas.

In 1973 the original one-room library on Ocampo was relocated to premises at Calle Constitucion 41, rented for 200 pesos a month from Aurelia Vega. The grand re-opening of the New Free Ajijic Library, with separate spaces for books and painting, was on 7 July.[3] James continued to pay the electricity bills, the salary of an art teacher, and provide all the necessary art materials; the Junta de Agua Potable waived the water bill.[4]

At about the same time, Dominga García, who supervised the La Colmena library, moved on to other things. The running of the library was entrusted to a group of well-meaning teenagers. After the library was badly vandalized, all remaining books and supplies were moved to the library on Calle Constitución.

Running a public library in rented facilities was not without its problems. In 1975, for example, the decision by owner Aurelia Vega to try to repossess her property led to an acrimonious dispute that threatened to cause a deep rift in the village. In the end the library remained there for another decade before being moved to Neill James' own property (Quinta Tzintzuntzan) on Calle 16 de Septiembre in 1984.[5] Here, the collection was expanded and merged with the small children's collection of the Lake Chapala Society, which had relocated here the previous year.[6]

The Children's Art Program

The innate artistic talent of local children was remarked upon by British novelist D H Lawrence, when he lived in Chapala in the 1920s:

"No wonder Mexican children are born to be painters!" exclaimed Lawrence. Several times he and Frieda led us to the village school to see artistry on display there, pictures imaginative, bold, alive. Again said Lawrence, as if feathering an arrow, "Better than Rivera!"[7]

Even before the advent of the Children's Art Program (CAP), the lives of many Ajijic children had been enriched by contact with artists living in the village. Surrealist painter Sylvia Fein, for instance, had given art materials and lots of encouragement to curious local children during her three years in Ajijic in the mid-1940s.

Neill James adopted a more formal approach. She offered young students who used the library the incentive of free art supplies and classes after they had completed their homework. Linking an art program to a library was a stroke of genius. The Biblioteca Pública and CAP became virtually synonymous, and the art program helped nurture the talents of many fine local artists. At one time or another, almost every family in Ajijic has benefitted from the program, which continues to this day to provide one of the stronger and longer-standing bridges between foreign residents and the local community.

In the history of the CAP, certain key individuals stand out. They are commemorated in a colorful mural at the Lake Chapala Society titled "Six Decades of Children's Art." The mural, financed by the Ajijic Society of the Arts, was painted by program alumni Jesús López Vega and Javier Zaragoza. Unveiled in March 2012, it pays special homage to the three remarkable women who ensured the program's success: Neill James, Angelita Aldana Padilla and Mildred Boyd.

James, both the founder and a generous patron, is the central figure. Recognizing student talent, she funded several scholarships that enabled promising artists to attend art schools in Guadalajara and San Miguel de Allende. The first to study at the Instituto Allende in San Miguel de Allende was Javier Zaragoza, followed by Florentino Padilla and Antonio López Vega.[8] Juan Navarro and Daniel Palma also benefited. Padilla moved to the US, but the others all later opened studio-galleries in Ajijic, as did many other CAP graduates, including Victor Romero, Dionicio Morales and Javier Ramos.

Teacher Angelita Aldana Padilla provided continuity of purpose for the program for almost three decades. Several generations of her family benefitted from the program. Her nephew, Florentino Padilla, studied in San Miguel de Allende on a scholarship from James for three years from 1960 to 1962.[9] On returning to Ajijic, he paid his good fortune forward by teaching the next generation of students. Padilla actively promoted the sale of children's art as a means to fund materials and supplies. Together with Paul Carson, the Lake Chapala Society president, he arranged an exhibition-sale at the Instituto Cultural Mexicano-NorteAmericano in Guadalajara in 1964 of over 50 paintings by "youngsters who have been taught at the Biblioteca."[10] Nearly all the paintings sold. Padilla's niece, Lucia Padilla Gutiérrez, is also a gifted artist who attended CAP classes, and her own son became the third generation of this particular family to benefit from the program.

Financial support for CAP over the years has come from sales of work, with a healthy percentage going to each individual student artist.

Student work was exhibited at the Tejaban Restaurant in Ajijic (then run by Jan and Manuel Urzúa) in 1973.[11] Peggy Duffield and the acclaimed American photographer Syliva Salmi (who had retired to Ajijic a decade earlier) were the show's principal promoters. Ajijic children's art even made it into a US motel. In 1974, Betty Lou and John Rip, frequent visitors to Lake Chapala, purchased paintings at the Ajijic Biblioteca to decorate all 44 rooms of their Mayan Motor Inn in Laredo, Texas.[12]

In 1977, José Manuel Castañeda, another Ajijic art student who had taken classes at the Art Institute in San Miguel de Allende, began teaching art classes at the Biblioteca whenever he was in Ajijic. He gave regular art classes to children on Saturdays; on Sundays he taught students how to make murals for the walls of their homes.[13]

Three years later an exhibition and sale of 175 watercolors by Ajijic students aged 8 to 14 was held at the Anglo-Mexican Cultural Institute in Guadalajara.[14] By this time, for a variety of reasons—including Neill James' advancing age and ill health—the CAP was running out of steam, and no regular art classes were held for a few years.[15]

Classes were revived in 1984 (after the children's library moved to Quinta Tzintzuntzan), first during summer vacation and then year-round, thanks to the joint efforts of the Lake Chapala Society and the Ajijic Society of the Arts, and to the tireless endeavors of American writer and volunteer Mildred Boyd, the third female figure in the mural.

Boyd, who died in 2010, stepped up at just the right time and directed the program for more than twenty years. To help the students, Boyd framed many of their original paintings and printed greetings cards featuring their art, with all the proceeds going back to the young artists concerned.

After Boyd unearthed a stash of long-forgotten works done by students who had been in the program decades earlier, she assembled, with the help of her daughters and others, a heritage exhibition of early works by several children who had become successful professional artists. Selected works from this heritage collection were exhibited at the Lake Chapala Society, the Ajijic Cultural Center and the Centro Cultural González Gallo in Chapala, as well as in a New York gallery and at the Casa Museo Allende in San Miguel de Allende. Boyd was especially thrilled with the San Miguel show, since its opening night in 2006 coincided with her 85th birthday and she had always wanted the children's art to reach a much wider audience. Two proud Children's

Art Program alumni—Jesús López Vega and his brother Antonio López Vega—helped host the San Miguel show.

At the 60th Anniversary of CAP exhibit in October 2014 at the Centro Cultural Ajijic, 130 works by alumni were displayed. The Legacy Art Collection (paintings and other works, some dating back to classes in the 1950s), the patrimony of all the people of Ajijic, is now being cared for by the Lake Chapala Society. Some 400 items from this collection can be viewed online.[16]

Artists of note who began their art careers by taking CAP classes include José Abarca, Armando Aguilar, Luis Anselmo Ávalos, Antonio Cárdenas, José Manuel Castañeda, Efrén González, Ricardo González, Antonio Lopéz Vega, Jesús Lopéz Vega, Bruno Mariscal, Luis Enrique Martínez, Dionicio Morales, Juan Navarro, Juan Olivarez, Lucía Padilla, Daniel Palma, Javier Ramos, Victor Romero and Javier Zaragoza.

Almost seventy years since its founding, as many as seventy local children continue to enjoy CAP classes each week. The children's library and CAP remain integral components of the important links between the Lake Chapala Society and the local community.

27

Foreign artists

Word of mouth and international advertisements spread Ajijic's fame as an art center far and wide during the 1950s. Among the many attractions Ajijic offered artists was that living costs were low, especially compared to prices north of the border. Furthermore, the wonderful light off the lake, beautiful scenery, exotic culture and hospitable people all enhanced the village's appeal to visual artists.

La Galería

La Galería, which had opened in 1948, remained a popular hang-out for members of the village art community into the 1950s. Hanging over the bar at one time was a fine portrait by Ernesto Butterlin of Herbert Johnson, the English engineer who had settled in Ajijic with his wife in 1939. At another time, the painting behind the bar was a battle scene with war helmets, bayonets and empty fields.[1]

The distinguished Canadian poet Earle Alfred Birney, who founded Canada's first creative writing program, traveled widely in Mexico in the 1950s. In an apparent dig at La Galería, in a poem titled "Ajijíc" (sic), Birney described a "hip gringo," who, after enjoying a morning tequila, brings out "from under the bar... his six feet of representational nonart."[2]

The 1957 *Life* magazine article about Ajijic described La Galería as a place where painters displayed their works and bought drinks. The article named the gallery's manager as Margo North de Butterlin. This betrays an unlikely love triangle.[3] Rich and beautiful Margo North was the long-time mistress of Otto Butterlin, who had died the previous year. They had lived together in one of the largest houses in Ajijic,[4] while Otto's wife, Peggy, and daughter, Rita, lived a few blocks away on Calle Constitución.

Margo had accepted that she could never marry Otto, but was so desperate to acquire the Butterlin surname that she married Lin, who had started the gallery.[5] Lin—friendly, polite, fun to be with (except when drunk), and gay—was the perfect choice for such a marriage of convenience. His fashionable "wife" was more than happy to help run the gallery.

La Galería lacked any competition until the arrival of Laura Bateman, who began a small gallery, Rincón del Arte, in about 1958 using rented space and the family home.[6]

Peter Arnold Art Studio

As noted in an earlier chapter, after the Mexican Art Workshop moved to Taxco in 1950, an enterprising pair of Englishmen—Peter Elstob and Arnold Eiloart—started a campaign to bring more visitors to Ajijic, with a special emphasis on attracting artists. One obituary of Elstob refers to this project as the Peter Arnold Art Studios,[7] though this name does not appear elsewhere and appears to have been a vanity expression, placing a bohemian spin on what was, in reality, a straight-forward tourist enterprise.

Regardless of name, the Elstob-Eiloart partnership certainly brought many artists to Ajijic, housing them in the Posada Ajijic and, if needed, other rental properties, such as the guest cottage of the Johnsons. Among those who rented the cottage was American artist Barbara Zacheisz, who later married Elstob. Zacheisz, from St. Louis, Missouri, had moved to Ajijic in the winter of 1949–50. Besides painting, she tutored Katie Goodridge Ingram, who exercised Peter Elstob's two horses and gave riding lessons to his art studio guests. After moving to the UK, Zacheisz married Elstob and held several shows in London of paintings completed in Ajijic.

The Scorpion Club

The cantina of choice for the artistic community in Ajijic in the early 1950s was a restaurant-bar called Club Alacrán (Scorpion Club). This was opened in 1950 at the northwest corner of Calle Constitución and Ramón Corona by Ernest (Alex) Alexander, an eccentric Black American painter-photographer from Chicago.[8] The building, a "small two-room adobe house with a patio and kitchen area" had formerly been the writing studio of Mort Carl, the American writer-artist who married Helen Kirtland and co-founded the Ajijic loom business.[9]

Alex was a US military veteran who had helped foment the nascent jazz and poetry scene in Chicago, where he developed a close friendship with poets Bob Kaufman, Gwendolyn Brooks (the first black writer to win a Pulitzer) and ruth weiss, who later visited Ajijic herself.

With Alex at the helm, Club Alacrán became a popular hangout for expatriate artists and writers, its numbers swelled at weekends by GI Bill students attending classes at the University of Guadalajara. It was also popular among locals, because Alex instigated a two-tier pricing system, offering them a discount on their drinks.

Alex was one of the many extraordinary characters that made Ajijic a lively place in the early 1950s. While living in the village, he met Dorothy Whelan, a Canadian whose husband was serving seven years in a Mexican jail for passing bad checks. Alex and "Dolly" set up house, with Dolly working (at least for a time) as a cook at the Posada Ajijic, while Alex ran his bar and painted. They hosted several massive barbecues on the beach and their son, Mark, was born in the village.[10]

Among Club Alacrán regulars were San Francisco Bay area sculptors Robert McChesney and his wife Mary Fuller. Fuller, who wrote a detective novel set in the Guadalajara art scene of the 1950s, later recalled how:

some of the artists were going to the University of Guadalajara on the GI Bill.... And some of them lived in Ajijic and they would go into Guadalajara once a week to pick up their checks and go in to school and that was about it.... [Others at the popular watering-hole included] a bunch of writers... some of them from New York. Some people who ran a bookstore. And they were published writers. And there was a mystery writer down there.[11]

McChesney, an abstract-expressionism pioneer and leading light of American modernism, and his wife painted the word *artistas* on the Model A Ford mail truck they drove to Mexico. They were delighted to find that:

People on the side of the road would wave at us. Kids would come running out of their house to see us. It wasn't until later that we learned that Mexicans used the word artista to mean 'movie actor.'[12]

In Ajijic at the same time were the McChesneys' good friends: abstract sculptor Blanche Phillips Howard and her husband, social-idealism and eco-activist painter John Langley Howard, considered one of the finest painters of his time in the San Francisco Bay area.

While running Club Alacrán, Alex was visited by the ethnomusicologist Sam Eskin. The second part of Eskin's historic sound recording *Mexican firecrackers: a prayer and a festival* was recorded from the patio of the Club; it features a religious festival in Ajijic, complete with church bells and pre-dawn firecrackers.[13]

Alex took many evocative photographs of Ajijic, including images of a typical rural lane on the outskirts of the village, and of fishermen tending their nets. He also painted Ajijic:

> One of them [his paintings] made a particularly strong impression on me: what appeared to be a fisherman's shack (I recall a net and floaters hung out on a wall to dry) in the full golden blast of a sundrenched late afternoon, while above and behind it the sky was bluegray with ominous storm clouds.[14]

The bar closed in 1953 when Alexander was "33-ed"[15] out of Mexico following a brawl which erupted after Dolly's husband (John Thomas Babin), having escaped or completed his sentence, returned to Ajijic and demanded his wife back. Dolly and Mark accompanied Alex to San Francisco, coincidentally at about the same time as their friends David and Helen Morris, who also lived in Ajijic, returned there.[16]

Tragically, life then spiraled downwards for Alex. After Dolly died while undergoing surgery in 1955, Alex slid towards insanity and never recovered.

Artists active in Ajijic in the 1950s

The dazzling range of artistic talent in Ajijic in the 1950s can best be illustrated by brief accounts of some of the dozens of artists, then resident in the village, whose work depicted the local area and its inhabitants.

Benjamin Shute, a co-founder of the Atlanta College of Art, painted in Ajijic at the start of the 1950s. His impressionist 1951 watercolor and ink work "Ajijic, Mexico" shows several people and animals on a village street with the church tower and mountains rising behind them.

Orley Allen Pendergraft, who became an ordained minister before dedicating himself to art, spent part of 1951 in Ajijic and lived the last thirty years of his life in Alamos, Sonora. One of his watercolors of Ajijic won a major prize at the 1951 Santa Cruz county fair in California.[17] Another painting from that time is titled "La Esquina del Carrisal Ajijic." By coincidence, Pendergraft's US agent, Joanne Goldwater, once resided in

Ajijic, and her father—former US senator Barry Goldwater—exhibited photos at the Centro Ajijic de Bellas Artes (CABA) in 1998.

When Pendergraft was in Mexico in 1959, trying to drown his sorrows after the death of his wife, he met Tennessee Williams and took the playwright to Puerto Vallarta, then a small, sleepy fishing village. Williams proceeded to write *The Night of the Iguana*, in which Pendergraft was the basis for the alcoholic priest.[18]

Charles Pollock, the oldest brother of Jackson Pollock—icon of the American abstract art movement—was a fine artist in his own right, and had a sabbatical year in Ajijic in 1955–56. He returned to the US only weeks before Jackson's untimely death in a traffic accident. Charles produced thirty large drawings and fifteen paintings in Ajijic, collectively known as the Chapala Series, which was first exhibited, to great acclaim, in a New York gallery more than fifty years later.[19]

Lothar Wuerslin lived with his wife, Ann, a poet and jeweler, and their new-born child in Ajijic from 1956 to about 1959. They rented a four-room adobe home in Ajijic, which had no tub, for the princely sum of $5 a month.[20] Lothar was busy preparing paintings for a solo show in New York. The 1957 *Life* magazine article about Americans at Lake Chapala includes photos of their home and Lothar's murals. It also shows the young couple playing chess. They returned to New York when their savings ran out.

Californian artist Alfred Rogoway and his wife, Marjorie, lived most of each year in Ajijic in the 1940s and 1950s. Rogoway, known for his ethereal elongated figures, had lived in France and was a friend of Pablo Picasso; the two regularly exchanged artistic ideas. The Rogoways' Ajijic house had a second-story viewpoint (*mirador*). On one unfortunate occasion, after imbibing one drink too many, the artist announced his intention to try to fly:

> He flew off the mirador, broke perhaps an arm, a leg, ribs and who knows what else. So he made tables in bed from the small mosaic tiles from Mexico which my mother found for him in Guadalajara. My mother, Helen Kirtland, was then the happy recipient of two of his tables created during his LONG convalescence.[21]

In the late 1950s artist and playwright Raphael Greno made several striking woodcuts of Ajijic subjects rarely chosen by other artists. They include a portrait of Neill James sitting at her typewriter in an *equipal*, cradling a pet parrot in one hand; women washing clothes on the lake-shore; and two images of silk production. Greno and his wife, Vee, later moved to Ajijic and lived in the village for a decade, where they joined the informal cultural group TLAC (Todas las Artes Combinadas) and taught art at the Galería del Lago.[22]

Pasadena painter Patricia Williams Tarbox spent the summer of 1958 in Ajijic, and then showed eight water colors and oils painted there at the Altadena Public Library. Tarbox was a frequent visitor to Mexico and held solo shows at the San Francisco Museum of Art and at Riverside Art Center.[23]

Robert Clutton, a British-born painter and sculptor, lived in Ajijic from about 1959 to 1961, and revisited several times. Clutton's works relating to Ajijic include one from 1959 showing the Posada Ajijic, and a powerful painting of a bullfight held in the village. Clutton eventually settled in San Francisco, where his solo shows included one at the prestigious Vorpal Gallery, which, over the years, hosted several solo shows for artists connected to Ajijic.

28

Creative Beats

The Beat movement, which began in New York in the early 1950s, subsequently made its way to California and then spilled south to Mexico and into Ajijic. It started as a literary movement, but also influenced, through social collaboration, music, dance and art. The Beat movement was essentially a reaction against conventional "square" society and its materialism and norms. Beats believed in experimentation and adopted styles of dress, language and behavior that rejected the status quo. Their experimentation led them to seek heightened sensory awareness via drugs, sex, jazz and Zen Buddhism.

Published writings by Beats were loosely structured, more stream of consciousness than formally organized prose, and more racy. Beat book and poetry readings were performances. Widely acclaimed Beat poet ruth weiss, for example, who visited Ajijic in 1959, recited her free form poems to live jazz. She had begun to do this a decade earlier, while living in Chicago, at the instigation of Black American artist Ernest Alexander, who ran the Scorpion Bar in Ajijic from 1950 to 1953.

During the early stages of the Beat movement several of its key figures lived in or visited Ajijic. The three key names always associated with the Beats are Jack Kerouac, Allen Ginsberg and William Burroughs. Convicted murderer Lucien Carr had first introduced the three men to each other.

Poet and novelist Ginsberg, accompanied by former college roommate Lucien Carr and Joan Vollmer, visited Ajijic to see Helen Parker in the summer of 1951. Redheaded Parker, Ginsberg's first lover, had been living in Ajijic for a few months with her then boyfriend, Yale Harrison, and two young sons.[1] Harrison, a New York Beat, appears as a minor character in *Where's Annie?*, Eileen Bassing's novel set in Ajijic.[2] Vollmer, the most prominent female Beat of the time, was living in Mexico City with Burroughs, who had fled his homeland when facing conviction for drugs charges. To complete the complex web linking these individuals, Volmer's former college roommate had married Jack Kerouac.

In May the following year Kerouac passed through Ajijic on his way to visit Burroughs in Mexico City. Writing to Ginsberg, he mentions having gone through "Ajijic little stone village of Helen [Parker]" and finding "no more beautiful a land and state than that of Jalisco."

Ginsberg's reply confirms his visit the previous year and refers to Ajijic as a "rendevous for Subterraneans."[3]

From Ajijic, Ginsberg, Carr and Vollmer continued on to visit Paricutín Volcano in Michoacán. Shortly after returning to Mexico City, Burroughs accidentally shot Joan Vollmer dead in their apartment.

Numerous other Beats had close links to Ajijic. They include poet ruth weiss, whose poems contain numerous references to Black American artist Ernest Alexander and several other significant Beats who lived in Ajijic. Her diary entry after visiting the village in 1959 includes a reference to Ernest Alexander (from her Chicago days), Anne McKeever and her good friend, Lori Fair.[4]

Artist and folksinger Lori Fair had moved to Ajijic in 1954 with her then partner Don Martin, one of the more innovative American painters ever to live in Ajijic. Anne McKeever had moved to Guadalajara in 1953, as had George Abend, a mutual friend and Beat jazz musician-artist who studied at the University of Guadalajara and maintained a studio in Ajijic.

This tight-knit group of friends had first met in the Beat circle of New Orleans in 1951 and was now reunited in Ajijic. The cover of the Summer 1956 issue of *Climax*, a Beat magazine published in New Orleans and printed in Guadalajara, is a photograph, taken by McKeever, of Don Martin's studio in Ajijic in 1955–56. Lori Fair is sitting by the drums and George Abend, a very accomplished musician, is at the piano.[5] This image neatly conveys the close friendship of these artistically talented individuals in Ajijic before their paths, and lives, diverged.

George Abend did not remain long in Ajijic. He became a prominent figure in the San Francisco Bay Area abstract expressionism movement and his striking abstracts were widely exhibited in the US.

Don Martin, who loved Ajijic, was able to keep afloat financially by selling the occasional painting in the Posada Ajijic prior to his first major solo exhibition in Guadalajara in August 1954. Both Fair and

McKeever attended that hugely successful show, as did Archie Mayo, the Hollywood movie director; Nicole Vaia Langley, daughter of violinist John Langley; Peter and Elaine Huntington of Ajijic; and Nayarit-born painter Melquiades Sánchez Orozco, who became a legendary soccer commentator.[6] Martin's Ajijic paintings were also shown in California.[7]

McKeever's photographs and Martin's paintings were exhibited on various occasions in Guadalajara and in Nayarit, where Fair gave a folk music concert in 1955.[8] McKeever also held an exhibit of her wonderfully evocative Mexican photos in New Orleans.

When Martin and Fair went their separate ways, he remained in Ajijic while she moved to Mexico City and changed her name to Bhavani Escalante. Shortly afterwards, McKeever left Guadalajara and joined Escalante in Mexico City, where she quickly became an integral part of the vibrant Beat scene, which included surrealist poet Philip Lamantia. On the fringes of this group was British-born artist Jeonora Bartlet, photographed for the 1957 *Life* magazine article about Ajijic.

Coincidentally, that *Life* article was the reason why Don Martin's future wife, Joan Gilbert, who read it while vacationing in Puerto Vallarta, immediately "took off for the storied enticements of Ajijic." The rest, as they say, is history.[9] The couple returned to live in California in 1961.

In 1959, McKeever and Lamantia were visited in Mexico City by jazz poet ruth weiss, near the end of her lengthy trip through Mexico. Several poems in weiss's *Gallery of Women* are about McKeever, who is also mentioned (as is Ernest Alexander) in a much later poem, "Post-Card 1995."[10] McKeever subsequently married a former bullfighter and started an English-language school in Tapachula, Chiapas.[11]

Beats from north of the border continued to seek out Ajijic into the late 1950s. Among the more noteworthy were Ned Polsky, author of the 1967 book *Hustlers, Beats, and Others*, and his Scottish writer friend Alex Trocchi, who hid out in Ajijic to complete his controversial novel, *Cain's Book*.[12] Polsky, a great admirer of Trocchi's work, later recalled how, in 1958 or 1959:

Alex and I had seen each other virtually every day while we were living in Mexico; there he had no difficulty in obtaining drugs, and under those conditions got much of the work done on his best novel, Cain's Book."[13] Polsky was with Trocchi a couple of years later in New York when the latter, aided by Norman Mailer, decided to jump bail and flee to Canada, rather than remain for his trial the following day on narcotics charges.

Veteran journalist John Ross, an early Beat who lived decades in Mexico, visited Polsky in Ajijic but did not stay long:

> Ajijic, packed with dissipated gringos, seemed to me a kind of leper colony and I soon bid it adios and grabbed the puddle-jumper down to Puerto Vallarta.[14]

The acclaimed American poet Jack Gilbert had a much more positive experience in Ajijic. He is often grouped with the Beat poets, though he himself denied this, saying that he did not "go in for freakish behavior nor esoteric knowledge."[15] Gilbert rented Zara's gold mill house in Ajijic in about 1959–1960, while working on *Views of Jeopardy*, which was nominated for the 1960 Pulitzer Prize for Poetry. While none of his published poems can definitely be linked to Ajijic, several refer to places and events in Guadalajara.

The Beats were not without their detractors, and onlookers were divided as to whether or not their presence in Ajijic was making things better or worse. Among those who defended the foreigners was local agrarian leader Juan Gutiérrez Comparán.[16] Apparently, the less desirable Beats did not stay long. One US journalist reported in 1960 that "Ajijic has tamed down and many of the bard and sandal set have moved on."[17] He was not to know that when the hippies began to arrive his optimism would prove to be totally unfounded.

A trickle of Beats continued into the early 1960s. This is when Black American artist and jazz-lover Arthur Monroe lived in Ajijic. Monroe grew up in New York and first traveled in Mexico (though not Ajijic) many years earlier to escape racism and discrimination. Strongly influenced by the rich spirituality and iconography of the Maya and other ancients, Monroe became an integral part of the abstract expressionist movement and Beat scene in California. Returning to Mexico in the early 1960s, he lived in Ajijic for three years in a house rented for $25 a month.[18] Strangely, it was in Ajijic where Monroe first met poet and writer Al Young, also based in California;[19] the two men became fast friends. Interviewed later, Young recalled how:

> At that time, Ajijic (near Guadalajara) was crammed with hippies … Arthur was one of the beatniks who had sort of lasted into the

hippie era ... The Mexicans loved him. They all called him by one name: Arturo. He was a very romantic figure, wearing the Mexican straw hat that the peasants wore. He was painting, and he was highly respected.[20]

Monroe, whose work was widely exhibited, including at the Posada Ajijic, was regarded as a leading light of the San Francisco cultural scene. Among Monroe's friends in Ajijic was Beverly Johnson, whose eldest daughter, Tamara, recalls visiting his house in about 1963 and:

> [meeting] Alan Watts who was having his first trip on LSD the day I met him.... I might add that I was tripping too, and had spent the whole day with my mother and siblings in El Manglar.[21]

A very different Beat, the multifaceted author Norman Mailer, winner of Pulitzer Prizes for both fiction and non-fiction, did not stop long when he first visited Ajijic in the late 1940s, and "did not succumb to the charms of the American expatriates."[22] However, he later returned with his second wife, Adele, to live in the village for a few months. He particularly liked the ready availability of marijuana: "In Mexico... pot gave me a sense of something new about the time I was convinced I had seen it all."[23] The couple also engaged in disturbing sexual shenanigans during their time in Ajijic. According to nine-fingered violinist John Langley, Mailer and his wife drugged their maid before sexually abusing her with an electric massager.[24]

In much more recent times, another former Beat, actor and author Norman Schnall retired to Ajijic with his wife, Claire, in 1998, and became active in the Lakeside Little Theatre. Schnall (stage name Norman Burton) was close friends of Kerouac and Ginsburg, and is Normie Krall in Kerouac's masterwork, *Visions of Cody* (1973).[25]

Part D

1960s: Free spirits

"[Chapala, Jocotepec and Ajijic] were originally native lake villages of great charm and a feeling of remoteness. But Americans, forever restless for a Utopian retreat, came, saw and eventually corrupted what had been a relatively uncomplicated existence."
—Carol Miller, 1963

29

Bohemians, hippies and drugs

By the early 1960s the Beat movement, which was certainly not without its vices, was morphing into the Bohemians, later known as the hippies.[1] The Bohemians were interested in political activism and experimented with ever-stronger consciousness-changing drugs. Many Beats embraced this shift of emphasis and became active Bohemians and hippies, so there is considerable overlap between the groups. In addition to writers, artists and musicians, the later movements appealed to young people who had no particular artistic aspirations but who sought some form of higher self-enlightenment.

Beats had kept a low profile and dressed conservatively, often in dark clothing; Bohemians and hippies stressed individuality and preferred bright colors. They often created their own small communities, living together, sharing responsibilities and resources cooperatively; in addition to drug use, they liked psychedelic music and embraced sexual freedom.

In Ajijic the Beats had scarcely ruffled the waters of the quiet village. A few villagers were rattled by the young foreigners who landed in their midst, but most were tolerant. The Bohemian-hippie era was a different story. The lifestyle of the young people who descended on Ajijic in droves in the mid-1960s openly challenged traditional attitudes and drew the ire of many villagers. The hippie movement took drug use to a whole new level, provoked run-ins with local officials, and gave foreigners, especially young ones, a poor reputation. In the eyes of many locals, the hippies, intentionally or not, were an undesirable influence on impressionable young village children.

Despite action by local authorities as early as 1962—"Ajijic has been cleaned up by the government. Its Bohemian colony had gotten a bit too

Bohemian"[2]—the following year Ajijic emerged as a major center for experimenting with LSD, at the heart of the maelstrom accompanying the shift from Beats to hippies throughout North America.

Timothy Leary and Ken Kesey were the two central figures in this shift. Frustratingly, no definitive documentary evidence has emerged that either spent any time in Ajijic. Indeed, there is such a paucity of documentary evidence about these events in Ajijic that this account is based largely on the recollections of individuals who were there. Given that most were written or recorded many years after the events transpired, they inevitably tend to raise as many questions as they answer.

Was Timothy Leary ever in Ajijic?

Dr Timothy Leary, a professor at Harvard, had been researching Mexico's magic mushrooms before starting experiments with LSD. He lost his supply of LSD when Harvard fired him in April 1963.

Sandoz, the Swiss manufacturer of LSD, had offices in Mexico City and Leary—some say—arrived in Ajijic to stock up, and was in Ajijic when he put the finishing touches to *The Psychedelic Experience*, an account of his work on LSD. If true, this places Leary in Ajijic in April 1963. But it could only have been for a few days, since Leary was in Zihuatanejo by 1 May for the second summer session of his psychedelic training center there; by early June, Leary and nineteen followers had been kicked out of Mexico.[3]

Received wisdom in Ajijic is that Leary rented Zara's gold mill house.[4] This does not square, however, with the account given by Jerry Kamstra in *Weed: Adventures of a Dope Smuggler*. According to Kamstra, who lived near Chapala from 1963 to 1964:

> When Leary was asked to leave Mexico [in 1963], a contingent of his colony under the leadership of a thin, messianic dude named Thad moved to Ajijic.... When Thad [Ashby] and his followers arrived in Ajijic, they set up shop in a place called The Mill, an abandoned granary that became a center for LSD experimentation for the next few years.... Shortly after his arrival in Ajijic, Thad talked the University of Guadalajara Medical School into conducting experiments with LSD-25, using members of the beat colony and some Mexican students as guinea pigs. These experiments were short-lived, however, because the scene was beginning to get out of control.[5]

Kamstra makes no mention of Leary, and his chronology, if correct, makes it virtually impossible for Leary to have ever spent more than a day or two in Ajijic.

At precisely the time in question (summer 1963), Loy Strother was visiting his mother (artist Tink Strother) in Ajijic: "I remember my mother warning me not to go around 'the mill' because "there were some real weirdos hanging around there." It was also the summer when Kit (Christopher) Bateman showed Strother a small medical vial filled with, he claimed, 1500 high (1500-microgram) doses of LSD. Strother told me that:

> most of the LSD that made its way to San Francisco in those days came from Kit. He somehow managed to get Sandoz Labs to send the vials to him through the mail!... Of course this was before the substance was pronounced illegal.

He also said that Kit's purchases of LSD were facilitated "probably through a British doctor."[6]

Kit's brother, Tony, later confided to Strother that he (Tony) had supplied the LSD used for the famous Acid Cool Aid Test in San Francisco, and that the drug had not been mixed with Cool Aid but smeared on the lips of soft drink cans. Tony was adamant that Leary himself had been in Ajijic for a short time in the summer of 1963.

Among the individuals participating in the LSD experiments was Beverly Johnson, who later worked briefly as a monitor for the "studies" conducted by Thad Ashby's group. In late 1963 she was visited by her younger half-brother, Scott Hampson, who had a "deeply transformative" experience when he tried LSD. Beverly, despite her proximity to the drug, was not an advocate and preferred to host alcohol-fueled gatherings where music and animated arguments enlivened the evening.[7] Even so, her oldest daughter, Tamara, described in an autobiographical short story a family trip to Barra de Navidad when she and her siblings had so little food to eat that they were given tiny amounts of LSD to ease their hunger pains.[8] The family visited Barra de Navidad several times, often at a moment's notice because immigration officials had arrived in Ajijic to carry out a sweep for undocumented foreigners.

As for Hampson, soon after he returned home in 1964 he received news that one of his friends had "successfully stolen a large shipment of LSD from Thad and Rita, who were the masterminds of the supply connection." Hampson returned to Lake Chapala for a few weeks; when he left, he had 1000 hits of Acid stashed in his underwear as he walked across the border.[9]

Jerry Kamstra's belief that the LSD experiments in Ajijic were short-lived is not supported by the personal testimony of Marsha Sorensen, who lived in Ajijic at the time and was a willing participant in trials organized by the University of Guadalajara:

> LSD studies occurred once a month during that time ('65-'66.) The man conducting the study didn't live in Ajijic, as far as I know, but would come once a month to conduct his study. He gave adults and children and once a standard poodle, LSD, and would film us and take notes.... When the man doing the study quit coming, I heard that he had been deported for jumping into a fountain in Mexico City naked.[10]

By summer 1965, just as the word hippie was entering the mainstream, Mexican authorities decided that they had had enough of the young *existencialistas* as they were labeled. A Guadalajara journalist contrasted the impacts of the maladapted young men, with their ragged clothes and Robinson-Crusoe beards, and young women, who had converted Ajijic into a "paradise," with the positive social benefits brought by longer-term residents such as Neill James. He complimented the authorities for expelling the young people and closing the Galería del Arte, where "every immorality had its place."[11]

Was Ken Kesey ever in Ajijic?

Whether or not Ken Kesey, author of *One Flew Over the Cuckoo's Nest*, ever visited Ajijic has proved equally impossible to verify. According to Michael Hargraves, Kesey told him personally that he'd never been to the Lake Chapala area.[12] However, Marcy Sorensen recalled that Kesey visited Ajijic with his psychedelic bus in 1966 or 1967, and that the occupants "poured out of the bus and ran naked down to the lake."[13]

Kesey and his Merry Pranksters were famous for seeking intersubjectivity through their use of LSD and other psychedelics. Journalist Tom Wolfe's popular account of Kesey's Acid Tests, the Hells Angels and the Grateful Dead, includes details about Kesey's time in Mexico. But it makes no mention of Kesey being any closer to Lake Chapala than Guadalajara, and then only for a very, very short time, and certainly without his bus.

While Wolfe acknowledged that Ajijic was "the true Acid Central of Mexico," he was unimpressed by "those poor sad Lake Chapala villages, Ajijic, Chapala, Jocotepec, with the lake drying up and the old suck-smack lily-pad scum mud showing and failed American aesthetes padding around earnestly in sandals."[14]

Drugs and music

Musician and composer Patrick Gleeson, a synthesizer pioneer, was in his late twenties when he visited his ex-wife, Karen, in Ajijic in 1963. Gleeson credits the start of his interest in electronic music to experiments with LSD while in Ajijic.[15]

Members of the rock band Jefferson Airplane, formed in 1965, were renting a house in Ajijic on Calle Marcos Castellanos when they were visited by American singer Mama Cass.[16] Jerry Garcia of the Grateful Dead apparently later lived in this house (Casa de la Tortuga).[17] This presumably explains why song writer Robert Hunter visited Ajijic, where he was sufficiently inspired to pen the lyrics of one of the Grateful Dead's most popular songs, "China Cat Sunflower," first performed in 1968:

> I think the germ of 'China Cat Sunflower' came in Mexico, on Lake Chapala. I don't think any of the words came, exactly—the rhythms came. I had a cat sitting on my belly, and was in a rather hypersensitive state, and I followed this cat out to—I believe it was Neptune—and there were rainbows across Neptune, and cats marching across the rainbow. This cat took me in all these cat places; there's some essence of that in the song.[18]

Chrissie Hynde also lived briefly in Ajijic in the early 1970s before going on to stardom after forming The Pretenders rock band.[19]

Drugs and literature

Drug dealing and use play an integral role in several literary works related to Lake Chapala. The most noteworthy is Willard Marsh's novel, *Week with No Friday*, set in the drugs and alcohol-fueled Ajijic of the late 1950s, early 1960s. The paperback edition was appropriately subtitled *Money, Marijuana and a girl named Martha Lowlife and highjinks South of the Border.*[20] In the novel a troubled expatriate playwright talks entertainingly and drinks a great deal. Depressed at a string of rejections, he becomes more positive after smoking pot. The arrival of a visiting schoolteacher from Iowa, and the return of his ex-wife, turn the story into a moving tragicomedy. Allyn Hunt described the opening chapter, first published in *Esquire*, as "deftly capturing the *ambiente* of Ajijic at that time."[21]

Marsh, an author and jazz musician, first arrived in Ajijic with his wife, George Rae Marsh, in the early 1950s to work on his Great American Novel. They witnessed firsthand how rapidly Ajijic changed over the next two decades. In 1964, George wrote to her brother (novelist John Williams) expressing misgivings about the village:

> Ajijic has been overrun with slobs quite a bit, too, but if it gets too bad, one can move a few kilometers down the lake to San Juan, Jocotepec, and on to Morelia. The lake is 25 miles wide and 50 miles long, so there's a lot of lakefront real estate still unoccupied.[22]

A few years later, she pointed out to a journalist, with a smile, that: "A lot of the Americans here don't mix too much with the Mexicans... although the Mexicans are a helluva lot brighter than some gringos." The number of Americans moving to the area had increased, they were "trying to change it to a suburbia," rents had doubled, and George (owner of the village's earliest discoteque) lamented that "now it seems we have too much of a retired crowd and not enough stimulating young people."[23] Willard Marsh died in 1970 and was buried in Ajijic. His remains were not at peace for long; two years later his grave was one of those desecrated by a bulldozer trying to carve a road through the cemetery.

Distinguished poet, novelist and academic Al Young, Poet Laureate of California 2005–2008, was a keen observer during his time in Ajijic in the 1960s. His 1975 novel *Who is Angelina?* includes several passages relating to Ajijic and Lake Chapala. The title character, Angelina Green, is an intelligent young life-loving woman living in Berkeley after the hippie phase who goes to Mexico to find herself. She has an affair with a tall, charismatic stranger named Watusi, and the couple house-sit for a while in Ajijic. Angelina asks Watusi if the village has many hippies:

> 'Use to', comes the reply, 'but the Mexican government done just about shut the door for good on that jive. They tolerate the native hippies cause all of em come from upperclass families that's got a lotta power and pull, but long-haired freaks from Gringoland got to straighten up when they step cross that border cause these crazy people down here don't be playin!'[24]

Allyn Hunt, publisher of the *Guadalajara Reporter* for many years, made his breakthrough as a short story writer in 1966 with "Acme Rooms and Sweet Marjorie Russell." Three years later, *Transatlantic Review* published his story "A Mole's Coat" about doing acid "jaunts" at Lake Chapala.[25]

A guest editorial in *Efanzine* described an insider's take on the marijuana scene in Ajijic at about this time:

> Total strangers would knock on your door and present you with sprays of pot. 'Welcome to Ajijic,' they'd say, and what a welcome it was once you got over the shock of the cultural differences and tried to think for yourself.... The social scene was something really running out of control.... The booze flowed endlessly as did the pot from machine-rolled joints to frosted brownies. In one form or another, you were smashed out of your gourd most of the time. At least between hangovers.... There was cocaine, too, at some of these parties, and various hallucinogenics, but most of us, by then, were die-hard potheads.[26]

Clearly, Mary Jane (María y Juana) was not hard to come by in Ajijic. When savings ran out, or checks from home or publishers dried up, one option was to trade weed to earn a few dollars. This did not always turn out as expected, especially for anyone unfamiliar with the seasonality of good weed. It led to tragedy for US writer Don Hogan who arrived in Ajijic with his family in the late 1960s with a very limited income.[27]

Hogan had been shortlisted for a Pulitzer Prize in 1959 for his role in a series exposing racketeering in the New York garment industry, and had lived with Castro's troops in Cuba immediately before they seized power. He was so desperate to maintain his lifestyle in Ajijic that he tried drug dealing. His first attempt was mistimed; a purchase of inferior quality grass barely covered his costs.[28] Hoping to make up for this error, Hogan asked friends for a loan in 1971 to buy a substantial stash, but came back penniless and empty-handed after several guns were pulled on him. A few weeks later, having borrowed yet more money, he tried again, this time packing a pistol. This attempt went horribly wrong: when Hogan reached for his gun the drug dealers shot him dead.[29]

Drugs and pornography

The literature of the Beats may have led to a relaxation of publishing standards in the US but this relaxation did not extend to erotic works and pornography. On being persuaded to leave California in early 1967, soft porn king Earl Kemp, previously a noted science fiction editor, rented a house at Constitución 14 in Ajijic. Over the next five years, Kemp, who subsequently served time in a California penitentiary for conspiracy to mail obscene matter, ran a stable of writers as a co-owner of San Diego-based publishing company Greenleaf Classics, a pioneer in gay and lesbian fiction, which churned out up to fifty titles a month.[30]

Kemp's residence—"La casa de mi corazón, the subconscious residence of my dreams"—was party central for multiple hedonistic houseguests. Booze and drugs flowed freely and guests were invited to sample "fresh Oaxacan mushrooms and acid-laced hashish brownies (frosted)."

In early 1970, Jerry Murray, one of the twenty or so writers who worked for Kemp, rented with this wife, Diane, "a partially furnished two-bedroom house on Calle Juárez, with a patio and a deep back yard, a gardener and a maid for $85/month." Murray wrote more than one hundred erotic novels, with titles like *Excess of Pleasure* and *Timid Stud*, under a dozen pen names including Ray Masters, Sonny Barker, Maude Jenkins, Ralph Basura, Lance Boil, Joyce Morrissey and Sam Diego.

Among the numerous Ajijic characters Murray later recalled were Neill James, Zara, John K Peterson, Trudy Campbell, Peggy Neal, Mercedes Boone, Wendell Phillips, Jan Dunlap, Manuel Urzúa, and "Red Raymond's mother Marge Bernardi (Official Supplier To The Grateful Dead!)" According to Murray, Bernardi was also reputed to deal in illegal firearms and was having an affair with Vern Lungren, a volatile member of Earl Kemp's stable of porn writers. One afternoon in April 1972 the romantically involved couple spent the afternoon together:

> She had a pistol with her when she and Vern went on a picnic, and Vern asked to see it, since he might want to buy it. As he examined it, he put its muzzle against his head and shot himself. Most people thought he'd simply angered Marge to the point where she'd killed him. Nobody really knew, but the cops and the crooks in Chapala knew that guns would be hard to come by if Marge went to prison for manslaughter, so Vern's death was listed as a suicide.[31]

30

Village photographer

In 1961, creative freespirit Beverly Johnson (1933–1976) fled a failed relationship in Oregon and drove south with her five young children, all under the age of nine.

The romantic version of how they arrived in Ajijic is that Beverly was headed for South America when her car broke down in Guadalajara. Unable to afford the repairs, Beverly, an up-and-coming singer, asked the mechanic if he knew where she could find some temporary work. He suggested Ajijic, telling her that the many Americans and Canadians there might pay to hear her sing.

Apart from occasional visits to the coast and periodic short trips to the border to renew her tourist papers, Beverly spent the remainder of her life in Ajijic. She became a fixture in the village, one of the completely unconventional characters that added spice and excitement to everyday life. As her second-eldest daughter, Jill, recalls, "She was amazing and crazy, and life with her was a roller coaster ride." Beverly used her many creative talents—as "singer, poet, writer, chef, painter, photographer and [artist of] mixed media like papier maché and rice paper balsa wood mobiles"—to eke out a living for herself and her children.

Beverly Estelle Johnson (née Hampson) was born in Grants Pass, Oregon, on 15 September 1933. On her way south with her children in 1961, Johnson stopped off in Los Angeles to record a promotional 45 record, hoping to make a living from singing and guitar playing. But this was not an era when music promoters were prepared to back a single mother with five young children. Among the other singers seeking stardom at the same time was a young Joan Baez; some years later, Beverly recognized Baez at the Beer Garden bar in Chapala and made a point of introducing herself.

Ajijic in the 1960s was bubbling with drug-related activity, not all of it welcomed by the local villagers. When an offshoot of Timothy Leary's group, led by Thad Ashby, arrived from Zihuatanejo in 1963, Beverly signed up to be a test subject (and later a monitor for tests) for the LSD "studies" conducted by Ashby's group with the help of the University of Guadalajara Medical School.

Beverly's half-brother, Scott Hampson, visited her that winter and also fell in love with Ajijic:

> There were flowers everywhere, immense mango and papaya trees, bananas, cobblestone streets lined with the walls and gates of houses and inside the gates courtyards with dazzling varieties of plants. Lake Chapala bordered the town and its waters stretched many miles toward high mountains. Ajijic's reputation was that of an "artist colony" for Americans, but the majority of residents were Mexican. Burros were more plentiful than cars and cars weren't really a necessity since buses ran everyplace, even up the dirt roads that accessed the little villages in the hills above town.[1]

Parties at Beverly's house were frequent:

> Almost every evening people would come over, Americans mostly of artistic stripe, to gather in Beverly's living room to talk, drink, smoke pot and generally entertain one another.... Some had written novels or had exhibited their paintings in major American cities.

As for LSD, Hampson says, Beverly did not experience any "transformative awakening" after taking it, was decidedly unimpressed, and believed that the idea it was going to change the world was "comically delusional."

At about this time Beverly began a lengthy relationship with a local contractor, Antonio (Tony) Pérez, which resulted in two more daughters, Sara and Miriam.[2]

Beverly was ever creative and resourceful. For example, when a village official at one point demanded that the exterior of her house be repainted, she quickly found a solution that satisfied officialdom as well as her need for individuality. Indeed, daughter Jill asserts that her mother's innovative response was instrumental in creating the colorful village we see today:

> Miss Beverly [as she was known around town] was the first person in Ajijic to paint her house in more than two different colors. The

bullies at El Municipio told her she had to paint her house or they would fine her 200 pesos. That being a week of groceries back then, she decided to enlist her artist friends and went around collecting any extra paint they had. Then she put us to work on that front wall: at least twenty different colors, simple long colorful stripes all the way down the wall. Those bullies were so mad at her and she simply claimed that they did not specify how to paint but just to paint. We had the very first colorful house in Ajijic and, as you can see, now that it started a trend, the whole town is painted in colors.[3]

In the latter part of 1969, Beverly traveled to California to renew her tourist papers and returned with two new loves: photography and photographer Michael Heinichen. They set up a darkroom in Ajijic where Heinichen taught her the techniques of developing and printing. While Beverly's love for Heinichen did not last very long (he fell in love with Laura Katzman and moved to Jocotepec), her love of photography lasted the rest of her life.

Working mainly in black and white, Beverly became Ajijic's unofficial village photographer, called upon for personal portraits, wedding photos, landscape shots, first communions, baptisms and even for portraits of the recently deceased for their families to remember them by. Her work was exhibited in Ajijic at the Galería del Lago (then occupying the building that is now the Ajijic Cultural Center) in about 1971. She also took the color photos used by the owners of the Hotel Danza del Sol to promote the hotel internationally shortly after it was built.

Beverly was active in numerous other art media. For example, in the 1970s she created the posters for special events at the Posada Ajijic. She also designed the weekly menu at the El Tejaban restaurant in exchange for a free meal each week for her family. Beverly's handpainted and colorful posters with expert calligraphy were so attractive that they were often stolen right off the wall.[4]

Beverly was one determined lady, who lived life to the full, in line with her personal motto of "Bring it on baby." Artist and author Henry Edwards, in *The Sweet Bird of Youth*, his autobiographical account of life in Ajijic in the 1970s, penned his first impressions on meeting "Sue Scobie":

She was a young woman in her late twenties or early thirties with blonde hair and blue eyes. Her hair, cut short, was very curly; she was quite fair but with a minor blemish or two on her face. I immediately noticed that her teeth were slightly tobacco stained and immediately judged the cause from the cigarette in her hand at the moment. She had on some very ordinary house dress and a pair of Mexican sandals. She was very friendly and invited us in in a rather offhand, distracted way.[5]

Beverly was always there when needed. When painter and muralist Tom Brudenell, living in Jocotepec, was stricken with hepatitis, she made it her mission to drive from Ajijic to Jocotepec daily for several weeks to take food and help care for him.

Sadly, Beverly was unable to overcome her own extended illness, which necessitated liberal doses of tequila to dull the pain. She suffered a fatal heart attack on 27 December 1976. Beverly was just 43 years of age, a shockingly short life for such a caring, compassionate and creative individual.[6]

To compound the family tragedy, Tony Pérez, father of the two youngest girls, died exactly one month to the day later. Jill, the de facto head of the family (given that her older sister Tamara was by then living in the US), made the difficult decision to leave Mexico and take her three younger sisters to stay with friends in California. Abandoning most of their possessions, they hopped a bus to Guadalajara in early March, caught a train to Tijuana, and crossed the border by taxi to stay with friends in Santa Barbara to start their lives anew.

The family has never forgotten Ajijic. Rebeca Prieto, one of Beverly's grandchildren, interviewed several members of the family in 2016 to compile a very interesting 28-minute YouTube video, *Mi Familia*, in which they reminisced about life in Ajijic and their journey north.

31

Posada Ajijic: parade of managers

As Ajijic entered the 1960s the managerial mantle of the Posada Ajijic passed to Murray Stone. Following the example set by previous managers, Stone advertised north of the border, in the *Los Angeles Times* and *Esquire,* proclaiming it was possible to live in Ajijic on $150 a month.[1] Little is known about Stone's previous life or his spell managing the Posada Ajijic—with the help of his partner, Virginia Knight—from about 1959 to 1962.

Dr Jim Vaughan, who stayed at the Posada almost every year for 35 years, told me that when Stone was manager the bar-tenders were Nacho and Gabriel.[2] Gabriel's son Victor Romero Llamas later worked at the Posada Ajijic, prior to becoming a successful visual artist.

The Posada was still praised as a great place to stay in 1962, when single occupancy with three meals cost $7.60 a day.[3] This is when former New Orleans schoolteacher Iona Kupiec arrived, having decided to stop off in Ajijic at the end of a two-year trip around the world. After a candlelight supper at the Posada:

> I spent the night in a suite of rooms in a little brick house set amid flowers, blossoms and fruits of a Garden of Eden. The rooms were spacious but cosy and were decorated with very colorful rugs, curtains, bed coverings and very large clay urns filled with bouquets of flowers. There was a beautifully designed fireplace and a glowing blaze from which issued the warmth of large burning logs.[4]

Kupiec, a particularly colorful, eccentric and generous character, became a long-time resident of Ajijic after renting a cottage from Zara (La Rusa).

Shortly afterwards, according to Vaughan, Murray Stone went back to the US, leaving his wife in charge. Unfortunately, she soon ran the Posada "into a hole."

Virtually nothing is known about Stone's short-lived successor as manager, Vic Aldridge, believed to have been in charge when Loy Strother and his friends affectionately dubbed one of the waiters "old lightn'n":

> because every plate delivered got cold in the time it took him to get from the kitchen door to your table. It was so frustrating because you could see your meal the whole time and he was making progress, but you knew the soup was getting cold as he shuffled along.... But he was about a hundred and eight years old and obviously needed the job, so what can you do?[5]

Strother's fondest memories of the Posada, though, "were the conversations deep into the night with Kit (Christopher Bateman) and the local men of knowledge and the fascinating people who had found their way to this inner circle."

Aldridge sold the business in 1963 to former Hollywood director Sherman Harris, best known for his work on *Lone Ranger* and *Lassie*. Harris had answered a classified advertisement in the *Los Angeles Times* for someone willing to invest $5000 "in a growing business," which turned out to be the Posada Ajijic. Immediately prior to moving to Ajijic with his second wife, Jane Goza, Harris had managed a 450-room hotel in Disneyland.[6]

When Harris and his wife took over in November 1963, they wasted no time making improvements to the Posada, such as upscaling the restaurant and adding a swimming pool, croquet court, poolside bar and a new patio, the Quinto Patio. A year later they announced that Canadians J D (Bob) Hannam and his wife, Phyllis, were joining them as partners.[7]

In 1964, Harris encouraged Gail Michel, an American businesswoman and dress designer, to open her own store, El Ángel, in the hotel. The store, which sold Michel's embroidered, handloomed dresses, jewelry, paintings, and select Mexican handicrafts, quickly outgrew its original location and moved to premises across the street.

The Harrises also organized an Independence Day swimming race from Chapala to Ajijic in 1964, with lunch and an awards ceremony afterwards at the Posada Ajijic. A few days earlier, American Bill Evans had swum across the lake from San Luis Soyutlán to Ajijic, apparently just for fun![8]

In a lengthy open letter to friends in 1964, Ralph McGinnis described how the Posada:

jumps on Friday and Saturday nights, when the brave men and fair women of the region gather there to make merry. The Posada has two bars and a glassed-in restaurant facing the lake and dominated by a walk-in fireplace. Two or three mariachi bands, with wandering single troubadours, supply the music. The food is good to excellent, depending on the sobriety of the chef.[9]

The following year the Harrises appointed Peter and Nancy Spencer, who had previously run the La Quinta inn in Jocotepec, to manage the Posada on their behalf. This gave a *Guadalajara Reporter* correspondent the opportunity to praise Sherm and Jane Harris for having transformed the Posada from "a drab, defunct inn" into one where:

beautiful gardens and swimming pool, comfortable rooms, good service in the bar and dining room and gay music for dancing in the delightful Quinto Patio...[attracted] a great many tourists from the States and Mexico.[10]

Harris continued to supply an informative booklet about Ajijic life and living costs to anyone who sent $2 for postage, and Spencer now introduced regular art exhibits.[11]

Guests at the Posada in November 1965 included Martin Litton, travel editor of *Sunset* magazine.[12] The October 1966 issue of *Sunset* featured a piece about Guadalajara and the lake: "In Ajijic, you will never regret the days or dollars you spend at the delightful Posada Ajijic, where poinsettias grow 10 to 20 feet tall to shade the walks and lawns."

Sherm and Jane Harris clearly did a great job of revitalizing the Posada during their time in charge. *Los Angeles Times* travel editor Jerry Hulse, who also stayed at the hotel in 1965, was effusive in his praise:

We have found a new paradise: a town with 4300 people and only a single telephone.... Posada Ajijic is run by an exHollywood film and television producer, Sherman Harris, and his wife Jane, who seem dedicated to the idea of spoiling their guests for any other life. A popular pastime involves nothing more strenuous than luxuriating in the sun beside the pool and gazing off at fishermen who spread their nets across the lake . . . Should this sound tempting, $15 will get you meals as well as a roof for two with private bath, comfortable beds, and a fireplace for when nights get nippy. Singles (with meals) come to $10 and suites are $18."

Hulse reported that a haircut cost 24 cents (3 pesos), beer was 18 cents a bottle, horses could be rented for 40 cents an hour and that homes with 2 or 3 bedrooms rented for $40 a month. He even liked the fact that the village had only one telephone, the Posada had a bilingual parrot (named Joe), and that the coffee served there came from beans grown in the gardens.[13]

The Spencers managed the Posada until September 1965, when they left for personal reasons because their marriage had disintegrated. Nancy had walked out and was living with Miriam Busby; the two women undertook a joint redesign of the Posada Ajijic bar but did not stay together for long.[14] With the Spencers out of the picture, Ismael Macías was appointed manager. Macías had formerly worked at the Chula Vista Holiday Inn restaurant and then at La Mansión in San Juan del Río, Querétaro.

After Harris sold his interest in the Posada Ajijic to Sue and Booth Waterbury in 1966, he and his wife continued to live at their lakeshore home (Morelos 33) in Ajijic. Barely two years later, Jane died unexpectedly in a Guadalajara hospital. Harris later remarried and moved to Houston, Texas.[15]

The Waterburys came to Ajijic from Newport Beach, California, in 1965, after reading Hulse's *Los Angeles Times* article. They met the Harrises, liked what they saw, and took over the Posada on Valentine's Day 1966.[16] Booth Waterbury, born on 4 January 1917, was a great grand-nephew of John Wilkes Booth, assassin of President Lincoln. He had acted in films, TV and at the Pasadena Playhouse, and ran a restaurant-bar business in California before moving to Mexico. His wife, Sue, was educated in Switzerland, where "her very first beau was Prince Bernhard von Lippe zu Blesterfeld, now married to Queen Juliana!"[17]

The Posada continued to attract celebrities from Hollywood and elsewhere, such as Isabelle Blodgett and Bob Swink, who honeymooned there at the end of March 1966. Blodgett had worked on movie crews for *My Fair Lady*, *The Collector*, *The Sun Also Rises* and *The Bravados*, the last two filmed in Mexico. Swink's credits as movie editor included *Friendly Persuasion*, *Roman Holiday* and *Big Country* (all nominated for Academy awards); he was currently working on *How to Steal A Million*.[18]

The Waterburys maintained the tradition of holding art shows at the Posada, and, in May 1966, offered the inn's premises for a well-attended fashion show, when more than 250 people packed the grounds to see the latest designs by Gail Michel, Helen Kirtland, Pat Williamson, Ethel Green, Alfredo, Neill James and Anita Pantoja.[19] The models included Susie Emery, Dorothy Rutherford, Helen West, Gerda Kelly (a former professional model in New York) and her daughter Jill, Lona Isoard, Allyn and Beverly Hunt, Bob Snodgrass, Josefina Gutierrez, Stephany Callis, Elena Pérez and Beverly Johnson's children.

The following year the Waterburys appointed Roberto Guerrero, formerly assistant manager at the Chula Vista Holiday Inn, as manager.[20] The rainy season that year was particularly bountiful. The lake rose so high that, by early October, Chapala was being called Little Venice as waves washed over its pier and flooded homes and schools. Ajijic was similarly affected.[21]

The Posada remained a regular stop for American motorists touring Mexico. Novelist and travel writer David Dodge and his family lived in Ajijic for several months in 1966. In *The Best of Mexico by Car* (1969) Dodge listed the Posada Ajijic as "a very attractive hotel on the lake shore" that welcomed visitors for lunch or dinner. Norman Ford, in his book published at about the same time, called the Posada, "A rustic and rambling but comfortable inn with colorful bar."[22]

Speaking of motorists and Ajijic, a big crowd gathered at the Posada bar in September 1968 to witness a memorable publicity stunt, when a Volkswagen dealership in Guadalajara arranged for a specially adapted Volkswagen Bug (*vocho*) to be driven across the lake. The vehicle left San Luis Soyatlán, on the south shore of the lake, in the early afternoon of Sunday 8 September and was expected to reach Ajijic two hours later. In the event, the crossing took twice as long, and it required another hour and a half or so to reach Chapala.[23] The car had traversed 24 kilometers of "lake highway" by the time it drove up onto the beach in Chapala to the loud applause of onlookers.

32

Other Ajijic hotels and Chula Vista

The Hotel Anita

In the early 1960s, when the Posada Ajijic temporarily lost its way due to more than one ineffectual manager, the Hotel Anita became the "in place." The Hotel Anita occupied a once extensive property (since subdivided into three) west of the plaza on Calle Juárez, north of Hidalgo.[1] It began life a few years earlier as the Hotel Laguna. The postcards of Hotel Laguna, and other scenes in Ajijic, taken by Jacques Van Belle in about 1957, are among the earliest postcard views of the village.

The Hotel Anita was owned by Anita Chávez de Basulto (La Muñeca), a close friend of Sara Fregoso de Nido, wife of Ramón Nido, owner of the eponymous hotel in Chapala. According to Natalia Cuevas, friends with both women, it was rumored that they had formerly run a brothel in Guadalajara.

Anita invested her ill-gotten gains in various properties in Ajijic, including the Hotel Anita and the village gas station. She also helped finance Natalia Cuevas' brother-in-law, Roberto Cuevas, when he purchased land in San Juan Cosalá to build the hotel and *balneario* (spa) that totally transformed that community. When Anita was diagnosed with a serious back problem, she wanted to go to Spain for treatment, but was persuaded to remain in Mexico by her much younger husband, Federico Basulto, and one of his friends. Anita died shortly after having an operation in a Guadalajara hospital.[2]

Loy Strother, who stayed at the Hotel Anita in 1961–62, described it as "the hot spot in town," with a bar that was "a classic watering hole for the rich and semi famous... and anyone else who wandered in." Its supremacy in this regard was later superceded by the Posada Ajijic bar.

Another noteworthy guest at Hotel Anita was artist Alfredo Santos. While serving four years for drug smuggling in San Quentin prison in California, Santos painted murals on the dining room walls showing a kaleidoscope of Californian history, including whimsical images of a sombrero-clad immigrant crossing the border. Following his release, he was a caricaturist at Disneyland and opened an art studio in San Diego. Fearing another arrest in 1961, he married his 19-year-old girlfriend and fled to Mexico. They lived initially in Guadalajara, where Santos painted a picturesque mural, "Ciudad de mujeres" (City of women), in the Café Madrid. The mural, which still survives, is said to have been painted in a single, liquor-fueled, fun-filled night.

When his wife left him to return to California, Santos moved to Ajijic to hole up for a while with a new companion in the Hotel Anita. Katharine Couto, whose family ran the hotel in 1963–64, recalls him as a long-time guest, who paid his bill, in part, with two paintings. One, showing people climbing the steps to a church, was later donated to the Latino Center in Omaha, Nebraska. The other painting, of a bridge connecting two cities, is still in the family.[3] After Ajijic, Santos opened art galleries in Mexico City and Acapulco before returning to live in the US.

The Hotel Anita closed in about 1965. It reopened in 1967 as the Hotel Villa del Lago, run by Luis de Alba, who had formerly managed the restaurant at Posada Ajijic, and his wife, Margaret.[4] Two years later, travel writer David Dodge, who lived in the village for a while, wrote that:

> The only place in town serving a la carta meals (good) that are consistently acceptable by gringo standards is the Villa del Lago, no phone yet, write A.P. Ajijic, Jal. $7, a nice small hotel in the middle of town one street west of the little central plaza.[5]

The Hotel Villa del Lago was relatively short-lived and lasted only until about 1970.

The Posada Rancho Santa Isabel

The Posada Rancho Santa Isabel, with its lovely gardens, first opened in the 1950s on what were then the eastern fringes of Ajijic; it remained a popular hostelry throughout the 1960s.[6] The 1965 Edition of *Terry's Guide to Mexico* describes it as a pleasant, informal, cottage-type establishment with ten units, a fair dining room and cocktail service. Double rooms, with private bath and veranda, were 120 pesos, meals included.[7]

The previous year, Mary Lou Keller, a correspondent for the *Red Rock News* in Arizona, described how she and her partner were driving an RV in the area when they realized they were running out of gas. The nearest gas station had closed because it had no power and the only place listed in their trusty AAA guide was the Rancho Santa Isabel, "an inn of high rating." They stayed overnight in this "veritable Garden of Eden," and were treated to a "delicious and memorable" breakfast the next morning.[8]

The Santa Isabel, on a lakefront lot on the western side of Calle Revolución, was named for Isabel Hunton, the daughter of the family that built Villa Virginia in Chapala.[9] Isabel owned and ran the hotel with the help of her husband, Carlos Ziener. One source describes Carlos as a "much-traveled, portly German gentleman," and claims that an original Diego Rivera graced one wall of the dining room. The property was a genuine ranch-hotel and the couple were great supporters of the local community. In December 1965, Isabel Hunton donated a Jersey bull calf for a secondary vocational school fund-raising bazaar held at the Posada Ajijic.[10]

Isabel, with occasional help from her two children, continued to run the hotel following her husband's death in 1966. The hotel appealed to longer-term visitors and advertised five bungalows with kitchenettes, and two double rooms with baths and a lakeview terrace. Breakfasts were available to guests, as were dinners on request. There was no bar, however, because Isabel did not want noise or problems.[11]

Isabel, born in Chapala in 1907, was an avid horse rider. Tragically, in January 1970, she died in Jocotepec following a fall from Gallo, her beloved chestnut quarterback horse.[12] Her daughter, Elizabeth Ziener Hunton, took over the reins of the hotel, which continued to attract regular visitors, including New York artist Walt Peters and his wife, Margaret. Peters visited every winter for several years and held an annual art show at the hotel of his meticulously executed plein air watercolors of scenes in Ajijic and San Antonio Tlayacapan.[13]

By the time the Posada Rancho Santa Isabel closed in March 1975, three small motels were operating in Ajijic: La Carreta on the village plaza, and Las Calandrias and Las Casitas on the main highway.[14] By 2020, Ajijic had more more than twenty hotels.

Chula Vista Subdivision and Holiday Inn

As the area began to attract more and more visitors, more hotels were needed. The first major new hotel to be opened was the Chula Vista

Holiday Inn in March 1960, alongside the entrance to the Chula Vista subdivision, the earliest US-style real estate development in the area.

Henry Albahtten commenced construction of Chula Vista in 1958. One of the first buildings to be erected, apart from the hotel, was the interdenominational Little Chapel by the Lake. Among the first Americans to build homes in the subdivision were Albert Wiegand, a retired salesman from Wisconsin, who later built several homes in Ajijic as rental properties, and Margaret Fleming and her husband.[15]

In his 1964 open letter "Lotus Land," Ralph McGinnis described how:

> Chula Vista sprawls on the slopes of a crescent of mountain about two miles west of Chapala on the lake shore. Chula Vista, with one or two exceptions, is exclusively Americano. Its luxury homes make a slight and condescending bow to the Mexican way of life by adding patios and walls, but it is essentially transplanted California.... Chula Vista sports a nifty golf club and most of the homes have pools, electric kitchens, and poodles.[16]

Chula Vista's sporty 9-hole hillside golf course opened in the early 1960s. The residents of Chula Vista also had access to a tennis court and swimming pool. The subdivision featured regularly in newspapers north of the border. One 1970 description called it:

> a planned US-style housing community... offering everything from $10,000 bungalows to $100,000 estates planted on a hillside slope. [It] already has a nine-hole golf course, hotel, restaurant, saloon and den for night-crawlers.[17]

More than 150 homes had been completed by 1974 when a New Mexico newspaper described how:

> Melvin and Dorothy Huffaker retired from Detroit six years ago and live on a hilltop in Chula Vista, a private community overlooking Lake Chapala. There is no pollution there, the only telephone is at the main clubhouse at the road below and the single civilized noise is the hum of swimming pool filters. Huffaker meets with his friends at Chula Vista's private golf course four or five times a week in the morning, takes a daily afternoon nap like most Americans who live in Mexico and plays a good deal of bridge.[18]

Perhaps the most famous of all the foreign residents who retired to Chula Vista in the late 1960s was Dr Walter Dornberger, who lived for about a decade at Calle del Fresno 114, with his wife, Doris.[19] Dornberger was the top German missile authority during the second world war. At the end of the war, he was interned and interrogated before being admitted into the US as part of Operation Paperclip.

Dornberger then developed guided missiles for the US Air Force and worked for the Bell Aircraft Corporation. His ideas and leadership were instrumental in the success of the Space Shuttle program. In retirement Dornberger was visited in Chula Vista in 1974 by his former assistant, Dr Wernher von Braun.[20]

The Dornbergers were not welcomed by all their Chula Vista neighbors. They were, for example, never invited by Art and Ginny Ganung to any of their (frequent) parties: "Walter looked like Frankenstein, with a prominent facial scar, and was known by locals as the General, and the Ganungs would have nothing to do with a Nazi general!"[21]

Von Braun and his family also lived in Chula Vista for a short time during the mid-1970s. Alexandra Bateman and her sister often saw his blond teenage son riding the local bus.[22]

The residents of Chula Vista were acutely aware of the economic gulf between their livestyle and that of the gardeners and maids they employed, who mostly came from San Antonio Tlayacapan. The Chula Vista Women's Society, founded in 1959, had more than forty members by 1980, and was helping fund the education of thirty local children.

As for the hotel, its joint managers from 1964 to at least 1974 were Antonio Shafer and Enrique Rojas, who had earlier managed the Posada Ajijic, and who had worked at the Chula Vista hotel from when it first opened. The hotel changed its name to Motel Chula Vista in about 1969, at which time a double room was $12 a night.[23] After it closed in about 1990, the motel was converted into apartments.

The bypass (*libramiento*)

By the 1970s, an estimated 7000 vehicles used the Guadalajara-Chapala highway every day, with peak flows of up to 20,000 vehicles on Sundays and holidays. As the size and number of subdivisions around Ajijic multiplied rapidly after the late 1960s, there was a desperate need for a short-cut so that traffic between Guadalajara and Ajijic avoided the center of Chapala.

Construction of the *libramiento*, offering a means of bypassing Chapala for drivers destined for San Antonio Tlayacapan, Ajijic and points west, began in 1974.[24] When it opened, in summer 1977, local columnist Ruth Netherton reported that "future links to roads leading from Chula Vista" had already been laid out. But she warned potential purchasers of adjacent building lots that:

> Much of the land traversed by the new road is 'ejidal' or zoned for government-controlled settlements. Individuals who might think of purchasing tempting homesites should make very sure the land in question is legally saleable.[25]

Netherton's comment was prescient. The first contentious development in this area, Chula Vista Norte, was begun in the 1990s; its legal situation was subsequently regularized. Currently, there are, however, at least four other real estate projects north of the *libramiento* which allegedly lack full and correct permitting at the municipal, state or federal level. The two most noteworthy are Las Minas and Colinas del Lago de San Antonio. Construction of Las Minas, a 17-hectare (42-acre) residential and hotel subdivision was halted only after workers had completed the all-too-visible and ugly road that forms a zig-zag scar on the lower slopes of Sierra El Travesaño. A short distance to the east, Colinas del Lago de San Antonio, a 40-hectare (100-acre) development in the hills north of Chula Vista Norte, was to have as its centerpiece a 40-million-dollar hotel-casino complex called Lake Chapala Hotel and Casino Resort.[26]

33

Zara meets flamboyant Iona

Zara had a life-long knack for making an indelible first impression on people, as did Iona Kupiec, another of Ajijic's many marvelous characters. Iona had been in Ajijic less than twenty-four hours in early 1962 when she met Zara for the first time, and the two women, from radically different backgrounds, soon became firm friends.

Iona was staying at the Posada Ajijic, having only just arrived, and had already fallen in love with the village. Walking along the beach the next morning, she also fell in love with one tiny lakefront cottage in particular, a "little white red-tiled house with a white picket fence, covered with roses," which reminded her of a favorite childhood book. Iona realized—from the white cloth hanging over its fence—that the lakefront cottage, a couple of blocks west of the pier, was for rent.

> While I was standing there entranced... what should I see suddenly appearing in front of me from around a bend in the road but a beautiful woman wearing a big red velvet, gold-embroidered charro sombrero with a red, satin, high-necked Russian blouse with a gold dragon embroidered on it from the belt up to the collar, black culottes, with red leather boots, riding a black satin horse which reared up on its hind legs when she suddenly tightened the reins. I was stunned![1]

Iona struck up a conversation and asked who owned the cottage. She was astounded when the woman (Zara) replied that she did, and that the rent was $30 a month. Iona agreed on the spot, before even seeing inside.

> I went back to the Posada, paid my bill, collected my few belongings and moved into Zara's "cottage", which originally was a *choza*

where the fishermen stored their belongings and their fishing gear, but which Zara had redesigned.... I was especially thrilled with the two glass walls of the kitchen which gave me a wide view of the lake. The water was just fifteen feet away from the wall of my small but flower-filled fruit garden and my horizon-long view took in the mountains on the south shore of the lake. The central window of the east wall gave me a panoramic view all the way to the Posada and the far distant shore of Michoacán state.

To get a receipt for her rent, Iona followed Zara back to her house, "a veritable art museum in one, very large, elegantly furnished, parlor." It was full of mementos from Zara's theater and ballet days, full length oils portraying her and her "brother", Holger, in their dancing costumes, gilded-framed portraits from her New York theater appearances, photographs, figurines and books.

Iona's handwritten receipt was dated 2 February 1962. Renting Zara's cottage was a very lucky break for Iona. First, Zara invited Iona to visit whenever she wished to play her grand piano. Then she insisted that Iona join her on her daily horse ride:

Zara was an equestrienne par excellence.... At the time of my arrival at her *huerta*, she had two mares and she rode one named Amaya; she let me ride the black one called by the very inappropriate name, Rosa. We rode every morning down to the old mill where the gold they had taken from the two mines that Zara owned was separated from the ore. The big iron grinding machine was still there, changing daily into orange and chocolate colored dust. Years before my arrival, Zara and her brother rode their horses into Guadalajara with the gold nuggets in their saddle bags, to the Assayer's office and then hid their treasure in a nunnery. Zara sold me two shares in the ownership of the mine called La Esperanza. Just when work was to begin again, the Mexican Government forbid the use of explosive as sumptuous summer homes were being built for two of the elite of Guadalajara on the hills above the mine.

Zara's gold mill house

Years earlier, while working her gold mine, Zara had built a house alongside the gold mill. When Zara had first had to put her mining plans on hold, she began renting out this house to earn some much-needed extra income, though she hoped this was only a temporary arrangement, and continued to harbor lingering hopes of striking it rich with gold.

Among those who loved the relative seclusion of the mill house was US poet Jack Gilbert in about 1960 when he was working on *Views of Jeopardy*. The house was also the perfect choice a few years later for LSD devotee Thad Ashby and his disciples.

Zara, who was New Age long before the term was fashionable, was a free thinker who believed in spiritualism, reincarnation, and the importance of karma.[2] She and her household had become lacto-vegetarians decades before the idea became mainstream.[3] While Zara had no time for anyone who drank alcohol, she thought that the LSD-taking hippies who stayed at her gold mill house in the 1960s were wonderful.[4]

Over the years a succession of artists resided at the mill house, including John K Peterson and Sid Schwartzman, and it was a venue for art shows. But perhaps the strangest of all the groups associated with the old mill house was the group called The Illuminated Elephants (Los elefantes iluminados) which camped there in 1982.[5] This traveling international theater family, once known as The Hathi Babas, had about twenty members; its co-founders included Mexican environmental activist Alberto Ruz Buenfil. Zara continued to own the mill house until at least the mid-1980s.[6]

Why was Iona Kupiec so loved?

Few of the colorful characters in Ajijic over the years were as creative or colorful as la Señora Iona. A retired school teacher, Iona dressed flamboyantly and often tucked a brightly colored hibiscus flower or pink ribbon in her hair. To walk to the village stores she customarily donned an extravagant hat.

Listening to Iona recount her adventures, her effervescent personality to the fore, was like watching a vaudeville showgirl performing on stage. To the delight of all who knew her, Iona told her life stories with a warm wit, a perfect sense of timing, and a healthy dose of hyperbole.

Iona Agnes Fick was born in New Orleans, Louisiana, on 22 August 1905, though vanity often prompted her to subtract a year or two from her age.[7] She grew up in a far-from-privileged household; her father worked as a mail clerk and then as a postman, and her mother, of Irish decent, rented rooms to boarders.[8]

A fine pianist, Iona also played the banjo and piano-accordion, and claimed that her fashion sense was instilled in childhood when her parents dressed her in "lots of buttons and bows."[9] After training as a teacher, Iona completed a degree in English at Tulane University; she later added a masters from Loyola University of the South.[10] She taught high school drama, English literature, music and rhetoric (persuasive public speaking) in New Orleans for more than thirty years prior to early retirement in 1960.

In her early thirties, Iona had married Walter Kupiec, an able bodied seaman who spent his life on the water. Ever willing to acquire new skills, Iona herself became an accomplished seafarer and was the first woman in Louisiana to hold a US Department of Commerce license to operate and navigate boats up to 65 feet in length.

Walter was often away for extended periods. On a trip to Tahiti he met and fell in love with a beautiful Tahitian girl. Iona was stunned on his return to find that he now had only half of his customary luxuriant beard; the other half of his face was clean shaven, reflecting, he said, his conflicting love for two women.[11]

Within weeks of retiring, Iona took a ship to Puerto Rico, the US Virgin Islands and the Dominican Republic, before spending most of the following year teaching English in the Madeira archipelago.[12] It was on her way home to New Orleans that she stopped off in Ajijic.

She adored Zara's cottage. Writing to a friend in New Orleans, Iona expressed how very much she enjoyed life in Ajijic:

My life here is sheer delight. I live in a little flower-bowered, picture-book adobe house right at the water's edge of gorgeous Lake Chapala. There are mountains all around. I have a beautiful copper-colored horse named 'Tapatio' and I go riding almost every day up in the hills to the gold mines and bat caves. I ride with five very handsome, very gallant, lively, fun-loving young Mexicans. We wear big sombreros and our saddles are picturesquely decorated with carved pommels and mine is inlaid with mother of pearl.[13]

The large garden attached to the humble cottage was the perfect setting for Iona's many and varied theatrical productions. It was the scene for some of Ajijic's most memorable garden parties. Iona would select a theme—such as *Alice in Wonderland*—allocate parts to guests, and cajole them into participating in an elaborately staged dramatic event, to the enjoyment and merriment of all.

One of the earliest events Iona organized was a gymkhana in April 1967 for "young Mexican and American equestrians of Ajijic" to compete in a series of riding and roping games she had devised. Journalist Anita Lomax called the gymkhana "a joy to watch" and "one of the most interesting contests we've had in the area for a long time!"[14]

After about five years renting Zara's cottage, Iona tried other locations in the village.[15] She also lived, apparently more than once, with Neill James at Quinta Tzintzuntzan. The two women took several foreign trips together, and Iona is the basis for the character Jana Saskova in *Kokio*, Stephen Banks' fictionalized biography of James.

Iona indulged her personal thespian interests by working with Betty Kuzell on early shows at the Lakeside Little Theatre. In 1977, Iona gave a workshop in which she directed and performed scenes from *The Mikado*.[16] This was apparently the Theatre's first ever mime show.

But it was her less structured, more creative, community theatrical events that became truly legendary. These included hosting, for several years, an annual party for children from the Hospicio Cabañas orphanage in Guadalajara. Up to 120 youngsters would choose costumes and participate in an impromptu performance.[17]

In 1976, Iona entertained friends at a mime and dance performance of *Carmen* by local children, under the direction of Manuel España Ramos, director of the Ajijic Folklórico.[18]

In the early 1980s, Iona returned to Zara's cottage, which then became her home for the remainder of her life.

Over the years, Iona's magic world of make-believe was the excuse for dozens of local children and adults to show off their previously unsuspected talents for an afternoon of fun while performing Christmas pastorelas and shows ranging from *Madame Butterfly* and *The Thief of Bagdad* to *Snow White*, *Little Red Riding Hood*, *Cinderella*, *Samson and Delilah*, *Romeo and Juliet*, and *The Pied Piper*.[19]

Iona was a committed supporter of the local community, content to live humbly, while contributing financially to help local children gain a better education. Her monthly social security checks were given to the Lakeside School for the Deaf in Jocotepec to sponsor students there; her pension and savings helped several Ajijic students further their education in Oak Hill School and in Guadalajara.

Even as age caught up with her, Iona refused to slow down, as shown by my wife's brief journal entry after she first met Iona, then in her late seventies, on 2 October 1982: "Iona in orange dress with huge orange bow in hair, organizing for party next day— 40 guests. She will perform a version (mimed) of *Hamlet*."[20]

At the age of 83, Iona took up painting. She completed dozens of charming, naif, full-length portraits of real and imagined characters, most depicted in suitably flamboyant and dramatic clothes, much like those favored by the artist herself.

Iona Kupiec was awarded a richly deserved Lifetime Achievement Award from *El Ojo del Lago* in April 1988.[21]

Neill James, Iona and Zara comprised a triumvirate of grandes dames living in Ajijic at the time. Unlike the unfortunate events that were to befall the other two women towards the end of their lives, Iona's final years were joyful and scandal-free. Only a few months before she died, her friends threw a fun-filled fiesta to celebrate her 94th birthday, with *botanas*, drinks, and music by the Mariachis Romántico Rústico de Ajijic.

After the party, Ruth Ross Merrimer remarked on "the mutual out-pouring of love between Iona and the neighborhood children... palpable in their greetings and hugs. She reminisced how:

> Up until a few years ago one of the most familiar sights on the streets of Ajijic was the slender form of Iona Kupiec, basket in hand, going about her daily shopping routine. Always dressed as colorfully re-splendent as the flowers and ribbons she tucked in her hair, Kupiec usually made slow progress with her many stops to chat with friends or to embrace a child.[22]

After living in Ajijic for her final 37 years, Iona Kupiec passed peace-fully at home on 27 September 1999. She will forever be remembered with affection by her long-term housekeeper, María Eugenia Sánchez, her friends, and all who knew her. A life well lived!

Zara's cottage had many other illustrious renters over the years, in-cluding Marcella Crump, Mimi Fariña (the younger sister of singer Joan Baez), Lona Isoard, and Ken Smedley and his wife, Dorian, but none as flamboyant as drama teacher and world traveler Iona Kupiec. Old-timers still have fond memories of the many zany parties and informal theatrical afternoons at "Iona's cottage."

34

Neill James the capitalist

During the 1960s, Neill James continued the Children's Art Program she had started a decade earlier and opened a second children's library at Seis Esquinas, even as she strived to build her weaving and silk business and consolidate her real estate rentals.

James had long entertained great hopes for her weaving enterprise, particularly since focusing on using home-produced silk, and now sought federal support for promotion and marketing. In 1960 she wrote to "El Director, Museo Nacional de Cosas Regional" (sic),[1] in Mexico City, enclosing information about natural silk, samples of material spun and woven in Ajijic, and a price list. A silk blouse with hand embroidery was 85 pesos, a rebozo of natural silk, hand made in Ajijic, 125 pesos. James also quoted for "original clothes made in Ajijic": girl's dress 75 pesos, girl's blouse 17, boy's shirt 25 and woman's blouse 30. Finally, James offered three woodcut prints by Raphael Greno of the silk industry in Ajijic at 10 pesos each.[2]

Two years later, in 1962, James successfully applied for her silk business to be granted a ten-year exemption from state and municipal taxes on manufacturing and real estate.[3] Her silk industry was in full flow at this time and garnered publicity far and wide. One US paper included photographs of silkworm cocoons and girls working silk, and another offered a detailed description of the processes involved.[4] Silk blouses were especially popular and commanded a much higher price than their cotton equivalents. Silk rebozos also sold well. One report claimed that "visiting Japanese silk experts pronounced the Ajijic silk supreme in the world."[5]

Such optimistic external validation helped give James the confidence to spend 24,206 pesos (about $2000) in 1964 to purchase a brand new, bright red, Volkswagen Bug, complete with white-walled tires, radio and antenna.[6]

But the following year, writing to a California silk enthusiast, James lamented the fact that she had failed to convinced villagers to plant mulberry trees or set up their own silk business:

"Not a single Ajijican was willing to abandon his milpa (which grew food for family, corn, beans) and set our established mulberry trees free for asking. A padre came from a distant village to learn to grow silk and spent two weeks with me. I gave away all my trees to be planted on golf course and in parks. A couple of farmers took some as food for animals."[7]

Despite the tax breaks, publicity and her own hard work, long-term financial success from silk proved to be elusive. James finally conceded defeat in about 1966.

A variety of explanations have been offered for why the silk industry flopped, ranging from the impatience of the local workforce to see quick results, a cold winter that killed the silkworms,[8] a lack of profitability,[9] problems with labor unions,[10] and a government campaign spraying pesticides to prevent malaria.[11] While the last reason is quite probable (a similar campaign in Oaxaca in the 1950s certainly wrought havoc in that state's silk industry),[12] James herself placed the blame on a single employee. Replying to a silk enthusiast in California to thank him for an unexpected gift of some silk eggs, she wrote that:

"My trouble was that the girl whom I taught all about silk ... and who took care of it for 15 years decided to leave my employ. Under Mexican law, if I discharge her I have to pay her 3 months salary for every year in which she has worked for me making a total of 45 months salary. Naturally I wouldn't dream of firing her. In desperation she finally left me without a day's notice and ran off with a lover. Last year when I went to the refrigerator to get eggs out for a new crop of silk, THERE WERE NONE! She had not saved a single egg! I had both the golden cocoons and the white Bagdad and could take care of half a million silkworms."[13]

James later admitted to a visiting journalist that "The silk I produced by hand cost me twice as much as I sold it for."[14] James quietly abandoned her silk-filled ambitions and went back to weaving cotton and wool.

Real estate

Prior to the mid-1960s—when the first specialist real estate firm was established in Ajijic—Neill James and Helen Kirtland had shared most of the expatriate real estate market between them. James, not surprisingly, turned out to be far better at garnering publicity for herself. For example, a full-page article in a California paper in March 1962, profiling Ajijic as an "unspoiled paradise," reported that Neill James rented out "comfortable Mexican-style homes with a gas stove, refrigerator, and fireplace for $65 a month," and that maid service was $4 a week.[15] By this time, Ajijic had a population of about 3500, including an estimated 300 Americans.

The two women faced formal competition after 1968, when Jim and Gerda Kelly opened a real estate firm called Servicios Unlimited. After eight months in temporary premises, their company moved next door to Helen Kirtland's looms, opposite the Posada Ajijic. A second company, Lakeside Homefinders was started by Dick Bishop and Agustín Velarde in 1973, along the street at Calle 16 de Sept 7. And yet a third firm, a branch of Guadalajara's Tierra Real, with Dereyk Berry as manager, opened its office on the highway in San Antonio Tlayacapan in 1976, the same year Richard Tingen opened Chapala Realty.[16]

Despite the competition, James further consolidated her real estate empire. According to her own handwritten records, she owned—and was paying the light bills for—eleven properties in 1962, twelve in 1963, and fifteen in 1972. In addition to her own house, Tzintzuntzan (Ramon Corona 20), the 1972 list included Quintanil (16 de Septiembre 14), Las Campanas (Guadalupe Victoria 8), the Biblioteca Central (Constitucion 41), Biblioteca La Colmena (Ocampo 107), Casa Colibri (Ramon Corona 22), five apartments—Tabachín, Bambú, Xalasuchil, Caoba and Tres Techos—at Ocampo 88, Casa Oro (Ocampo 90), and three apartments—Margarita, Ciruela and Arayán—at 16 de Septiembre 11.

James' archive at the Lake Chapala Society includes numerous letters highlighting the challenges she faced in managing so many properties while still running her gift shop, weaving and silk production businesses. Prospective renters had questions about costs, stores, schools, transport, pets and safety. In 1965, for example, recently widowed Carrie Joseph, with three children aged 11, 13 and 15, wanted to know whether they travel daily to school in Guadalajara from Ajijic, or also rent an apartment in Guadalajara. She was, above all, concerned about food:

35

Art community consolidates

Continued publicity for Ajijic during the 1960s brought an extraordinary variety of international artists to the village and its ever-growing art scene. It also led to the opening of Ajijic's first purpose-built art gallery.

Galleries

Laura Bateman had begun a small gallery, Rincón del Arte, in about 1958, using rented space and the family home. About a year later, Laura and her artist-architect husband, Jack, bought land and then built three homes, one of them specifically designed as a gallery with garden.[1]

The Rincón del Arte opened at its new location in April 1966.[2] After Laura Bateman left for New York in 1967, the gallery, run in her absence by a cooperative of artists, struggled on for a time before finally closing. Among the artists who exhibited there were Alfredo Sánchez Larrauri, Jesús Alcalá, Whitford Carter, Carlos Coffeen and Inga Berkman.

La Galería, the long-running gallery founded in the 1940s in El Tejaban, continued to be a lively hang-out for the village art community until after the death of Ernesto Butterlin in July 1964. Less than a year later, it had acquired such a bad reputation that it was closed, a closure celebrated in *El Informador*:

> The authorities, following numerous complaints... finally expelled the 'existentialists' and closed the so-called 'Galería del Arte', which never was an art gallery only a site for scandal where every immorality had its place.[3]

At about this time the building was acquired by Lou Wertheimer. La Galería reopened in December 1968 when he leased the building to

Grupo 68, a group of artists organized by Peter Huf and others.[4] Upkeep had been neglected. Huf recalls how they were surprised one evening to discover that thousands of swallows had returned to their nests high up in the ceiling, but decided not to chase them away.[5] According to Allyn Hunt, this incarnation of the gallery "produced more ideas, more interesting serious works than have been seen in the Guadalajara area in decades."[6] Artists who showed there included Peter Huf, Eunice Hunt, Tom Brudenell, Jack Rutherford, Don Shaw, John K Peterson, John Brandi, Bob Snodgrass, Cynthia Siddons, Paul and Casey Hachten and Alejandro Colunga.

In addition to Rincón del Arte, La Galería, and art shows held in local hotels like the Posada Ajijic and the Holiday Inn in Chula Vista, other galleries in this decade included Galería del Arte Casa Blanca in 1967,[7] and Galería Lincoln, a one-hit wonder in 1968 for a show titled "20 Años del Arte en Ajijic," organized as part of the Guadalajara Cultural Program for the 1968 Mexico City Olympics.[8]

Another gallery that lasted less than a year was Galería Ajijic (Galeria Ajijic Bellas Artes, AC), which opened in March 1968 at the intersection of Calle Marcos Castellanos and Calle Constitución.[9] Established by Hudson Rose and his wife, Mary, who claimed it was "the first truly professional independent gallery in this area," it hosted several group shows, an exhibit of unique wool paintings by José Gutiérrez Olmedo, and a solo show of works by Tom Brudenell.[10]

Visual artists working in Ajijic

Among the many, many artists active in Ajijic during the 1960s whose work showcased the village and its residents were some truly memorable characters.

Ohio-born Walter Thornton, founder of the eponymous modeling agency famous for its second world war-era pin-up girls, like Susan Hayward and Lauren Bacall, retired to Ajijic in 1958. He married Candelaria Navarro; the couple had six children and built an ostentatious house of mosaic tiles in upper La Floresta, one of the stranger architectural gems in the village.

After solo shows in Washington DC and New York, Colombian-born Carlos López Ruíz lived and painted in Ajijic for several years in the early 1960s. He specialized in fine portraits of people, horses and toreadors, as well as village scenes. In Ajijic he began a seven-year relationship with fellow artist Tink Strother; the couple moved to California and opened a joint gallery-studio there in 1963. Strother had arrived in Ajijic, where she worked as a portrait artist and taught art, in 1960.

Fashion designer, artist and entrepreneur Gail Michel, from South Dakota, arrived in Ajijic in her mid-twenties in 1961 and stayed seventeen years. In 1964 she started El Ángel Boutique, which made the pages of *Harper's Bazaar* and *Vogue Paris* for its embroidered handloomed dresses, original jewelry, paintings, and select Mexican handicrafts. At one point Michel employed "a dozen seamstresses and a staff of wood and stone carvers who cut anything from small figurines to water fountains."[11] Imitation is the sincerest form of flattery, and copies of Gail Michel's original dress designs can still be found in Ajijic stores. Michel had a lengthy relationship with local contractor Marcos Guzmán, with whom she had four children. The late Tom Faloon, who greatly admired her art, laughed when he recalled how Michel had once been so furious when her beau had started seeing a new girlfriend that she had deliberately crashed her car into the girlfriend's vehicle. The next day, a contrite Michel hurried to the police station to confess, only to learn that the police had absolutely no interest in looking into this or any other crime of passion.[12]

Lily Dulany Cushing (1909–1969), from Newport, Rhode Island, had her first solo exhibitions in New York at the age of twenty-one. She spent some time in Ajijic in the early 1960s and two of her Lake Chapala paintings, including one titled "Posada Garden with a Monkey," were on extended loan for more than a decade to the US Supreme Court.[13]

John Lee and his second wife, novelist Barbara Moore, spent a year in Ajijic in 1962–63 and made numerous return summer visits. Lee was a prolific writer, photographer and educator who penned thousands of newspaper articles, several nonfiction books and a dozen novels, including two NY Times bestsellers. In retirement, using the moniker Bestjonbon, Lee assembled several YouTube videos about Ajijic, including "Ajijic 50 years ago" and "Fiesta Ajijic—45 Years Ago."

Some of the artists who tried living in Ajijic were far less enamored with the village. For example, renowned painter and social rights activist Mary Lovelace O'Neal—urged to visit Ajijic by Black American artist Arthur Monroe—stayed only a very short time:

> I was going to be this great expatriated African American woman artist. And then I got down there and those Mexican men were acting

like Italian men. I'd say, "If you put your hands on me, I'll kill you."
And the weather got funky, and my Spanish was rotten. That was
not my spot. I wasn't supposed to be there. And so I came back.[14]

Indianapolis-born artist Mary "Beth" Avary was just beginning
her career when she moved to Ajijic with her husband, Don, in the mid-
1960s for several years. Avary showed her naturalistic expressionist works
in dozens of major invitational and juried shows in the US, Mexico,
Spain, Japan and Russia. Don Avary's nephew, Roger Avary, spent part
of his childhood in Ajijic before working in film and television. He and
Quentin Tarantino were awarded a joint Oscar for their screenplay of
Pulp Fiction (1994).

The renowned Mexican-American artist Eugenio Quesada, a key
figure in the history of Mexican-American art, lived in Ajijic in the mid-
1960s. Quesada is best known for his small paintings, sketches and exquisitely executed charcoal portraits, which include several of Ajijic children,
and a masterful portrait of guitarist Carlos Espíritu. Quesada's work has
featured in several major traveling exhibitions of Mexican-American art.

Artist and art instructor Jo Lee Rodke Storm spent several winters
in Ajijic in the 1960s. Several of her Mexican paintings won prizes in
exhibitions in Arizona, including "The Vendors," a Mexican street scene
which won a prize for oils in 1967.

California-born Jack Rutherford, a former Director of the School of
Fine Art in Long Beach, California, lived with his wife, Dorothy, and
their four children in Ajijic from about 1966 to 1971. He held numerous
solo and group exhibitions and was a co-founder of the Grupo 68 art
collective. Many of his intriguing and beautifully executed paintings
depicted Ajijic, or were inspired by the village.

John Kenneth Peterson (1922–1984) ran his own art gallery in the
San Francisco Bay area before settling in Ajijic in 1965, where he taught
art, opened a gallery and was active in the community for two decades.
Peterson was a founding member of both Grupo 68 and Clique Ajijic and
held several solo shows. One 1968 review described him as "probably the
area's most provocative artist when dealing with conventional nudes."[15]
Peterson completed up to thirty paintings a month, and his artistic ver-
satility extended to murals, stained glass, fresco, sculpture, water colors,
oils and wood blocks.[16] He painted dozens, perhaps hundreds, of scenes
in Ajijic, including the hills, boats, fishermen and women washing clothes

in the lake. He was truly one of Ajijic's larger-than-life characters. His partner in later life was sculptor Margo Thomas.

Noted expressionist artists Abby and Jules Rubinstein lived in Ajijic from 1966 to 1976. Abby, who had been taught by famous Mexican artist Rufino Tamayo at the Brooklyn Museum Art School, developed an emotion-tugging style dubbed "humanist expressionism" by one art columnist.[17] Their home and studios in Ajijic welcomed a steady stream of international visitors and collectors. The Rubinsteins held several solo and joint shows in Guadalajara, including some organized for the 1968 Mexico City Olympics,[18] and were quoted at length in an extended newspaper piece about American retirees in Mexico.[19]

Another artistic couple—Canadian-born Eunice Hunt and German-born Peter Paul Huf—first met in Mexico in the 1960s. They married in Ajijic, had two sons, and lived there from 1967 to June 1972, before relocating to Europe. In addition to numerous solo shows, they co-founded the small art collective Grupo 68 and the cooperative gallery, La Galería. Their final studio-home in Ajijic was at Calle Constitución 30, a building later shared by artists Adolfo Riestra and Alan Bowers. Before leaving Mexico, the Hufs illustrated a small booklet of poems written by Ajijic resident Ira Nottonson.[20] The illustrations are Mexican naif in style, whereas their own art is more abstract or surrealist. In 2007 their elder son, Paul (Pablo) Huf, also a professional artist, retold the story of his parents' romance in an enthralling art display in Mexico City.[21]

Impressionist painter Daphne Aluta lived in Ajijic from the late 1960s for about twenty years. In September 1985 she broke a glass ceiling by becoming the first female artist featured in the Chapala area monthly *El Ojo del Lago*; all its previous art profiles had been of male artists. In addition to painting and sculpting, Aluta designed and built several homes in the village.

The intricate linoleum block prints of Charles Surendorf are often compared favorably in quality to the much-acclaimed work of Thomas Hart Benton. Named by *Art Digest* in 1959 as one of the top twenty-five woodblock artists in the world, Surendorf traveled to Mexico with his family in 1968 to make the preliminary block print sketches needed to carve printing blocks back in California. The linocuts include several mysterious and powerful images of Ajijic.

Renowned German-American painter Emil Eugen Holzhauer, who exhibited at the 1939 New York World's Fair, visited and traveled in

Mexico numerous times before he painted "Ajijic" in 1968. Another of his paintings, titled "Lake Chapala," was featured on the back cover of *Museum and Arts* (Houston's Art Journal) in 1993.

British painters Richard and Nancy Carline visited Ajijic in 1967 and 1975 to spend time with their good friends Jack and Laura Bateman. One of Richard's paintings—"After Rain Ajijic Mexico 1967"—was shown in London, UK, in 1968, and a 1975 painting by Nancy—"Ajijic Mexico Lake Chapala"—was sold at auction there in 2020. The Batemans' oldest daughter, Alice, after studying art for a year at the University of Guadalajara, stayed with the Carlines in London in the 1960s to continue her studies. Now based in Texas, Alice is an internationally recognized sculptor.[22]

Grupo 68

The initial members of the Ajijic art cooperative Grupo 68, active between 1967 and 1971, were Peter Huf, his wife Eunice (Hunt) Huf, Jack Rutherford (who dropped out after about a year), John K Peterson and Don Shaw. Painter and muralist Tom Brudenell joined them for some shows.[23] The group exhibited regularly at the Hotel Camino Real in Guadalajara, and also held many shows in Ajijic, at the Rincón del Arte gallery, and at its own collective gallery, La Galería. Grupo 68 also held shows in Guadalajara, including one for the Cultural Program of the International Arts Festival for the 1968 Olympics.

Grupo 68 disbanded in 1971 when the individual artists went their separate ways. Rutherford returned to the US, and later settled in Spain, while Huf and his wife left for Europe. The only member of Grupo 68 to remain in Ajijic was John K Peterson, who later joined forces with seven other artists to form a new group named Clique Ajijic.

The Chula Vista happening

Three young artists—John Brandi, Tom Brudenell, and Don Shaw—combined in June 1969 to stage a Cocktail Party "MythMass" or "happening" in Chula Vista.[24] They wanted attendees to experience as well as observe their work. Shaw told me that the performance was intended to challenge the area's artistic status quo. The choice of venue was deliberately provocative. Many American retirees living in Chula Vista, the first subdivision in the area, were, Shaw argued, only there because it was so much cheaper than the US. However, he continued, although they had chosen to live there, many of them "hated" the *campesinos*, maid and gardeners who worked for them.[25]

The Chula Vista happening was held in a building adjacent to the Chula Vista motel on, perhaps appropriately, Friday 13th June. It seems to have been Mexico's first ever artistic happening and came only a few years after the earliest happening in the US and at roughly the same time as the first in Canada. Cocktail in hand, some 150 visitors walked through the building, and became more than merely passive observers as they were immersed in, or exposed to, a variety of visual, auditory, tactile and olefactory stimuli. The final room featured a vintage 1910 Ford truck, complete with *campesino* driver sounding the vehicle's horn every few minutes, and an indigenous woman in one corner preparing handmade tortillas over a wood fire.

Shaw and Brudenell both stressed to me that the event needed to be understood in its historical context. It was held less than a year after the Tlatelolco student massacre in Mexico City, and was an attempt to draw attention to the racial and societal injustices found in both the US and Mexico, while challenging the community to engage more actively with local artists.

This 1969 Chula Vista event occurred right in the middle of a particularly fecund period of artistic experimentation and exploration in Ajijic. The artistic vacuum left in the mid-1970s, as many of these artists moved on to seek new challenges and inspiration elsewhere, took some time to fill.

Somewhat paradoxically, the growing tide of incomers that had prompted the Chula Vista event was simultaneously creating new opportunities for other artists to achieve a degree of commercial success by producing art that matched the tastes of the new residents of the many residential developments then springing up along the lakeshore.

36

Lakeside Little Theatre

Unlike the Chula Vista Golf Club and the Lake Chapala Society, which had formal and structured beginnings, many other community organizations came into being more organically. This was especially true of theater groups. The first English-language play performed in the area is thought to be the comedy *You Can't Take It With You*, staged in the open patio of a small inn in Chapala in 1949. John and Claudia Upton joined another couple, Helen Kirtland and Mort Carl, to arrange the show. The play, in which John Upton took the lead role, ended with spectacular pyrotechnics as fireworks were ignited and rockets shot skywards.[1]

The Lakeside Little Theatre (LLT) emerged from this, various other early informal theater shows, and the private musical evenings arranged in the 1960s by newer arrivals such as Betty and Dudley Kuzell, who lived for many years in Chula Vista, an area which attracted an unusually high proportion of actors, singers, dancers and musicians. Betty and Dudley were both accomplished musicians. Dudley was a professional actor and singer, with film credits for *Thank Your Lucky Stars* (1943), *Hail the Conquering Hero* (1944) and *Faithful in My Fashion* (1946). But he was best known as a baritone in the Ken Lane Singers (a group that sometimes accompanied Frank Sinatra, including for his iconic recording of "White Christmas") and in The Guardsmen quartet, which sang on the sound tracks of more than 800 motion pictures from the 1930s to the 1950s, including Walt Disney's *Snow White and the Seven Dwarfs* (1937), where the quartet played four of the dwarfs.

In early 1964 the Kuzells held a musical evening at their home, with Betty on the organ, Paul Carson playing the piano, and with Dudley, William Stelling and Kenneth Rundquist all singing.[2] This was a very distinguished gathering. Carson had 38 years of experience on NBC Radio as organist, pianist, composer and presenter. Rundquist was scheduled to sing a few months later at the World's Fair in New York.

Within a few weeks the Kuzells identified several like-minded residents and formed a Little Theatre Group. The group's first production was at the Chapala Country Club (in the former railroad station) and opened on 20 June 1964. With Betty Kuzell directing, a cast of four put on George Kaufman's brilliant satire, *If Men Played Cards as Women Do.*

Early the following year, on 18 February 1965, a formal business meeting established the Lakeside Little Theatre (LLT), with Betty Kuzell as founding director. Ellen and Kenneth Kirk were also founder members. Regular membership was set at 25 pesos ($2) a year. Sponsor members paid 100 pesos and were given four free tickets.[3] It was some years before the LLT name stuck; in its early days, the group was often referred to as the Lake Chapala Little Theatre.

By June 1965, LLT had 130 members, and announced that membership would close when it reached 150. In mid-June, it presented its first official show—*The Saddle Bag Saloon, Duke Reagan, Prop.*—at the Chapala Country Club. The play, with a cast of over forty, was written and directed by Betty Kuzell, who also arranged the music.[4]

The LLT continued to present shows at the former railroad station until 1968, when the lake rose and flooded the building. After staging a few shows at the Balneario in San Juan Cosalá, the theater accepted an offer to use the second floor of the clubhouse at the Chula Vista Country Club, where they remained for the next seventeen years.

Several of the shows performed at Chula Vista were also presented in Guadalajara. In 1973, for instance, LLT presented *The Pleasure of His Company*, by Samuel Taylor and Cornelia Otis Skinner, at the Anglo-Mexican Cultural Institute. This was directed by former Hollywood actor Rocky Karns, who had retired to Ajijic two years earlier with his wife, Kate. This particular sell-out show is noteworthy because the lead role was taken by Tony Villegas, the "first Mexican to have a lead in one of the Lakeside productions."[5] It would be another twenty years before a Mexican directed a show at LLT: that honor went to Lionel Fernández in 1993, when he directed *Last of the Red Hot Lovers*.

When, in 1986, the Chula Vista Country Club declined further use of its clubhouse, LLT board members voted to find a suitable site to build their own theater. Construction of a permanent theater, designed by Jack Bateman, began in 1986 on land donated by Ricardo O'Rourke. During planning and construction, shows were staged at the Hotel Real de Chapala. The new 112-seat playhouse opened in January 1988 with Woody Allen's *Don't Drink the Water*, also directed by Rocky Karns. In LLT's first fifty years, Karns directed nineteen LLT shows in all, more than any other director.

Over the years, a lot of other famous names have graced the boards of the Lakeside Little Theatre or directed shows there. Professional dancer turned choreographer Anya Flesh moved to Chapala in 1998 and directed a dozen musicals and dramas in the last decade of her life, including *The Miracle Worker* (2000); *A Streetcar Named Desire*—which Tennessee Williams was working on when he visited Chapala in 1945—(2002), *Cabaret* (2006), and *Quilters* (2007).

Tod Jonson and his partner Ektor Carranza moved from adult films and documentaries in Hollywood to Ajijic in 1984. Todd was a long-time movie gossip columnist and one-time centerfold model for *In Touch* magazine.[6] At LLT, he appeared in more than twenty plays and directed several. During their twenty-five years in Ajijic, the pair created more than fifty LLT sets.

Roland Varno, the only Dutch actor to play in films alongside Marlene Dietrich, Greta Garbo and Katherine Hepburn, retired to Chapala Haciendas in the early 1970s. Varno, whose best known scene in Hollywood was a dance with Greta Garbo in *As You Desire Me* (1932), directed two plays for LLT: *The Bad Seed* in 1976 and *Harvey* in 1979.

Richard Vath and his wife, Joyce Langford Vath, retired to Ajijic in 1987 and were avid LLT supporters. Richard, a former Pasadena Playhouse President, acted in numerous US movies and TV shows in the 1950s and 1960s. He directed sixteen shows at LLT between 1988 and 2002. Joyce, a professional actress, had roles in more than thirty LLT plays.

Other notables, each of whom directed at least ten LLT productions, include, in approximate chronological order, reporter Ruth Netherton (fourteen directing credits, 1976–1996); Californian actress Norma Troiani Lyerly (twelve credits, 1980–2009; ex-professional dancer Barbara Clippinger (fourteen since 2000); and Canadian actor-director Roseann Wilshere (twelve since 2006).[7]

LLT stalwarts over the years included English couple Mickey and Reg Church. Reg worked on cruise ships after the second world war, becoming head waiter on the *Queen Mary* and then the *Mauritania*, where he met Mickey, a stewardess. They owned a restaurant in California prior to moving to Mexico, where they became active in charity work and managed the Villa Formoso garden bungalows in La Floresta. Their good friends and fellow Brits, Angela and Albert Rouse, were also active in LLT. Albert was a box office manager for numerous London shows in the 1950s, having been musical director for a 1940 wartime revival of *The Chocolate Soldier.*

Also active in LLT, prior to his untimely death in an auto accident in 2003, was actor and author Norman Schnall (stage name Norman Burton) who had appeared in dozens of TV programs and more than forty movies, including *Pretty Boy Floyd* (1960), *Planet of the Apes* (1968), *Diamonds Are Forever* (1971) and *The Towering Inferno* (1974).

And on the other side of the coin? Perhaps the most infamous actress and director at LLT ever was Donna McCready, the alleged serial killer in the mid-1980s, who was herself murdered in January 1987, only a few blocks from the theater, by Joe Kovach, her lesbian lover's husband.[8] McCready had directed Kovach at the LLT when he played the psychiatrist in *Duet for One*. The entire sordid story was the basis for Jan Dunlap's novel and screenplay titled *With Money Dances the Dog.*

The LLT has been going strong for more than fifty years. Though not the earliest English-language theater group in Mexico, it is now the longest-running.

Plays set in Ajijic

Curiously, the Lakeside Little Theatre has never put on either of the two English-language plays set in Ajijic published by mainstream publishers: Fred Carmichael's *Mixed Doubles: A Comedy in Two Acts* and George Ryga's *A Portrait of Angelica.*[9]

Carmichael's play, published in 1973, was written after visiting his brother, Thomas Carmichael, who lived at Lake Chapala from 1966 to 1972. The play is set in a small hotel in Ajijic called the Casa Pericolo.[10] The first act is about a separated middle-aged couple who occupy connecting suites and have a romantic fling. In the second act, the suites are respectively occupied a few months later by an unmarried golden-age couple and a band of inept drug smugglers. The Mexican premiere of *Mixed Doubles*, performed regularly in US community theaters, appears to have been at Rosarito Beach, Baja California, in April 2010.

Canadian playwright and novelist George Ryga owned a home in San Antonio Tlayacapan for many years. *A Portrait of Angelica*, written during the 1972–73 winter, was first performed in Banff, Canada, the following summer. *A Portrait of Angelica* is a Canadian perspective on the interaction between a group of tourists and the Mexican townsfolk who live in Angelica. Ryga's plot, centered around frustrated lives and loves mixed with tales of lust, violence and drunkenness, explores some serious themes, including the conflicts and contradictions created in a rapidly globalizing world.

Of plays set locally that were never published, the most interesting is *The Lions and the Tigers*,[11] written in 1951–52 by American author and playwright Vance Bourjaily, a close friend of artist-explorer Tobias Schneebaum and novelist Willard Marsh, both of whom were living in Ajijic at the time. The verse play is about the Ajijic literary and artistic colony, and was written shortly after Bourjaily stayed at "the now defunct Posada Navarro, run by Doña Feliz."[12] The main character is a Mexican painter whose first US show was a great success. Critics have given up waiting for his second show, so his former flame, a lusty New York art critic, turns up in Ajijic, hoping she can push aside the many distractions he faces and get him back on track.

37

El Charro Negro

One of the more memorable characters in Ajijic in the 1960s and 70s was El Charro Negro, a very handsome, very elegant and fun-loving American who dressed as a *charro* and rode his magnificent horse at the end of every village procession. He was, to quote Milagros Sendis, "more Mexican than the locals," and all the girls loved him.

Dickinson Bishop junior, the son of Dickinson H Bishop and his wife, Sydney, had an extraordinary life. Indeed, if his father had not survived the sinking of the Titanic, junior would never even have been conceived. His father was in the first lifeboat lowered from the stricken vessel, and Dick could trace his lineage as a Son of the American Revolution all the way back to Isaac Bishop (1758–1846).[1] On his mother's side, Dick was the grandson of William Boyce, founder of Boy Scouts of America.

Born in San Francisco on 13 January 1917, Dick was only a child when his well-to-do family, who employed a live-in maid and a live-in cook, moved to Ottawa, Illinois. The family spent some summers in Europe and avoided the coldest months in Illinois by spending winters in the luxury Idlewyld section of Fort Lauderdale, Florida, or in Honolulu, Hawaii. Dick claimed to have been brought up in Biaritz, France, and to have spoken French before he learned English.[2]

It was at his preparatory school in Aiken, South Carolina, that Dick was first introduced to horses and the sport of polo. Despite being injured at school when a car struck the horse he was riding, Dick became an expert equestrian.[3] As a teenager he worked as a bronco buster on a ranch in Wyoming. When he competed in the famed Cheyenne Frontier Days Rodeo, he was unlucky and drew Midnight, a champion bucker who usually threw riders on the first jump. To his delight, Dick managed to last two jumps![4]

In 1938, shortly after turning 21, Dick married Melissa Hilfinger in Kansas City, Missouri.[5] Following service in the US Army from 1941 to 1943, and the breakdown of his marriage, Dick settled in Hollywood, California, where in 1948 he took Puerto Rican-born Ligia Rivera as his second wife. That relationship had also broken down by 1957 when Dick—enabled by an allowance from his family to live in luxury wherever he fancied—decided to drive to Panama. He got only as far as Ajijic, and never left.[6]

Wealthy, handsome, available bachelors in Ajijic were in short supply, and Dick was immediately pursued by an attractive, strong-willed, dark-haired beauty named Margo North de Butterlin. Margo had been the long-time mistress of artist Otto Butterlin (who had died in 1956), and she had even married his brother Ernesto in order to acquire the Butterlin surname. Doubts about the precise circumstances of Otto's death led some villagers to nickname Margo "La Viuda Negra" (The Black Widow).[7] Whether or not she ever had any formal annulment or divorce from Ernesto is undetermined, but Margo soon "married" Dick Bishop. Katie Goodridge Ingram, who knew all those involved, neatly summarized why the majority of villagers had little respect for Margo:

> Margo married a rich good looking shallow companion/escort... [who] wore pale blue Brooks Brothers pin-stripe suits, and SHE CALLED HIM PINHEAD. Eventually no one could tell you what his real name was. Her capacity for diminution was infinite. For all of her beauty, the red roses in her pulled back black hair, for her expensive black dresses,... she was really quite vulgar.[8]

Dick's other loves were alcohol, his horses and his bespoke saddle. Bill Atkinson chuckled to me as he recalled how Dick "kept track of his drinks in a ledger, noting down each time he had a drink,"[9] and Loy Strother described the special saddle Dick had for his favorite black thoroughbred Arabian, the fastest horse in town:

> The saddle for that horse had a bar in it. Yep, the pommel of that saddle was raised on a square structure (covered in carved leather as part of the saddle), with little sliding door compartments that held glasses, small bottles of booze and even a little ice bucket.... Oh yeah,

and a tiny martini shaker. His booze didn't hang on the side of the saddle like some itinerant cowboy, he had a custom built-in wet bar![10]

Strother, a teenager in 1962–63, rode that horse (minus the saddle) in several local races:

I jockeyed on him myself when the local race track was a section of the 'old road' dirt track between San Antonio and Ajijic. We raced bareback with nothing but a knee strap (that big thoroughbred was too wide for my knees to grip) on a windy dirt road lined with rock walls on both sides about a mile long in [an] all out sprint with two to five horses jostling for position; thrills and spills, the nearest hospital sixty kilometers away.

Horse races between San Antonio Tlayacapan and Ajijic, such as the one Strother rode in, were not uncommon. In 1965, when the owners of the four competing horses were Dick Bishop, Marcos Guzmán, Marianne Fowler and Alonso Anaya, Bishop's *Chiceada* and Anaya's *Colorado* were declared the winners.[11]

After Margo's death (date not currently known), Dick inherited (or bought) the spacious home at the corner of Ocampo and Privada Ocampo that she had once shared with Otto Butterlin.[12] Dick also owned real estate several blocks further west, at Ocampo 186, where he stabled his horses.

In about 1961, presumably not long after Margo's death, Dick Bishop married Nina Ketmer, a 42-year-old Danish-born naturalized American citizen. Three years later, in memory of Margo, Dick and Nina gave the Chapala hospital an X-ray machine.[13] They also gave "a rare pair of pre-Columbian ceramic figurines" from Nayarit to a museum in Central Florida.[14]

Nina Ketmer died suddenly of liver failure on 5 January 1965 and was interred in the local cemetery. In her heartfelt tribute to Ketmer, author Gina Hildreth, calling her a beautiful and gracious hostess, expressed how her friends "respected her as an artist of great talent... admired her wit and have marveled at her devoted interest in developing a stable of fine horses."[15]

Among Nina and Dick's circle of close friends in Ajijic were Bill Atkinson, John and Margaret Mersereau, Gina and Phillip Hildreth, Bob Somerlott, Lou and Cathy Wertheimer, and Helen Kirtland and her husband, Larry Hartmus. Gina Hildreth and the men formed an Ajijic chess club which held multi-week competitions.[16]

The Mersereaus, who commissioned Marcos Guzmán to build them a house west of Ajijic at Rancho Nuevo, were also horse-lovers, and Nina had sculpted, as a gift, an equestrian statue of Margaret Mersereau, who loved *charro* and rode her young Arab thoroughbred filly in all the village parades.[17]

Dick was understandably shocked at losing Nina, but made it his mission to find another tall beautiful woman to woo and marry as soon as possible. Bill Atkinson explained how:

> Before Dick met Mary, he would send a young boy down to meet the bus each day when it arrived in Ajijic (from Guadalajara/Chapala), and to run back and tell him if a tall blonde arrived. Mary was American, 6' 2" and that is how Dick met her.[18]

When Mary—in Ajijic to visit a girlfriend—learned that Dick was interested, she offered to introduce him to her mother. 'What's wrong with you?' asked Dick. Five days later they were wed.[19]

Dick and Mary became famous for their lively parties, including huge annual bashes at Xmas and New Year. After 1973—when Dick Bishop and Agustín Velarde started Lakeside Homefinders—the only people specifically not invited were Jim and Gerda Kelly and Bill Atkinson, because they owned a competing real estate business, Servicios Unlimited.[20] Artist Peter Huf laughed heartily when he recalled how the climax of one of the Bishops' most riotous parties ever, in about 1968, was a game of "Burro Polo," where both teams tried to cajole their donkeys into chasing the ball, with a certain inevitable degree of futility.[21]

In their stables, the Bishops raised thoroughbred race horses, quarterbacks and Arabians, mainly for sale to wealthy Mexicans. One of the horses they refused to part with was one acquired from a former governor of Nayarit. Paloma had a greyish-white coat, stood sixteen hands high, and was "the only purebred Arabian mare in this part of the country."[22]

In a curious twist of fate, Dick and Mary Bishop became very good friends with Otto Butterlin's daughter, Rita, and visited her in Mexico City at Christmas time in 1968. The following April the Bishops entertained Rita's eight-year-old animal-loving daughter, Monique Señoret, in Ajijic.[23] Monique, a "blond moppet with huge, lushly fringed brown eyes," left her sixteen hamsters in the care of her mother and enjoyed a memorable time in Ajijic, though she was far too young to recognize the complicated connections linking her hosts, and their home, to her grandfather.

In the early 1970s, Mary Bishop handled local sales for the Hotel Danza del Sol development. The photographer for the hotel's publicity materials was Beverly Johnson, whose portrait of Mary at about this time shows her sporting a double strand pearl necklace around her neck, with a fur stole draped over one arm, wine glass in hand. Her other hand, holding a cigarette, rests lightly across the shoulders of Tom Faloon.[24]

Dickinson Bishop junior died in Ajijic on 17 May 1979, aged 62, and was buried in the family plot in Ottawa, Illinois, far to the north of his beloved adopted village.

38

Music since 1960

Ajijic has a long musical tradition, fomented over the years by the presence of many stellar performers, from Alex von Mauch, Tula Meyer and Justino Camacho to pianists Kate Wolff and Elena Cavalcanti. Many of these musicians, as well as several outstanding amateur jazz musicians in the 1950s, appear in other chapters. This chapter highlights some important contributions made to the local music scene since 1960 by foreign musicians and those of international standing.

Guitarists

During the 1960s, Ajijic was a musical hotbed for guitarists. The resident guitar teacher was Carlos Espíritu, a well-known musician who had his own trio, which performed regularly at the Posada Ajijic. His students included singer-photographer Beverly Johnson and Juan José Luvian (Juanjo), who was a member of Espíritu's string trio.[1] Espíritu also taught Geoffrey Goodridge (1943–2016), who was raised in Ajijic and went on to study in Spain, where he changed his name to Azul, and became a noted professional flamenco guitarist based in the Netherlands. Goodridge gave concerts in Ajijic whenever he visited his family, including performances at the Posada Ajijic in January 1968 and August 1978.[2]

Also active in Ajijic in the 1960s and 1970s was the multitalented artist-guitarist Gustavo Sendis (1941–1989), whose family, based in Guadalajara, owned a vacation property in Ajijic. Sendis studied with some of the guitar greats, including Jack Buckingham in California, and Alvaro Company and Emilio Pujol in Spain. He gave concerts in Mexico and Europe, and in 1972 performed nightly in Ajijic at the El Tejaban restaurant-gallery. Sendis made recordings and was also a composer; his compositions for the guitar included "Danza Nahuatl" and "Paisajes."

Two later guitar-related events are also worth noting. In 1996 a concerto for guitar and orchestra composed by Ajijic-born Victor Manuel Medeles was performed by the Jalisco Philharmonic Orchestra.[3] A decade later, guitarist Bobby Fisher recorded "Sueños De Ajijic" as one of the tracks on his album *Guitar Prayer*.

Rock bands

The earliest mention of a rock band in Ajijic is the announcement of the formation of the Supersonics, a very youthful quartet described as "Mini-Monkees, Petit Beatles or, if you will, Rolling Pebbles."[4] After rehearsing for three months, they started making public appearances in 1967. The musicians, all aged between 10 and 12, were Chas Elam (rhythm guitar), David Michel (bass guitar), Eric Johnson (drums) and Steve Robinson (vocalist).

A much more mature rock band, Los Axixis, was founded in 1969.[5] Modeled on the Bee Gees, it had five members: Daniel Solís (drums), Jesús Moreno (accompaniment), Miguel Ramírez (bass guitar), Lee Hopper (vocals) and Juan José Luvian (guitar). This band of twenty-something-year-olds was the first group in Ajijic to use amplifiers, and its publicity photos were taken by Beverly Johnson. It sang mostly in English, interpreting songs popularized by The Beatles, The Rolling Stones, Credence Clearwater Revival, The Bee Gees, Santana, Los Solitarios and Los Bukis.

Los Axixis gave several performances in the building used until the early 1970s as the village cinema (Morelos 5), played at the Hotel Real de Chapala on weekends, and gave concerts in Guanajuato, Nayarit and elsewhere. It played at the inauguration of Plaza del Sol, Mexico's first shopping center, and was frequently hired for student parties. The musicians went their separate ways in 1974, not long after lead vocalist Lee Hopper left to get married.

Classical and choral music

Until relatively recently, live classical music was in short supply at Lake Chapala. Filling this cultural gap was the reason for the formation in Ajijic in 1965 of a Guadalajara Concert Guild to arrange bus trips to symphony concerts in the city.

Seven years later, in 1972, two music lovers—Enid McDonald and her friend Josephine Warren—formed Lake Chapala Festivals. They brought chamber music groups to Ajijic by organizing, starting in November 1972, events at the Camino Real hotel and the Club Náutico (Yacht Club) in La Floresta, as fund-raisers for a Lakeside Auditorium.

Chamber music remains an important part of Ajijic cultural life, as evidenced by the annual Northern Lights Music Festival. Since its inception in 2003, this famed festival has brought an extraordinary number of high calibre international musicians to Ajijic. Main-stage concerts, predominantly either classical or jazz, are normally held in the Auditorium (now Estación Cultural Chapala), but subscribers are also treated to an ever-growing number of chamber performances in private homes. The festival's artistic director is Toronto-based violinist Christopher Wilshire.

The longest-running community choir in the area, Los Cantantes del Lago, was formed in the year 2000. Many of its founder members had previously sung in Bonnie Wolff's Ecumenical Choir which presented a Christmas Cantata, with up to fifty singers, annually from the mid-1990s. After Wolff's death in 2000, Millicent Brandow, a former member of the Hamilton Opera Company and the Harlequin Singers in Canada, helped reassemble the choir into Los Cantantes del Lago. Darel Walser was the founding director of the choir; Timothy G Ruff Welch took over as conductor and artistic director in 2003. The choir, whose members hail from Mexico, Canada, the US and elsewhere, has performed internationally in Canada, Cuba, Greece, Turkey and Ecuador, and presents two major concerts each year.[6]

Popular music

Ajijic has had dozens of popular music groups over the past hundred years.[7] But one particular Ajijic musical dynasty—the musical Medeles family—merits a special mention. Four generations of this family have enhanced the musical scene in the village.

Patriarch Rutilio Medeles, an outstanding flautist, was born in about 1889 and was a bohemian long before it was fashionable. He married Epigmenia Flores and their son Jesús Medeles Flores was born on Christmas Day, 1912.

Jesús made his living as a carpenter but taught himself to play the church organ, violin, trumpet and guitar. He married Ana María Romero Ybon in 1940,[8] and the couple had eleven children: six boys and five girls, all of whom graduated with professional qualifications. Their eldest daughter, Alicia, was the first female *delegada* of Ajijic. All the boys learned to play musical instruments. Together with a brother-in-law, Manuel Martínez, they formed a band named Los Hermanos Medeles, which played regularly at the Posada Ajijic and at the Hotel Camino Real (Real de Chapala) and was popular throughout the sixties and into the seventies.[9]

Jesús' eldest son, Victor Manuel Medeles Romero (1943–2009), completed a bachelor's degree as a music instructor at the University of Guadalajara, and a master's degree in composition at the Instituto Nacional de Bellas Artes in Mexico City. One of the best contemporary composers of his generation in Mexico, Victor Manuel actively promoted classical musicianship and, in 1990, established CREM (Centro Regional de Estudios Musicales), a classical music education program in Ajijic. CREM began with a youth choir which sang Sunday Mass in the parish church, before expanding to offer lessons for the piano, violin and other orchestral instruments. It later established a village youth chamber orchestra. Two CREM alumni (violinist Diego Rojas and violist Manuel Oliveras) are members of the Jalisco Philharmonic Orchestra.

Victor Manuel's son, Emmanuel Medeles Medina, a violinist, grew up in the CREM choir and studied music and vocal technique at the University of Guadalajara, before taking over CREM when his father fell ill. He is assisted by his two siblings, Areli and Azael, who teach cello and piano respectively. More than fifty students benefit from CREM classes.

Emmanuel's cousins include the three sons of classical guitarist Jesús Medeles Romero, the youngest of Los Hermanos Medeles: Juan Pablo, Jesús (Chuni) and Daniel Medeles Córdova. The three brothers founded Orquesta Ajijic in 2011, an ensemble that bridges the cultural divide and has foreign retirees playing alongside town youth. In addition, Chuni teaches music in schools and manages Mariachi Real de Axixic, which Daniel established in 2016.

Many of Emmanuel's other cousins are also active in music, including Alejandro Martínez Medeles, a jazz drummer who toured the world with a Los Angeles band, and his brother Álvaro, a jazz guitarist with projects in Ajijic and Guadalajara.

Ajijic's traditional Fiesta de Los Músicos (Fidelomus) has been held in mid-November almost every year since the late 1960s; the 2021 event marked its 50th anniversary. The event raises funds to celebrate the religious feast day of Saint Cecilia (the patroness of musicians) on 22 November, aka Día del Músico.

Ajijic Huapango

Terence "Diego" Smedley-Kohl, the son of Ken Smedley and his wife, Dorianne, was born in Ajijic at the end of the 1970s, and lived in the village until the age of ten. He later joined Mariachi Los Dorados (of Canada), which was honored with an invitation to play in Guadalajara at the prestigious International Mariachi Festival. Kohl is the composer of "Ajijic Huapango," a short piece written in traditional style that "celebrates the peace, innocence and beauty of the Mexican people and the positive spirit of Mexico."[10]

Mi Lindo Ajijic

The song "Mi Lindo Ajijic"—"En México entero no hay otro pueblito / así de bonito como mi Ajijic" (In all of Mexico there is no other little town / as beautiful as my Ajijic)—was written by Ajijic-born Cresencio Ramos Heredia (1916–1994). A mural commemorating the composer and his song was unveiled by artist Bruno Mariscal in 2021.[11] Most villagers agree with the song's admirable overall sentiment, though many might question—given Ajijic's rampant development in recent decades—the validity of the line near the end of the song that "Tus nuevas colonias son tu fortaleza" (Your new subdivisions are your strength).

Part E
1970s on: Modernizers

"Resort living for Mexicans and expatriates alike is the new order of the day and you are reminded of it on all sides: new houses abuilding, new developments laid out, old houses getting a facelift. Flying Dutchmen, waterskiers, and sightseeing boats give the lake a busy look."
—James Kelly, 1973

39

Neill James the philanthropist

Ajijic underwent rapid change in the 1970s. Its growing population, coupled with an ever-increasing influx of outsiders, triggered all manner of social, cultural and environmental pressures. At the same time, complying with ever more complex legal, immigration and tax requirements posed problems for those foreigners and small businesses who wanted to do things by the book.

Among the challenges James faced in running her multiple business ventures was how to retain a loyal workforce while minimizing those expenses related to taxes and benefits. Mexican sociologist Francisco Talavera was not being complimentary when he described James as a classic combination of capitalist and philanthropist.[1] James could apparently be somewhat creative in her approach to legal and accounting issues. She allegedly insisted on some occasions, for instance, that her helpers were members of a cooperative, and therefore not entitled to all the protections afforded regular employees. But Mexican labor laws are very protective of workers, and labor unions tend to win in the end.

James' labor troubles began in 1971 when Miguel Rojas, the leader of the Chapala branch of the all-powerful union confederation CROC (Confederación Revolucionaria de Obreros y Campesinos), visited James' store and unionized her workforce. Two years later, on 26 October 1973, James fired Rosario Morales, the sole operator of her gift shop, for "being one hour late every day" and for "robbing the till."[2] Morales rejected James' offer of severance pay and sought the help of Rojas and CROC. Rojas visited James, ordered her to close the shop, and then, according to James, persuaded her two gardeners to down tools in solidarity. To bolster the case against James, Rojas convinced two of the eighty or so women who did piecework embroidery that they were really full-time employees and were therefore owed considerable amounts of vacation pay and overtime.

Recognizing that the odds were stacked against her, James fought back as best she could. Enlisting the help of supposedly influential friends in Mexico City, she was able to reopen her shop, provided she was the only one who worked there. For a time she lived in perpetual fear. In a letter to a friend, James explained that "The *presidente* of Chapala sent two policemen to guard my place at night. They say they are watching the day too. Am so happy to have them as have had *molestaciones*."[3]

CROC stepped up the pressure in 1974 by launching cases against James in the labor conciliation court on behalf of five former workers: the shop girl, the two gardeners and the two piecework embroiderers.[4] Conveniently for CROC, the court failed to notify James of the cases until after the hearings had already concluded. The total indemnification against James, having lost all five cases, was 153,876 pesos ($12,310). Her lawyer was eventually able to bargain this amount down to 100,000 pesos.

Even though James paid up immediately, she was seriously worried that the other 78 or so piecework embroiderers might follow suit in demanding indemnity for past work. In the worst case scenario, she estimated that she might have to find almost 3 million pesos ($240,000) to settle all potential claims.[5] Fortunately for James, CROC did not file any further claims. However, the damage had been done. As James explained to the director of the Mexican Tourism Department in Washington, DC: "The CROC Syndicate headed by Miguel Rojas killed a thriving tourist industry and were the cause of the Tropical Gardens [Quinta Tzintzuntzan] being closed."

James closed her handlooms business, stopped embroidery piecework, and shuttered her tourist shop. A small display advertisement in *El Informador* in November 1974 announced that she had retired and that her store and tropical gardens had closed to the public.[6] More than forty years later, the Lake Chapala Society, ably assisted by María Lupita Vega Velázquez—who learned the art of embroidery with James—has revived classes in artistic embroidery for local women.[7]

James was also becoming tired of having to administer so many rental properties. She retained most of them well into the 1970s, by which time her one bedroom apartments were renting for between $50 and $60 a month, plus light and water. After several renters fell behind with their payments, James bemoaned the fact that several renters had "cheated me out of large sums of rent, light and water," and that the "government tax on house for permission to rent" was equivalent to $14 a month.[8]

Social events and civic improvements

From her early years in Ajijic, James (later ably assisted by her good friend Iona Kupiec) held an open-house every Christmas Eve at Quinta Tzintzuntzan, serving eggnog and fruitcake to all visitors, young and old alike. This quickly became an established tradition.

For her Christmas party for local children in 1951, James organized a piñata-making competition. Hot chocolate was served (James gave youngsters hot chocolate once a week) and sixteen piñatas were judged, with prizes for the best three made by girls and the best three by boys. When a friend offered her $50 towards clothing for the poorer children, James matched that amount, bought material and paid her employees for "seventy well made shirts to distribute among the poorer boys and girls."[9] This is the earliest record of an organized effort to provide clothing for the area's disadvantaged families, but certainly not the last.

James also held a lavish annual New Year's party to which all were invited. Katie Goodridge Ingram recalls that, "Her garden at Tzintzuntzán was jammed. There were huge long tables decorated with poinsettias and laden with food, punch bowls and hors d'oevres."[10]

James is quite rightly revered today for her many positive contributions to the health and education of her adopted village. In the 1940s, Chapala and San Antonio Tlayacapan had electricity, but Ajijic did not, making it difficult to preserve perishable food items. Ice was brought in daily from Guadalajara; by the time it arrived in the mid-afternoon it had already half-melted. Local lore (impossible to verify) is that James wanted to open her own ice factory in the village, using the knowledge she had gained working in similar factories in Hawaii and Florida. She cajoled villagers into action, pressured the mayor of Chapala, and argued for the electricity system to be extended to Ajijic. Within months, the poles and wires were up and supplying power, albeit intermittently in those early years.

As an ancillary benefit, the same poles could be used to string telephone lines to Ajijic, thereby reducing the village's dependance on a single phone in the post office.

The provision and reliability of power, water and telephone service remained problematic for decades. The credit for Ajijic finally getting

24-hour electricity service in October 1957 is due to Juan Gutiérrez Comparán, one of Ajijic's agrarian leaders.[11] Temporary power outages remained common long after that date. The opening of an exhibition at La Galería in May 1969 was marred by a power failure which followed on the heels of Ajijic having endured two weeks without water![12] And, as recently as the mid-1970s, electricity supply was frequently interrupted for up to twelve hours a day.[13]

The vagaries of the power system led award-winning Canadian poet Al Purdy to choose "Let There Be Light—Perhaps" as the title for a travel piece about Ajijic. Purdy was at the peak of his creative powers when he and his wife rented an apartment overlooking Ajijic for several weeks over the winter of 1978–79. Despite the roads, roadkill, police, and the sketchy electricity supply, Purdy loved Mexico. On the "luxuriant green" Ajijic lakeshore:

> Mexican kids play their game in the dust, gabbing together; fat mothers feed their babies, thin mothers feed their babies; old men totter thru the cobbled streets, a flash of their eyes responding to friends' flash of their eyes in greeting.[14]

Problems with electricity were extremely inconvenient and costly for businesses such as Cine Ajijic, which had no choice but to acquire its own auxiliary generator to cope with lengthy outages.

Glamorizing Ajijic

In 1977, a few years after retiring, James donated three buildings at Seis Esquinas for the village's first Health Center, the story of which is told later in this book.[15]

Notes in her personal papers from that time show that James was also actively trying to form a group of like-minded individuals to undertake "the glamorization" of Ajijic. To improve the village's appearance, James suggested adding signs to explain the names of each of the central streets, writing Aztec maxima (slogans) on street walls, and persuading property owners to paint Mexican scenes on exterior walls.[16] Though not implemented immediately, the last of her glamorization ideas was the genesis of the remarkable variety of mural art now beautifying Ajijic. Classes devoted to teaching Ajijic students how to make murals for their homes began in May 1977. They were given by José Manuel Castañeda, a graduate of the Children's Art Program, who had studied at the Art

Institute in San Miguel de Allende. Castañeda taught children at the library, offering regular art classes on Saturdays and a special class about making murals on Sundays.

Following James' retirement in 1974, the wonderful gardens of Quinta Tzintzuntzan had been closed to the public. However, in 1977, James agreed to reopen her property on Sunday afternoons as an art garden (*jardín del arte*) for a new artists' group, the Young Painters of Ajijic (Jovenes Pintores de Ajijic), most of whom had taken classes at the children's libraries.[17] The following year the artists held what was billed as Ajijic's "first annual cultural week" in the gardens, with art exhibits, guitar concerts and ballet recitals, among other attractions.[18]

James had undertaken a round-the-world trip in 1971. Six years later she took a trip to the Orient.[19] On her return to Ajijic, her close friend Iona Kupiec (an equally extraordinary character in her own right) gave the Petticoat Vagabond a fun and fancy brunch which featured festive Far East cuisine served by hostesses dressed in the appropriate national costumes.[20]

In 1983, James offered the Lake Chapala Society the use of part of her Quinta Tzintzuntzan property rent-free for five years. Seven years later, in January 1990, the legal title to all 5000-plus square meters of Quinta Tzintzuntzan, with its buildings, fish ponds and gardens, was transferred to the society, which agreed to care for James for the remainder of her life.[21] Later that year, James was declared Woman of the Century and presented with a Lifetime Achievement Award.

Neill James died on Saturday 8 October 1994, only three months shy of her 100th birthday; her ashes were interred in her beloved garden.

Were James still alive today, she would be the first to point out that many of her worst fears from seventy-five years ago have been realized. Her chosen paradise—Ajijic—is now visibly suffering under the strain of so much rapid growth.

A legend in her own lifetime, Neill James loved Mexico and was always intent on improving the opportunities for its women, children and young people. Whatever her flaws as an entrepreneurial capitalist, she was a committed philanthropist: her persistence was instrumental in bringing electricity, libraries and a health clinic to Ajijic, and she jump-started Ajijic's transformation into a nationally important center for the visual arts.

40

Canadians revive Posada Ajijic

At the start of the 1970s the Posada Ajijic was still very much the social center of the village, a fact instantly recognized by writer Jerry Murray when he arrived in town with his wife, Diana, in 1970 to stay with Earl Kemp, the veteran porn publisher. Murray wrote dozens of erotic books for Kemp's Greenleaf imprint, under a variety of pen names, and this is how he described the Posada:

> La Posada, the Inn, was the hub of the evening's activities, which often began with a fine dinner in the Inn's very good restaurant. It was a two-block walk from Earl's house, on the beach of Lake Chapala, where strollers could hear the band warming up in the Inn's bar. This nightly happening called for an after-dinner drink, and by the time the second was ordered, the dance floor was filling up with gringos and Mexicans doing variations of the twist, the samba, the New Yorker, and the Mexican Hat Dance. It could get very sweaty out on the dance floor, but a cold *cerveza* or a margarita remedied that. And if a dancer or drinker got a bit sleepy, they could check into one of the dozen or so rooms at the Inn for the night.[1]

The Posada Ajijic's success was rudely interrupted when owner Booth Waterbury died of a heart attack on 10 July 1974. His widow, Sue, distraught at her recent loss, took to the bottle as she tried to run the inn on her own. While she continued to advertise in the local newspaper,[2] the business was in serious trouble. By a very fortunate coincidence, only weeks after she placed her final advertisement trying to revive the business, serendipity brought a Canadian couple—Judy and Morley Eager—to the hotel. As Judy later recounted, their first encounter with the Posada was entirely fortuitous.

In Canada, the Eagers had built and run a hotel in Port Alberni on Vancouver Island, before Morley Eager pursued a career in marketing health products across Canada. They were living in Toronto in May 1975, when Morley was invited to a conference three time zones west in Victoria, British Columbia. The timing coincided with an Air Canada promotion which allowed them to fly from Toronto to Victoria via Guadalajara, so the Eagers decided to have a few days in Mexico, and made reservations at the newly opened Hotel Real de Chapala in Ajijic. When they tried to check-in, the clerk was unable to find their reservation, the hotel was fully booked, and they ended up staying at the Posada Ajijic. It was during their short stay there that one of the gardeners admitted that the hotel was for rent.[3]

Talking things over after returning to Canada, the Eagers decided to up sticks and move to Mexico for a change of lifestyle. They negotiated a lease with Josefina Ramírez, the sole owner of the Posada after the death of her husband, Casimiro, a few years earlier. Then, with two of their three children and the family dog in tow, the Eagers returned to Ajijic in September to take possession.

They were shocked to find the Posada padlocked and closed, and stripped bare of all fittings and furniture. Sue Waterbury had shuttered the premises and left for California when the business went bankrupt soon after their initial visit. Once she left, creditors and looters had stripped the inn of anything that could be carried off, including tiles, electrical fittings and bathroom fixtures.[4]

Undeterred at finding a derelict building, the Eagers rehabilitated the hotel and had the Posada Ajijic up and running again within six months. The restaurant opened on 17 February 1976, and the first guest rooms two weeks later.[5] The Eagers progressively fixed up more rooms and, before long, the Posada regained its former status as the village's social hub, with the bar and restaurant becoming especially crowded at weekends. In the early days, rooms cost 100 pesos ($5) a night, an eat-all-you-can dinner was 45 pesos ($2) and drinks were 12 pesos.[6]

Some people were jealous of the Eagers' success. Michael Eager shared with me what happened when a rival hotelier in Ajijic alleged that the family was working illegally in Mexico and tried to get the Posada closed down. A quick trip to Mexico City resolved matters in their favor.[7]

The Eagers gradually gained the confidence of the village by virtue of their honesty, generosity to worthy local causes and civic events, and the support they gave their own workers. One Christmas, Morley Eager persuaded rotund, bearded artist John K Peterson to dress up as Santa Claus and distribute presents (bought by the Eagers) to all the village children. Peterson may have been the first Santa the village kids had ever seen; apparently the earliest paintings of Santa in the Lake Chapala Society's Children's Art Program date from about this time.[8]

The Posada's support for the local community extended to offering an annual Christmas *posada* for up to 800 schoolchildren and sponsoring a fireworks *castillo* in the annual village fiesta. It was all part of the enduring commitment of the Eagers to the place they called home.

Relations with the village were further boosted when Morley and Judy's eldest son, Michael, who had stayed in Canada to attend university, arrived for spring break, fell in love, and married into the Ajijic community.[9] Michael and his wife, María Elena Hinojosa, helped run the hotel. The Eagers' younger son, Mark, later founded a real estate company in Ajijic.

Morley was very much an "ideas man," never short of vision for the future. Once he grabbed hold of an idea, he was indefatigable and allowed nothing and no one to get in his way. He restarted regular art shows and was happy to promote local artists by hanging their work on the walls of the restaurant-bar. In 1977, when Morley hosted two group shows for Clique Ajijic, a loose-knit cooperative of nine artists, a portion of the proceeds went towards helping deaf children in Jocotepec.[10] The Eagers also supported the local weavers and other indigenous artisans.

In 1977, Morley introduced the Easter Bunny to Ajijic, organizing a spirited event in which local artist Saúl Gutiérrez (then about 20 years of age) dressed up as the bunny. 1977 was also the year of the first (and last) Annual Greater Ajijic Raft Race. With the lake level so high that waves lapped against the steps to the beach, the Posada bar was the perfect vantage point from which to watch this crazy event.

A good breeze on Sunday 27 March 1977 ensured that the lake was suitably choppy. The challenge was to build and sail an improvised raft—made of materials costing no more than $25—out beyond the pier, round a marker, and back to the Posada, a total distance of about 150 meters. All rafts had to carry a flag, and no hand or foot paddling was allowed. The three main prizes were for best racer, most original raft and saddest attempt.[11] Several of the eight teams that entered sank during construction. One noteworthy entry was Dragon Baggies, built by Georg Rauch and Oliver Johnson, which was buoyed by inflated plastic bags and had two luxurious armchairs for the crew. In the end, the Posada declared everyone a winner and awarded all participants a free dinner.[12]

Morley always encouraged the musical and theater scene, and was quick to offer the Posada as the venue for special events. One of the first groups to take advantage of this opportunity was the informal combined arts group TLAC. He was also a tour-de-force in 1978 when he helped organize the community's first chili cooking event which later morphed into the Mexican National Chili Cookoff.[13]

Over the years, all manner of guests stayed at the Posada Ajijic. They included Dick and Fran Norman, who always brought a life-sized wooden "Indian" with them in their car, and always stayed in Room 9, where their silent friend could have his own chair.[14] Room 11 was the favorite of concert pianist and piano teacher Kate Wolff, who visited a score of times. Wolff had been a soloist with the Berlin Philharmonic before joining the faculty of Bard College in New York State. Wolff gave numerous private concerts in Ajijic over the next two decades for the family and guests of her close friend Helen Kirtland.

During the Eager's tenure, Room 101 became known as Suites Vaughan, because Dr Jim Vaughan, who first stayed at the Posada in about 1955, returned almost every year until it closed in 1990.[15] When he first visited, the lake was a long way from the beach. When his daughter honeymooned at the Posada in 1957, the lake had recovered and was threatening to overflow the Posada's retaining wall. When interviewed, Vaughan recalled the havoc wrought by the 40-mile-an-hour gale on the day of the raft race, the occasion when a boat ended up in the garden, and a night which ended with seven bullet holes in the front door![16]

Other noteworthy Posada guests included actress Elizabeth Taylor, Charles Bronson, Robert Young (Dr Marcus Welby), Larry Hagman (J R Ewing, Dallas) and his wife, the list is endless....

The Posada bar, with its view of the Ajijic pier and across the lake to the mountains beyond, became the setting for more discussions, plans and arguments than anywhere else in Ajijic. At weekends, Tapatíos arrived from Guadalajara to party at the Posada and dance to live music until the early hours. The Posada positively hummed with energy and provided the basis for so much of Ajijic village life, it was a legend in its own lifetime, and featured in several books. These included *The Lair*, a thriller by prolific novelist Louis Henry Charbonneau about the ramifications of a kidnapping. One evening the protagonists are on their way to meet someone at the lakefront bar:

> The streets of Ajijic seemed crowded with Americans out for a stroll or Mexicans standing in open doorways. The tiny plaza at the center of the village was busy. There was a movie theater featuring Sean Connery in a James Bond rerun. On the corner opposite was a small, brightly lit and very modern *supermercado*, its shelves lined with American canned goods, cigarettes and magazines.
>
> "You've been here before?" Blanchard asked, as Charmian Stewart turned along a dark, oneway street leading away from the plaza.
>
> "I bought this skirt at one of the gift shops here. It's a pretty little town. You should see it in daylight."
>
> "Do any Mexicans still live here?"
>
> She laughed. "Of course, Who do you suppose the servants are?[17]

The Posada was far more than simply a place of rest and entertainment where visitors found a warm welcome and friendly, informed advice about a host of village matters, it also provided an important stepping stone for many villagers who sought an opportunity to open their own small businesses. Many of the shopkeepers and craftsmen of Ajijic started out by working in the Posada kitchen, bar, or restaurant.

The Posada Ajijic had been a successful commercial venture and the social center of Ajijic for decades when Josefina Ramírez, who owned the buildings, passed away in 1986. After the Eagers learned that her heirs planned to raise the rent without contributing to long overdue upgrades, they designed and built their own new hotel—La Nueva Posada—on a lakeshore lot they owned three blocks further east. The Eagers closed the doors of the Old Posada in August 1990 and opened their new hotel a few days later. By a strange twist of fate, the site of their new hotel had once been owned by Paul Heuer who had started Ajijic's earliest, much more modest, lodging establishment at the other end of the village in the 1930s.[18]

The original Posada never reopened as an inn, but Javier Mercado modified one section in 1991 into a restaurant, which was renamed the María Isabel when the Cornejo Aguilar family took over in 2013. The former entrance to the Posada on Calle 16 de Septiembre has since been remodeled into the popular Cocinart restaurant, one of more than seventy restaurants now in Ajijic. Most patrons of Cocinart, owned by one of Josefina Ramírez's great grandsons, have little or no idea of the many and varied twists of fate that the building has witnessed during its long history.

Built to look old, La Nueva Posada, the Eager's new hotel, opened in September 1990, with Michael (who designed it) at the helm. It established a new standard for hotels in Ajijic, and set out from the start to appeal to both former and new clients, including weekend visitors from Guadalajara. The elegant dining room (later remodeled into a private apartment) was originally named La Rusa, in homage to Zara, who had died the previous year. In 1999 the Posada's ever-genial host Morley Eager died unexpectedly in a Guadalajara hospital while undergoing treatment for emphysema. Morley's widow, Judy, and their son Michael and his family continue to run the hotel, which remains deservedly popular.

41

Art in the 1970s

The gallery in El Tejaban marched on well into the 1970s. From about 1972 to June 1975 it was run as a restaurant-gallery-boutique by Jan Dunlap and her husband Manuel Urzúa. Dunlap was especially proud that her exhibit of Ruth Anaya paintings there led to El Tejaban (and Ajijic) being listed in *Who's Who in American Art*.[1] She also showed works by Mexican artist María Cristina O de Einung, whose painting "Paloma Herida" had won a National Art Award.[2] Dunlap moved on in June 1975 to open a boutique, The Blackfoot Contessa, and later an art gallery, the Wes Penn Gallery, on Calle 16 de Septiembre.

El Tejaban continued to be used intermittently as an art gallery, restaurant and even, briefly, as a secondary school into the 1980s. It had fallen into a sad state of disrepair by the time it was drastically remodeled a few years ago.

1971 Fiesta de Arte

One of the largest single art fairs held in Ajijic during the 1970s was the Fiesta de Arte held on Saturday 15 May 1971 at Calle 16 de Septiembre 33, the home of art patrons Frances and Ned Windham. Originally billed as the First Lakeside Artists Fair, the show was organized by John K Peterson and Peter Huf, helped by Beth Avary and Donald Hogan. About thirty artists participated in the one-day show, which included paintings, photography, block prints and serigraphs; more than 500 people attended.[3]

While most of the exhibitors were foreign artists, there was one especially noteworthy local artist: Fernando García, a self-taught carver, who worked for Robert de Boton (husband of painter Alice de Boton)

who dabbled in carving and sculpture after retiring to Mexico. G
watched his employer at work, expressed an interest in learning to c
and then worked by candlelight late into the night for several weeks to
complete several "small primitives of extraordinary beauty and sensitivity,"
all of which sold within minutes.

Galería del Lago

The most important and influential Ajijic art gallery in the 1970s was
La Galería del Lago de Chapala, often called simply Galería del Lago. It
was a cooperative non-profit founded on 27 November 1971 by Arthur
and Virginia Ganung, assisted by Charlotte McNamara, Jack Williams
and John Frost.[4] It also received the support of Hudson and Mary Rose
after the demise of their Galería Ajijic.

Galería del Lago ran for about a decade and held temporary shows
alongside permanent exhibits by about twenty founder members. Almost
180 artists had purchased memberships by the time the gallery opened in
the former Ajijic public market on the north side of the plaza (now the
Ajijic Cultural Center), next door to what was then the village cinema.
In 1972 the gallery published *A Cookbook with Color Reproductions by
Artists from the Galería*, a 48-page booklet of recipes which includes
color images of works in varied media by twenty artists then active in
Ajijic. The gallery continued to thrive even after the Ganungs departed
Ajijic in 1974.

The gallery was determined to be inclusive and appeal to the entire
community, both Mexican and non-Mexican. It arranged evening lectures
on topics such as the haciendas of Mexico, and a massive village fiesta on
the plaza with mariachi music, dancing, fashion show and exhibitions of
artwork. It offered classes in painting, craft-making and ceramics. Among
the exhibitors at its original location on the plaza were sculptor Leonie
Trager, photographer Sylvia Salmi, Sheryl Stokes Sourelis, and painter
Alicia Sendis and her very gifted painter-guitarist son, Gustavo Sendis.[5]
In August 1974 the gallery moved to Colon 6, across from El Tejaban.
Participating artists could rent three linear meters (ten feet) of gallery
space for 100 pesos a month.[6]

Katie Goodridge Ingram took over as president of the gallery in
1975. Having grown up in the village, she was particularly determined to
encourage young Mexican talent and immediately established a fund to
pay for materials and framing. The gallery also branched out by offering

a Christmas exhibit of batiks in the garden of Quinta Johnson (then owned by Ingram's mother, Helen Kirtland), concerts, an Art and Craft Bazaar, and a series of gourmet candlelight dinners.[7]

By August 1976 the gallery had outgrown its Calle Colón location and moved to larger premises (formerly Decoraciones del Hogar, a store run by Mercedes Boone) on the north side of the highway near the gas station.[8]

The list of artists shown at Galería del Lago is a Who's Who of the artists then working in Ajijic. Noteworthy exhibitors included Frank Barton, Jean Caragonne, Conrado Contreras, Gustel Foust, Priscilla Frazer, John Frost, Antonio López Vega, Dionicio Morales, Bob Neathery, John Peterson, Julián Pulido, Georg Rauch, Eleanor Smart, Sylvia Salmi, Frank Kent and Betty Warren. The gallery also displayed and sold paintings by the young artists of the Childrens Art Program.

Jalisco State officials invited Galería del Lago to mount a group show in Guadalajara during the 1976 Fiestas de Octubre, and also supported a collective exhibition in December 1976 at Plaza de la Hermandad in Puerto Vallarta. When organizers arrived at the coastal resort, they discovered, to their horror, that the building was incomplete and still lacked windows or any security.[9]

After Galería del Lago closed in 1977, Ingram arranged monthly shows until 1983 at a smaller gallery in her mother's store, Mi México.

Blossoming art scene

The number of art shows, and of small galleries run by individual artists, exploded after 1972. This growth reflected the large number of working artists living in the village—more than fifty by the end of the decade—as well as the the rising number of well-heeled foreigners living in the area and the tremendous increase in demand, mainly for commercial art, that coincided with the building of new subdivisions.

Noteworthy among the many shorter-lived galleries of the 1970s were Galería de los Artistas Cooperativos, directed by Juan Olivarez Sánchez, which opened at 16 de Septiembre 9 in 1975, and became Jan Dunlap's short-lived Wes Penn Gallery the following year;[10] and the José Clemente Orozco Gallery, organized by Dionicio Morales and Julian Pulido, on Calle Guadalupe Victoria. Its opening show in 1976 featured their work, alongside that of Honstan Aparicio, Frank Barton, Antonio Cárdenas, Henry Edwards, Antonio López Vega, Sid Schwartzman and Havano Tadeo.[11]

Clique Ajijic

Clique Ajijic was a group of eight varied and gifted artists who formed a loosely organized collective for three years in the mid-1970s: Tom Faloon, Hubert Harmon, Todd (Rocky) Karns, Gail Michel, John Peterson (the only member of the group who had previously been in Grupo 68), Synnove (Shaffer) Pettersen, Adolfo Riestra and Sidney Schwartzman.[12] The group's first shows were arranged by Ingram at the Galería del Lago. In addition to regular shows in Ajijic and Guadalajara, Clique Ajijic also exhibited in Manzanillo (1975) and Cuernavaca (1976). By the end of 1976 two of the original eight members had left the village—Pettersen to the US and Riestra to Tepoztlán (Morelos)—and Richard Frush had joined the group. Clique Ajijic's final show was at the Posada Ajijic in December 1977.[13]

Talented artists

The short profiles of individual artists which follow offer only a partial glimpse into the wealth of artistic talent that graced Ajijic in the 1970s.

Visual artist and architectural designer Tom (Tomás) Faloon arrived with his wife and young daughters in Ajijic in 1970, and never left. Faloon loved Mexican handicrafts and folk traditions, and integrated seamlessly into village life and. In the 1980s he began to remodel village homes, often incorporating some whimsical elements: *las locuras de Tomás*, as he called them. Faloon was an "icon of Ajijic's expat community" and "one of the community's most prominent and endearing longtime foreign residents."[14]

Alice de Boton, born in what is now Israel, studied in Paris and gained her international reputation as a versatile artist while living in California after the second world war. She and her husband, Robert, lived in Ajijic from 1969 to about 1975. De Boton's acrylics, collages, assemblages, encaustics and tapestries were social commentaries.

Norwegian-born Synnove (Shaffer) Pettersen studied at the Art Center College of Design in Los Angeles before living in Ajijic from 1973 to 1976. Now a much sought-after portrait painter, she painted dozens of fine paintings of the village and people of Ajijic.

Leonie Trager, born in Austria, held a solo exhibition at the Galería del Lago in April 1973, when she was living in Chula Vista.[15] She had previously had one-person shows in London and New York. The Ajijic show featured 32 sculptures in a range of media, from jacaranda and pink alabaster to Carrara marble and Indian jade, with titles such as "Mothers and Daughters," "Snowflake," "Sensuousness" and "Despair."

Pennsylvania-born fashion illustrator and painter Jean Caragonne first visited Mexico, with her husband, George, a portrait photographer, in 1949. The couple rented a home in Chapala in 1968 before moving to Ajijic in 1971. Jean's attractive representational paintings, which included views of Ajijic, were displayed locally and one became an Amigos de Salud fundraising card.

Eugene Nowlen and his wife, Marjorie, had a long connection with Mexico and first visited Ajijic in 1950. They returned regularly into the 1970s. Eugene, an architect, held several solo shows in Laguna Beach, California. Marjorie was a painter and pianist. Examples of their work were included in *A Cookbook with Color Reproductions*.

Austrian-born Georg Rauch, who lived thirty years in Jocotepec, exhibited regularly in Ajijic and was a founder member of CABA. Rauch had an adventurous early life; his riveting memoirs, translated by his wife, Phyllis (also an artist), were published as *Unlikely Warrior: A Jewish Soldier in Hitler's Army*. Rauch prepared a series of posters for the Guadalajara Committee of the 1968 Mexico City Olympics and held numerous solo shows.

Painter and jeweler Hubert Pickering Harmon junior studied in Europe before moving to Taxco in the 1940s to design whimsical silver jewelry, often featuring angels and dogs, worn by the likes of Hollywood glamor icon Dolores del Río.[16] Harmon moved to Ajijic in about 1970 and became a bright light on the social scene. His paintings varied from humorous to overtly homoerotic. Harmon was later conned out of his valuable personal collection of silver by a fraudster; the internationally recognized designer lived his final years in extreme poverty in an old folks' home in Chapala.[17]

Roscoe (Rocky) Karns retired to Ajijic with his wife, Kate, and family in 1971, after acting in Hollywood and working in public relations. Karns played Harry Bailey in *It's a Wonderful Life* (1946). In Ajijic, Karns shared his talents by directing and producing several shows at the Lakeside Little Theatre. He also honed his painting skills; his endearing naïf paintings remain very popular.

New York-born artist Betty Warren (later Herzog), one of the highest paid female portraitists of the twentieth century, first visited Ajijic in 1974 when she rented the Helen Kirtland home for a month. Two years later

Warren held a solo show of oils and drawings at the Villa Montecarlo, sponsored by the Galería del Lago.[18] She was a regular winter visitor and maintained a studio in the village year-round.

Clark Hulings, an acclaimed American realist painter, visited Mexico numerous times from 1964 onward. His keen eye for detail, notably of people engaged in their daily activities, resulted in powerful paintings of street and market scenes in Chapala and Ajijic. His Mexican paintings usually include a donkey or two; fortunately for art-lovers, Hulings ignored the advice of a New York gallery owner early in his career who told him that there was no market for paintings of either Mexico or donkeys.[19]

Visual artist Sidney Schwartzman moved to Ajijic in about 1973, after living in Woodstock (Vermont) and Los Angeles. In Ajijic he married a local girl, Regina Galindo, and helped raise her four daughters, one of whom married Ajijic painter and muralist Efrén González. Mustachioed, bushy-haired Schwartzman, who specialized in pencil sketches and paintings of nudes, shared his studios and expertise freely with many up-and-coming local artists; Schwartzman's legacy lives on through their efforts. Local art patron Sally Sellars helped Schwartzman open a gallery in the late 1980s at Felipe Angeles 12, where shows included annual art auctions to benefit Oak Hill School.

Artist and print-maker Alvin Sandler studied in Mexico City, had his first solo show in New York in 1953, and lived in Ajijic from 1969 to 1974. His exhibit of more than fifty Ajijic works at the Runyon Winchell Gallery in New York in 1977 is surely the largest exhibit of Ajijic-related works ever held in that city.

Bulgarian writer, artist and explorer Dimitar Krustev married a former student, American-born Helen Marie. The couple were regular visitors to Ajijic from the early 1970s before they moved permanently to the village in 2000. Krustev, who documented and painted indigenous groups such as the fast-disappearing Lacandon people in Chiapas, taught art in Ajijic and often painted local scenes. Helen Marie specializes in detailed acrylic portraits of Mexico's indigenous peoples.

Multilingual Polish-born artist and educator Harry Mintz was a frequent visitor to Chula Vista and Ajijic from 1974 into the 1990s. Many of his works were images of the village.[20] Mintz held more than forty solo shows in Ajijic, including one at ARTestudio.

Photographer Toni Beatty and her husband, Larry Walsh, lived in Mexico for several years after visiting retired Hollywood actor Roland

Varno in 1976. Varno introduced them to American photographer Sylvia Salmi, who let them rent her Ajijic casita and encouraged Beatty to explore black and white portrait photography.

Beatty's work was also inspired by Adolfo Riestra, arguably the most famous of all the Mexican painters and sculptors to have lived in Ajijic for any prolonged period of time. Riestra, whose own work was strongly influenced by western Mexico's archaeology and folk art, as well as by political events such as the 1968 Mexico City student massacre, painted and sculpted in Ajijic from about 1971 to 1976. His paintings include two portraits of Alan Bowers, an American artist friend then living in Ajijic.

Painter and batik artist Gustel Foust studied art in Germany, and had already been in Mexico twenty years before she lived in Ajijic from 1978 to 1984. She exhibited regularly in local galleries and elsewhere. Foust's Ajijic works include impressionist landscapes of women doing their laundry in the lake and of villagers chatting in the street. One of these street scenes was chosen for an Amigos del Lago charity card.

Impressionist painter Sheryl Stokes Sourelis grew up in Guadalajara and studied art in Europe. Her first recorded exhibition in Ajijic, a joint show with Gustavo Sendis and his mother, Alicia Sendis, was in 1974. Sourelis lived year-round in the village for the last five years of her life. Greetings cards featuring her lively Mexican village scenes and landscapes sold well in Ajijic and elsewhere.

Gustavo Sendis, a virtuoso guitarist as well as an exceptional artist, painted many superb expressionist paintings of Ajijic. Sendis had studied drawing with Juan Navarro and Ernesto Butterlin in 1958–59, and first exhibited in Guadalajara in 1968. In the 1970s and early 1980s he exhibited widely in Mexico and Europe, as well as in Canada.

Hungarian-born artist and accomplished violinist Stefan Lökös escaped from a POW camp in Odessa, Russia, in 1945. Lökös and his wife, Ingeborg, lived in Ajijic from about 1977 to 1980. Lökös held a solo show of his semi-abstract watercolors at Galería del Lago in February 1977, and gave two violin recitals at Posada Ajijic in December that year.[21]

Young Painters of Ajijic

The Young Painters of Ajijic (Jovenes Pintores de Ajijic) was a group formed in 1977. The group included Dionicio Morales, Antonio López Vega, Daniel Palma, Julián Pulido, José Manuel Castañeda, Alejandro

Martínez and Victoria Corona, most of whom had started out by taking the free weekly classes at the children's libraries founded by Neill James.

James graciously opened her home—Quinta Tzintzuntzan—every Sunday afternoon as an art garden (jardín del arte) for them to show off their work. The group's first show, on Sunday 28 August 1977, of oils, acrylics, watercolors, charcoal drawings and prints, resulted in combined sales of over 12,000 pesos ($550). Accompanying entertainment was provided by the Folkloric Dance Group of Ajijic and the wind music group of Luis López. The Sunday garden of art shows were a regular weekly event for some time. Other exhibitors, besides those already named, included Antonio Cárdenas, Victor Romero, Diana Powell and Sid Schwartzman.

The following March, the group held what was billed as Ajijic's first annual cultural week in the gardens, with art exhibits, guitar concerts, ballet recitals, and other attractions. This occasion included performances by the Folkloric Dance Group and the School of Music of the University of Guadalajara, and a stage play—*El Demonio Azul* (The Blue Devil)—directed by Félix Vargas.[22] Regrettably, this week-long show was not repeated in later years.

State recognition as an Art Center

The significance of Ajijic as an art center was finally recognized at the state level in 1976, when Jalisco governor Alberto Orozco Romero instructed the Department of Fine Arts (Departamento de Bellas Artes) to draw up a "master plan for the Lake Chapala area to become a major cultural and art center in Mexico," centered on the Lakeside Auditorium (now Estación Cultural Chapala), which was nearing completion at the time. The master plan included workshops for Mexican and foreign students in painting, photography, theater, writing and silkscreen techniques.[23] Unfortunately, completion of the auditorium was delayed, Orozco Romero left office, and this laudable scheme never really got off the ground.

42

Medical and health services

As Katie Goodridge Ingram has written, "modern" medicine was only just beginning to reach Ajijic during her childhood there in the late 1940s:

There were serious health threats in the 1940s and the 1950s, among them malaria, dysentery from contaminated water, black widows, scorpions, diarrhea, undulant fever from un-pasteurized milk, typhoid fever, tetanus and rabies. The usual childhood diseases of whooping cough, measles, mumps and chickenpox and polio were rampant. Smallpox and scarlet fever were being eradicated by vaccination.[1]

And she should know: in the days before antibiotics were commonly available, she endured excruciating treatment for rabies, and her brother John survived typhoid fever. Fortunately, in succeeding decades, vaccines, antibiotics and public health campaigns made Ajijic a much healthier place.

In the mid-1960s cultural anthropologist Carol Shepherd McClain spent eighteen months in Ajijic investigating traditional birthing practices. She found a mix of old and new in the village:

Ajijicans were more than willing to incorporate modern medical practices as they could easily see that many were effective (e.g. surgery, antibiotics) but that they retained very traditional beliefs about the causes of illness (e.g. witchcraft, fright).

McClain returned in 1973 to interview mothers, grandmothers, *curanderas* (native healers), *parteras* (midwives) and *espiritistas* (spiritual-ists) about childbirth and midwifery. She got to know four local *parteras* quite well. Doña Carmen, a curandera, had studied under a *hierbero* (herbalist) for five years and had "traveled as far as Mexico City to bring patients back to Ajijic." Her daughter, Josefina, first became a *partera* at the age of 25. Doña Josefa, in her seventies, had worked both as a *partera* and a *curandera*. Doña Petra, also in her seventies and born in San Juan Cosalá, began practicing as a *partera* in 1920 and spent nine months working under a doctor in Guadalajara; she was the most "modern" (and expensive) of the four.[2]

McClain discovered that local women believed a fetus was affected by four external factors: food taboos, sibling jealousy, eclipses of the sun and the moon, and a father who drank to excess. It was widely held, for example, that "cold" foods might cause illness in the newborn child. Another belief—that a lunar eclipse may cause babies to be born with extra fingers or toes, while a solar eclipse could result in deformities resulting from incomplete development—can be traced back centuries. To counteract risks from eclipses, women wore "a metal object such as a safety pin beneath their clothing." McClain's overall conclusion was that:

> Whatever advantages traditional obstetrical care offers women and their children in Ajijic (and these may be considerable), they will be lost if it is completely displaced by modern hospital services. A partial compromise may be the alternative method of home delivery under the care of a physician.

Even in retirement, McClain continues to research folk medicine beliefs and practices in Ajijic, and presented a paper on the subject to the American Anthropological Association in 2012.

The 1970s were a particularly significant time for the provision of health services in Ajijic; the decade offered examples of both the best and the worst of foreign involvement.

Dubious doctor

Areas with high numbers of foreigners, especially elderly foreigners, invariably attract more than their fair share of con artists, quacks and unlicensed practitioners of all kinds. In this regard, Ajijic more than kept pace with the outside world.

The *Guadalajara Reporter* broke the story in March 1976 of how 34-year-old Walter Paul Kitonis III, an American who had opened a medical practice in Ajijic, was not a licensed medical doctor, but an ex-convict, parole violator, and convicted thief for whom US authorities had issued eleven arrest warrants. Kitonis had lived in Guadalajara and at Lake Chapala for several weeks. He rented a house in Chapala and opened an office in Ajijic—facing the plaza at Parroquia 16—in February 1976, calling himself Dr Paul Kitonis Morris, and offering "general and surgical medical services."[3] Accompanying Kitonis was a 22-year-old former barmaid from Detroit. Only weeks after she left penniless to return to Detroit, Kitonis reportedly married a 20-year-old Guadalajara receptionist, María Nieves.

Subsequent investigation showed that the only evidence for his right to call himself "Doctor" was a certificate from the Universal Life Church of California. When interviewed by the *Guadalajara Reporter*, he claimed that "we often treat many of our poor Mexican patients for practically no payment, just a few vegetables, or a chicken, or whatever work they can help us with in the clinic."[4] Once outed, Kitonis fled to Puerto Escondido and then Guatemala.

Kitonis was apprehended by the FBI in Sacramento, California, in 1977, while working as an administrator of weight loss clinics. From his jail cell, he tried to fund his defense by selling a cornea or a kidney. The serial con man later resurfaced in Detroit, posing as a psychologist with a degree from a university in Guadalajara; this finally earned him a lengthy sentence behind bars.[5]

Ajijic Health Center

Such masquerades only underscored the need for a professionally staffed clinic in Ajijic. In 1977, Neill James donated 1083 square meters of land, on which she had built three rental units, at Seis Esquinas for the village's first Health Center (Centro de Salud). Casa Oro, the largest of the three units, was converted into an eight-bed clinic. The adjacent unit, Casa Bambú, became the doctor's office with lecture rooms, while Casa Xalasuchil was used as a residence for two nurses.[6]

The clinic opened in May 1977, supported by state and federal funding that provided three doctors, all graduates of the University of Guadalajara: Ajijic native Dr Jorge Ibarra, as the clinic's administrator, Dr Salvador Pérez, a gynaecologist, and Dr Helena Hermosillo, a pediatrician. The clinic offered free family planning and was equipped to handle minor surgeries. It received its first patients even before it had a phone line. A few months later it had its own ambulance, a converted station wagon donated by New Yorker Alice Pariaplano, which arrived at the same time as adjustable hospital beds, examination tables and assorted operating room equipment donated by Riverside Hospital in Studio City, California.[7]

With the aid of numerous local and American volunteers, James helped ensure that the plan remained on track. As local columnist Ruth Netherton wrote at the time, benefactress Neill James "rises above petty local attempts to embroil her in legal squabbles and goes on doing good."[8] After a somewhat bumpy start, additional government funding and a fresh group of volunteers brought the project to the finish line.[9] The property (Ocampo 90) now also houses a DIF day care and kindergarten.

Port of Health

Port of Health, "Lake Chapala's beautiful new health spa," touted hyperbaric oxygen rejuvenation in March 1977.[10] The spa, at the Villa Formoso Apartments, also offered "natural nutrition, super-juice therapy, colon irrigation, etc." that could "heal arthritis, asthma, ulcers, diabetes, arteriosclerosis [and] high blood pressure… via natural therapies without toxic drugs, mutilating surgery or burning cancer-causing radiations." Accepting that hyperbaric oxygen treatment can be useful for a variety of conditions, evidence is lacking for it helping either asthma or diabetes.

The spa, directed by Dr Edward L Carl, installed Mexico's first multiple-person hyperbaric oxygen health chamber. Dr Bernard Jensen, "chiropractor, author and teacher of iris diagnosis," and director of Hidden Valley Ranch Health Spa in Escondido, California, had a series of rejuvenation treatments at Port of Health in July 1977.[11] A few months later, several members of Hope Foundation from San Diego, California, including its director Dr Robert Reynolds, spent three weeks at "Port of Health International Naturopathic Healthatarium" in Ajijic.[12] A subsequent issue of *Hope News*, the foundation's monthly magazine, was entirely devoted to endorsing Port of Health to its members. For better or worse, the spa was short-lived and dropped off the radar shortly after moving to the Chula Vista Motel in December 1977.[13]

Touch of Eden

Another local spa, the Touch of Eden, was closed by state and federal authorities in August 1978. This health venture had operated out of the Hotel Real de Chapala on the eastern edge of the village.[14] The two men running the spa—Richard Shaar and Ernesto Cordova Ibarra—were arrested by police and taken into custody. The accusations leveled against

Shaar included distribution of illegal drugs, fraudulent claims of curing patients of arthritis, rheumatism and senility, and lacking the proper documentation to work in Mexico.

In association with a related company in Pasadena, California, they had offered package trips to Lake Chapala, including room, meals, treatments, medical service and air fare, starting at $1189 a person for seven nights, six days. The treatments included manual and electrical massage, therapeutic baths and sauna, vitamins, and injections of the controversial anti-aging drug Gerovital H-3. According to Touch of Eden literature, Shaar was a US citizen of French-Syrian ancestry, with a degree in naturopathy and credentials in dermal therapy and cosmetology, while Cordova Ibarra was a surgeon who graduated from the University of Guadalajara and had held medical positions in Puerto Vallara and elsewhere.

The closure of Touch of Eden in Ajijic followed complaints received at two Mexican consulates in California and various local government offices in Mexico by US citizens who had taken so-called treatments at the self-styled rejuvenation spa. One of these complainants may have been Mrs Robert Prestie, better known as the prolific, best-selling author Taylor Caldwell, who had stayed two weeks at the Touch of Eden with her husband only a month before its closure.[15]

Ajijic Development Clinic (Sylvia Flores)

Social activist Sylvia Flores, a registered nurse and midwife, began counseling low income families at the west end of the lake about nutrition and family planning in the 1970s. She founded CEDEJO (Centro De Desarrollo Jocotepec, AC) in 1986 and has since trained dozens of young women to help expand knowledge of health, environmental and sex education in schools and the wider community. CEDEJO moved to Ajijic (Calle Ocampo 45A) in 1991. Flores received United Nations recognition for her contribution to common unity and women's development. The Ajijic center and its mobile medical care unit continue to provide socially important services related to prenatal care, family planning (including contraception) and medical consultations, as well as sex education and empowerment workshops in schools and elsewhere.

And the medical situation today? Ajijic and San Antonio Tlayacapan now boast an impressive range of medical and dental facilities, as well as easy access to the world-class specialists and hospitals in Guadalajara.

43

The performing arts

In 1973 a community meeting was held in support of a proposal to build an auditorium on a vacant lot adjacent to the Artisans School and the Museum. The lot was owned by the municipality and funding was to be divided between the municipality, the state and the local community. The foreign community and Mexican community united to gain the financial support of the state government and raise the necessary funds. Several small-scale music and theater groups existed at Lake Chapala, but they were always struggling to find suitable venues for productions, so the decision to aim for a purpose-built auditorium can not have been a hard one to make.

Music lovers Enid McDonald (a Canadian flying pioneer) and Josephine Warren (mother of Chris Luhnow, founder of the long-running *Traveler's Guide to Mexico*) registered Lake Chapala Festivals as a non-profit to manage all local fund raising. A second non-profit, Patronato Pro Construccion del Auditorio Municipal AC, was formed, with Hector Márquez as president and McDonald as secretary, to negotiate with state authorities in Guadalajara to finalize details of the design and construction. The original idea, for an open-air auditorium, was upgraded to a fully enclosed building with specialist facilities. The first big local fund raiser, The Amethyst Ball, was held in April 1974.

Serving on the Lakeside Auditorium (Auditorio de la Ribera) Building Committee, established the following month, were McDonald, Márquez, Manuel Pantoja, Warren and Dr William Winnie. The construction of the 500-seat auditorium was the responsibility of the Jalisco Public Works Department, and the architect appointed to design the auditorium was Julio Ornelas Davila.[1] After seeing the initial plans, the committee suggested minor modifications, including the expansion of the proposed foyer to make it more suitable for art exhibits. Final plans were approved by state administrators in September 1974, and construction, expected to take eight months, started almost immediately. Groundbreaking was on 24 September 1974, and the cornerstone of the new building was laid by Jalisco State Governor Alberto Orozco Romero on 10 December that year.

In April 1975, La Floresta's Club Náutico was the scene of one of the largest fund raising events ever held at Lake Chapala. Raffle prizes at the April in Paris Ball included a trip for two to Paris, and a weekend in Acapulco. The Aquamarine Ball, held the following year with actor-singer Roger Cudney as guest star, raised another $13,000 for the auditorium.

Delays in construction caused the scheduled formal opening of the auditorium to be pushed back to 25 September 1976. The inaugural event was to have been a concert by internationally acclaimed Mexican pianist Manuel Delaflor, who had just played at New York's Carnegie Hall. This concert was canceled at the last minute, when it was discovered that the smooth walls of the new auditorium created abysmal acoustics. The auditorium's near-completion was celebrated, instead, with a garden party.

Eighteen months later, after the sound problem and other flaws had been rectified, the inaugural concert at Lakeside Auditorium on 15 March 1978 featured soprano Lucille Sabella, the Guadalajara Symphony Orchestra and the Jalisco Philharmonic Chorus.[2]

One particular musical expatriate family, the Campbells, had a special connection to the building. The auditorium's $8000 Baldwin concert grand piano was donated by Hilary Campbell, in memory of her sister Elsa.[3] The piano was officially christened in its new location on 25 March 1978 by internationally known pianist Elena Cavalcanti. Colorado-born Cavalcanti, who had played with the BBC and the London Symphony Orchestra, and recorded for Decca, emerged from her Ajijic retirement to give a superb recital.[4]

Those early supporters, together with many others who have contributed to the facility's maintenance and renovations over the years, can be justly proud of their efforts. The Lakeside Auditorium became an enduring tribute to a fine spirit of cooperation between local residents, foreign visitors, and municipal and state officials. After major renovations in 2020, the auditorium reopened as Estación Cultural Chapala, a regional cultural hub run by Jalisco's Department for Culture.[5]

Of the many creative arts groups formed at Lake Chapala over the years, one of the most original and innovative was TLAC (Todas Las Artes Combinadas, All The Arts Combined). TLAC is also a Nahuatl prefix meaning 'person.'[6] Founded in April 1977, one of its early ventures was organizing a logo-design contest. The winners were Barbara Faste for a TLAC logo and Sue Hadley for a special dinner theater logo; Morley Eager awarded each winner drinks, dinner and wine for two at the Posada Ajijic.[7]

TLAC members included Jack and Laura Bateman, Hank Edwards, Suci Emery, John Lychek, Ray Rigby, Hubert Harmon, Patricia Wightman, Helen Kirtland, Katie Goodridge Ingram, and photographer Sheldon Lychek and his future wife, Kelly Stauffer.[8] Soon added to the play-reading committee were Georgia Hill, Tio Kitzmiller, Phyllis Rauch, Andy Rubin and Roland Varno. At its peak the group had about forty members, with three main subgroups—for writers, actors and painters—hosted by Suci Emery, Patricia Wightman and Gail Michel respectively.[9]

Most meetings of TLAC were held in members' homes. It was especially active during its first eighteen months when it published a handful of editions of a literary magazine, *Connections*, with a different editor taking charge each month.[10] It also put on a number of experimental dinner theater plays, with tables for fifty couples, in the Quinto Patio at the Posada Ajijic. The first of these, in June 1976, featured three short plays: *American Still-Life*, written by Jack Bateman, *Patty Doll* by Patricia Wightman and *Lovers of Beethoven*, by John Lychek.[11]

Visitors to a similar show in September were treated to another trio of short plays: *Cushions*, set in Ajijic, written by Rafael Greno, *Hail the Conquering Hero* by Ray Rigby (author of *The Hill*), and *The Last Stab* by Suci Emery. Rigby's play was praised for its high humor, biting satire and crisp dialogue. The actors on that occasion included Reg Church, George Finch, Gloria Hill, Don Holliday, Pat Murphy, Ruth Netherton, Wayne Palfrey and Fred Wright.[12]

In December, the audiences enjoyed *Dr Acula's Clinic* by "Ivon Korisikoff" (Jack Bateman), a five-act play which was "campy, full of laughs, [and] suitable for young and old." The cast comprised Barbara and Sam Zagoria, Inga Holland, Reg Church and John Lychek.[13]

The following year, in May 1978 TLAC had an evening of *Monty Python's Flying Circus*, consisting of nine skits ably performed by Mickey Church, Wayne Palfrey and Sheldon Lychek. The last TLAC dinner theater on record was held in August, with performances of *Recycled* by Rafael Greno, *Fat* by Jack Bateman and *The Burglars* by Peggy Koll, noteworthy because Ajijic's resident Hollywood star, Rocky Karns, played a leading role.[14]

On the visual arts side, TLAC held a week-long art show in July 1977 at the Batemans' house with paintings and sculptures by Andy Ruben, Sid Schwartzman, Gustel Foust; Christina Journey, John K Peterson, Hubert Harmon and Dionicio Morales.[15]

For April Fool's Day 1978, TLAC organized a Self Portrait Show (any medium allowed) at the Posada Ajijic. First prize went to Grace Castle for a needlework on denim portrait using applique and embroidery. Among the other artists competing were Bob Snodgrass, Howard Skulnick, John K Peterson, Lona Isoard, Jim Marthai, Jean Caragonne, Lisa Hilton, Bee Dunham, Ramiro Magaña, Bob Neathery, Vee Greno, Rafael Greno, Hubert Harmon and Sheldon Lychek.[16]

To quote Alexandra Bateman, "TLAC was all about being irreverent, modern, experimental and above all light-hearted."[17]

In addition to Lakeside Little Theatre and TLAC, innumerable smaller groups have put on plays locally, often at dinner theater evenings in hotels. Deserving of mention is this regard is Canadian couple, Ken Smedley and his wife, Dorian Smedley-Kohl, who lived in the area from 1978 until 1989, initially in George Ryga's home in San Antonio Tlayacapan and later in Ajijic. Smedley, a professional director, oversaw several productions at Lake Chapala, including plays by Joanna Glass, Jack Heifner, David Marnet and Harold Pinter.

Perhaps his single most noteworthy production was the dinner theater offering at the Posada Ajijic in 1979 of *Portrait of a Lady, a Tribute to Margaret Laurence*. Dorian Smedley-Kohl, a professional model and actor, gave an acclaimed portrayal of heroine Hagar Shipley in this play, which was based on George Ryga's seminal adaptation of Margaret Laurence's classic novel *The Stone Angel*. Smedley-Kohl reprised this role numerous times afterwards in theaters across western Canada.

In 1988 the Smedleys were instrumental in mounting El Fringe, the first (and only) Ajijic Fringe Theater, which included performances by Dorian in *Circle of the Indian Year*, and by Ken in *Ringside Date with the Angel*, alongside various other events.

44

Zara's final years

By 1970, Zara had become a village fixture. Villagers accepted her eccentricities and the foreign community was duly respectful, either on account of her illustrious artistic career or for the length of time she had been a local resident. She was even considered, in some quarters, a spokesperson for all non-Mexicans living in Ajijic.

One of Zara's hallmarks in later life was shopping by horseback. Journalist Jack McDonald explained in his account of Zara, why she declined to get down from her horse to purchase anything: "It's unlawful to hitch a horse out in front, so she calls out her order and they fill her saddlebag with groceries."[1] This is a good story, but it is equally likely that the once-famous and entitled Zara felt disdain having to enter a rustic commercial establishment, when she could order a shopkeeper to come out and serve her on the street. Equally, as she aged, she found it more difficult to dismount and remount her horse.[2] Zara continued to shop from her horse well into the 1970s. Michael Eager recalls her stopping in the street outside the Posada Ajijic to demand that someone come out and weed the roadway because blades of grass could be seen emerging from the cobblestones.[3]

Zara was a great cook and Katie Goodridge Ingram has never forgotten the dinner Zara prepared for her and several friends one afternoon:

> She made the best chile enchiladas I have ever tasted... She made crepes, roasted dark green chiles, stuffed the crepas with rajas of the roasted chile, then bathed them in a most delicious white sauce. It was magical.... as Zara, trailing her long wide-leg pants across the floor, went from pot to pan to flames making her creation![4]

By the end of the 1960s, villagers and tourists alike had become alarmed about a new environmental threat to the health of the lake: pollution. The immediate cause was untreated sewage entering the lake. Zara was one of four signatories representing the Comité Pro-Defensa del Lago de Chapala on an open letter to the public.[5] The Comité had been largely inactive since 1958, when it helped avert the first major crisis. Now it campaigned for a water treatment plant in the town of Chapala, the major source of untreated sewage. Telegrams from political heavy-weights and community leaders to the President of Mexico and Governor of the State of Jalisco in August 1971 were co-signed by Zara, J González Gortázar, Fernando Luna de la Paz, Raúl Navarro, and José Guadalupe Zuno.[6] The campaign was successful and the area's first water treatment plant was duly installed.

By 1976, Zara, now well into her seventies, was starting to slow down, though she retained a keen interest in what was happening in the village. The bountiful rainy season that year filled the lake to overflowing. The rising waters flooded the kitchen of Zara's lakefront rental cottage, washed away parts of a retaining wall, and damaged the well. She wrote to a friend, acknowledging that she was distracted:

I don't have time to fight against pollution although it is so urgent. Have had endless difficulties with publishers who never fulfill an agreement and have cheated me abominably.... Also I have many problems here.[7]

At about this time *Guadalajara Reporter* correspondent Ruth Netherton described Zara as "a picturesque figure, with her long, full divided skirt, her long grey hair, her large hat, her sweet smile and blue gaze." Like many others before and since, Netherton accepted Zara at face value, including the myth that she had been born in Russia, and that she and Holger "came on horseback from Guadalajara, pausing to perform impromptu revolutionary ballets before astonished Mexican children, and being feted by rich *hacendados* along the way."[8]

In 1980, Zara regained her activist energy when an entirely new cause arose. The Comité Pro-Defensa del Lago de Chapala campaigned in support of building the La Zurda dam and reservoir, arguing that it would help relieve pressure on Lake Chapala and provide a much-needed alternative source of potable water for the people of Guadalajara.[9] Zara warned readers of the city's daily paper that allowing the lake to dry up "would completely ruin the traditionally good climate of Guadalajara."[10] The following year she persuaded the Jalisco Fine Arts Department and FONAPAS[11] to present her ballet *Amor Sublime* at the Degollado Theater as a fundraiser for the project, which "had still not yet got underway, despite the obvious benefits it would bring to Lake Chapala."[12]

In 1983 the original Comité Pro-Defensa regrouped into a new non-profit: the Sociedad Pro-Defensa del Lago de Chapala, AC. Zara was one of those present at the first meeting, along with Annabelle de Rigby (wife of British strawberry grower Jim Rigby, a long-time Ajijic resident), Luis Manuel Ochoa Altamirano, Alejandro González Gortázar, Luis Medina Jiménez and Alejandro Casillas Moreno. A few days before the group's formal meeting in Guadalajara in February 1983 to elect officers, an open letter in *El Informador* expressed concern about the level and pollution of Lake Chapala, and called for further discussion about the wisdom of extracting any more water for Guadalajara. The signatories, in addition to Zara Alexeyewa St. Albans (as Zara signed herself), included J Jesús González Gortázar, priest Raúl Navarro Ramos, Fernando Cuevas García and Ramón Rubín.[13]

Activism like this did eventually result in official action to protect the lake. The multiple state governments in the drainage basin of the Rio Lerma and Lake Chapala agreed to cooperate in sharing the region's limited water resources. These agreements were strengthened after the lake level fell so low in 1988–1992 that it required a lengthy walk or short taxi ride in Chapala to cross the wide expanse of exposed lake bed to the tourist boats.[14]

Zara would have loved Ajijic photographer and activist Xill Fessenden's idea, for World Environment Day 2000, of a giant expression of grassroots unity in which people held hands and tried to encircle the lake. More than 10,000 people took part in the event, called Hand in Hand We Embrace the Lake (Mano a mano abracemos el lago), held on 3 June.[15]

While nothing should ever be taken for granted where ecology is concerned, the activism of Zara and many other Ajijic residents over the years has brought only positive benefits to the village and to the entire region.

Return to the stage

Zara also fulfilled, in the 1970s, her long-time ambition to return to the stage. Zara and Holger had promised each other that neither would ever dance without the other. But Zara's mother, on her deathbed, made her daughter promise to return to the boards and perform again. In 1976, Zara, now almost 80 years old, decided to fulfill that promise to her mother and emerge from retirement to dance again. She confided to a friend that: "I am so eager to produce the Aztec Ballets. It is all I care about in life.... My mare is saddled and am off for the Post Office as it is mail time."[16]

A few weeks later, she wrote a follow-up letter confirming that:

> My only wish is to sell the mill house and produce the Aztec Ballets after which I am ready at any time to leave this planet. I so dearly love those who have gone beyond and believe I will rejoin them. I would like them to say "Well done!" I expect the ballets to be a sensation and most of the profits to help the Indian tribes. Holger and I loved the lake at first sight when it appeared before us as we rode over the mountains from Guadalajara. Perhaps hundreds of years ago we lived here belonging to some Indian tribe.[17]

Zara persuaded a young Mexican dancer, Sergio Lasso, to take Holger's roles in the two ballets she had created while vacationing in Chapala in 1925: *The Princess of the Moon* and *Nauollin*. These ballets were scheduled to be performed at the Teatro Juárez in Guanajuato on 23 September 1977.[18] Lasso later developed ambivalent feelings about Zara. Despite being friends with her in his twenties, he later realized that Zara had tried to mold him into a clone of her beloved Holger. As for Zara's love life, Lasso, author of an unpublished novel about the dancer, believed that she died a virgin, "having invented more lovers than there are stars in the sky."[19]

Final curtain call

Zara's final farewell performance was at the Degollado Theater in January 1978. Lasso spent weeks helping Zara repair costumes that had been stored away in trunks for decades, prepare the staging, hire a dance corps and chorus, arrange publicity, and rent the theater. Lasso played, opposite Zara, the leading roles in *The Princess of the Moon* and *The Red Terror*.[20]

Several bus loads of Zara's friends and other interested spectators from Ajijic attended the event. The front page of the *Guadalajara Reporter* featured a John Frost photo of Zara performing. The paper's review explained how Zara:

staged two of her own ballets as a farewell performance Friday January 20, with the aid of the chorus of the School of Music of the University of Guadalajara and the Helen Hoth Ballet plus Lakeside figures Wayne Palfrey, Katherine Karns and Gail Michel.... In both ballets, Zara was magnificently supported by premier danseur Sergio Lasso. The conception and execution of both pieces may be termed grandiose, strengthened by astounding scenic effects such as the eruption of the volcano with both fire and smoke, followed by a tremendous storm.[21]

Zara's final performance was certainly memorable, though not entirely for the right reasons. During the show, the ballet star posed theatrically and was twirled around by her partner as the rest of the cast danced around them. The finale featured an exploding volcano, meant to kill all the dancers apart from Zara (Princess of the Moon) and Lasso (Prince of the Sun), whose eternal love would—according to Zara's notes—protect them from the eruption. The volcano blew its top as planned, but set the stage on fire. Attempts to douse the flames flooded the orchestra pit, where the musicians suddenly found themselves ankle-deep in water. At the impromptu close, the audience erupted into applause, presumably more in relief than gratitude. Zara was delighted with her final standing ovation![22]

Ignominious end

Zara had long wanted her Ajijic home, which had received only minimal maintenance during her lifetime, to become a museum for the village as a tribute to the memory of Holger and herself.[23] Iona Kupiec told two young Canadian teachers in 1982 that she had talked Zara into opening her home as a museum to display her collection of incredible costumes, including those of the white peacock and the moon princess, which was silver mesh covered with pearls. When they then asked if Zara still cooked for herself, Iona replied, "No! She lives on mist!"[24]

This museum idea may be what motivated Zara to self-publish a booklet in 1982 titled *The Espectacular Artistic Life of Zara Alexeyewa Khyva St. Albans - Autobiography.*[25] A four-page autobiography was followed by dozens of excerpts from reviews and letters from adoring fans. After her opening line—"Ayenara Zara Alexeyewa Khyva St. Albans has probably had the most spectacular career in the history of the theatre"—Zara thanked God for giving her "three great gifts: actress, ballet dancer and writer."

Sadly, the museum idea was never acted upon. Even more sadly, in her final years an unscrupulous gardener-companion with drinking and money problems used intimidation and deceit to steal many of her treasured belongings and empty her house of anything valuable.[26] Most foreigners had no idea what was happening. But a local Spanish-language periodical alerted readers in 1986, three years before her death, that Zara was infirm, that her faithful horse Amaya (her best friend) had died, and that her current companion was "violent and without scruples."[27] The author called, quite justifiably, for Zara to be shown more respect.

Zara's unsavory companion gained control of her affairs, and moved her out of her own house—and away from her familiar memories and spirits—to a single room elsewhere on the property. Despite the protestations of Laura Bateman and others, he then sold off Zara's possessions and land.[28] Instead of the museum that Zara herself had wanted to be her legacy to the village, her property was subdivided for a dead-end street (*cerrada*) and several new homes.

Zara died in poverty on 12 January 1989 at the age of 92, and was buried in Ajijic cemetery, alongside her adored mother and her beloved soul mate Holger.

Many local residents still have fond memories of Zara. In 2013 local reporter Domingo Márquez wrote that Zara's mausoleum in Ajijic cemetery was in desperate need of renovation and that, to enhance the work, local artist Juan Navarro was painting a mural of Zara on one side.[29]

This remarkable woman, perhaps the only person ever to reach stardom as an actress under one name (Khyva St. Albans) and as a dancer under another (Ayenara Zara Alexeyewa), was, without question, one of the more complex and colorful characters ever to live in Ajijic.

And what became of the remnants of Zara's estate? Land registry documents show that there is still a small remnant of property that technically remains hers. When her properties were subdivided and sold, fifty-five square meters of Ajijic "fell between the cracks."[30] Even in her higher celestial world, Zara still owns a tiny piece of the village she called home.

45

Ajijic expands east

Neill James described Ajijic, when she arrived in 1943, as having "six streets which parallel the lake, cut by six others extending from lake to the sierras."[1] Prior to the mid-1960s, Ajijic was still only a fraction of its current size. From the plaza, the village stretched about five blocks in each direction, with the eastern edge of the village more or less coinciding with Calle Francisco I Madero.

In the early 1960s, Ajijic had added two subdivisions on its western outskirts: Rancho del Oro, begun in 1960 on land owned by Jorge Parada from Mexico City, and Villa Nova, which was started in 1964.[2] By the end of that decade some residents were already expressing discontent at how their village was changing. In 1967, for instance, *Guadalajara Reporter* columnist Anita Lomax lamented that:

> Ajijic's plaza, surrounded by small, typical tiendas (of brightly paint-ed exteriors and cool cave-like interiors) on three sides and the tiny, ancient chapel on the fourth, will never be the same. Several weeks ago, down came la tienda Rafles... and in its stead is being built a "super" market certain to be of the stark steel, glass and neon design so prevalent. Who needs it?[3]

La Floresta

Urban sprawl changed Ajijic for ever in the 1970s with the comple-tion of Fraccionamiento Aguilar, an urban infill project for an area west of Calle Revolución, and the construction of the massive La Floresta subdivision further east. Both were developed by José Aguilar Figueroa and his sons, Ignacio and Javier Aguilar Valencia.

The few blocks south of the highway that comprise Fraccionamiento Aguilar were given a street pattern similar to the preexisting streets of Ajijic. However, La Floresta, which extends for several blocks either side of the highway, was built with distinctive broad, cobblestone streets and a decidedly non-village feel, completely different in style to the core of Ajijic.

La Floresta, originally known as Ajijic Dos Lagos, was by far the largest real estate development in Ajijic at the time, and, indeed, the first major tourist-residential integrated complex anywhere in Mexico. Designed as an "Ajijic tourist hub," the huge multipurpose project was the brainchild of Aguilar Figueroa and his sons, working with Guadalajara engineer José Calderón Robert.

José Aguilar believed he owned La Floresta's 96.26 hectares (about 240 acres) of land, variously called San Nicolás de la Pesquería, Caballerías de Los Heredia or San Nicolás de Chiapa, on the strength of the deed drawn up when he bought it in 1945 from a 90-year-widow, Josefina de Alba. During the time her family owned it, Ajijic *campesinos* had been allowed to farm it.[4]

In 1957, confident that they had owned the land for more than a decade, the Aguilars decided to start development, and ejected the campesinos.[5] Unfortunately for them, the Ajijic Indigenous Community (Comunidad Indígena de Ajijic)[6] immediately lodged a competing claim, arguing that it had the rights to this land from centuries earlier, and that its rights had subsequently been confirmed in court.[7] The indigenous group claimed it planned to use the land for a new farmers' village (Colonia Popular Campesino) and offered to pay the Aguilars 37,000 pesos to settle the matter. This was the start of a lengthy, contentious and complex legal battle.

The Aguilar family obtained a federal certificate (*certificado de in-afectabilidad agrícola*) stating that the land was ineligible for communal management.[8] It was later alleged in court that this bore a falsified signature of the federal president. Years of thrust and counterthrust, offers and counteroffers, followed. The indigenous group continued to fight, surmounting bureaucratic hurdles at every turn as it navigated its way through Mexico's labyrinthine legal system, with its often arbitrary, and sometimes corrupt, decision-making processes.

As the case proceeded, the Aguilar family sought to curry favor (and influence state and federal decision-making) by donating land for the Escuela de Artes y Oficios, opened by President Gustavo Díaz Ordaz in July 1966, and for a sports field. The family also presented houses to both the president and the state governor, Francisco Medina Ascencio.[9] The 12,439-square-meter property given to the president was priced at $1.9 million when it went on the market in 1998.[10]

In 1967 the indigenous community was granted an injunction by the Second District Court in Guadalajara temporarily halting all work on the property. The community occupied the land, only to be violently removed within days by judicial police, who threw the leaders in jail. Peaceful protests outside Guadalajara cathedral by the mothers, children and friends of the detained men were broken up violently by state police. One of the conditions of the men's eventual release several months later was that they had to report, in person, to authorities in Guadalajara every week; this was relaxed to once a month in 1970. Only in 1977 were they finally declared innocent.[11]

In May 1968 heavy machinery began preparing the groundwork for Ajijic Dos Lagos. Despite the ongoing ownership conflict, a banner headline on the front page of *El Occidental* in January 1969 screamed "The Tourism Complex 'Ajijic' will become a reality."[12] According to the state Tourism Department, developing the first 50-hectare section of the project would cost around $9.6 million. A brief mention of the project in *Esquire* magazine noted that Ajijic Dos Lagos included a one-hundred-room hotel and a marina."[13] Greatly alarmed, the indigenous community wrote to the president, complaining about Ajijic Dos Lagos and informing him that the state governor had been given a "majestic lakefront house" built on community land.[14]

Notwithstanding all the protests, construction of Ajijic Dos Lagos began in earnest in March 1969. An area of 75 hectares was transformed into hundreds of residences, a luxury hotel, a trailer park, a nautical club (marina) and a shopping center. On the initial plans, half of the entire area was set aside for streets or green space. The subdivision was to have three deep wells for potable water and its own drainage plant. Within the first three years, the value of homes already completed represented total investments of more than $12 million (150 million pesos).[15] When the original plan to create two large artificial lakes was abandoned, the name Ajijic Dos Lagos was changed to La Floresta.

The conflict over land rights had rumbled on for so long that it was straining the internal bonds of the indigenous community to the limit. The bonds finally snapped in December 1969 when several community leaders signed an agreement with a different developer to renounce all rights over 38.5 hectares of land in a different part of Ajijic. In exchange for 30,000 pesos (shared between the leaders and their lawyer), ownership of a dozen or so separate parcels of land passed to Promotora Inmobiliaria Mexicana, SA, a company established by Louis Wertheimer Fuchs, whose name soon became synonymous with irregular land deals in the Ajijic area.[16] Most members of the indigenous community knew nothing about this deal until after it had been consummated; in the ensuing chaos they elected a brand new slate of officers.[17]

For the indigenous community, setback followed setback. It complied with a request in from a government agency in 1973 to submit additional paperwork, only for the package—containing more than 1000 pages of documents—to disappear in transit. When it finally turned up three months later, several key documents were mysteriously missing.[18]

When plans were announced for an auditorium on the highway near the sports field, the indigenous community renewed its protests, arguing that an auditorium offered no benefit to the local community, and that a secondary school or other educational establishment would be far more appropriate on what it considered community land. The indigenous group's opposition to La Floresta slowly petered out as the members of the group became older and fewer in number. Despite lingering resentments, their voices were stifled. The group—now called Grupo Indígena de Axixik—remains active; its main focus in recent years has been to protect the hills behind Ajijic from further development.

Club Náutico La Floresta

The long-running land dispute with the Aguilar family had failed to prevent the completion of La Floresta. Its luxury Camino Real hotel was later purchased by the Universidad Autónoma de Guadalajara and renamed Hotel Real de Chapala.[19] Adjoining the hotel, the Club Náutico La Floresta, now the Nimue Marina Residence & Sport Club, was completed in 1971. Its clubhouse lounge has some of the oldest surviving murals at Lake Chapala. Painted by Guadalajara artist Guillermo Chávez Vega, they show local historical events, from pre-Columbian Indian rituals to the heroic resistance of insurgents occupying Mezcala Island during Mexico's War of Independence. An additional mural, of a woman reposing in a fishing net hammock, was an unfortunate casualty when the members-only boating and social club was renovated in the 1980s.

The club began holding annual summer regattas in 1971. While primarily a sailing club, with more than 300 members at its peak, it organized the first motorboat rally on the lake in August 1974, a four-stage race, starting and ending in La Floresta, via Isla del Pato, Isla de Alacranes and San Luis Soyatlán.[20] In 1976 twelve Flying Dutchman yachts competed in Olympic Sailing Trials organized by the Club Náutico to select Mexico's top sailors for the 1976 Summer Olympics in Montreal, Canada. The club also organized the First Waterskiing Classic (Primer Clásico de Esquí) in November 1989, with a mix of Mexican and US participants.[21]

The La Floresta Trailer Park (later the Hotel La Floresta, and now La Floresta Village) was particularly popular during the mid-1970s. Compared to north of the border, monthly rates were extremely accessible. In the winter of 1973–74, for example, a small space with a patio cost $35 a month, while a large space with patio was just under than $60. Among other amenities, the walled (secure) park of 125 spaces offered full hookups and a communal heated swimming pool.[22]

In 1994 the section of the highway through La Floresta was renamed Boulevard Jin Xi in honor of Chapala's sister city relationship with the Chinese city of Jin Xi (more commonly Jinxi) in the province of Liaoning.[23] In 2010, citing the difficulties caused by using distinct names for different sections of the same highway, Chapala officials voted to rename the entire road—as far as the limit with the municipality of Jocotepec—Paseo del Centenario de la Revolución Mexicana.[24]

With all the component parts of La Floresta complete, the transformation of Ajijic into a tourism hub was well under way. However, land tenure conflicts, such as the controversy exemplified by La Floresta, continue to resurface periodically along the north shore of Lake Chapala. Such conflicts have inevitably stirred an undercurrent of dissatisfaction among some sections of the local populace and fomented spirited debate about the positive and negative effects of the so-called "progress" brought by tourism.

One thing is certain; there is no going back. Paraphrasing Mexican sociologist Francisco Talavera: on the north shore of Lake Chapala *campesinos* have been forced to abandon their plows and nets to take up brooms and pruning shears.[25]

46

Ajijic expands west

Ajijic also expanded rapidly towards the west during the 1970s. Unlike the planned, orderly, garden suburb approach that characterized La Floresta, development west of the village was more piecemeal and the results far less uniform.

Hotel Danza del Sol

The Danza del Sol, now owned by the Universidad Autónoma de Guadalajara, is about ten blocks west of the plaza and dates back to the early 1970s. The first brochures used for international promotion featured photographs taken by Beverly Johnson. Mid-way through the project, the developers—the wealthy and influential Leaño family from Guadalajara—added US architect George Heneghan to the design team, on the strength of the home he had just completed for his family on Calle Zaragoza in Ajijic.[1]

Heneghan and his wife, Molly, moved to Ajijic with their two young sons in 1971, after building numerous commercial buildings and residences in Aspen, many in an architectural style best described (to borrow a phrase from his son Eric) as Wrightian/Organic.[2] The Heneghans, who were very active in the Lakeside Little Theatre, left Mexico in 1975 for New Mexico, and later settled in Hawaii, where Heneghan continued his award-winning architectural career.

In Ajijic, Molly, an artist and graphic designer, drew and published "Sunny Ajijic," an informative color postermap of Ajijic. This valuable social history document dates back to about 1973 and boasts a wealth of details about the location and identity of individual stores and services.

Subdivisions further west

Many of the residential developments further west were built on land amassed by Louis Wertheimer.[3] Wertheimer (1912–1994) was a Buffalo-born entrepreneur, who owned the historic Silverthorne House in that city and had been a regional manager for the Davis Distributing Corporation.[4]

Wertheimer and his wife, Cathy, first arrived in Ajijic in about 1960. He quickly recognized that the area offered a magnificent opportunity for real estate speculation. Among the buildings he owned in the 1960s was El Tejaban, the historic former home of Juan Jaacks. Wertheimer leased this for a short time to the Grupo 68 artist collective, a fitting choice given that the building had once belonged to the Butterlin family, who had opened the village's first art gallery there twenty years earlier.

Wertheimer managed his land and property deals through a Mexican-registered firm, Promotora Inmobiliaria Mexicana, SA. In a notarized agreement dated 9 December 1969, the Ajijic Indigenous Community gave this firm full rights over various Ajijic properties in exchange for 30,000 pesos, shared between those who had signed on behalf of the community and their lawyer.[5]

The agreement identified each parcel by means of a single distance and compass direction from the church.[6] Some of the properties in this agreement were on the north and north-west outskirts of the existing village, while others were on the lakeshore to the west. To the north, the largest transfer (10.23 hectares) combined three rural properties named El Tacote, Las Salvias and Piedra Rayada. The largest single property to the west was La Cristina (9.4 hectares). Between Ajijic and La Cristina, Promotora Inmobiliaria Mexicana also acquired the land rights for Tio Domingo, Alceseca, La Canacinta and Arroyo Colorado.

Within months, Wertheimer began developing his newly acquired land. Building lots were sold in Fraccionamiento La Cristina as early as June 1970. According to advertisements, all relevant permits had been approved by the municipality. Wertheimer had developed strong political connections in the area, strengthened no doubt by being the only non-Mexican appointed to a Tourism Development Group established by the *sub-delegado* for tourism in Chapala in 1967.[7]

According to Francisco Talavera—who estimated that Wertheimer owned, at one time or another, a total of between 600 hectares and 800 hectares of urbanized and urbanizable land in the Lake Chapala area—most of the land was acquired fraudulently, without proper title, and for less than $0.15 a square meter. The same land, once legal deeds were obtained, sold for between $16 and $32 a square meter, depending on its proximity to the lake.[8] Such profit margins only made Wertheimer's decision to dress as Robin Hood for a Halloween Costume Dinner Dance in 1973 all the more audacious.[9]

Only a year earlier, Wertheimer had gained notoriety in Ajijic when he was accused of having ordered a road to be driven straight through the middle of the village cemetery to improve access to an area he was developing. More than a hundred graves were desecrated before work was halted.[10] Among the bodies disturbed on the morning of 17 October were those of novelist Willard Marsh and writer, turned would-be-drug-dealer, Don Hogan. One of the graves destroyed was that of a young child killed in a house fire on Calle Ocampo in 1932.[11] Wertheimer published a vehement denial in *El Informador*, claiming to have no connection to the work, directly or indirectly, and stating that he did not even own any land adjacent to the cemetery.[12] In the wake of serious threats, Wertheimer and his wife left town.

A few days later several municipal officials were detained for having arranged the bulldozer incident as some kind of political stunt, presumably to incriminate Wertheimer. A long-time American resident of Ajijic, Peggy Neel, wrote to her daughter, shortly after visiting the cemetery for a burial service, that the bulldozed road was only a few feet from the plot where Zara's mother and her dance partner, Holger Mehnen, were both buried.[13] In her next letter she explained how, believing Wertheimer was responsible, "local Mexican people had risen up and by the hundreds walked to the cemetery and piled huge boulders across [the] road to block [it]," and how, two weeks later, "the local mayor and about 5 key men" were put in jail for the incident. Even so, she continued, some local villagers "say Americans have no right to come here and spend such huge amounts of money on everything—ruin the town—or rather take over—while the locals have next to nothing—which God knows is true."[14]

Foreign ownership

Wertheimer was, as we have seen, far from being the first or only foreigner to profit from property deals in Ajijic. But just how much land had fallen into foreign hands by the 1970s? Helpfully, Talavera compiled a map in 1977 of who owned what in Ajijic, distinguishing between foreign owners, owners from Guadalajara (Tapatíos), and local (native Ajijic) owners.[15] Even excluding La Floresta, Las Salvias and Rancho del Oro (none of them owned by villagers), his map shows that barely 50% of Ajijic was still owned by locals in 1977; Tapatíos from Guadalajara owned about 27% and foreigners 23%.[16] Strikingly, the entire lakefront—bar the 4% corresponding to Posada Ajijic, which was owned by Mexicans but managed by foreigners—was already in either Tapatío or foreign ownership; the fate of 96% of the entire lakefront of the village was already controlled by outsiders.

A decade later, when Wertheimer—then in his seventies—was interviewed in Ajijic by *Time* correspondent John Moody, an estimated 5000 foreigners resided in the Chapala-Ajijic area. Wertheimer told Moody that the question that "flashed through his mind when he first saw the sparkling waters of Lake Chapala and realized how cheaply he could live there" was why everyone else was not also there, and that, even 27 years later, he still wondered why Ajijic was "not overrun with gringos looking for the good life."[17] Wertheimer enjoyed the good life for many years, as have so many other incomers to the area. But at what price in terms of long-term impacts on the local community?

Misión del Lago and Lomas de Ajijic

Fast forward a few years to the early part of this century and a conflict similar to that in La Floresta erupted over two developments on the hillside immediately north of Ajijic: Misión del Lago and Lomas de Ajijic. Developer Jaime Hernández claimed to hold legal title to all the property in question. But parts of both developments allegedly occupied a small section of the 481 hectares of hillside that a 1983 presidential decree had formally awarded after the La Floresta dispute to the Ajijic Indigenous Community.

Legal actions between the indigenous community and Hernández bounced around various courts for over a decade. The eventual outcome, in early 2006, was that the indigenous community won the right to restitution of its land. According to the decision, the responsibility for rectifying the situation lay with the local municipal government which had approved the building permits. It offered to pay the *comuneros* the pre-development value of the land; the *comuneros* held out for the value of the land post-development.[18]

And history quickly repeated itself. Only a few months later, Chapala municipal officials approved the construction of Tres Cañadas—a hillside subdivision four kilometers west of Ajijic—despite claims that its land, too, belonged to the Ajijic Indigenous Community.[19]

El Ojo de Agua, a casualty of development

A short distance west of Misión del Lago, at the northern end of Calle Colón, is the site of El Ojo de Agua, the spring and small pool once used by villagers for washing clothes and bathing. Novelist Barbara Compton, who visited Ajijic in 1946, included a first person description of the pool in *To The Isthmus*:

> I follow a stony path up and out toward the mountain slope which crowds the village to the flat strip along the lake.... As the path winds up, the few dry stunted thorn trees give way to a tall and slender growth clinging to the hillside. The path dips, and there is a rich shining grove of eucalyptus trees, and the sound of water and voices. It is a deep emerald pool set in a basin of rock, round which some half dozen women are doing their washing.[20]

The spring was a vital source of fresh water, and its use was closely monitored, as shown by a 1937 inspection when an official from the Secretaría de Agricultura y Fomento determined that an unnamed individual had commandeered the water from the spring (which belonged to the nation) for personal use to the detriment of other *ejidatarios*. The inspector decreed that the water must be shared more equitably.[21]

With the lowering of the water table in Ajijic over the years—due more to the extraction of water via wells than climate change—the Ojo de Agua, now on private property, dried up. This is particularly ironic, given that the name Ajijic derives from the Nahuatl for "navels of water that spill" or "place of springs."[22] According to local lore, this is where the village of Ajijic was founded by Queen Xóchitl.

Before village homes had piped water, residents either relied on spring water from the Ojo de Agua, collected water from the lake, dug their own well, or bought water from the water cart that belonged to Jesús "Pipón" Romero.[23] By the early 1950s the spring water was piped down to a holding tank (*pila*) and fountain in the plaza, making it easier for households to access the water they needed. This quickly became the 'water fountain' where women met and gossiped daily before carrying water home.[24]

In the 1960s a municipal system was installed. This supplied piped water to homes from village wells, the first of which was at Carretera and Marcos Castellanos, and the second at Aquiles Serdán and Zaragoza.[25] Even this did not resolve all the water issues. In 1970, for example, Ajijic went without town water for several weeks, and residents had to rely on private wells.[26] Supply was improved (for a time) after a third well was drilled in 1974 at Tempisque and Antonio Torres. The local administrator for potable water stated at that time that the Ajijic system served 717 Mexican households and 215 non-Mexican households.[27] To this day, the provision of potable water in Ajijic struggles to keep up with the pace of expansion.

47

Traditions and festivals

Ajijic celebrates a large number of religious and civic occasions each year with fiestas, parades, dances, fireworks and culinary delights. This chapter considers five annual events that have a unique and distinct Ajijic flavor.

Carnival

Carnival (*Carnaval*) celebrations in the village are said to pre-date those in Chapala, and to be more authentic, relying on traditional community organization rather than a top-down approach. Ajijic Carnival, including the main parade, is entirely financed by local residents and organized for their enjoyment. For instance, the costs of "The hosting (*Recibimiento*), Bull of Eleven (*Toro de Once*), and the band (among other things) are covered by members of the Asociación de Charros."[1]

The most distinctive feature of Ajijic Carnival is the presence of *sayacos* and *sayacas*, who possibly represent the amused reaction of indigenous people when weird-looking Spaniards arrived and tried to impose their strange foreign religion and customs. Male *sayacos* and female *sayacas* participate in a series of pre-Carnival parades (which do not have any floats) as well as in the major parade with floats on Mardi Gras.

The *sayacos* traditionally wear a mask (dark-colored wood or paper maché) adorned with beards and bushy eyebrows, as well as a bandana, an old hat with a wide brim, a long-sleeved shirt, an old vest, formal pants and boots; they carry a woven bag full of confetti. Some *sayacos* dress up as old men to dance with their partners.[2]

Most *sayacos*, however, dress up as women, with an elegant lady's hat, colorful blouse, skirt and boots or high heels; they carry confetti in their handbags.³ Strategically placed balloons or balls accentuate their femininity. The masks of these cross-dressing *sayacos*, who often don blonde or red wigs, are painted with full red lips and bright rosy cheeks.

In the old days, all *sayacos* carried confetti; the trend of substituting flour for confetti began relatively recently, as did the participation of girls and women as *sayacas*. As the *sayacos* and *sayacas* wander the streets or accompany a parade, they throw liberal amounts of flour at onlookers, and engage in mock fights with mischievous youngsters. After the main parade the *sayacos* hold their own dance contest as part of the celebrations.

The *sayacos* date back at least to the 1940s, probably earlier.⁴ According to local oral tradition, the antics of *sayucos* derive from "native rituals practiced during the pre-Hispanic era" and link back "to the legendary village matriarch Xicantzi, a direct descendent of the area's ancestral tribal ruler."⁵

Inevitably, as Ajijic has grown, this event, like so many elsewhere in Mexico, has gradually become more touristy. Preserving old traditions enriches cultural heritage and is usually a laudable thing to strive for. However, some former Carnival traditions have—probably fortunately—died out. Zoe Kernick, for instance, who witnessed Carnival in 1949, was horrified by one particular aspect of what she saw:

> A less great moment is Carnival time; tired street oxen are herded into an arena where tequila-reeling men bite their tails to goad them into attitudes of fury; the whole town cheers on flimsy stands so crowded that both orchestra and audience are liable to imminent collapse. The Hero of each day is He Who Gets Gored, and each citizen contributes money to pay for the hero's hospital bills, or for his funeral.⁶

Easter Passion Play

By far the most dramatic community event at Lake Chapala during Holy Week is Ajijic's Easter Passion Play or Via Crucis, first conceived and organized in 1980 by Eduardo Ramos, Martha Elva Romero and Abdulia Zamora.⁷ Back in 1980 they apparently managed to organize the entire event in just three days, with sixteen villagers as actors. A working script for the following year required volunteer actors for forty-five roles. By 1985 the number of participants had grown to eighty-five; it now exceeds a hundred. The cast reenacts, over three days, the arrest, trial and crucifixion of Christ. Months of intensive preparations are involved and the costuming, acting and open-air sets are absolutely magnificent.

On Palm Sunday, a week before Easter Day, a procession wends its way through Ajijic with Jesus riding the donkey. On the evening of Maundy Thursday, Roman soldiers lead Jesus in a candle-lit procession from upper Ajijic to the San Andreas church. The main event, the Passion Play held in the atrium of the church on Good Friday, is one of the most memorable and extravagant anywhere in Mexico. Huge crowds gather to watch.

Ajijic Sun Dance

The Ajijic Sun Dance (Danza del Sol), now held each summer to thank the Great Spirit for the gift of life, may have very ancient roots. The event is held at a large circle of stones on a grassy meadow in the hills overlooking western Ajijic and the Hotel Danza del Sol. The meadow has structures made of branches that can be covered with blankets to make sweat lodges (*temazcales*). In its modern incarnation, first held in 1991, more than 100 dancers participated. This was no event for the faint-hearted since the dancers had to go four days without any food or water, and had to offer themselves in honor to the earth by piercing their skin. All participants had to have been active members of the local indigenous group for at least two years prior to the event.[8]

According to Aldo Arias, who wrote his masters thesis on the Ajijic Sun Dance, the origins of its revival stem from a meeting of indigenous chiefs from the Americas held in Mesa, Arizona, in 1980.[9] The Ajijic Sun Dance is an unusual example of a long-forgotten Mexican ritual being revived and returning to its place of origin.

Hot-air balloons (*globos*)

Ajijic's annual hand-made hot-air balloon competition, Globos de Luz, held every September to coincide with Mexico's Independence celebrations, is one of the longest-running annual events unrelated to religion in the village. The history of making the glorified sky lanterns out of tissue paper and other materials dates back centuries.

Herbert Johnson's photo album from the 1940s includes two undated photos, presumed to have been taken in Ajijic, of conical-shaped hot-air balloons rising above the heads of a throng of young people, to their obvious enjoyment, so their manufacture in Ajijic certainly dates back at least seventy years and probably even further.

Ángel Chacón believes his uncle, Absalón García from Zapotitán de Hidalgo, was the true pioneer of making tissue paper balloons. Chacón recalled how, in 1945, his uncle told him that he would share the necessary skills (which the uncle had learned from his own father, Adelaido García) but only if Ángel first promised never to teach anyone else. His uncle then took him to the home of a friend, Juan Pérez, where the mosaic floor tiles made it easier to cut and paste strips of paper. Chacón, however, subsequently broke his word and taught several others, including Antonio Pantoja, Salvador Gutiérrez and Javier Paes.[10]

Many years later, Chacón was living with his family in Tijuana. One day he rescued a box of tissue paper squares from a dumpster, intending to amuse himself by making a *globo*. Coincidentally, his mother saw an advertisement seeking people who knew how to make them. After demonstrating his design, Chacón won a contract to supply 100 similar balloons in time for the September fiesta. He earned $7 for every balloon that rose well, but only $5 for those that failed.

On his return to Ajijic in April 1963, Chacón was surprised to find that people were preparing for a *globo* competition, and that classes on *globo* making were being given in the library. Hence, he claims, his disobedience was directly responsible for Ajijic's annual balloon event.

Marcella (Malle) Crump, an amateur photographer who was very active in Ajijic in the late 1950s and early 1960s, documented many village events. One of her photos of a *globo* competition in about 1962 shows several spectators watching the event, including her daughter Hilda, Laura Bateman, Neill James and Alicia Sendis.[11] In that particular year, the balloon made by the Bateman family dwarfed all others, with the author-artist Jack Bateman proving his design and construction skills. Bateman is credited in one newspaper article as the co-founder (in 1958), with Sid Williamson, of Ajijic's *globos* competition, when the two men stirred interest by flying *globos* from their own back yards.[12]

By 1965 the *globos* competition was an annual fund-raiser. The proceeds that year went towards the new regional Vocational School which opened a few months later. The judges of the balloon races that September included Rubén Chacón, Charles Murray, Gus West and Chick Hopkins; betting on the event was organized by Lou Wertheimer and Bob Werk.[13]

Globo-making was put on a sound footing in the 1970s when several foreign artists, including Jerry Murray, not only entered their own designs, but also taught the necessary skills to eager local youngsters to enable them to become the next generation of sky lantern enthusiasts. In recent years the annual balloon regatta (*regata de globos*) has attracted as many as 300 entrants and more than 3000 curious onlookers.

Chili Cookoff

As more and more charities were formed at Lake Chapala, fund raising became an integral part of the social scene. The variety of fund-raising activities and events held over the years is stunning, ranging from all manner of sponsorships and gourmet dinners to house and garden tours, masked balls and art auctions.

The largest single annual fund-raiding event is the Chili Cookoff, first held in July 1978 on the beach in front of the Posada Ajijic. Morley Eager was master of ceremonies for the inaugural four-day event. When the lake rose to the Posada steps, contestants were forced to set up their kitchens either on the pier or in the Posada Ajijic gardens.[14] Journalist Dale Hoyt Palfrey was there, and summarized the first competition in this memorable paragraph:

> Those who were there remember it as a wild bash revolving around a chili cooking match-up between three of the community's most colorful characters: Scrabblemaster Bill Teunis, bagpipe blower Dave Bennett and lady-about-town Reni Rice, who famously laced her chili pot with a full bottle of Scotch whiskey. Most everyone present got rip-roaring drunk, and Bennett threw a full-blown tantrum when Teunis was declared the winner.[15]

A few years later, the inimitable Morley Eager contracted a circus to set up on the beach next to the pier, and proudly rode the troupe's prize elephant at the head of the first ever Cookoff parade. Wayne Palfrey, the director of Oak Hill School, translated for Morley Eager in early shows, before taking over the microphone and demonstrating his prowess as an immensely talented bilingual MC for many years.

In March 1979 the Chili Cookoff became the Mexican National Cookoff, an event sanctioned by the International Chili Society (ICS), which meant that the winner automatically gained a spot in the ICS World Championship. The organizers that year included Mickey Church, Ronald Dorsey, Morley Eager, Joan Frost and Ann Whiting. Ann Whiting recalls that Jocotepec residents Allyn Hunt (long-time editor of the

Guadalajara Reporter) and his wife, Beverly, were instrumental in getting this first ICS-sanctioned event off the ground.

Contestants that year included Rita and Al Kilpatrick (Viva's Chili), Curtis Foust and Roberto Mosqueda (Chili Choncho), Dick Moore (Grandma's Chili), Madeline Sophie Gray and son (Real Down Home Chili), Wayne and Dale Palfrey (Zoo Kids), Luis Chávez and Elva Patricia Gómez (Chili Tapatio), Nancy González and her Xalisco Xalapeños team (Secret Recipe), Francis Hopper (Chili Tecolote), Art and Vicki Keough (Eat, drink and beware) and Ron Mitre (Ron's Heavenly Chili). Accompanying music was from the Carlos de la Torre jazz band, the Bobby Haggart jazz group, Los Mariachis de Ajijic, the Jocotepec Piper (Dave Bennett), and the Ajijic Brass Band. A large team of judges, including chili specialists from California, New York and Puerto Vallarta, declared Don England of California the winning chef.[16]

The ICS continued to sanction the Mexican National Chili Cookoff in Ajijic until 2008. Local competitors rarely took the top prizes, but many had a knack for zany antics that put a special stamp on the event.

Among the local non-profits to benefit from the Chili Cookoff over the years are Amigos del Lago, Casa de Ancianos, Lakeside School for the Deaf (now School for Special Children), Mexican Red Cross (Cruz Roja Mexicana), Niños de Ajijic, Niños de Chapala, Niños de San Antonio Tlayacapan, Niños Incapacitados, and Niños y Jovenes de San Juan Cosalá.

Art and creative writing since 1980

Many of the galleries that opened in the 1980s had only a short life span. They included print-maker Bill Gentes' gallery at Independencia 5, which held an exhibit of 100 of Jim Moran's "Naromji" works in 1986. Few of Ajijic's many colorful characters over the years had as many true tales to spin as serial prankster Moran, who was almost eighty years old when he retired to Ajijic. As a publicity stunt he once painted the worst abstract he could, and had it accepted by a juried Los Angeles Art Association show as the work of Naromji, a previously unknown artist.[1]

Galeria de Arte Los Amigos, active during the second half of the 1990s on Calle 16 de Septiembre, was another interesting gallery that did not last long. This was a joint venture of Ajijic-born artist Victor Romero, a graduate of the Children's Art Program, and Californian Robert O'Connell. Later exhibiting members included Isela Martinez (Romero's wife), Judy Eager, Ann Tunnell, Luisa Julian and Isidro Xilonzochitl.[2]

The first gallery of note in San Antonio Tlayacapan was opened in the late 1980s. The Studio Art Gallery, organized by Luisa Julian de Arechiga, ran for three years from 1988 and held shows by, among others, Peter D'Addio, Xill Fessenden, Bill Gentes, B R Kline, Dimitar and Helen Krustev, Sid Miller, Georg Rauch and Sid Sklar.[3]

Ajijic Society of the Arts

The early meetings of the Ajijic Society of the Arts, founded in 1986, were held at Posada Ajijic, and its first president was Xavier Pérez Aguilar. Membership of the society has grown from 120 artists in 2003 to about 230 in 2020. The society initiated an Annual Studio Art Walk in 2012;

by 2020 this included around 100 artists at 30 different locations. The Ajijic Society of the Arts supports the Children's Art Program and the Ajijic Balloon Festival (Festival de Globos). It also organizes an annual Art Camp for about 150 lucky young artists.

Weekly art fair

Despite all the galleries that had come and gone, the opportunities available in the 1980s for home-grown artists to exhibit remained relatively limited. As a direct result of being excluded from one of Ajijic's "elite" galleries, Jesús López Vega, Jesús Higuera, Daniel Palma and others combined forces in August 1989 to hold an open-air art show, Expoarte Ajijic 89.[4] The event, on Calle Galeana (behind the church), had art displays, performances and food stands offering local culinary specialties. This was the forerunner of El Callejón del Arte (Art Alleyway), the open air art fair held weekly, weather permitting, along the north side of the plaza.

Ajijic Cultural Center

López Vega and his colleagues then organized a second event, Artistic and Cultural Pavilion Ajijic 89 (Pabellón Artístico y Cultural Ajijic 89), in which they commandeered the building on the north side of the plaza (now the Ajijic Cultural Center) in November 1989, during the annual fiesta de San Andrés, for an exhibition of paintings and photographs.[5] The activism of these artists led to the building being designated a Casa de Cultura in 1992.

Further lobbying resulted in it being transformed, with the help of architect Luz María Briseño, into the Centro Cultural Ajijic (Ajijic Cultural Center), which opened in 2004 and was officially inaugurated the following year.[6] A building which had been used from the 1980s for (successively) a market, storeroom, dances, cockfights and an evening *secundaria* finally received a new lease of life as a central venue for visual, music and theater arts in the community.

The first director of the Cultural Center was Luis Anselmo Ávalos Rochín, a graduate of the Children's Art Program. Ávalos was a successful commercial artist who had run the Galeria Eclipse art and interior decoration workshop-gallery in Ajijic.[7] He was especially active in all annual village celebrations and festivities, and the mastermind behind Ajijic's Day of the Dead cultural festival, held annually since 2003.

Ajijic Center for Fine Arts (CABA)

The art cooperative CABA (Centro Ajijic de Bellas Artes), organized by sculptor Estela Hidalgo and photographer Xill Fessenden, opened on Calle Colón in 1993. Each of its nine founder members—Estela Hidalgo, Xill Fessenden, Carole D'Addio, Peter D'Addio, Guadalupe Rivera, Sergio Cuevas, Georg Rauch, Pat Apt and Bill Gentes—had their own exhibit space. Additional rooms were set aside for temporary shows and folk art, and the center had a garden restaurant run by Ricardo González and Isabel Pedroza.[8] At its height, CABA had about seventy members, each of whom could enter works in bimonthly juried group shows. CABA ran for about eight years and its legacy includes a book of color photographs of works by fifty artists then active in the Lake Chapala area.[9]

Social activist Fessenden has regularly exhibited her superb artistic photographs in Ajijic. Mexico City-born artist-environmentalist Estela Hidalgo has undertaken commissions for a UNESCO event and for the Pan American Games in Guadalajara; the carved tree stump on Ajijic plaza is a particularly fine example of her work.

Foreign artists

Sociologist Francisco Talavera's unkind take on art in Ajijic in the late 1970s and early 1980s was that, "exhibitions abound. Every 'gringo' believes themselves to be an artist."[10] Ajijic has certainly been home to a plethora of foreign artists since 1980. But Talavera failed to appreciate how many of them had a well-deserved international reputation. Though not necessarily a representative sample, the following artists illustrate the amazing variety of individuals who have found creative inspiration in Ajijic in recent decades.

Visual artist and lecturer Buddy Ryan Kline, lived in Ajijic from 1983 to 1992. Kline toured the world and amassed a collection of 91 paintings, one for each country he had visited.[11] At his home-studio at Aquiles Serdan 3, he did commercial art for *El Ojo del Lago*.[12] The Lake Chapala Society owns a fine Kline portrait of Neill James. Both Kline and Sid Schwartzman had a profound influence on exceptionally skilled artist and muralist Efrén González.

Brooklyn-born William (Bill) Gentes specialized in lithographs, woodblocks and (later) linoprints during the decades he lived at Lake Chapala. Gentes retired to Mexico in 1970 to live initially in San Miguel de Allende. He explored the country on local buses seeking inspiration, before settling at Lake Chapala in 1979. A founder member of CABA, Gentes employed his art and his impish sense of humor to engage with social and political injustices. His artworks from the 1980s often portrayed scenes in Ajijic, including the Posada Ajijic.

Also born in Brooklyn was accomplished saxophonist and amateur artist Sid Miller, who bore an uncanny resemblance in later life to Albert Einsten, and moved to Ajijic to paint and sculpt in 1982. Miller made no effort to commercialize his highly original sculptures and paintings, and preferred to give them away to friends and family.[13]

Two Japanese-born artists made San Antonio Tlayacapan their home in recent years. Mine Oka arrived in Mexico in the mid-1970s to study in Mexico City and was living in San Antonio by 1985.[14] He has held numerous exhibits in Mexico and his native Japan, as has Masaharu Shimada, who specializes in sumi-e pen and ink drawings. Shimada settled in San Antonio Tlayacapan in 1986. His works include numerous evocative impressionist landscapes of Ajijic and San Antonio Tlayacapan.

Wisconsin-born Carol Hoorn Fraser, who spent most of her art career in Canada, lived in Ajijic over the winter of 1989–1990. She made several superb drawings and paintings of the village and of her temporary home there, including a watercolor posthumously titled "All the Trumpets Sounded," based on the gates of the Ajijic cemetery.[15] Fraser's realist-expressionist landscapes have been favorably compared by some critics to the works of Frida Kahlo and Georgia O'Keeffe.

Professional photographer Jack Weatherington moved to Ajijic in 1988 and quickly became fascinated with Mexican masks. Weatherington, often working with local photographer José Hinojosa, took some magnificent images of Ajijic, which were marketed as postcards. Active in the Ajijic Society of the Arts, Weatherington also took sensitive portraits of some of Ajijic's most famous residents, including Neil James.

Commercial artists

Three of the more interesting examples of the many commercial artists active in Ajijic over the past forty years are Josefa Ibarra, Rebeca Jonsson and Billy Moon.

Ibarra, born in 1919, was almost ten years old before her birth was registered in Coahuila, northern Mexico. Raised mainly in the US before returning to Mexico as an adult, she was the creative genius behind the fashion label Josefa. Her elegant and original dresses and blouses, inspired by indigenous textile patterns, were worn by the likes of Elizabeth Taylor, Glenda Jackson, Sophia Loren, Diana Ross, Nancy Reagan and Deborah Kerr. Josefa built her own home-studio near San Juan Cosalá in about 1980; her company, active from the 1960s to the 1980s, won a National Export Prize seven years in a row, and she is widely regarded as "the mother of Mexican fashion," responsible for first showcasing Mexican styles on the world haute couture stage.

Jonsson opened a soft sculpture atelier producing "whimsical Christmas dolls" and teddy bears in San Antonio Tlayacapan in the early 1980s to supply retail stores throughout Mexico. With a couple of helpers, her workshop (*taller*) was turning out dozens of original designs and as many as 15,000 figures a year, all with individually handpainted or embroidered faces.[16]

Texas-born entrepreneur Moon built up a veritable business empire in Ajijic in the late-1980s, designing and manufacturing his bespoke furniture and household accessories at his own exclusive factory and showrooms, the Moon Collection, on Río Zula in west Ajijic. At its peak, the company was employing more than 100 workers and shipping a container-load of items to the US each week.[17] Moon's designs, sold in outlets ranging from Neiman Marcus to Disneyland, won numerous international decorative art awards. Moon closed his Ajijic premises in 1998 to move to Asia.

Creative Writing

Dozens of poets have found inspiration at Ajijic over the years. Of those active in the latter part of the twentieth century, three deserve a special mention: Regina deCormier Shekerjian, Aileen Melby and Jan Richman.

Poet, author and illustrator Regina Shekerjian and her husband, photographer Haig Shekerjian, were regular visitors to the village from the 1950s to the 1980s. The dining room of La Nueva Posada in Ajijic has a permanent exhibition of Haig's evocative photographs of what the Lake Chapala area was like years ago, evidence, if any were needed, of the couple's immense enthusiasm for the area and its people. Several poems in Regina's book *Hoofbeats on the Door: Poems* (1993) are about life in Ajijic.

Aileen Melby, a poet and children's novelist, lived at Lake Chapala from 1970 to 1973 and then retired to Ajijic in 1986. Melby published

Song for Mexico, a collection of poems about the Lake Chapala area, in 1991. Many of her poems encapsulate the winds and storms that characterize Ajijic's annual summer rainy season.

California poet and novelist Jan Richman's poem "Ajijic" was first published in 1994,[18] and reprinted in her first poetry collection, *Because the Brain Can Be Talked Into Anything*, which won the 1994 Walt Whitman Award from the Academy of American Poets.

The stand-out novel from the final years of the twentieth century related to Ajijic is (despite its title) *A Chance to See Egypt*, written by Sandra Scofield following her visit in the early 1990s. The action takes place against a backdrop of two villages—Lago de Luz and Tecatitlán—that are a fictionalized mash-up of Ajijic and Chapala. The novel won the Best Fiction award from the Texas Institute of Letters in 1996. Scofield acknowledges that her writing was helped by the book *Village in the Sun*, by Dane Chandos, and it was clearly also influenced by my own travel guide to the region. I am greatly flattered that Scofield found my book useful!

The central character, Tom Riley, a widower, joins a writing class at the Lakeside Society Library given by the novel's narrator, Charlotte Amory. The two strike up a friendship and Amory helps Riley navigate his way through doubts and uncertainties towards a new and different life. The novel delves deeper into the cultural differences and resulting tensions between local townsfolk and their American visitors than other twentieth century novels set at Lake Chapala. The depictions of village life in *A Chance to See Egypt* are far more even-handed than those in Eileen Bassing's *Where's Annie?* or Willard Marsh's *Week with No Friday*, which both focus squarely on the expat community to the near-xclusion of their Mexican hosts.

Fast forward to this century, a whole slew of novels set in Ajijic have been published. They include Ruth Ross-Merrimer's *Champagne & Tortillas* (2001), William Schrader's *Kiss My Tears Away* (2002), T M Spooner's *Notes from Exile* (2006), John Hoopes' three Lake Chapala Serenade works (2011 onwards), two books by Carolena Torres—*Dust on their Hearts* (2013) and *Castles by the Lake* (2017)— Lilian Levy's *Death comes to Lake Chapala* (2016) and Jan Dunlap's *Dilemma* (2017). The first and the last named are especially interesting in terms of their historical perspective.

Ross-Merrimer (1925–2011) first visited Ajijic with her husband in 1966 when a film company contracted them to make seven documentary films for the Mexican National Tourist Department ahead of the 1968 Mexico Olympics. Ross-Merrimer returned to live in Ajijic from 1999 to 2004. *Champagne & Tortillas* is set in a retirement community called Lake Azul that is surprisingly like Ajijic, despite the customary disclaimer. It is a tale of loving, hating and backbiting that led to murder in a tightknit group of mainly US expatriates. Ross-Merrimer reported on local news for the *Guadalajara Reporter*, *El Ojo del Lago* and other English language publications, and was a founder member of the Ajijic Writers Group.

Texas-born Dunlap, who died in 2018, lived in Ajijic for more than thirty years (from 1967 to 1998). Known as Big Mama, she was one of the village's more colorful and warm-hearted characters. Dunlap ran a succession of restaurant-bars, boutiques and galleries, including El Tejaban, the Blackfoot Contessa Boutique, the Wes Penn Gallery, Big Mama's and El Tapanco, and headed the Rowdy Bunch which contributed its positive energy to many Ajijic events in the 1980s. *Dilemma*, her novel set in Ajijic, and loosely based on bar room gossip and her personal experiences, is an exciting tale about a drug-dealing cartel *capo* and a beautiful, youthful female DEA agent.

Fully deserving of the final word in this chapter, and in a category all of its own, is *According to Soledad*, the creative non-fiction memoir by Katie Goodridge Ingram, which recounts her childhood in Mexico City and Ajijic. Soledad (Ingram's persona in the book) considers herself part American and part Mexican: "My skin is white but my soul is brown." She knows city life with her family's sophisticated, multicultural, artistic friends; she also knows village life with no running water or electricity. Soledad manages two languages every day and is hyper-observant of the sometimes shocking differences among the Mexicans, Americans and foreigners in her life. This absorbing and stunningly well written book is an unrivaled account of what one young girl living in Ajijic in the 1940s and 1950s felt, thought and experienced.

49

Press and academic articles

Newspapers and magazines play an important role in communication, help educate people about news, events and issues, and provide a mirror for a community. The two main English-language print publications reporting news and events in Ajijic are the *Guadalajara Reporter* and *El Ojo del Lago*.[1] The earliest online publication related to Ajijic was *Mexico Connect*.

Guadalajara Reporter

The first edition of the weekly *Guadalajara Reporter*, originally known as *The Colony Reporter*, was on 19 December 1963. Its first regular Ajijic correspondent was Texas-born Anita Lomax (1915–1987), who arrived in Ajijic in 1956 and started as a columnist in 1964.[2] She was succeeded in about 1971 by Joe Weston. Two years later, Beverly Hunt started writing the Lake Chapala column.

The paper's content related to Ajijic (and Lake Chapala in general) increased significantly after Beverly and her husband, Allyn, purchased the paper in 1975. The Lake Chapala column was then written by Joan Frost for a year before Ruth Netherton took over.

After gaining a degree in Spanish from the University of Chicago, Netherton (1922–2002) and her husband, John, lived for many years in Central and South America and the Caribbean before they retired to Ajijic in 1974. Described by publisher Allyn Hunt as "both a sympathetic and probing columnist as well as a nononsense reporter," Netherton worked for the *Guadalajara Reporter* from 1977 to 1994.[3]

After relatively short stints by Tim Hogan, Merry Barrickman and Teresa Kendrick reporting Lake Chapala events, the next long-time correspondent was Jeanne Chaussee, who recorded the local news and social scene from about 2000 to 2013. Chaussee was succeeded by Dale Hoyt Palfrey, whose grandparents lived at Lake Chapala in the early 1950s, and who became a resident of Ajijic, with her husband, Wayne, in 1973. Bilingual journalist Palfrey has gained an enviable reputation as an intelligent, penetrating and thoughtful columnist, with an uncanny ability for writing succinct and accurate prose, however complex the issues.

El Ojo del Lago

The first issue of *El Ojo del Lago*, a free monthly, was printed in September 1984. Published by Richard Tingen, at the instigation of June Nay Summers (1916–2001) and her husband, Cody (1937–2011) who had only just retired to Ajijic, the magazine had Diane Murray as editor.[4] All the early issues were written by the Summers, who contributed to *El Ojo del Lago* for about a decade. Cody, a former US Navy officer, served as US Consular Warden at Lake Chapala.

Tod Johnson was appointed Editor-in-Chief in 1988, the same year the publication organized its first annual El Ojo del Lago Awards Show. Award-winning writer Rosamaría Casas, recently retired from the Mexican Foreign Service, took over as editor four years later. Casas was succeeded by Hollywood screenwriter Alejandro Grattan-Domínguez at the end of 1994.

Mexico Connect

Ajijic's presence on the internet began in 1996 when Canadians David and Dona McLaughlin moved to the village and used their retirement savings to launch an online monthly called *Mexico Connect* (now *MexConnect.com*). Its contents, in its early years, were heavily biased towards Ajijic and Lake Chapala. Mexico Connect gained a reputation for publishing high quality articles, managed several moderated forums for readers to exchange information and ideas, and provided the earliest online publicity and promotion for dozens of Ajijic organizations and businesses.

Studies of the Ajijic retirement community

By the 1970s the Ajijic retirement community was sufficiently established that it attracted academic attention. The earliest study, never formally published, was by Dr Edwin G Flittie, a professor of sociology at the University of Wyoming. Flittie visited in 1973 and subsequently presented copies of "Retirement in the Sun," his analysis of the retirement community, to the Lake Chapala Society Library.[5] Like several later studies of foreign migrants, Flittie considered the Chapala-Ajijic region as a single unit, and not as two communities with their distinct histories as regards tourism and retirement. Flittie interviewed more than 100 retirees and found that many had failed to appreciate the substantial cultural differences between the US and Mexico, or recognized that the emphasis for many local residents was "not on material gain but rather on the attainment of a satisfying existence traditionally based upon agrarian economic self-sufficiency."[6]

Flittie estimated that about 60% of retirees were aged 60 to 74, and 14% were 75 or older. Very few were fluent in Spanish and 88% reported that their social life centered on fellow expatriates and other English-speaking individuals. Flittie found that most retirees lived much as they would have lived in the US. The main problems they faced were related to excessive drinking, marital and family discord (men adapted better than women), boredom, bribery, interactions with the local community, domestic help and old age. Flittie returned briefly in December 1977 to research the impacts of the massive 1976 devaluation of the peso from 12.5 pesos to a dollar to about 22.5 pesos to a dollar.

Juan José Medeles Romero, in his 1975 thesis proposing an urban development plan for Ajijic, detailed how the village had approximately tripled in size between 1900 and 1950, and then doubled in size the following decade. And this was even before the addition of numerous subdivisions such as Rancho del Oro and La Floresta. Curiously, Medeles ignored the impacts of foreigners and only mentioned them in passing.[7]

In the late 1970s sociologist Francisco Talavera examined the varied impacts of foreign residents on Ajijic, as explained elsewhere in this book.[8]

This was also when anthropologist Eleanore Moran Stokes homed in on Ajijic. She divided the evolution of the village after 'Discovery' into three phases: Founder (1940s to mid 1950s), Expansionary (mid 1950s to mid 1970s) and Established Colony (mid 1970s into the 1980s).[9]

Several of her informants considered the representation of Ajijic in the Dane Chandos novels (Founder phase) to be non-fiction; to Stokes, this was "the local equivalent to a creation myth." The nature of migrants changed in each stage. During the Founder phase, Ajijic served, in her view, largely as an artists' colony. These "young single well-traveled" artists were resourceful and independent individuals who had little impact on the village beyond the employment of domestic help; most of them learned the language, liked the cuisine, and blended into the local community.

Later (Expansionary phase) arrivals tended to be members of the affluent and retired middle class, many of whom had traveled widely, either in the military or working for international corporations. These newer arrivals did materially change the village. The cash they infused into the local economy created "a new wage labor class in the village." They upgraded village homes to distinguish them from those of local families. By retaining their language, food and lifestyle preferences, these incomers established a social distance from their host community, even forming "privileged associations for recreation, friendship and religion." In essence, many of these migrants wanted to make many aspects of life in Ajijic more like the US.

Such tendencies continued into the Established Colony phase. Vacant houses became increasingly scarce, and agricultural land was parceled for vacation and retirement homes. The foreign community boosted philanthropic activities, especially those helping children, though this stage also saw a marked social stratification develop within the foreign community.

Stokes estimated that foreigners occupied about 300 of the 950 houses in the village in 1979, but comprised less than 8% of the population. Like Talavera, she viewed retirees as agents of change, not merely spectators of ongoing social processes, though they felt a sense of powerlessness in regards to what they saw as deficiencies in the provision of such services as water, electricity, telephone, garbage collection and police.

Sociologist Charlotte Wolf, who moved to Ajijic with husband Rene in the early 1990s, was interested in how individual retirees adapted and constructed a new life for themselves in Ajijic.[10]

Among the conclusions in 1997 of Lorena Melton Young, who looked specifically at US retirees, was that they created new jobs, donated to charities and hastened "modernization," but that their presence was driving up the cost of living for local people. In a later paper, Young offered a detailed description of the mourning ritual and other customs in Ajijic following the death of a child (*angelito*).[11]

The evolutionary framework developed by Stokes was used by geographer David Truly to examine how the type of migrant has changed over the years and to develop a matrix of retirement migration behavior. Like Stokes, Truly concluded in 2002 that newer visitors (including retirees), and unlike earlier migrants, had less desire to adapt to the local culture and were more keen on "importing a lifestyle" to the area.[12]

Stephen Banks, while living in Ajijic in 2002–2003, studied the identity narratives of retirees.[13] Interviewees depicted Mexicans, both generally and individually, as "happy, warm and friendly, polite and courteous, helpful and resourceful." However, at the same time, many shared instances in which they thought Mexicans had been untrustworthy, inaccessible, lazy and incompetent. The responses revealed:

a struggle to conserve cultural identities in the face of a resistant host culture that has been colonized.... The Lakeside economy is dominated by expatriate consumer demand; ... prices for real estate (routinely listed in US dollars), restaurant dining, hotel lodging and most consumer goods are higher than in comparable non-retirement areas; traditional Mexican community life centered around the family has been supplemented, and in some cases supplanted, by expatriate community life centered around public assistance and volunteer programs... and the uniform use of Spanish in public life is displaced by the use of English.

Lucía González Terreros is the lead author of two recent papers that explore the complexity of defining residential tourism and how alternative definitions relate to property rights, transaction costs and common goods. The research arose from her personal concerns about the rapid increase in the number of foreigners in Ajijic since 1990.[14]

Equally interesting is the work of Francisco Díaz Copado, who looked at how Ajijic is being shaped by both local and foreign "rituals," such as the annual Fiesta of San Andrés and the Chili Cookoff respectively. In his 2013 report, Díaz Copado also examined "the different ways in which people describe and name the different zones of Ajijic... [which] reflect some historical conflicts." Two annotated maps sharply contrast traditional locations and names with those used by retirees.[15]

Marisa Raditsch investigated the impacts of international migrants settling in the municipality of Chapala "based on the perceptions of Mexican people in the receiving context." This 2015 study found that these perceptions tended:

to be favorable in terms of generating employment and contributing to the community; and unfavorable in terms of rising costs of living and some changes in local culture. It is suggested that measures should be taken to better take advantage of the presence of migrants who may introduce human and financial capital into the community.[16]

Social anthropologist Vaira Avota, writing in 2016, looked at the relations between foreigners and locals in Ajijic. She contrasted "traditional immigrants," who had wanted to "integrate in Mexico, truly understand its culture, traditions... [learn] Spanish and willingly participate in local activities," and "new immigrants" who wanted to live in a version of the US transplanted to Lake Chapala.[17]

The impacts of this shift in migrant type were further explored by Mexican researcher Mariana Ceja Bojorge, who focused squarely on the relationships and interactions between local Ajijitecos and foreigners.[18] She concluded in 2021 that the shift "endangers the acceptance of the presence of the other," and that

> Although the presence of foreigners has generated economic well-being in the area, it has also been responsible for the reconfiguration of space, where locals have been forced to leave their territory.

This change of space is precisely the reason why a popular restaurant on Ajijic plaza was selected for the cover of this book. The plaza was originally a Mexican space, where locals filled water containers, met friends, gossiped, socialized and bargained at the weekly market. The chapel and all the stores around the plaza were exclusively run by village residents to meet local needs. In those years, if there was a center for foreigners it was the Posada Ajijic bar, restaurant and gardens.

The use of the plaza has changed. After Cine Ajijic opened on the north side of the plaza in 1969, its weekly English-language films actively encouraged foreigners (en masse) to share the same social space as the local community. The supermarket on the south side of the plaza also became a shared space for locals and foreigners, a dual role which continued after the premises became a bank. Stores and restaurants either owned by, or designed to serve, foreigners were established around the plaza. An even stronger foreign focus is evident in the plaza coffee shops which spill over onto what was formerly public space. This has inevitably resulted in a debate about the appropriateness of a private enterprise occupying public space, and whether even paid use, via concessions, is an acceptable tradeoff for the loss of such space. Compromise is needed by all; there will never be any one-size-fits-all solution to any of the issues arising from migration and cultural change.

Acknowledgments

This book would not have been possible without the extremely generous assistance offered by dozens of individuals and institutions.

The staff of the Archivo Histórico Municipal de Chapala have been unfailingly helpful. My particular thanks go to the late Armando Hermosillo Venegas, who oversaw the archives from 2001 to 2006, Zaida Cristina Reynoso Camacho, who was in charge of the archives from 2012 to 2015, and to Rogelio Ochoa Corona, who continues to actively promote the area's history via online videos since first managing the archives from 2015 to 2018.

Lake Chapala Society archivist Marianne O'Halloran and the Society's then executive director Terry Vidal graciously gave me free reign to scour the LCS archives in Ajijic, including its Neill James collection.

I am hugely indebted to Michael Forbes and Sean Godfrey for providing access to the invaluable archives of the *Guadalajara Reporter*, and to Lic. Blanca García Floriano, coordinator of the Hemeroteca Histórica del Biblioteca Pública del Estado de Jalisco "Juan José Arreola." The staff of the Archivo Municipal de Guadalajara were also extremely helpful.

Special thanks to archivist Heather Home and her administrative assistant, Lisa Gervais, for material from the Purdy archives at Queen's University in London, Ontario, Canada; and to J Weston Marshall, Archival Associate of the Special Collections Library of Texas Tech University; Frances Kaplan, Reference and Outreach Librarian, California Historical Society, San Francisco; Mary O'Neill, Visual Resources Librarian at Sewanee: The University of the South, Tennessee; and to the staff of the Seattle Public Library, of Bowdoin College in Brunswick, Maine, and of the Bancroft Library at UC Berkeley, Oakland, California.

Katie Goodridge Ingram's detailed recollections of life in Ajijic, and her thoughtful and eloquent responses to scores of random queries over several years, have greatly improved this book. Michael Eager enthusiastically shared his perspectives on the history of Ajijic and helped resolve several specific queries. Journalist Dale Hoyt Palfrey, a long-time resident of Ajijic, has been hugely supportive of this project from the start; her enthusiasm and willingness to share research materials in her possession has proved invaluable.

A special heartfelt thanks to Dr Kimberly Lamay Licursi for entrusting to my care her chance find, at an estate sale, of the 1940s photograph album once owned by the Johnsons (chapter 9).

Dozens of other individuals have also contributed, in a wide variety of ways, to this book. They include: Marcia Ackland-Sorensen, Pat Apt, Bill Atkinson, Dr Stephen Banks, Jeanora Bartlet, Alexandra Bateman, Toni Beatty, Dr Louise Bergman, Stephen Best, Alan Bowers, Dr R B Brown, Tom Brudenell, Penelope Caragonne, Janice Carter, Moreen Chater, Jane Clutton, Katharine Couto, Hilda Crump, Raymond Crump, Dinah DeVry, Elizabeth Hulings Diamond, Jan Dunlap, Pamela Duran, Michael Eager, Judy Eager, Sukey Elstob, Tom Faloon, Jane Farrar, Sylvia Fein, Xill Fessenden, Curtis Foust, Joan and John Frost, John Burdett Frost, Bill Gentes Jr., Efrén González, Ingrid Goodridge, Angelina Guzmán, Scott Hampson, Colette Hirata, Lee Hopper, Peter and Eunice Huf, Maricruz Ibarra, Tamara Janúz, Hans-Reinhard Koch, Iona Kupiec, Ana Andrea Javier McKeever, Rachel Lyn Johnson, Judy King, Nicole V Langley, John Lee, Mark Lewis, Antonio López Vega, Jesús López Vega, Agustín Velarde, Jill Maldonado, Joan Gilbert Martin, Dr Carol Shepherd McClain, Hilda Mendoza, Gail Michel de Guzmán, Judy Miller, Sari Mintz, Arthur Monroe, Nafeesa Monroe, Dionicio Morales, Nicolas Morris, Carmen Suzanne Mosqueda Melendy, Nancy Neel, Dr Marijane Osborn, Alan Pattison, Synnove Pettersen, Dani Porter-Lansky, Monica Porter, Phyllis Rauch, Abby Rubinstein, Thomas Ryerson, Ricardo Santana, David Schwartzman, Sandra Scofield, Milagros Sendis, Monique Señoret, Don Shaw, Charles J Shields, Marsha Sorenson, Loy Strother, Tom Thomson, Dr David Truly, Jorge Varela Martínez Negrete, Dr Jim Vaughan, Enrique Velázquez, Stephanie Wallach and Timothy G Ruff Welch. Sadly, several of those named passed away before they could see their contributions in print. I am extremely grateful to all these individuals—and to any I have inadvertently omitted—for so willingly sharing their knowledge, ideas, memories and insights, without which this book could never have been completed.

Kudos also to artist Peter Shandera for his generosity in allowing his watercolor of Ajijic plaza to be used on the cover.

Last, but certainly not least, I owe an immense debt to my soulmate, Gwen, for her continued, unwavering support and good humor throughout the extended process of researching and writing this book.

Chapter notes

Abbreviations

AHA: Archivo Histórico del Agua.
AMG: Archivo Municipal de Guadalajara.
AHMC: Archivo Histórico Municipal de Chapala.
BPEJ: Acervo Histórico del Biblioteca Pública del Estado de Jalisco "Juan José Arreola."
CMAC: Catastro Municipal del Ayuntamiento de Chapala.
GR: *Guadalajara Reporter*, previously *The Colony Reporter* (1963–1987) and *The Colony Guadalajara Reporter* (1987–2006).
HNDM: Hemeroteca Nacional Digital de México.
LCSA: Lake Chapala Society Archive.
LSPY: Laura Stedman papers, Yale Collection of American Literature, Beinecke Rare Book and Manuscript Library.
NJA: The Neill James Archive, held by the Lake Chapala Society.

Introduction

1. All figures in this section, unless otherwise stated, come from the results of Mexico's national census, held every ten years. The 2020 census listed Ajijic and San Antonio Tlayacapan as a single district with 13,031 inhabitants. The estimates are based on trends.

2. Alex von Mauch may have been the only foreigner living in Ajijic in 1930, but he was not the first foreigner to live or own property in Ajijic.

3. GR, 6 March 1976.

4. These figures were derived by deducting the number recorded as born in Jalisco and the number for those born elsewhere in Mexico from the total population figures.

Chapter 1. Ajijic before 1940

1. Antonio Tello, *Libro segundo*. Translated excerpts of this and several other early accounts are available, with commentary, in *Lake Chapala Through the Ages: an anthology of traveler's tales*.

2. Menéndez Valdés, *Descripción y censo general*.

3. Bárcena, *Ensayo estadístico*. Quote is from translation published in *Lake Chapala Through the Ages*, chapter 34.

4. Embree, *A Dream of a Throne*, 155.

5. *La Gaceta Comercial*, 5 December 1899, 3.

6. Stephens, *Louis E. Stephens*.

7. Yogananda, "Ode to Lake Chapala."

8. *El Informador*, 16 November 1919, 3 October 1920.

9. *El Informador*, 22 August 1931.

10. *El Informador*, 15 May 1934.

11. *El Informador*, 14 April 1935.

12. Leo L. Stanley. "Mixing in Mexico", 1937. Leo L. Stanley Papers, MS 2061, California Historical Society. Vol. 1, 46.

13. Old and new names compiled from land records; Milagros Sendis, personal communication; and Federico Frances Navarro. "How I knew Ajijic," in *Conecciones* (LCS), two parts: May 2020, 26; June 2020, 13.

14. "The Idols of San Juan Cosala" was first published in the December 1936 issue of *American Junior Red Cross News*.

15. Katie Goodridge Ingram. "Helen Kirtland Goodridge," in Bateman and Bollenbach, *Ajijic*, 92–93.

16. Parsons' comments are quoted in Desley Deacon. 1999. *Elsie Clews Parsons: Inventing Modern Life*. University of Chicago Press.

17. Talavera Salgado, *Lago Chapala*, 71.

18. Gallop, *Mexican Mosaic*.

Chapter 2. German land-grabber

1. Hans Jaacks' parents were Heinrich Bernhard Jaacks (1832–1909) and Louise Dorothea Catharina Vest (1833–1908), known in Mexico as Doris Vest de Jaacks.

2. Jaacks acquired the pharmacy from "Enrique Weitenaver" (probably a transliteration of Heinrich Wiedenhöfer).

3. Jalisco State Archives, Caja 1, Expedientes 32 and 43, both from 1892. Example of advertisement: *Heraldo-Seminario,* 28 April 1895, 1.

4. See note 21, p 32, of Araceli Ibarra Bellon. 1995. "La consolidación de las relaciones entre México y Estados unidos en el Porfiriato; su impacto en Jalisco, 1876–1910" in Arroyo Alejandre, *Ajustes y desajustes.*

5. Morales López, *Santos Rico*, 35.

6. AMG: Gobierno del Estado de Jalisco. 1897. *Memoria del Estado de Jalisco*, 1894–1896, 159. The report is dated 16 November 1896, a few weeks after Jaacks had been murdered.

7. Rogelio Ochoa Corona, personal communication.

8. Morales López, *Santos Rico*, 35.

9. Documents from Chapala municipal archives, quoted in Cristina, *Chapala, Siglo XIX, Tomo II*, 130–132. The counter-claim names the mayor as a Señor Barba. However, according to the official list of Chapala mayors, the mayor in 1896 was Pablo Serna.

10. *Diario del Hogar*, 7 November 1896.

11. *El Nacional*, 6 November 1896, 1; *Diario del Hogar*, 7 November 1896; Rogelio Ochoa Corona, personal communication, March 2020.

12. *Diario del Hogar*, 7 November 1896.

13. Carreño, *Guad-alhajero*. Multiple sources identify the humble local as Sra Pomposa Ortega.

14. Rogelio Ochoa Corona, personal communication, May 2018.

15. Juan Jaacks, aged 20, the "son of Juan Jaacks and Rosario Covarrubias," married Maximina Contreras (16) on 16 November 1912. José Jaacks (aged 26, same parents) married María Briseño (22) in Mexico City on 2 February 1921.

16. Legal notice in *El Informador*, 4 April 1969.

17. Sebastian Sainz Peña (ca 1851–1927), married to Maria Dolores Stephenson Zambrano (1869–1958), was a wealthy Spanish farmer and merchant with property interests in Ajijic and Chapala at the start of the twentieth century. The land included a

lot sold to the Victor Hunton and his wife for Villa Virginia. See chapter 31 of Burton, *If Walls Could Talk*.

18. Morales López, *Santos Rico*, 34–39.

Chapter 3. Ajijic gold rush

1. Cresencio García, "Impresiones de un Viaje a Chápala," *El Constitucionalista*, Morelia, 29 June 1868.

2. AHMC, "La Mineria en Ajijic."

3. AHMC, "La Mineria en Ajijic."

4. AHMC, "La Mineria en Ajijic."

5. *El Siglo Diez y Nueve*, 21 June 1887, 3.

6. Sources for Table 2 are AHMC. "La Mineria en Ajijic." *Arizona Republican* (Phoenix, Arizona), 23 January 1906. *Diario Oficial de la Federación*, 1905-1912. *El Nacional*, 14 August 1888, 3. *El Tiempo*, 19 October 1906. *Jalisco Times*, 6 February 1904; 20 February 1904; 12 July 1907. *La Voz de Mexico*, 5 August 1887; 15 November 1887, 2; 24 May 1907, 2. *The Daily Herald* (Brownsville, Texas), 28 December 1895. *The Mexican Herald*, 21 March 1898; 22 August 1909, 3; 8 February 1911, 9.

7. Boehm Schoendube, "Cartografía Histórica."

8. *The Mexican Herald*, 23 March 1904, 3.

9. *Los Angeles Times*, 6 March 1926, 1.

10. *Arizona Republican* (Phoenix, Arizona), 23 January 1906.

11. *Jalisco Times*, reprinted in *El Paso Daily Times*, 13 September 1906, 5.

12. Dollero, *México al día*.

13. A ten-stamp mill crushes ore using two groups of five 750-pound stamps which rise and fall about 6 inches, 35 times a minute.

14. *Jalisco Times* 20 September 1907.

15. *The Mexican Herald*, 4 February 1909; reprinted in *Los Angeles Herald*, 8 February 1909, 12.

16. *The Mexican Herald*, 22 August 1909, 3.

17. *The Mexican Herald*, 15 December 1909, 15.

18. Idella Purnell had taken poetry classes in California with Witter Bynner; she and her father became friends with D H Lawrence when he and Bynner stayed in Chapala in 1923.

19. *The Mexican Herald*, 15 December 1909, 15.

20. *El Paso Herald*, 23 December 1909.

21. See Burton, *If Walls Could Talk*.

22. *Diario Oficial de la Federación*, 3 August 1917.

23. William S Stone. "La Soñadora," *Mexican Life*, March 1947, 13-14, 74-84.

Chapter 4. Zara "La Rusa"

1. Charlotte Welles Saenger (1865–1949), aka Nayan Saenger and Charlotte Welles Nayan St Albans Saenger, was born in Wayne, New York, and died in Ajijic. Saenger was the organist at the historic Episcopal Church of the Incarnation at Madison and 35th Street in New York, and was one of just four female organists in the 145 founders of the American Guild of Organists in 1896, the year Zara was born. (*New York Tribune*, 13 January 1896; and Stephen Best, personal communication.) Despite claims to the contrary, Zara's maternal grandfather, Charles D Welles (1830–1909), had no direct connection to Gideon Welles (1802–1878).

2. The Saengers had a box at the gala opening of the Metropolitan Opera season in 1907, as did the Duchess of Marlborough, the Pulitzers and the Guggenheims. (*New York*

Times, 5 November 1907). See "The Little Girl who always had her own way" in *Salt Lake Tribune*, 23 January 1916; and "What would you do with a million?" in *Buffalo Courier* (Buffalo, New York) 25 June 1916, 76.

3. *Penn Yan Democrat*, 26 February 1915, 2; Bide Dudley. 1915. "About Plays and Players", *The Evening World*, 12 November 1915; *The Nation*, 2 December 1915.

4. *The New York Dramatic Mirror*, 15 April 1916. The cities included New York; St. Louis, Missouri; Taylor, Texas; Bryan, Texas; and Wichita and Junction City in Kansas.

5. *The Owensboro Messenger* (Owensboro, Kentucky), 29 December 1916, 2.

6. *Los Angeles Evening Express*, 19 October 1918, 8. *The New York Dramatic Mirror*, 2 November 1918.

7. J P Wearing. 2014. *The London Stage 1920–1929: A Calendar of Productions, Performers, and Personnel*. Rowman & Littlefield Publishers.

8. (a) *Ottawa Evening Journal*, 26 November 1921. A special benefit performance was later organized to help pay the cast, with Ruby Miller appearing in Zara's role. (b) *Pittsburgh Post-Gazette*, 8 February 1922; *The Evening World* (New York City), 9 February 1922.

9. *El Informador* (Guadalajara), 15 August 1944.

10. The artistic directors of Ballets Suédois included Swedish artist Nils Dardel, who later lived in Chapala while completing paintings for a major exhibition in New York. George Dorris. 1999. "The Choreography of Jean Borlin, A Checklist with the Tours and Personnel of Les Ballets Suédois," *Dance Chronicle*, Vol. 22, No. 2 (1999), 189–222.

11. Ayenara Zara Alexeyewa. 2001. "El Hermanito." *La Pirouette Danza*, #33, May–June 2001: Guadalajara: Gobierno del Estado de Jalisco (Secretaría de Cultura), 8.

12. *The Red Terror* was a ballet by Max Marceau based on a poem by Leonid Andreyev and arranged by Zara; *The Black Swan and the Lily* was based on a story by a family friend Kaia Heliostalakti, with music by Russian composer Vladimir de Butzow. Itinerary based on press clippings; de Brundige, *Quilocho*, 189–193; LSPY: Undated booklet compiled by Zara (YCAL MSS 291 Box 5 f. 67).

13. LSPY: Letter from Zara (on Vapor Palerma) to Laura Stedman (YCAL MSS 291 Box 5 f. 67).

14. de Brundige, *Quilocho*, 210.

15. LSPY: Letter, 12 July 1924, from Nayan Saenger (Mexico City) to Laura Stedman; letter, 14 Sept 1924, from Zara (Mexico City) to Laura Stedman (YCAL MSS 291 Box 5 f. 69).

16. LSPY: Letter, 14 September 1924, from Zara (Mexico City) to Laura Stedman (YCAL MSS 291 Box 5 f. 69).

17. *El Informador*, 7 December 1924, 4; 11 December 1924, 7; 12 December 1924. José María Cuéllar, Guadalajara mayor, offered the use of the theater, and the Guadalajara Symphony Orchestra provided the music; the performance was on Saturday 10 January 1925.

18. *El Informador*, 12 December 1924, 4, 6. Villa Reynera is pictured on the cover of Burton, *Lake Chapala Through The Ages*.

19. GR, 23 September 1977. The curious choice of Nauollin as a title presumably alluded to Nahui Olin, the name adopted by Carmen Mondragón, the nymphomaniac lover of the famous painter Dr Atl (Gerardo Murillo).

20. Jackson, *Burros and Paintbrushes*, 23, 27.

21. (a) LSPY: Letter, 29 June 1925, from Zara (Mexico City) to Laura Stedman (YCAL MSS 291 Box 5 f. 67). (b) Letter, 14 July 1925, from Zara (Chapala) to Idella Purnell, in possession of Purnell's daughter, Dr Marijane Osborn. The mentalist was "Professor" W Bert Reese, a celebrity sleight of hand performer.

22. Letter, 14 July 1925, from Zara (Chapala) to Idella Purnell, in possession of Purnell's daughter, Dr Marijane Osborn.

23. Letter, 14 July 1925, from Zara to Idella Purnell, in possession of Dr Marijane Osborn. The letter was signed "Zara Saenger."

24. LSPY: Letter, 30 June 1925, from Nayan (Guadalajara) to Laura Stedman.

25. LSPY: Letter, 29 July 1925, from Nayan (Chapala) to Laura Stedman.

26. *Reading Times* (Pennsylvania), 21 April 1927.

27. *East–West*, Vol. 2 #4 (May–June 1927).

28. *East–West*, Vol. 4 #3 (Nov–Dec 1929). See "Spiritual leader and poet Paramahansa Yogananda (1893–1952)." https://lakechapalaartists.com/?p=1445.

29. The performances were originally scheduled for Saturday 22 June and Sunday 23 June. The Saturday performance was canceled because Zara was unwell and replaced by a Monday performance.

30. *El Informador*, 7 November 1929, 4.

31. de Brundige, *Quilocho*, 326.

32. de Brundige, *Quilocho*, 329, 340–341.

33. *El Informador*, 15 August 1944, 9.

34. CMAC: historial catastral.

35. *El Informador*, 15 August 1944, 9.

36. Katie Goodridge Ingram, personal communication.

37. Pennsylvania State Archives, Land Office Records, W2. F&W 335.

Chapter 5. Zara's gold mine

1. Letter, 14 July 1925, from Zara (Chapala) to Idella Purnell (California) in possession of Purnell's daughter, Dr Marijane Osborn.

2. LSPY: Letter, 29 June 1925, from Zara (Chapala) to Laura Stedman.

3. The mentalist was W Bert Reese, whose exploits attracted massive audiences. Reese fell ill in Mexico in 1925 and died the following year in his native Germany. (*The Burlington Free Press* (Vermont) 12 July 1926, 2.)

4. LSPY: Letter, 29 July 1925, from Nayan Saenger (Chapala) to Laura Stedman.

5. Susan Taylor, personal communication via Stephen Best.

6. Talavera Salgado, *Lago Chapala*, 66.

7. James, *Dust on my Heart*, 2801; NJA: James and Ivon, undated document : "Gold in Ajijic 35 years ago."

8. de Brundige, *Quilocho,* 337 on. In *Quilocho*, the mine is La Misericordia and the lawyer Catalino Rameño.

9. James, "Mexican Story."

10. de Brundige, *Quilocho*, 347, 385.

11. *El Informador*, 19 November 1934, 1

12. *El Informador*, 8 March 1935, 1; 27 March 1935, 6; 29 March 1936, 6. SCL = Sociedad Cooperativa Limitada.

13. *El Informador*, 1 August 1935, 4, 6.

14. Ruth Netherton. 1977. GR, 13 August 1977, 17.

15. Archivo Histórico del Agua (AHA) caja 2108 exp 31803.

16. CMAC: historial catastral. The administrator of Minerales de Chapala, SA, was Benjamin Gaysinsky, a Russianborn Jewish banker and businessman who lived in Guadalajara. Federal concession: See Talavera Salgado, *Lago Chapala*, 16, and Archivo Histórico del Agua, Caja 1357 exp 18300.

17. CMAC: historial catastral.

Chapter 6. Austrian lakefront orchard

1. *El Informador*, 28 November 1932, 5.

2. *El Informador*, 10 December 1922, 3, 5.

3. *El Informador*, 14 February 1923, 6; 16 February 1923, 8; Pierre Noziere. 1923. "El Concierto de Anoche en el Degollado", *El Informador*, 17 February 1923, 7.

4. CMAC: historial catastral for Calle Independencia 26 (formerly Calle Independencia 20). Strohbach, born in California on 17 August 1891 to two German born immigrants, William and Paulina Strohbach, graduated from the University of California Berkeley in 1914 and joined the American Institute of Mining in 1916.

5. AHA (Archivo Histórico del Agua), Caja 796 exp 11536.

6. *El Informador*, 19 February 1929, 4.

7. *El Informador*, 6 June 1930, 4.

8. CMAC: historial catastral includes record of improvements dated 26 May 1934 to Von Mauch property.

9. *El Informador*, 13 May 1934, 4.

10. *El Informador* 18 July 1935, 7.

11. (a) Ida Harris. 1935. "Eleanor Armstrong Bride of Former Army Officer." *Los Angeles Times*, 31 July 1935, 30. (b) Anon. "Laguna Beach Artist, Baron Wed in Mexico", *Santa Ana Register*, 29 July 1935, 13.

12. James, *Dust on my Heart*, 284.

13. *El Informador*, 17 November 1935.

14. *El Informador*, 22 November 1935, 1, 2. Jalisco death certificate.

15. *El Informador*, 3 May 1936, 4; 8 May 1936, 4.

16. *Los Angeles Times,* 02 January 1937, 3; 26 September 1937, 66.

17. For example *El Informador*, 24 July 1937, 4.

Chapter 7. Ajijic in the 1940s

1. Talavera Salgado, *Lago Chapala*, 71.

2. Leo L. Stanley. "Mixing in Mexico", 1937, two volumes. Leo L. Stanley Papers, MS 2061, California Historical Society.

3. Parmenter, *Stages in a Journey*, chapter 3.

4. *El Informador*, 27 August 1945.

5. Brian Boru Dunne. 1946. "Village Gossip," in *Santa Fe New Mexican* (Santa Fe, New Mexico) 3 October 1946, 9. Though the precise number is unknown, there were more than fourteen foreigners living in Ajijic in 1946.

6. Renée George. "Ay Naranjos." *Modern Mexico*, Vol 22, #2, Mar–Apr 1949, 16–17, 28–29.

7. Helm, *Journeying Through Mexico*, chapter 9.

8. Upton, "Ahheeheek."

9. Kernick, "Ajijic."

Chapter 8. Rustic German inn

1. Katie Goodridge Ingram, personal communication.

2. Classified advertisement in *El Informador*, 21 May 1933.

3. James, "Mexican Story."

4. Compton, *To The Isthmus*, 167.

5. Laura Bateman, "Mexico 1952", in Bateman and Bollenbach, *Ajijic*, 72.

6. Compton, *To The Isthmus*, 143–150.

7. Kernick, "Ajijic."

8. Netherton, "More about the Way it Was."

9. James, *Dust on my Heart*, 272, 275, 276.

10. James, "Mexican Story."

11. James, *Dust on My Heart*, 114–118.

12. Laura Bateman, "Mexico 1952" in Bateman and Bollenbach, *Ajijic*, 72.

13. *El Informador*, 27 August 1945.

14. Sylvia Fein, personal communication.

15. Katie Goodridge Ingram, personal communication.

16. *El Informador*, 27 September 1945, 19.

17. Kenesaw M. Landis II. 1946. "Revolution jitters develop quickly in Mexico Tourists." *The St. Louis Star and Times* (St. Louis, Missouri) 17 April 1946, 23.

18. The harrowing story of Nola, a brilliant young girl who descended into schizophrenia, is compassionately told by Robin Hemley (Gottlieb's younger son by Cecil Hemley) in *Nola: A Memoir of Faith, Art, and Madness* (University of Iowa Press in 2013).

19. *Kingston Daily Freeman*: 12 September 1947.

20. Katie Goodridge Ingram, personal communication.

21. Text from images of postcard sold on eBay.

22. This version, albeit with several factual inaccuracies, appears in Talavera Salgado, *Lago Chapala*, note 42, 159–160.

Chapter 9. English squire's famous garden

1. Edgar Ellinger, Jr. 1953. "Mexican Town Offers Peaceful Way of Life." *Arizona Republic*, 2 August 1953, Section 2, 8.

2. 1911 UK Census.

3. Herbert Johnson. Handwritten weather log in possession of the author, 94.

4. NJA: James, "Mexican Story."

5. Gail Eiloart, personal communication.

6. NJA: James, "Mexican Story."

7. Katie Goodridge Ingram, personal communication.

8. Milagros Sendis. Unpublished manuscript "Recuerdos de Ajijic" shared with author 7 January 2021.

9. Elizabeth Schuler. 1964. *Gardens of the World*. (Translation of *Mein Garten Mein Paradies*, published in Germany in 1962). London: MacDonald, 160–161.

10. Parmenter, *Stages in a Journey*, 86–91.

11. *Diario Oficial de la Federación*, 13 March 1943.

12. Archivo Histórico del Agua (AHA), Caja 1193 expediente 16197.

13. Katie Goodridge Ingram, personal communication.

14. Article (written by James herself), *El Informador*, 19 December 1944, 12.

15. James, *Dust on my Heart*, 293; Sylvia Fein, personal communication.

16. *El Informador*, 18 November 1944, 6.

17. Sylvia Fein, personal communication.

18. Katie Goodridge Ingram, personal communication.

19. Milagros Sendis. Unpublished manuscript "Recuerdos de Ajijic" shared with author 7 January 2021.

20. Katie Goodridge Ingram, personal communication.

21. Netherton, "More about the Way it Was."

22. Katie Goodridge Ingram, personal communication.

23. Photo album in possession of author.

24. Colette Hirata (Helen's daughter), personal communication.
25. *El Informador*, 9 September 1949.

Chapter 10. Posada Ajijic

1. Rogelio Ochoa Corona, personal communication, May 2018.
2. Morales López, *Santos Rico*, 34–39.
3. Toby Smith. 1986. *Romantic Inns of Mexico: A Selective Guide to Charming Accommodations South of the Border*. Chronicle Books Inc.
4. Their home at that time was 16 de Septiembre 312; Posada Ajijic was 16 de Septiembre 317.
5. Mary Frances Kennedy Fisher. 1943. *The Gastronomical Me*. New York: Duell, Sloan and Pearce.
6. This marriage was on 18 January 1947.
7. *El Informador*, 10 March 1945.
8. *El Informador*, 27 August 1945, 11.
9. James, "Ajijic Carrousel."
10. Katie Goodridge Ingram, personal communication.
11. Frances Toor. 1948. *New Guide To Mexico* (New Revised Edition 1948). New York: Crown Publishers, 182.

Chapter 11. Dane Chandos books

1. *Britannia and Eve*, 1 July 1948, 41.
2. Marquis of Ruvigny and Raineval. 1907. *The Plantagenet roll of the blood royal: being a complete table of all the descendants now living of Edward III....* London: T C & E C Jack.
3. *The Oxford University Calendar*, volumes for 1923 to 1927 inclusive.
4. A T Michell (reviser). 1929. *Rugby School Register*, vol 4, 488, 571. The ancestor was Richard Oke Millett (1749–1832). Millett's other works included *Wanton Boys* (1932), *India's Coral Strand* (1934), and *Strange Island Story* (1939), which was published after he had moved to Mexico.
5. *London Gazette*, 26 January 1937, 596.
6. NJA: James, "Mexican Story." I have been unable to find the column James refers to.
7. Catherine A. MacKenzie. 2011. "Three Authors in the Sun", *Lake Chapala Review*, vol 13 #1, 15 January 2011.
8. Rodney Gallop. 1948. "Rural Mexico: Village in the Sun. By Dane Chandos." (Review), *The Spectator*, 17 June 1948, 22.
9. Several details in Gallop's account suggest he visited in 1938 rather than 1937.
10. CMAC: land transactions.
11. Herbert Johnson. Handwritten weather log (1939 on) in possession of the author.
12. Bedford, *A Visit to Don Otavio*, 109, 248, 251.
13. *El Informador*, 18 November 1944.
14. *El Informador*, 19 December 1944, 12.
15. *El Informador*, 27 August 1945.
16. Back cover text of 1999 reprint of *House in the Sun*.
17. Los libros de Frida: http://regionplural.com/los libros de frida/
18. Nigel Millett died in Guadalajara on 25 March 1946.
19. Mary Chase Hardy Woodward, 1985. "Posada Ajijic." Sixteen-page promotional booklet. Guadalajara: Impresora Chapalita.
20. Letter, 8 October 1991, from Anthony Stansfeld (Macon, Georgia) to Moreen Chater, in possession of Moreen Chater.

21. Letter, 24 July 1946, from Witter Bynner (Santa Fe) to Hari Kidd and Edythe Wallach. Special collections of the University of the South, Sewanee, Tennessee.

22. Chandos, *House in the Sun*, 101.

23. Chandos, *House in the Sun*, 191–194.

24. Chandos, *House in the Sun*, 84.

25. Letter, 8 October 1991, from Anthony Stansfeld (Macon, Georgia) to Moreen Chater, in possession of Moreen Chater. Millett attended Oxford University from 1922 to 1927; Stansfeld studied there from 1932 to 1938.

26. Curiously, Stansfeld's death certificate refers to his Dane Chandos persona.

27. Bruce Buckingham (pen name) wrote *Three Bad Nights* (London: Michael Joseph, 1956) and *Boiled Alive* (London: Michael Joseph, 1957).

28. Facebook post, August 2020, by María Elena Enciso Hernández.

29. Grupo Acalli San Antonio Tlayacapan. 2019. *San Antonio Tlayacapan: Recorriendo su historia*. Grupo Acalli, 6768.

30. Lilley left three beneficiaries: Marcos Clemente Maza, Thomas Servington Savery and Leslie Chater. Leslie and his wife, Moreen, subsequently bought the other two out and moved to Mexico in 1983. (Moreen Chater, personal communication)

31. Quotes from Sophie Annan Jensen. 1999. "Candelaria's Cookbook" (review) on MexConnect.com [25 May 2018]

Chapter 12. Violinist and the Pepsi House

1. *El Ojo del Lago*, November 1984, 2.

2. Farías, Casos y cosas de mis tiempos. Members included painter José María Lupercio, violinist and painter Félix Bernardelli, Tomás V. Gómez, Luis Pérez Verdía, Alberto Santoscoy, artist and author Gerardo Murillo (Dr Atl) and Salvador Villaseñor.

3. *El Informador*, 11 December 1922, 2; 4 July 1926, 6.

4. *El Informador*, 14 February 1923, 6; 16 February 1923, 8; 17 February 1923, 7; 25 July 1924, 5; 17 January 1926, 1, 5.

5. Even the 1930 Mexican population census gives her place of birth as Germany.

6. *El Informador*, 30 September 1960, 5.

7. Milagros Sendis. Unpublished manuscript "Recuerdos de Ajijic" shared with author 7 January 2021.

8. *El Informador*, 5 October 1945, 16; 21 October 1945, 5.

9. CMAC: Historial Catastral for Pedro Moreno 75, Ajijic, includes public deeds dated 7 March 1951 and 24 May 1961.

10. *El Ojo del Lago*, November 1984, 2.

11. Milagros Sendis. Unpublished manuscript "Recuerdos de Ajijic."

12. GR, 6 January 1968.

13. Milagros Sendis. Unpublished manuscript "Recuerdos de Ajijic."

14. GR, 3 June 1967.

15. CMAC: historial catastral.

16. (a) *La Jornada*, 26 January 1998. Negocios ficticios y ligas con narcos, los cargos a Romero de Velasco." (b) *Crónica*, 7 July 2007. "Sentencian en Jalisco a integrante del Cártel de Sinaloa."

Chapter 13. Neill James the writer

1. The 1910 US Census lists James' parents as Willie Anna Wood (1861–1901) and Charles Campbell James (1857–1911).

2. Anon, "Philanthropist." This lists her as a member of the class of '18.

3. This has been suggested by Judy King, Stephen Banks (the author of *Kokio: A novel based on the life of Neill James*) and Elizabeth Tomlinson. Tomlinson, a distant relative of James, presented "The Petticoat Vagabond: Writer, Adventurer, Philanthropist, Spy" at the 59th Annual Convention of the Rocky Mountain Modern Language Association in 2005.

4. *The Capital Journal* (Salem, Oregon), 27 March 1937, 5, 10.

5. Madeline Miedema (1909–1994), an educator and historian in Ventura, California, visited James several times. In June 1947 she witnessed the signing of the book contract for *Dust on My Heart*, in which she is given the pseudonym Marion Morris.

6. James, "Ajijic Carrousel."

7. James, *Dust on My Heart*, 272 on.

8. Ruth Netherton, "More about the Way it Was."

9. NJA: Photo albums.

10. NJA: Document dated 1947.

11. James, *Dust on My Heart*, 290.

12. James, "Ajijic Carrousel."

13. Ruth Netherton, "More about the Way it Was."

14. NJA: Unpublished document, "Why I Wanted to Build a House."

15. James, *Dust on My Heart*, 291.

16. Delfino Flores, born in Ajijic on 22 December 1926, died of malaria at his home (Ocampo 110) on 14 April 1936.

17. NJA: Unpublished manuscript "A Peso for the Moon" dated 1948.

18. Letter, 4 September 1944, from James (Ajijic) to Jane.

19. Letter, 4 September 1944, from James (Ajijic) to Jane.

20. Anon, "Neill James in Mexico."

21. James, *Dust on My Heart*, 303–304.

22. Anon, "Neill James in Mexico."

23. James never claimed to have originated the saying, an almost identical version of which—"Once the dust of Mexico has settled on your heart, you have no rest in any other land"—is labeled a proverb by Anita Brenner in *Your Mexican Holiday* (1932).

24. James, *Dust on My Heart*, 292.

25. *El Informador*, 19 December 1944, 12.

26. Anon, "Neill James in Mexico."

27. Sylvia Fein, interviewed at her home 5 February 2015.

28. *The Des Moines Register*, Iowa, 13 February 1949, 36.

29. Anon, "Neill James in Mexico."

30. NJA: Neill James. Unpublished manuscript "Mexican Story" dated 26 October 1948.

Chapter 14. Neill James builds dream home

1. Unless otherwise noted, all the letters and documents on which this account relies are in the NJA.

2. NJA: Neill James. Unpublished manuscript "Mexican Story" dated 26 October 1948.

3. The 2700-square-meter lot, once jointly owned by Major Carlos Cendejas Paguia and María Elena Ramírez Jaime (one of the daughters of Casimiro and Josefina Ramírez, owners of Posada Ajijic), was bought from General Marcelino Garcia Barragán and his wife, Maria Montañes de Barragán, who had acquired it in May 1944.

4. In identifying herself as Neill James Campbell, James was using her US married name. Her legal name in Mexico was either (Nellie) Neill James Wood or, if she went by her married name, (Nellie) Neill James de Campbell.

5. James, "Ajijic Carrousel."

6. NJA: Neill James. Unpublished manuscript "Mexican Story" dated 26 October 1948.

7. Swiss-born Irma Heinrich, who lived in Guadalajara, had been a witness to some earlier land documents relating to James. Heinrich bought lot B, with its buildings, from María Guzmán, and E, also with a building, from Andrés Rochín García and Mateo Saucedo Rochín. The joint purchase by James and Heinrich was from Sra. Aniset Antolín.

8. James, "I Live in Ajijic."

9. James later sold about 380 square meters, including most of lot B, to John and Doris Molinari, who moved to Ajijic from California in about 1985. In 2021 the Lake Chapala Society bought this property to extend its existing facilities.

10. Katie Goodridge Ingram, personal communication.

Chapter 15. Art community begins

1. Jackson, *Burros and Paintbrushes*, 68, 71. Jackson further claims that they were "the only Americans living in Ajijic," despite American dentist George Purnell, for one, having a home in Ajijic at that time.

2. Quote from Sylvia Fein's website sylviafeinpainter.net [27 April 2015]

3. *El Informador*, 3 December 1944, 11. Annual shows were held in 1945, 1946 and 1947.

4. *The Santa Fe New Mexican*, 5 June 1945, 5.

5. Jane Farrar, personal communication.

6. James, "I Live in Ajijic" Virginia was a long time girlfriend of López Bermúdez, not his wife.

7. James, "I Live in Ajijic."

8. *The Dispatch* (Moline, Illinois), 05 September 1946, 12; *The Des Moines Register* (Iowa), 13 February 1949, 36.

9. *The Daily Times* (Davenport, Iowa), 16 October 1948, 16.

10. Renée George. "Ay Naranjos." *Modern Mexico*, Vol 22, #2, Mar–Apr 1949, 16–17, 28–29.

11. *New York Times*, 28 October 1951, 104.

12. *Terry's Guide to Mexico*, 1947, 476.

13. Schneebaum, *Wild Man*, 11.

14. Schneebaum, *Wild Man*, 12, 15.

15. Kernick, "Ajijic."

16. Irma Seeligman Jonas. 1953. "Schooling South of the Border", in *Barnard Alumnae Magazine*, Volume XLII, April 1953, #5: 14-15.

17. *The Michigan Daily*, 5 May 1948.

18. Kernick, "Ajijic."

Chapter 16. International tourists

1. Gail Eiloart, personal communication.

2. It is unclear if Peter Arnold Studios SA was the same company as Peter Arnold SA or a separate business entity only just established.

3. AHMC: documents kindly shared by Rogelio Ochoa Corona.

4. Gail Eiloart, personal communication.

5. Elstob and Barbara married in 1953 and later had a second child, Sukey.

6. *El Informador*, 3 November 1951. The signatories included Leonora Barry, Esther Pantoja, Juan Ibarra, George F Ballin, Nicolós Vázquez, José Ramos Pérez, Martha Kirk, Francisco Ramos P, Ignacio Ruiz, D Whelan de Babin, Nieves Castellanos and Ernesto Alexander.

7. This extraordinary adventure led to Arnold Eiloart and Peter Elstob. 1959. *The Flight of the Small World.* London: Hodder & Stoughton.

8. *Florence Morning News* (Florence, South Carolina) 13 February 1958; *Los Angeles Times*, 13 April 1958, 107.

9. *Los Angeles Times*, 11 December 1955, 153.

10. *Kansas City Times*, 12 January 1955, 8.

11. *Los Angeles Times*, 11 December 1955, 153.

12. *Post-Standard* (Syracuse, NY) 6 March 1955, 42.

13. *Los Angeles Times*, 27 January 1957, 201; 14 Sept 1958, 231.

14. Eleanor Morehead. "How to Live the Good Life on $150 a month." *Esquire*, March 1958, 53, 55.

15. GR, 27 August 1964; 27 November 1971.

Chapter 17. Hotel health spa

1. *El Informador*, 27 August 1945; 27 September 1945, 10.

2. Mabel F Knight. "Ajijic - The Gem of Jalisco." *Pemex Travel Club magazine*, 1 February 1952: 2-4.

3. Anon. "San Andres en Ajijic." *Club de Viajes Pemex*, Vol XV, Num 338 (1 December 1956).

4. Hilda Crump, personal communication, November 2017; Katie Goodridge Ingram, personal communication, March 2016.

5. The registration of the marriage, on 21 June 1940, describes Lytton Bernard as age 50, single and a journalist. Almost exactly a year earlier, his first wife had sought (in Windsor, Ontario) a divorce that would be valid in the UK, as she planned to return there; her petition was rejected because her husband was no longer living in Canada.

6. Roy Kelsey. 1968. "Discovering Mañana Land – A Paradise Where a Hot River Flows Amid Cactus and Volcanic Chasms." *Floridian*, 1 December 1968, 58.

7. International Vegetarian Union. Undated. "15th World Vegetarian Congress 1957." https://ivu.org/congress/wvc57/souvenir/blessings.html 2 May 2018

8. "The Vegetarian World Forum." Note in *World Forum*, #4 Vol. XII (July 1959), 30 36. https://ivu.org/history/world forum/1959ivu.html 2 May 2018

9. Michael Eager, personal communication.

Chapter 18. Advertising and marketing

1. For example, *New Yorker*, 6 May 1950 and *Arizona Republic*, 16 August 1950, 16.

2. Laura Bateman, "Mexico 1952" in Bateman and Bollenbach, *Ajijic*, 69. I have never located the advertisement seen by the Batemans in the New York Times.

3. Mabel F Knight. "Ajijic - The Gem of Jalisco." *Pemex Travel Club magazine*, 1 February 1952: 2-4.

4. For example, *The American Legion Magazine,* December 1954; *The Des Moines Register* (Iowa), 10 October 1954, 130; *Los Angeles Times*, 31 October 1954; *The Rotarian*, October 1954, 62.

5. *Elk Magazine*, July 1956.

6. Norman, *In Mexico*, 241.

7. For example, *Los Angeles Times*, 27 January 1957, 201; 23 November 1959, 57.

8. For example, *Esquire*, February 1960, 26.

9. Shekerjian, "You can Afford a Mexican Summer."

10. McCombe, "Yanks Who Don't Go Home."

11. *Reading Eagle*, 26 April 1934; *Calgary Herald*, 1 November 1934, 3.

12. Eleanor Morehead. "How to Live the Good Life on $150 a month." *Esquire*, March 1958, 53, 55.

13. Patricio Escalante Guerra. "Ajijic is Fun", *Pemex Travel Club Bulletin*, Vol XX, num 324, 1 January 1960, 4-5.

14. Irma McCall. "Ajijic–Paradise Under the Mexican Sun." *Independent Press-Telegram*, 11 March 1962, 82.

15. *Time* magazine, 22 May 1964. "Retirement Down Mexico Way."

16. GR, 9 July 1964, 7. The letter writer sent copies to several newspapers and magazines, including Time.

17. McGinnis, "Lotus Land."

18. Clifton also wrote *Wooden Leg John. Satire on Americans living in Mexico.* (1971)

Chapter 19. Radio, TV and silver screen

1. TV listings, *San Bernardino County Sun*, 16 October 1957.

2. GR, 6 April 1968. The episode was released on 23 April 1968.

3. CTVA. "The Classic TV Archive - US Documentary Series: Jack Douglas Adventure Documentaries" online. https://ctva.biz/US/Documentary/JackDouglasDocumentaries.htm

4. *The Desert Sun* (Palm Springs), 8 August 1960.

5. GR, 22 October 1964; 22 November 1964.

6. GR, 3 June 1967.

7. GR, 14 December 1974.

8. Katie Goodridge Ingram, personal communication.

9. Antonio López Vega, personal communication.

10. Antonio López Vega, personal communication.

11. Katie Goodridge Ingram, personal communication.

12. Carmen Suzanne Mosqueda, personal communication.

13. Antonio López Vega and Carmen Suzanne Mosqueda, personal communications.

14. Dinah DeVry, personal communication, based on interviews with Ricardo Mosqueda; and Carmen Suzanne Mosqueda Melendy, personal communication. Born in 1939, Carol Ann Melendy died in 2008. Roberto Mosqueda, born in Guadalajara in 1928, died in Ajijic in 2009.

15. Dinah DeVry, personal communication, based on interviews with Ricardo Mosqueda.

16. Karen Talbot. 2016. "Jardin Plaza Ajijic: A popular meeting spot, people watching." GR, 14 July 2016. Dale Hoyt Palfrey, personal communication.

17. *The Marion Star* (Ohio), 10 March 1957, 18. "Couple Leaves Movie Capital and Finds Success in Mexico."

18. *El Informador*, 13 August 1953.

19. *Daily Notes* (Canonsburg, Pennsylvania), 11 February 1963; *Pasadena Independent*, 9 April 1963.

20. Many characters in *Where's Annie?* are based on foreigners living in Ajijic at the time, including Leonora Baccante, Willard and George Marsh, Helen Kirtland, Mort Carl, Ernest Alexander, Dolly Whelan, Nicolas Muzenic, Ernesto Butterlin, Toby Schneebaum and Zoe Kernick.

21. Glendon Swarthout. 1958. "Ixion." *New World Writing*, #13.

22. Miles Swarthout, personal communication via emails.

23. GR, 18 November 1967; 28 August 1971.

24. GR, 16 April 1964; 15 April 1967.

25. Alex Grattan. 1995. Remembering Ray Rigby, *El Ojo del Lago*, July 1995. See also "Novelist and playwright Ray Rigby (1916 –1995) lived at Lake Chapala in the 1970s." https://lakechapalaartists.com/?p=2222

26. James, "I Live in Ajijic." Cinema Reporter. No. 482, 11 October 1947, 16.

27. Jack McDonald. "Sherm Harris. Posada Ajijic's former owner was top Hollywood Producer.", GR, 7 March 1970, 15–16.

28. GR, 19 May 1973; 21 February 1976.

29. *El Ojo del Lago*, July 1989.

Chapter 20. Ajijic Hand Looms

1. E W Nelson. 1904. "A Winter Expedition into Southwestern Mexico." *National Geographic*, vol XV, #9 (September 1904), 341357.

2. Katie Goodridge Ingram, personal communication; *Kingston Daily Freeman* (New York): 12 September 1947.

3. *Diario Oficial de la Federación*, 20 February 1947.

4. Dale Palfrey. 1988. "Weavers' Magic", *El Ojo del Lago*, 1-2: January 1988.

5. Katie Goodridge Ingram, email 15 July 2019.

6. Katie Goodridge Ingram, email 11 March 2021.

7. Katie Goodridge Ingram, personal communication

8. Katie Goodridge Ingram, personal communication

9. *Kingston Daily Freeman* (Kingston, New York): 8 October 1952, 15.

10. Katie Goodridge Ingram, personal communication.

11. Bob Lamont and Margaret Lamont. 1955. "Guadalajara One Of Picturesque Places In New World." *Phoenix Arizona Republic*, 3 April 1955, 65.

12. Norman, *In Mexico*, 241242.

13. Katie Goodridge Ingram, personal communication.

14. For details of the mourning ritual and other customs in Ajijic following the death of a child (angelito), see Lorena Melton Young Otero. 1999. "Death and Civil Society." *Annals of the American Academy of Political and Social Science*, Vol. 565, 193-206.

15. Katie Goodridge Ingram, personal communication.

16. GR, 7 February 1976, 9.

17. John Abney. 1974. "Lightest Mexico: Mariachi Mass Fills The Church." *Waco Tribune Herald*, 18 September 1974, 14.

18. GR, 7 February 1976, 9.

19. Katie Goodridge Ingram, email, March 2016.

Chapter 21. Neill James the businesswoman

1. Mabel F Knight. "Ajijic - The Gem of Jalisco." *Pemex Travel Club magazine*, 1 February 1952: 2-4.

2. Katie Goodridge Ingram, email 15 July 2019.

3. Norman, *In Mexico*, 241-242.

4. NJA: Notes by James on the history of her silk making project.

5. Claims that James introduced sericulture to Mexico, or to Ajijic, are spurious. See Rebeca Vanesa García Corzo. 2016. "Intentos de implementación de la industria de la seda en la Nueva España en el siglo XVIII." *Fronteras de la Historia*, v 21 #1, 118–144.

6. Dr Varton Kriekor Osigina came from an Armenian family of silk experts and had perfected a process whereby silkworms spun silk in any one of eighteen distinct shades. (*Popular Science*, November 1920).

7. NJA: This (exaggerated) claim comes from the extensive notes kept by James on her silkmaking project.

8. NJA: Letter, 31 December 1951, from James (Ajijic) to Hazel Kerper (Cody, Wyoming).

9. NJA: Handwritten list of salaries paid to her employees in James' notebook.

10. NJA: This letter, 11 January 1954, promises that a diploma is being sent separately.

11. Mabel F Knight. "The Silkworm returns to Mexico". *Mexican American Review* (Mexico City: American Chamber of Commerce of Mexico), Vol XXIII #8 (August 1955) 16, 33.

12. NJA: Entry for 31 August 1954 in James' notes about her silk business.

13. Anon, "Philanthropist."

14. McCombe, "Yanks Who Don't Go Home."

15. Bill Atkinson, interviewed at Rancho Los Colorines on 7 April 2016.

Chapter 22. Save the Lake

1. Compton, *To The Isthmus*, 165.

2. Tello, *Libro segundo de la Crónica Miscelánea*, 696.

3. *La Voz de México*, 13 August 1880.

4. GR, 17 September 1988.

5. Herbert Johnson. Handwritten weather log in possession of the author.

6. *Country Life*, 20 May 1949. "The shrinking Caspian Sea."

7. B Manuel Villagómez R. 2016. "La Colosal Defensa Por El Lago De Chapala," *Semanario de la Laguna*, 27 January 2016. http://semanariolaguna.com/15092/ 7 March 2021

8. *El Informador*, 2 August 1955, 7 (paid advertisement).

9. In addition to Zara (Khyva Welles St. Albans), the signatories were: Malva C. Cluff, P. Lytton Bernard, E. Golden, Irving H. Golden, John A. Younger, Flora Chávez, Christine R. Howard, Richard H. Odgers, James C. Linehan, Mrs J. C. Linehan, Duke Hichman, B. F. Martin, Howard B. Rockfold, Lovisa Y. Ayres, Camilla Bersu, Louise Peyton, Lelia R. Kelley, Ethel Golden, Erny R. Noschke, Pearl Hunter and Lillian Witcher.

10. McCombe, "Yanks Who Don't Go Home."

11. *El Informador*, 11 August 1959, 8.

Chapter 23. Violent Crime

1. CGTN America. 2017. Report/film by correspondent Mike Kirsch; quotes are from minute 7.54 of the video.

2. AMG: Informe Municipal: Departamento de Chapala (16 September 1896 to 15 September 1898), 99.

3. *El Informador*, 18 December 1935.

4. *El Informador*, 4 March 1922, 1.

5. *El Paso Herald*, 15 March 1922, 2.

6. Letter, 18 June 1956, from the German Embassy in Mexico City to Rudolf Quehl, now in the archives of Rhenania, a fraternity of the University of Bonn (Rheinische Friedrich Wilhelms Universität), brought to my attention by Hans-Reinhard Koch.

7. Friedrich Butterlin's letter is quoted in a letter, 19 February 1957, from Fritz Rung to Hermann Schaefer in the Rhenania archives.

8. Kenneth McCaleb. 1968. "Conversation Piece: How To Be an Art Collector." *The Corpus Christi Caller Times*, 15 February 1968, 17. Monique Señoret (Rita's daughter), personal communication, 2015.

9. *San Francisco Examiner*, 21 July 1968, 24.
10. *El Informador*, 8 July 1975; GR, 12 July 1975, 21.
11. Joan Frost, writing in GR, 4 October 1975.
12. Letter, 25 November 1976, from Zara (Ajijic) to Nancy Neel in possession of Nancy Neel.
13. GR, 28 January 1978, 18.
14. GR, 17 January 1987, 1, 8, 16.
15. Jan Dunlap. 2018. *With Money Dances the Dog* (screenplay). Canada: Sombrero Books.
16. GR, 17 January 1987, 16.
17. Jack McDonald, "Engineering Whiz Ralph Mathews Had Varied and Exciting Career" GR: 10 January 1970, 1112.
18. GR, 17 September 1999. *The San Francisco Examiner*, 21 September 1999, A1, A10.
19. *The Seattle Times*, 17 June 2000.
20. GR, 29 November 2011.
21. GR, 9 February 2014.
22. GR, 30 October 1976, 22.
23. Terry Reed and John Cummings. 1995. *Compromised: Clinton, Bush and the CIA.* Clandestine Publishing.

Chapter 24. Lake Chapala Society

1. Details of dates, members and officers come from minutes of meetings and other documents in LCSA.
2. LCSA: Information sheet dated 18 June 1955.
3. GR, 9 July 1964.
4. NJA: Membership roster.
5. Images of this newsletter were posted on eBay 22 February 2021.
6. GR, 1 May 1976, 29.
7. GR, 17 September 1983, 18.
8. Quote from Tom Faloon during 2013 interview with Harriet Hart for the LCS Oral History project. https://www.youtube.com/watch?v'OwrNr-JE34M
9. Arthur Melby. 2009. "History and Vision for the Lake Chapala Society". *El Ojo del Lago*, December 2009.
10. Lake Chapala Society. Undated. "History of the Lake Chapala Society." https://lakechapalasociety.com/public/history.php 21 November 2018
11. Stephen Banks, *Kokio*, 235.
12. Lake Chapala Society Official May 1989 Bulletin, published in *El Ojo del Lago*, April 1989, 2.
13. James was granted copyright for *Dust on My Heart. Petticoat Vagabond in Mexico* on 24 June 1946 and renewed it on 18 July 1973.
14. Lake Chapala Society *Membership Directory* for years 2016-2019 inclusive. Slightly over 90% of members came from the US or Canada. Other countries listed include Argentina, Bahamas, Australia, Belgium, Belize, Bermuda, China, Colombia, Costa Rica, Denmark, Ecuador, Egypt, Fiji, Finland, France, Germany, Ireland, Italy, Jamaica, Kenya, Lithuania, Netherlands, New Zealand, Peru, Poland, Puerto Rico, Singapore, South Africa, Spain, Sweden, Switzerland, Thailand, United Arab Emirates, United Kingdom, Venezuela and Zimbabwe.

Chapter 25. Educational initiatives

1. AMG: Gobierno del Estado de Jalisco. 1897. *Memoria del Estado de Jalisco*, 189496. AHMC: Untitled document in Box: Chapala 1826–1999 Varios II.

2. *The Brooklyn Citizen*, 22 July 1898, 3.

3. *El Informador*, 3 October 1923.

4. *El Informador*, 10 December 1932. Fausto Márquez, personal communication via Facebook (June 2021).

5. According to local lore, Castellanos was buried in this graveyard, though there is documentary evidence that he was actually interred in Jocotepec. (Manuel Flores Jimènez, personal communication.)

6. Dionicio Morales, posting on Facebook, 26 April 2021.

7. *El Informador*, 18 July 1951. In addition to local and state politicians, the guests included Dr Cristino Sendis, Herbert and Georgette Johnson, Grace Wilcox, Neill James, Nicolas Muzenic, Arnold Eiloart, Peter Elstob, Mort Carl, Esther Merrill, Bob Bassing, Rob Storm, Pablo and Louisa Heuer, Tula Meyer, Juan Butterlin (father of Otto and Ernesto), John Upton and Ernest Alexander.

8. NJA: Letter, 31 December 1951, from James (Ajijic) to Hazel Kerper (Cody, Wyoming).

9. The name was in honor of Saúl Rodiles Piña (1885–1951), a career educator who had headed the Teachers' College in Guadalajara and helped establish the state secondary school system.

10. Raymond Crump, personal communication.

11. Lee Hopper and Raymond Crump, personal communications.

12. GR, 6 May 1965; 20 May 1965.

13. GR, 10 June 1965.

14. GR, 2 July 1966.

15. *Semanario de la Laguna*, 16 June 2016 http://semanariolaguna.com/17872/

16. Albert Kelley. 1977. "Ajijic waits for med equipment. *Valley News* (Van Nuys, California) 27 May 1977, 16.

17. My thanks to Antonio Moreno, Antelma Plascencia, Elda Conchas, Veronica López Orozco and others for their Facebook comments explaining this sequence of events.

18. (a) GR, 16 August 1975; 10 September 1977, 19. (b) Shep Lenchek. 2001. Salute to the Oak Hill School. *El Ojo del Lago*, March 2001.

19. GR, 23 January 1964.

20. GR, 28 May 1964.

21. Anon. 1972. "Sociedad de Estudios Avanzados del Occidente de Mexico, A.C.", *El Mensajero*, Vol 1 Number 1.

22. (a) GR, 22 June 1974; *Pecos Enterprise* (Texas), 8 April 1974, 2. (b) American Association of Teachers of Spanish and Portuguese. *Hispania*, March 1975.

23. Luis Gómez Gastélum, Cristina Ramírez Munguía and Mayela Guzmán Becerra. 2014. "Distant Neighbours: Different Visions about Mexican Archaeology" in *Bulletin of the History of Archaeology*, 2014.

24. Betty Bell (ed). 1974. *The Archaeology of West Mexico*. Sociedad de Estudios Avanzados del Occidente de Mexico, A. C. / West Mexican Society for Advanced Studies.

Chapter 26. Children's libraries and art

1. NJA: Letter, 7 April 1952, from George B Smith (Los Angeles, California) to James (Ajijic).

2. Katie Goodridge Ingram, personal communication, July 2019.

3. NJA: Guest Book celebrating the inauguration of the New Free Ajijic Library. Among those who signed were Katharine Karns, Dorothy Grier, Clyde Mitchell, Ann and Donald Robertson, Gail Michel, Betty Kuzell, Ben and Elena Lemon, Antonio H de Vázquez, Ma Concepción Higuera Hernández and Ana María Ramos.

4. NJA: Various unpublished documents.

5. Andres Ivon. 1984. "New Mexican Library in Ajijic. Building donated by Miss Neill James", *Welcome*, 30 March 1984, 4.

6. The Lake Chapala Society began a children's library in Chapala (the first library in that town) in the mid1950s, located first at Francisco I Madero Nte 248, and then, from December 1975, at Zaragoza 334. (GR, 6 December 1975, 20.)

7. Bynner, *Journey with Genius*, 98.

8. NJA: A letter, 19 December 1959, from James (Ajijic) to Stirling Dickinson (the director of the art school in San Miguel) asked for a first report on the progress of Favier Zaragossa (sic) and requested that Florentino Padillo (sic) start classes there in January.

9. GR, 1 October 1964.

10. GR, 24 September 1964, 10.

11. GR, 10 November 1973.

12. GR, 16 March 1974.

13. NJA: Neill James. 1977. "Ajijic." Unpublished notes.

14. *El Informador*, 19 April 1980, 10C.

15. Mildred Boyd. 2001. "Children's Art Alive and Well in Ajijic!". *El Ojo del Lago*, Vol 17 #10 (June 2001). The hiatus appears to have begun later than 1979, the year stated by Boyd.

16. CAP heritage collection accessible online via https://www.lakechapalasociety.com

Chapter 27. Foreign artists

1. Alexandra Bateman, personal communication, 2016. The portrait is almost certainly the portrait now in the possession of the Sendis family in Guadalajara. Interview with Bill Atkinson at this home in Chapala in April 2016.

2. Earle Alfred Birney. 1962. *Ice Cod Bell or Stone: A Collection of New Poems*.

3. McCombe, "Yanks Who Don't Go Home."

4. Margo's house, with huge paintings on tall walls, was at Ocampo 58 (Privada Ocampo 1). Later owners included Dick Bishop, and Joe and Jane Osburn. It was from here, in 1988, that my fiancée left for the church on our wedding day. Otto's painting studio was in an adjoining orchard (presumably owned by himself or another family member) that extended to the lakeshore.

5. The marriage between Ernesto Butterlin and Margo North was corroborated independently in personal communications by both Katie Goodridge Ingram (in March 2016) and Agustín Velarde (in April 2016).

6. Alexandra Bateman, interviewed in Ajijic in April 2016.

7. Ben West. 2002. "Obituary: Peter Elstob; Writer and Activist for International Pen", *The Independent* (London, UK), 9 August 2002.

8. See "Ernest Alexander (1921–1974), artist and photographer" (lakechapalaartists.com)

9. Katie Goodridge Ingram, personal communication.

10. Katie Goodridge Ingram, personal communication.

11. Oral history interview with Mary Fuller McChesney, 1994 Sept. 28, Archives of American Art, Smithsonian Institution.

12. M V Wood. 2002. "It's a colorful life / Robert McChesney, Mary Fuller celebrate art and their marriage with a joint show." *SFGate*.

13. *Mexican firecrackers: a prayer and a festival* (Smithsonian Folkways, 2001).

14. Sean Wilder. 2011. *Alex*. Lulu.com, 173.

15. "33ed" refers to expulsion from Mexico under the infamous Artículo 33 of Mexico's constitution which allows authorities to expel "undesirable" foreigners without due process.

16. In the late 1940s, David Morris used GI Bill funds to complete a Masters degree in Fine Arts at the University of Guadalajara. By mid 1951 he and his wife were living in Ajijic. After moving to San Francisco they gained international renown for their jointly designed ceramics.

17. *Santa Cruz Sentinel*, 28 September 1951, 5; 7 October 1951.

18. Álamos History Association. Álamos Interviews: Allen Pendergraft. 21 June 2011. This wonderful story has a ring of truth, though there is a counter claim elsewhere that the fictional priest was based partly on the Reverend Sidney Lanier.

19. See "Charles Pollock and his Chapala Series (1955–56)" (lakechapalaartists.com)

20. *Bennington Banner* (Bennington, Vermont), 24 July 1965, 5.

21. Katie Goodridge Ingram, personal communication.

22. GR, 19 July 1975; 7 February 1976; 1 May 1976, 22.

23. *Independent Star-News* (Pasadena, California), 21 December 1958; 12 May 1963.

24. Jane Clutton, personal communication, October 2016.

Chapter 28. Creative Beats

1. Mark Lewis, personal communication by email. Parker stayed in Ajijic for about six months. Lewis thinks that Parker probably returned to the lake in 1958–1959 and may have returned to live at Lake Chapala in the 1970s.

2. Mark Lewis, personal communication, based on information from Bob Bassing.

3. Two letters—Jack Kerouac (Mexico City) to Allen Ginsberg (New Jersey) 10 May 1952 and Allen Ginsberg (New Jersey) to Jack Kerouac (Mexico City) 15 May 1952—quoted in *Jack Kerouac and Allen Ginsberg: The Letters* (Penguin 2010).

4. weiss, *Can't stop the beat*.

5. *Climax*, #2, Summer 1956.

6. *El Informador*, 15 September 1955.

7. *Sausalito News*, #52, 31 December 1954, 3.

8. *Prensa Libre* (Tepic, Nayarit), 24 April 1955.

9. Joan Gilbert Martin, personal communication.

10. (a) ruth weiss. 1959. *Gallery of Women*. (b) weiss, *Can't stop the beat* includes "Compass" and "Post Card 1995."

11. The Instituto Cultural de Inglés Javier McKeever was the first English language school in Chiapas and is now run by McKeever's grandsons.

12. John Ross. 2004. "Afterword: The Heart of it All." *The Texas Observer*. https://www.texasobserver.org/1711 afterword the heart of it all/ 29 April 2021

13. Ned Polsky, Letter to the *New York Times*, 1995.

14. John Ross. 2004. Afterword: The Heart of it All. *The Texas Observer*.

15. Gordon Lish. 1962. "Interview with Jack Gilbert." *Genesis West* #1.

16. Talvera Salgado, *Lago Chapala*, 134.

17. Burke Johnson. 1960. "Ajijic Tears from Laughter." *Arizona Republic* (Phoenix) 16 October 1960.

18. This house, on the west side of Calle Colón immediately south of Calle Zaragoza, was later the home of photographer Sylvia Salmi, and three other photographers—Toni Beatty, Bruce Greer and Diane Murray—also lived there at one time or another.

19. The late Arthur Monroe, personal communication, 2016.

20. Judith Broadhurst. 1991. "The beat goes on for artist Arthur Monroe", *Santa Cruz*

Sentinel, 25 January 1991, 11.

21. Tamara Janúz, personal communication.

22. Pete Hamill. 2007. "In Memoriam: Mailer y Norman." Published, translated into Spanish, in *Letras Libres,* December 2007, 42–44.

23. Quoted in Mary V. Dearborn. 1999. *Mailer: A biography.* Houghton Mifflin Harcourt.

24. Reynolds, *The Expatriates.*

25. Dave Moore (compiler). 2010. "Character Key to Kerouac's Duluoz Legend." http://www.beatbookcovers.com/kercomp/ 28 April 2018

Chapter 29. Bohemians, hippies and drugs

1. The term "hippie" was first used in publications on the US east coast in 1964 and on the west coast in 1965.

2. L Burr Belden. 1962. "Guadalajara, Both Large, Beautiful." *The San Bernardino County Sun* (California), 22 March 1962, B2 (17).

3. *St. Louis Post Dispatch* (St. Louis, Missouri), 15 June 1963, 2; George Dusheck. 1963. "Paradise Lost by Mexico LSD Colony." *San Francisco News Call Bulletin,* 2 July 1963.

4. For instance, as stated in (a) Kate Karns. "Old Ajijic." *Lake Chapala Review,* Vol 12, #1 (14 February 2010). (b) Bateman and Bollenbach, *Ajijic.*

5. Kamstra, *Weed,* 118–119. Thad was Thaddeus Ashby, called by British philosopher Alan Watts in *In My Own Way* "an inspired eccentric" and "undoubted genius", who had been instrumental in making him realize that vegetables were intelligent.

6. Loy Strother, personal communication via email, 20 December 2017. LSD possession was not illegal in the US until October 1968. The British doctor may have been Dr Bernard Lytton-Bernard, who was certainly in Ajijic at the time.

7. Scott Hampson. 2016. "Beverly and Mexico 63–64." Unpublished document dated 2016 shared with author December 2020.

8. Tamara Johnson. 1997. "The Beach: My Self in the Mirror," in Bernard Selling. 1997. *Writing from Within: A Guide to Creativity and Life Story Writing.*

9. Scott Hampson. 2016. "Beverly and Mexico 63–64." Unpublished document dated 2016 shared with author December 2020.

10. Marcy Sorensen, personal communication.

11. Gabriel A Menéndez. 1965."Undesirable Immigration." *El Informador,* 1 June 1965.

12. Hargraves, *Lake Chapala.*

13. Marcy Sorensen, personal communication.

14. Tom Wolfe. 1968. *The Electric Kool-Aid Acid Test.* New York: Picador, 300–301.

15. Danny Sofer and Doug Lynner. 1977. "Interview with Patrick Gleeson." *Synapse* (magazine), Vol. 1 #5 (January–February 1977), 21; Jill Maldonado, personal communication, December 2020.

16. Kate Karns. "Old Ajijic." *Lake Chapala Review,* Vol 12, #1 (14 February 2010).

17. Contribution 21 May 2015 by "alex45920" to chapala.com webboard. [27 April 2021]

18. Anon. Undated. "China Cat Sunflower by Grateful Dead." https://www.songfacts.com/place/lake chapala jalisco mexico/china cat sunflower [20 April 2021]

19. Oscar Torres de León, personal communication via Facebook.

20. Marsh, *Week with No Friday.*

21. Marsh, "Mexican Hayride". H Allyn Hunt, "Writers on the lam in Mexico," *GR,* 29 March 2008.

22. Letter, 16 April 1964, from George Marsh to John Williams (Williams papers, University of Arkansas, Fayetteville).

23. John Platero. 1970. "Guadalajara Lures, Keeps Retiring Americans." *The Corpus Christi Caller*, 19 Nov 1970, 53.

24. Young, *Who is Angelina?* 86–87.

25. Allyn Hunt: (a) 1966. "Acme Rooms and Sweet Marjorie Russell." *Transatlantic Review*, Spring 1966; The story was included in Martha Foley and David Burnett (eds). *The Best American Short Stories 1967*; (b) 1969. "A Mole's Coat." *Transatlantic Review*, Summer 1969.

26. Lloyd Penney. 2002. "Outside Looking In." Ce*I*3C (Vol. 1 No. 3) July 2002.

27. According to Jerry Murray (see note 31), Hogan was living on a modest monthly remittance from his father of $700 a month.

28. Peter Huf, personal communication.

29. GR, 28 August 1971.

30. Earl Kemp. (a) 1976. "Pleased to meet you, too..." in Ce*I*9C (Vol. 2 No. 4) August 2003 - https://efanzines.com/EK/eI09/index.htm, and (b) 2006. "Preface 1980: Twenty Reconstructed/Fragmented Years" in Who Killed Science Fiction? Ce*I*29C (Vol. 5 No. 6) December 2006.

31. Jerry Murray. 2008. "SLODGE". Ce*I*40C (Vol. 7 No. 5) October 2008 https://efanzines.com/EK/eI40/index.htm.

Chapter 30. Village photographer

1. Scott Hampson. 2016. "Beverly and Mexico 63–64." Unpublished document dated 2016 shared with author December 2020.

2. This account of Beverly's time in Ajijic is based on personal communications from three of her daughters (Tamara Janúz, Jill Maldonado and Rachel Lyn Johnson) and on interviews with several Ajijic residents of the time, including Tom Brudenell, Janice Carter, Jan Dunlap, Peter Huf, Don Shaw and Marsha Sorensen.

3. Jill Maldonado, personal communication.

4. Jan Dunlap, personal communication.

5. Edwards, *The Sweet Bird of Youth*.

6. Obituary in GR, 15 January 1977.

Chapter 31. Posada Ajijic: parade of managers

1. *Los Angeles Times*, 14 October 1959, 55; 23 November 1959, 57. *Esquire*, February 1960, 26; March 1960.

2. Dr Jim Vaughan, interviewed by author in August 1990.

3. Irma McCall. "Ajijic–Paradise Under the Mexican Sun." *Independent Press-Telegram*, 11 March 1962, 82.

4. Iona Kupiec, interviewed by author, August 1990.

5. Loy Strother, personal communication.

6. Jack McDonald. "Sherm Harris. Posada Ajijic's former owner was top Hollywood Producer.", GR, 7 March 1970, 15–16.

7. GR, 9 January 1964, 5; 3 September 1964; *Los Angeles Times*, 28 February 1965, 108.

8. GR, 17 September 1964.

9. McGinnis, "Lotus Land."

10. GR, 3 June 1965.

11. GR, 5 August 1965.

12. GR, 25 November 1965.

13. Jerry Hulse. 1965. "A 24-Cent Haircut in Paradise." *Los Angeles Times*, 11 April 1965, 116.

14. Joan Frost. 2011. "Jocotepec and Area in 1966," in Bateman and Bollenbach, *Ajijic*, 121–2. Miriam returned to California; Nancy later married a minister and divided her time between Mexico City and La Manzanilla.

15. GR, 1 October 1977, 27.

16. GR, 20 May 1965; 19 February 1966; 14 May 1966.

17. GR, 14 May 1966.

18. GR, 2 April 1966.

19. GR, 28 May 1966.

20. GR, 15 April 1967.

21. GR, 7 October 1967.

22. Dodge, *The Best of Mexico*, 138. Ford, *Fabulous Mexico*, 117.

23. (a) Adverts in *El Informador*, 6 September 1968, 21; 7 September 1968, 20; 11 September 1968, 24. (b) "Jalisco Bizarro: El vocho que cruzó el Lago de Chapala," *Mural*, 22 April 2020.

Chapter 32. Other Ajijic hotels and Chula Vista

1. The three parts are, today, Calle Juárez 30, 30A and 32.

2. Cristina, *El Chapala de Natalia*, 4246, 8283.

3. Katharine Couto, personal communication, November 2014.

4. GR, 19 March 1966; 18 June 1966; 8 July 1967.

5. Dodge, *The Best of Mexico*, 138.

6. It is unclear whether the hotel opened in December 1953, or was built by Carlos Ziener after he retired in 1956. Jack McDonald. "Inn's Charming Hostess is Chapala 'Native'." GR, 29 June 1968, 12 gives both versions.

7. Terry, *Terry's Guide to Mexico*, 250.

9. Mary Lou Kepper. 1964. "Adventures in Mexico." *Red Rock News* (Sedona, Arizona), 27 February 1964, 6.

9. Normally known as Isabel or Isabela, Victoria Elizabeth McCullough Hunton was the daughter of Victor and Elizabeth Hunton. See chapter 31 of Burton, *If Walls Could Talk*.

10. GR, 25 November 1965.

11. GR, 12 August 1967.

12. GR, 10 January 1970.

13. GR, 4 February 1967; 12 January 1974.

14. James Kelly, writing in *Traveler's Guide to Mexico*, January 1973, G10–G11. La Carreta opened in about 1970 (GR, 15 September 1973, 10).

15. *Freeport Journal-Standard* (Illinois), 8 September 1976, 8. Fleming's sister, Alice Frankfort, an abstract-expressionist, exhibited her work at El Tejaban gallery in 1974 (GR, 18 May 1974).

16. McGinnis, "Lotus Land."

17. Horace Sutton. 1970. "Chapala is Retiree's Dream Cost of Living Big Attraction," in *TimesP-icayune* (New Orleans), 15 November 1970, 30.

18. Anon. 1974. "American expatriates enjoy different life in Mexico." *The Santa Fe New Mexican*, 6 February 1974, 97.

19. *The Kansas City Times*, 15 May 1968, 32.

20. GR, 16 February 1974.

21. Jim Dunlap (Art Ganung's son-in-law), personal communication.

22. Alexandra Bateman, in Bateman and Bollenbach, *Ajijic*, 144. Bateman must be referring to Peter Constantine von Braun, born in 1960.

23. Dodge, *The Best of Mexico*, 138.

24. GR, 9 November 1974.

25. GR, 16 July 1977, 17.

26. *Proceso* #1818, 4 September 2011; *El Informador*, 7 de marzo de 2012, 3-B.

Chapter 33. Zara meets flamboyant Iona

1. Excerpts in this chapter are from a handwritten manuscript by Iona given to the author in summer 1990. Iona's description conflates real-life Zara and the artwork on the dustjacket of *Quilocho and the Dancing Stars*.

2. Laura Bateman, interviewed in February 1990.

3. NJA: "The Espectacular Artistic Life of Zara Alexeyewa Khyva St. Albans Autobiography", printed in Guadalajara in 1982.

4. Tom Faloon, interviewed in February 2014.

5. See "The Illuminated Elephants visited Ajijic in 1982." https://lakechapalaartists. com/?p=9818.

6. This date is supported by rentals of the property. However, Alexandra Bateman writes elsewhere that Zara sold the mill house in the late 1970s to the then state governor Flavio Romero de Velasco and his wife.

7. Her birth record names her Agnes Iona Fick. But almost all other sources, including the 1910 US census, call her Iona Agnes.

8. US censuses for 1910, 1920 and 1930.

9. Ruth Ross Merrimer. 1999. "Birthday Party For Iona Kupiec." GR, 28 August 1999.

10. Julie Arnoldy. 1947. "Seagoing school ma'am." *The Times Picayune*, 23 March 1947, 109.

11. Iona Kupiec related this tale to Gwen Chan Burton in about 1988.

12. Jack McDonald. 1969. "Ajijic Woman Looks Back on Life of High Adventure." GR, 31 May 1969, 910.

13. This excerpt is from a letter to Mrs Laura Kattengeli, a friend in New Orleans, quoted in *The Times Picayune*, 28 April 1967, 11.

14. GR, 22 April 1967.

15. Iona lived at several different addresses before returning to Zara's cottage again in the early 1980s. Hilda Mendoza reported that Iona had lived for a few years on Calle Ocampo; a 1968 Lake Side Directory lists Iona's address as Zaragoza 22.

16. GR, 1 October 1977, 27.

17. Anon. 1985. "Profile Present." *El Ojo del Lago*, December 1985, 56.

18. GR, 22 May 1976, 22.

19. June Summers. 1992. "Living Legend: Iona Kupiec." *El Ojo del Lago*, September 1992.

20. Gwen Chan Burton, personal journal entry for 2 October 1982.

21. Tod Jonson. 1988. "Portrait of the Artist." *El Ojo del Lago*, May 1988.

22. (a) Ruth Ross Merrimer. 1999. "Birthday Party For Iona Kupiec." GR, 28 August 1999; (b) Ruth Ross Merrimer. 1999. "Iona Fick Kupiec" (Obituary). GR, 1 October 1999.

Chapter 34. Neill James the capitalist

1. This refers to "El Museo Nacional de Artes e Industrias Populares", located at the time in the former Corpus Christi Church in downtown Mexico City.

2. NJA: Letter, 22 May 1960, from James (Ajijic) to the director of the "Museo Nacional de Cosas Regional" (Mexico City).

3. *El Estado de Jalisco* (Periodico Oficial del Estado), 20 December 1962, Tomo CCXVIII, Num 3, 29.

4. (a) Irma McCall. "Ajijic–Paradise Under the Mexican Sun." *Independent Press-Telegram*, 11 March 1962, 82. (b) Rex and Catherine Magee. "Petticoated Benefactress: State Woman is First Lady of Sleepy Mexican Village." *Clarion-Ledger* (Jackson, Mississippi), 20 February 1962, 7.

5. Netherton, "More about the Way it Was."

6. NJA: This is referred to by LCS volunteer archivist Marianne O'Halloran in the LCS newsletter for August 2016, 3.

7. NJA: Letter, 3 January 1965, from James (Ajijic) to Mr Leong (Los Angeles).

8. Hargraves, *Lake Chapala.*

9. Netherton, "More about the Way it Was."

10. June Summers. 1992. "Happy 97th Birthday..." *Chapala Riviera Guide*, Vol 3 #3.

11. Banks, *Kokio*, 205.

12. Leslie Grace. 2004. "460 Years of Silk in Oaxaca, Mexico." *Textile Society of America 9th Biennial Symposium* (2004). Univ. Nebraska Digital Commons, http://digitalcommons.unl.edu/tsaconf/482/ 21 November 2018

13. NJA: Letter, 8 March 1968, from James (Ajijic) to Bill Johns (Downey, California).

14. Anon, "Philanthropist Leads an Eventful Life."

15. Irma McCall. "Ajijic–Paradise Under the Mexican Sun." *Independent Press-Telegram*, 11 March 1962, 82.

16. GR, 10 November 1973; 5 June 1976, 15.

17. NJA: Letter, 28 July 1965, from Layton, Utah, to James.

18. NJA: Copy of letter, 28 July 1968, from James to Dr Victor Bloom in London, UK.

19. NJA: Letter, 8 December 1975, from Hundley Thompson to James.

20. Letter, 27 July 1968, to the editor in *El Informador*, 8 August 1968, 5-A. Mexican signatories included Carlos Gómez Arias, María Guadalupe A de Segura, María Guadalupe Avila and Guillermo Valdés. Foreign signatories, besides, Neill James, included Helen Kirtland, Dickinson Bishop and Sally P Kingsbury.

21. Dale Hoyt Palfrey. "Lakeside's new guardians: natural resource defense group takes shape." GR, 11 October 2018.

Chapter 35. Art community consolidates.

1. Alexandra Bateman, interviewed in Ajijic in April 2016. The address of the gallery at that time was Hidalgo 41.

2. GR, 2 April 1966; 28 May 1966.

3. Gabriel Antonio Menéndez. 1965. "Emigración Indeseable" (Undesirable Immigration), *El Informador*, 1 June 1965.

4. GR, 21 December 1968.

5. Peter Huf, interviewed at his home in Bavaria in 2014, and subsequent emails.

6. GR, 26 April 1969.

7. GR, 18 March 1967.

8. *El Informador*, 26 November 1968.

9. GR, 24 February 1968; 25 January 1969.

10. GR, 24 February 1968; 27 April 1968; 18 May 1968; 25 May 1968; 8 June 1968.

11. Jack McDonald. 1968. "Ajijic Woman Carved out Business for Herself." GR, 22 June 1968, 15.

12. Tom Faloon, interviewed in February 2014.

13. Annual Reports, US National Gallery of Art (Washington DC), 1971 and 1986.

14. Quote from page 85 of catalog for exhibition "Mary Lovelace O'Neal. Chasing Down the Image" at the Mnuchin Gallery in New York in February 2020.

15. Allyn Hunt, GR, 9 November 1968.

16. Joe Weston, GR, 1 July 1972.

17. *The Sun Gazette*. March 22, 2017. "Renowned artist shows 'humanist expressionism' at Exeter gallery."

18. GR, 15 June 1968; 6 February 1971; 3 April 1971.

19. Edward J Sylvester. 1975. "So you'd like to retire in Mexico?" *Tucson Daily Citizen*, 13 September 1975, 9–11.

20. Nottonson, *Mexico My Home*.

21. The exhibition "40 Años/40 Years" was part of a group show titled "Vistazo, La transformación de lo cotidiano" at the Museo Carrillo Gil in Mexico City in 2007.

22. See http://alicembateman.com/about.html.

23. Interviews with Peter Paul Huf, Eunice Hunt, Tom Brudenell and Don Shaw.

24. Loosely defined, a happening is an artistic performance or event, usually multi disciplinary, which involves the active participation of the audience.

25. Interviews with Tom Brudenell and Don Shaw.

Chapter 36. Lakeside Little Theatre

1. Katie Goodridge Ingram, *Mexico City News*, 3 July 1977, and personal communication in 2019.

2. GR, 2 April 1964.

3. GR, 14 June 1975; 18 February 1965.

4. Evidence is lacking for the claim made elsewhere that LLT's first official production was *From Kokomo to Mexico*, a musical by Betty Kuzell. LLT website lists this as first performed in March 1968.

5. GR, 10 November 1973.

6. "A Man Called Beautiful," in *In Touch: The Magazine for a Different Point of View*, #17 (April May 1975). Beverly Hills, California: In Touch, Inc.

7. Data from LLT Playlist of 53 seasons http://www.lakesidelittletheatre.com/app/download/7244501237/LLT+Playlist+up+to+Season+53.pdf [28 January 2018]

8. Anon. "Murder among expats shocks lakeside", GR, 17 January 1987, 1, 8, 16.

9. (a) Fred Carmichael. 1973. *Mixed Doubles: A Comedy in Two Acts*. Samuel French Inc. (b) George Ryga. 1973. *Portrait of Angelica / A Letter to My Son*. (2 plays) Winnipeg: Turnstone Press, 1984.

10. The Casa Pericolo is fictional. But, coincidentally, Bruce Ackland ran a small bed and breakfast called The Posada del Perico in Ajijic in the late 1950s.

11. A copy of this play resides in the library of Bowdoin College, Bourjaily's alma mater.

13. Hargraves, *Lake Chapala*.

Chapter 37. El Charro Negro

1. "30 years ago" in *Detroit Free Press*, 19 April 1932, 6.

2. *Fort Lauderdale News*, 4 November 1937, 5. McDonald, "Horses, Hobby and Business."

3. *Aiken Standard* (South Carolina), 2 April 1930, 4.

4. McDonald, "Horses, Hobby and Business."

5. The marriage took place on 12 April 1938.

6. McDonald, "Horses, Hobby and Business."

7. Agustin Velarde, interviewed in Ajijic on 12 April 2016.

8. Katie Goodridge Ingram, email, 17 May 2019.

9. Bill Atkinson, interviewed 7 April 2016.

10. Loy Strother, personal communication, 31 October 2017.

11. GR, 22 July 1965.

12. This property later became the Hacienda del Lago boutique hotel.

13. GR, 24 September 1964.

14. *The Orlando Sentinel* (Orlando, Florida), 22 November 1964, 26; 26 November 1964, 45. The museum later became the Orlando Science Center.

15. Gina Hildreth, quoted in GR, 14 January 1965, 9.

16. GR, 10 December 1964.

17. John Mersereau Jr., personal communication by letter in 2008.

18. Bill Atkinson, interviewed 7 April 2016. Dick and Mary Bishop celebrated their fifth wedding anniversary in August 1971. (GR, 28 August 1971).

19. McDonald, "Horses, Hobby and Business."

20. Bill Atkinson, interviewed 7 April 2016.

21. Peter Huf, interviewed at his home in November 2014.

22. McDonald, "Horses, Hobby and Business." The governor was Francisco García Montero (not García Montara as stated in the article).

23. GR, 19 April 1969.

24. Photograph in possession of Beverly Johnson's daughter Jill Maldonado.

Chapter 38. Music since 1960

1. Tamara Janúz, personal communication.

2. GR, 20 January 1968; 5 August 1978, 3.

3. Laura Castro Golarte. 1996. *El Informador*, 28 January 1996.

4. Anita Lomax. 1967. GR, 19 August 1967.

5. Jocelyn Cantón. 2016. "Los Axixis, primera banda de rock de Ajijic." *Laguna, Periodico Semanal*, 7 March 2016. The band was initially known as Los Alacranes Cubanos (The Cuban Scorpions).

6. Timothy G Ruff, personal communication.

7. Victor Manuel Medeles Romero. Undated. "Semblanza de nuestros pilares musicales." *PAGINA Que sí se lee!*

8. Name as on marriage registration; elsewhere named María Ana Romero Ibon.

9. Britton, Sandy. 2020. "The Medeles family: A Musical Legacy," in *Conecciones* (LCS), in two parts: April 2020, 67; May 2020, 1011.

10. *The Penticton Western News* (Canada): 17 February 2012. Ajijic Huapango can be found on YouTube.

11. Sofía Medeles. 2021. "Terminan mural en honor al compositor de 'Mi Lindo Ajijic.'" *Semanario de la Laguna*, 7 February 2021.

Chapter 39. Neill James the philanthropist

1. Talavera Salgado, *Lago Chapala*.

2. NJA: Copy of letter, 26 March 1974, from James (Ajijic) to Antonio Guzmán Rodríguez, Director, Mexican Government Tourism Department in Washington DC.

3. NJA: Copy of letter, 12 December 1973, from James (Ajijic) to "Raymond."

4. NJA: James names the five individuals, in letters, as Reyes Villanueva, Isabel Rojas, Rosario Morales Castilla, Otilio Flores and Celedonia Flores.

5. NJA: Letter, 22 May 1974, from James (Ajijic) to Antonio Guzmán Rodríguez, Director, Mexican Government Tourism Department in Washington DC.

6. *El Informador*, 20 November 1974, 2C.

7. Karl Homann. 2020. "Artistic Embroidery: An LCS Program that Enriches the Lives of Local Women." *Conecciones* (LCS), May 2020, 1213.

8. NJA: Letter, 19 February 1976, from James to Lic Agustín Velarde.

9. NJA: Letter, 31 December 1951, from James (Ajijic) to Hazel Kerper (Cody, Wyoming).

10. Katie Goodridge Ingram, email 15 July 2019.

11. Talavera Salgado, *Lago Chapala*, 134.

12. GR, 17 May 1969.

13. GR, 3 May 1975.

14. I have failed to locate the published version of this article. The quotes come from the manuscript version in the Purdy archives at Queen's University, London, Ontario.

15. Documents in NJA, and see chapter about health services.

16. NJA: Neill James. 1977. "Ajijic." Unpublished notes.

17. GR, 13 August 1977, 19; 10 September 1977, 18.

18. GR, 8 April 1978, 19.

19. Anon, "Philanthropist."

20. GR, 10 December 1977, 19.

21. Lake Chapala Society. AHistory of the Lake Chapala Society." Undated post on LCS website https://lakechapalasociety.com [21 November 2018]

Chapter 40. Canadians revive Posada Ajijic

1. Jerry Murray. 2008. "Slodge". Ce*I*40C (Vol. 7, No. 5), October 2008. http://www.efanzines.com/EK/eI40/index.htm#slodge [9 June 2018]

2. eg GR, 3 May 1975.

3. (a) Judy Eager, interviewed by Nancy Bollembach, 10 July 2008. Interview transcript published as "Eager Interview", Bateman & Bollembach, *Ajijic*, 117–120. (b) Judy Eager, personal communication, February 2020.

4. Toby Smith. 1986. *Romantic Inns of Mexico: A Selective Guide to Charming Accommodations South of the Border*. Chronicle Books Inc., 967. Sue Waterbury later returned to Ajijic and married George Reed there in 1978. (GR, 30 September 1978, 18)

5. GR, 7 February 1976.

6. Morley Eager, personal communication, 1990.

7. Michael Eager, personal communication.

8. Terry Vidal, personal communication.

9. GR, 5 November 1977, 17.

10. GR, 19 February 1977, 18; 5 March 1977, 17; 10 December 1977, 19.

11. GR, 19 March 1977, 8.

12. GR, 2 April 1977, 19.

13. Dale Hoyt Palfrey. 2018. "Flashback to the birth of the Mexican National Chili Cookoff", GR, 15 February 2018, 9.

14. Michael Eager, personal communication.

15. GR, 7 January 1965; 6 January 1968; 12 January 1974.

16. Dr Jim Vaughan, interviewed by author in August 1990.

17. Charbonneau, *The Lair*.

18. The Eagers bought the property from Guadalupe Jauregui Martínez and Alfonso Solórzano Campos, who had acquired the property from Paul Heuer on 3 September 1955.

Chapter 41. Art in the 1970s

1. GR, 17 January 1976, 29.

2. GR, 14 September 1974.

3. GR, 3 April 1971; 24 April 1971; 8 May 1971; 22 May 1971; 5 June 1971.

4. GR, 23 October 1971; 27 November 1971

5. Haciendas lecture by noted authors Paul and Elizabeth Bartlett on 22 May 1972. GR, 9 September 1972; 22 April 1973; 26 January 1974; 16 March 1974.

6. GR, 17 August 1974.

7. GR, 15 November 1975, 20; 6 December 1975, 20; 21 February 1976; 30 October 1976, 23; 11 December 1976; 12 February 1977, 17.

8. GR, 17 July 1976, 20.

9. GR, 2 October 1976, 22; Katie Goodridge Ingram, personal communication, 2015.

10. GR, 13 December 1975; 17 January 1976.

11. GR, 13 March 1976, 21.

12. This section is based on interviews with Synnove Pettersen, Tom Faloon, Katie Goodridge Ingram, Gail Michel and her daughter Angelina Guzmán.

13. (a) *Mexico City News*, 13 February 1977. (b) GR, 19 February 1977; 5 March 1977; 10 December 1977.

14. Dale Hoyt Palfrey. 2014. "Remembering Tomás Faloon, icon of Ajijic's expat community," GR, 29 November 2014.

15. GR, 14 March 1973.

16. Penny C Morrill. 1997. "Hubert Harmon Whimsy and Humor in Mexican Silver", in *Jewelry* (Journal of the American Society of Jewelry Historians.) 1 (1996 97): 64 –77.

17. Tom Thompson, personal communication.

18. GR, 23 February 1974; 27 March 1976; 12 February 1977, 17.

19. Elizabeth Hulings Diamond, personal communication.

20. A feature article about his daughter's stylish Chicago home in the September 2008 issue of *CS* (Modern Luxury Media) includes a photograph of a Mintz monotype titled "Tree in Ajijic, Mexico."

21. GR, 12 February 1977, 14; 3 December 1977, 19. The story of Lökós is told by Ingeborg Lökós (his wife) and Martha LaCasse in their *Still Life with Violin* (Santa Fe: BelleCora Press, 2004).

22. (a) GR, 13 August 1977, 10 September 1977, 8 April 1978 (b) Interviews with Dionicio Morales and Antonio López Vega.

23. GR 11 September 1976, 21. Theater, writing and silkscreen classes to be given by Conrado Contreras, Zaida Contreras and John Frost, respectively.

Chapter 42. Medical and health services

1. Katie Goodridge Ingram. 2011. "Helen Kirtland Goodridge," in Bateman and Bollenbach, *Ajijic*, 95.

2. Carol Shepherd McClain. 1975. "Ethno-obstetrics in Ajijic," *Anthropological Quarterly*, 40: 38 56.

3. GR, 6 March 1976, 1, 8, 14; 10 April 1976, 1; 23 July 1977, 1; *Mexico City Daily News*, 17 July 1977.

4. GR, 6 March 1976, 14.

5. *Detroit Free Press*, 3 June 1981, 40; 10 November 1981, 10.

6. Anon, "Philanthropist Leads an Eventful Life."

7. (a) GR, 21 May 1977, 17. (b) *Valley News* (Van Nuys, California), 27 May 1977, 16.

8. Netherton, "More about the Way it Was."

9. GR, 2 September 1978, 14.

10. GR, 5 March 1977, 26.

11. GR, 23 July 1977, 19.

12. GR, 8 October 1977, 27.

13. GR, 31 December 1977, 19.
14. GR, 26 August 1978, 1, 10.
15. GR, 29 July 1978, 19.

Chapter 43. The performing arts

1. GR, 18 May 1974; 20 March 1976, 8.
2. Dale Palfrey. 2016. "Lakeside Auditorium's birthday woes." GR, 22 September 2016
3. GR, 3 May 1975.
4. GR, 18 March 1978, 19, 22; 8 April 1978, 21.
5. GR, "Lakeside auditorium to close for renovation." GR, 23 January 2020.
6. Alexandra Bateman, "Into Modern Times," Bateman and Bollenbach, *Ajijic*, 141–147.
7. GR, 16 April 1977, 19; 17 September 1977, 18.
8. GR, 17 Sept 1977, 18; Katie Goodridge Ingram, personal communication.
9. GR, 7 May 1977, 18; 28 May 1977, 17.
10. Alexandra Bateman, "Into Modern Times," Bateman & Bollembach, *Ajijic*, 144–145.
11. Katie Goodridge Ingram. 1977. "Dinner Theater at the Inn." *Mexico City News*, 3 July 1977.
12. GR, 24 September 1977, 19; 1 October 1977,
13. (a) GR, 3 December 1977, 18. (b) Alexandra Bateman, "Into Modern Times," Bateman & Bollembach, *Ajijic*, 144–145.
14. GR, 6 May 1978, 19; 20 May 1978, 17; 19 August 1978, 15; 9 September 1978, 17.
15. GR, 9 July 18.
16. GR, 8 April 1978, 19.
17. Alexandra Bateman, "Into Modern Times," Alexandra Bateman and Nancy Bollenbach, *Ajijic*, 145.

Chapter 44. Zara's final years

1. Jack McDonald. 1969. "'La Russe' Familiar Figure in Village of Ajijic", GR, 22 February 1969, 1112.
2. Ken Smedley, personal communication.
3. Michael Eager, personal communication.
4. Katie Goodridge Ingram, personal communication.
5. *El Informador*, 7 August 1970, 34.
6. *El Informador*, 21 August 1971, 32.
7. Letter, 25 November 1976, from Zara (Ajijic) to Nancy Neel (San Diego) in possession of Nancy Neel.
8. Ruth Netherton, GR, 13 August 1977, 17.
9. *El Informador*, 21 December 1978, 11. This was a reversal of policy. In its early years the Comité Pro-Defensa del Lago de Chapala had actively opposed the La Zurda project. See *El Informador*, 9 April, 1957, 2.
10. *El Informador*, 2 June 1981, 31.
11. FONAPAS: Fondo Nacional Para Actividades Sociales (National Fund for Social Activities).
12. NJA: Uncredited unpublished biography of Zara. The ballet was performed by the Ballet Azteca, directed by Carlos Ochoa, and the Ballet Clásico de Jalisco, directed by Deborah Velázquez.
13. *El Informador*, 4 February 1983, 26; 15 February 1983, 5A.
14. Tony Burton. 1997. "Can Mexico's Largest Lake be Saved?" *Ecodecision*, Volume 23, Winter 1997.

15. (a) Sean Mattson. "'Hands around the Lake' set for June 3". GR, 15 April 2000. (b) Dale Hoyt Palfrey. "Eco-enthusiasts gather to embrace Lake Chapala." GR, 22 June 2000.

16. Letter, 7 December 1976, from Zara (Chapala) to Nancy Neel (San Diego) in possession of Nancy Neel.

17. Letter, 29 January 1977, from Zara (Chapala) to Nancy Neel (San Diego) in possession of Nancy Neel.

18. GR, 23 September 1977; *El Informador*, 21 December 1978, 11.

19. After a career as a contemporary dancer, Sergio Lasso (1952–2007) directed and adapted works for theater and dance shows, and worked in radio and TV. See articles by Sergio Lasso and Fernando Mendoza in *La Pirouette Danza* in issues 31 (January–February 2001) and 33 (May–June 2001).

20. *El Informador*, 4 December 1977, 20.

21. GR, 28 January 1978, 1, 17-18.

22. Sergio Lasso. 2001. "Mi Hermana, la Rusa de Ajijic." *La Pirouette Danza*, #33, MayJune 2001, 1,4,5.

23. Fernando Mendoza. 2001. "Ayenara Zara Alexeyewa, La Rusa de Ajijic. Parte 1." *La Pirouette Danza*, #31 January–February 2001, 57.

24. Unpublished diary entry for 2 October 1982 by Gwen Chan Burton, one of the teachers.

25. NJA has a copy of this autobiography, printed in Guadalajara.

26. Ken Smedley, personal communication.

27. *Aquí en la Ribera de Chapala*, vol 1 #49, 18 January 1986.

28. Katie Goodridge Ingram, personal communication.

29. Domingo Márquez. 2013, "Remozarán el mausoleo de Khyra Zara Alexeyewa 'La rusa'", *Chapala en vivo*, 16 October 2013. http://www.chapalaenvivo.com/2013/10/16/remozaran el mausoleo de khyra zara alexeyewa la rusa/

30. CMAC: Historial catastral and property transfer details. The land in question was originally part of Calle Independencia 20 (formerly 387).

Chapter 45. Ajijic expands east

1. James, *Dust on My Heart*, 277.

2. Laura Bateman. "Mexico 1952," Bateman and Bollenbach, *Ajijic*, 76.

3. GR, 11 February 1967.

4. Talavera Salgado, *Lago Chapala*, 8385.

5. Talavera Salgado, *Lago Chapala*, 86.

6. According to Allyn Hunt and Ruth Netherton ("Citizens Blocking Apparent Agrarian Reform 'Land Grab' Attempt in Ajijic" in GR, 23 November 1985, 1, 15, 18): "The 'Communidad Indígena,' recognized in 1940, consisted of 310 or 320 members. Today 1985, it is generally agreed, only 10 or 12 of the 'comuneros' are Ajijic natives, no more indigenous than 10,000 or so others. The remainder are Guadalajara residents who are said to want free land for vacation homes."

7. For details of this extraordinary conflict, see Talavera Salgado, *Lago Chapala*. The community had won a case against neighbors in San Antonio Tlayacapan in 1797, and their rights were reconfirmed by the Jalisco State Department of Asuntos Agrarios in 1945.

8. Talavera Salgado, *Lago Chapala*, 912.

9. Talavera Salgado, *Lago Chapala*, 109, 113.

10. Sol Fortoul. "La construcción despierta en la ribera de Chapala." *Público*, 24 January 1998.

11. Talavera Salgado, *Lago Chapala*, 113-114.

12. *El Occidental*, 25 January 1969

13. Richard Joseph. 1969. "Travel Notes." *Esquire*, June 1969, 178, 180.

14. Talavera Salgado, *Lago Chapala*, 1489.

15. Martínez Réding, Chapala, 5861.

16. Talavera Salgado, *Lago Chapala*, 126, 150152.

17. Talavera Salgado, *Lago Chapala*, 125.

18. Talavera Salgado, *Lago Chapala*, 127128.

19. The university bought the hotel in late 1976. (Letter from Zara to Peggy Neel, 29 January 1977.) The earliest advertisement in *El Informador* using the name Hotel Real de Chapala was 3 August 1986, 24.

20. *El Informador* 24 August 1974, 13.

21. *El Informador*, 24 November 1989, 24.

22. Brochure for La Floresta RV park advertised on eBay, November 2021.

23. The change of name was approved by municipal authorities on 28 February 1994. By unfortunate timing the city of Jinxi was renamed Huludao later that year.

24. Gilberto Padilla García. 2010. "El tramo de la carretera Chapala–Ajijic: Avenida Kilométrica." *Página, Que Sí Se Lee*, 3 December 2010, 13.

25. Talavera Salgado, *Lago Chapala*, 143.

Chapter 46. Ajijic expands west

1. GR, 8 May 1971.

2. Eric Henneghen, personal communication.

3. Known in Mexico as Louis Wertheimer Fuchs.

4. (a) Jane Hamilton. 2007. "History Silverthorne House." Post at Buffalo Architecture and History. https://buffaloah.com/a/del/877/hist.html [15 February 2021]. (b) *Billboard*, 10 April 1948, 112.

5. Talavera Salgado, *Lago Chapala*, 150–152

6. Giving only the distance and direction from the church to each property is a totally inadequate way to identify location and boundaries. In addition, several of the compass directions in the document are meaningless, including those which confuse *sureste* (southeast) with *suroeste* (southwest).

7. *El Informador* 23 February 1967.

8. Talavera Salgado, *Lago Chapala*, 54. The land acquired by Wertheimer included the hillside in the municipality of Jocotopec developed in 1972 for the Racquet Club in San Juan Cosalá.

9. GR, 10 November 1973 (Tejaban advertisement).

10. Talavera Salgado, *Lago Chapala*, 56–57.

11. Fausto Márquez, personal communication via Facebook. (June 2021)

12. *El Informador*, 25 October 1972.

13. Letter from Peggy Neel to Nancy Neel, 6 November 1972, in possession of Nancy Neel.

14. Letter from Peggy Neel to Nancy Neel, 31 November 1972, in possession of Nancy Neel.

15. Talavera Salgado, *Lago Chapala*, 64.

16. Author's analysis of Talavera's map. Some known minor inaccuracies on the original map were corrected prior to analysis.

17. John Moody. 1987. "Paradise, Down Mexico Way." *Time Magazine*, 24 August 1987.

18. (a) Hector del Muro. 2006. "Lomas de Ajijic y Misión del Lago regresan a la

comunidad indígena." *El Charal.* (b) Javier García Duarte. "Lomas de Ajijic, despojo y farsa." Editorial in *El Charal,* 21 January 2006. (c) Dale Hoyt Palfrey. 2006. "Land dispute reports alarm home owners." GR, 27 January 2006.

19. Dale Hoyt Palfrey. 2006. "Subdivisions approval stirs heated debate." GR, 24 November 2006.

20. Compton, *To The Isthmus,* 148–149.

21. *El Informador,* 22 April 1937, 4, 8.

22. (a) Alejandro Mendo Gutierrez. 1996. *Ajijic: su significado toponímico. Ajijic: Axixik Temaskalpulli.* (b) Anon. 2011. "Colores Ancestros: Dionicio Morales." (Entrevista) *Meretrices: revista cultural de la ribera de Chapala,* 7 December 2011.

23. Antonio López Vega, personal communication.

24. Katie Goodridge Ingram, personal communication.

25. Antonio López Vega, personal communication, 24 March 2021.

26. GR, 24 January 1970.

27. GR, 28 September 1974, 16.

Chapter 47. Traditions and festivals

1. Domingo Márquez, Facebook message, 25 January 2018.

2. Micki Wendt. "Fiestas, January through Easter", undated contribution by Micki Wendt, edited by *Ajijic News,* http://www.ajijicnews.com/pages/jan_easter2018

3. D Arturo Ortega. 2016. "La Sayaca será este martes la figura central del Carnaval Ajijic 2016." *Seminario Laguna,* 8 February 2016.

4. Jocelyn Cantón. 2016. "Ser sayaco, una tradición de familia." *Seminario Laguna,* 13 February 2016. http://semanariolaguna.com/15569/

5. Dale Hoyt Palfrey. 2017. "Mysterious roots of the wacky Sayaca." GR, 23 February 2017.

6. Kernick, "Ajijic."

7. *El Ojo del Lago,* March 1986.

8. Carlos Alvarez Gallegos. 2017. "El camino rojo, una forma de vida espiritual." *Revista Aló San Luis,* 14 April 2017. https://www.alosanluis.com/2017/04/14/el camino rojo una forma de vida espiritual/ 7 June 2018

9. Aldo Daniel Arias Yerena. (a) 2011. "La Danza del Sol de Ajijic: un ritual nodo en la red de espiritualidad alternativa." Masters thesis in Social Anthropology, Guadalajara: CIESAS-Occidente. (b) 2012. "Significados y apropiaciones mexicas de la Danza del Sol. Estudio de caso de Axixik Temazkalpulli", *Cuicuilco* #55 (Sep–Dec 2012), 195–217.

10. Ángel Chacón. 2011. "The history about the beginning of hot air balloons, made out of tissue paper, in the town of Ajijic, Jalisco." AjijicNews.com, 12 September 2011 http://www.ajijicnews.com/pages/globo_history

11. Crump, born in Estonia, married a US Air Force officer after the second world war. Her husband died in a flying accident in 1955. Three years later, Crump and their six children, all under the age of nine, moved to Ajijic.

12. GR, 30 September 1965.

13. GR, 9 September 1965.

14. Ruth Netherton. 1978. "Great Chile Cookoff", GR, 5 August 1978, 17.

15. Dale Hoyt Palfrey. 2018. "Flashback to the birth of the Mexican National Chili Cookoff", GR, 15 February 2018, 9.

16. "Down Memory Lane," article from the GR reprinted in the 1997 Cookoff Program.

Chapter 48. Art and creative writing since 1980

1. Additional biographical details for most of the artists named in this chapter can be found at lakechapalaartists.com.

2. Jackie Hodges. "Focus On Art" (ca 1999) in *El Ojo del Lago*.

3. *El Ojo del Lago*, October 1988; March 1989; May 1990.

4. Jesús López Vega. 2016. "Historia del Movimiento Cultural de Ajijic." *Semanario de la Laguna*, 27 November 2016. http://semanariolaguna.com/22710/ [12 April 2021]

5. The organizers of this event included Jesús Escamilla, Alejandro Martínez, Moctezuma Medina, Pablo Márquez, Saúl Gutiérrez, Filiberto Higuera, Antonio Cárdenas and Anselmo Avalos. (Jesus López Vega, 2016, see note 4)

6. This group included Alejandro Martínez, Dionicio Morales, Jesús López Vega, Jesús Escamilla, Rodolfo Rivera, Anselmo Avalos and Moctezuma Medina. (Jesus López Vega, 2016, see note 4)

7. Avalos' painting "Primavera," completed when he was 12 years old, appears in Ganung, *A Cookbook with Color Reproductions*.

8. Xill Fessenden, personal communication via email, 22 April 2021.

9. CABA (Centro Ajijic de Bellas Artes). 2000. *Cincuenta Artistas: expresión plástica en la ribera de Chapala*. Ajijic: CABA.

10. Talavera, *Lago Chapala*, 50 (caption to photo).

11. *El Ojo del Lago*, January 1985; May 1990.

12. June Summers. 1993. *Lake Chapala: Villages in the Sun*. (Self published.)

13. Judy Miller, personal communication.

14. *El Ojo del Lago*, May 1985.

15. John Fraser. "The Educated Imagination: Carol Hoorn Fraser, Artist." Lecture at the University of King's College, Halifax, Nova Scotia, 11 April 2008.

16. Dale Palfrey, *El Ojo del Lago*, December 1987.

17. Hendrik Eleveld, *El Ojo del Lago*, March 1992.

18. Richman, "Ajijic."

Chapter 49. Press and academic articles

1. Since the 1980s there have been numerous other English-language print publications, including the *Chapala Riviera Guide* (1989–1993), edited by Jorge Romo, and the *Lake Chapala Review* (1999–2014), founded by Helyn Bercovitch, whose later editors included Darryl Tenenbaum and Judy King. The most noteworthy more recent publication is *Conecciones*, the bilingual monthly begun in January 2019 by the Lake Chapala Society.

2. GR, 25 February 1967, 10.

3. GR, 25 November 1978, 17.

4. Dale Hoyt Palfrey. 1994. "In the beginning were the words." *El Ojo del Lago*, September 1994.

5. GR, 4 February 1978, 17. Flittie's study is summarized in Gordon Finley. 1983. "American Retirement Abroad." 276–291 of D Landis & R W Brislin (Eds) *Handbook of intercultural training*, Vol III. New York.

6. Quoted by Finley (note 5).

7. Juan José Medeles Romero. 1975. "Plan de Desarrollo Urbano para la Poblacion de Ajijic." Tesis profesional que presentan facultad de Arquitectura Universidad de Guadalajara. Mexico. Comments based on account in Stokes (1984), see note 9.

8. See Francisco Talavera Salgado. 1977. "La ribera norte del lago de Chapala. La otra cara de una zona turística." *Controversia*, 1, 26–35, and Talavera, *Lago Chapala*.

9. Eleanor M Stokes. 1984. "La Colonia Extranjero (sic): an American retirement community in Ajijic, Mexico." PhD Thesis, University of New York, Stony Brook.

10. Charlotte Wolf. 1996. "Expatriate Identity: Construction of Another Life." Paper presented at University of Nottingham, UK, July 1996. (Reported in GR, 30 December 1995 and in *El Ojo del Lago*, February 1996.)

11. Lorena Melton Young Otero. (a) 1997. "US Retired Persons in Mexico." *American Behavioral Scientist*, 40, 7, 914–22. (b) 1999. "Death and Civil Society." *Annals of the American Academy of Political and Social Science*, Vol. 565, 193-206.

12. David Truly. (a) 2002. "International retirement migration and tourism along the Lake Chapala Riviera: developing a matrix of retirement migration behaviour". *Tourism Geographies*, Volume 4, Number 3, 261–281. (b) 2006. "The Lake Chapala Riviera: The Evolution of a Not So American Foreign Community" in Nicholas Dagen Bloom (ed). 2006. *Adventures into Mexico: American Tourism Beyond the Border*.

13. Stephen P Banks. (a) 2004. "Identity Narratives by American and Canadian retirees in Mexico." *Journal of Cross-Cultural Gerontology*, 19: 361–381. (b) 2009. "Intergenerational ties across borders: Grandparenting narratives by expatriate retirees in Mexico." *Journal of Aging Studies*, 23: 178–187.

14. (a) Lucía González Terreros, José Luis Santana Medina and Rosalba Castañeda Castro. 2018. "Ajijic, Jalisco ¿turistas residenciales o residentes? Un analisis desde los Derechos de Propiedad, Costos de Transaccion y los Bienes Comunes," in Mazon, Tomas (ed.) (2018). *Turismo residencial. Nuevos estilos de vida: de turistas a residentes*. Alicante, Spain: Publicacions de la Universitat d'Alacant. (b) Lucía González Torreros, José Luis Santana Medina, Katia Magdalena Lozano Uvario and Rosalba Castañeda Castro. 2020. "Airbnb en Ajijic, Jalisco. Una nueva forma de turismo residencial e impulso al desarrollo inmobiliario. Un analisis desde la Nueva Teoria Institucional." *Pasos*, Vol. 18 #1, 143-158.

15. Francisco Vladimir Díaz Copado. 2013. "Shaping multiple Ajijics and development. A Mexican town in the context of the international retirement migration." Thesis for doctorate in Rural Development Sociology, Wageningen University, Netherlands, 44–46.

16. Marisa Raditsch. 2015. "North-South Migration: The Impact of International Immigration in the Municipality of Chapala, Jalisco, Mexico." in *Hagira* (Israel Journal of Migration), 4, 94–111.

17. Vaira Avota. 2016. "Ahihika: amerikāņu sapnis, tikai Meksikā" ("Ajijic: American dream, just in Mexico"). Thesis, MA in social anthropology, Riga Stradins University, Latvia.

18. Mariana Ceja Bojorge. 2021. "Migración internacional de retiro: imaginarios sociales, memoria y cambios en el espacio de Ajijic." *Revista IUS* (Instituto de Ciencias Jurídicas de Puebla), Vol. 15, Núm. 47 (2021), 343–376.

Key dates, 1856–1990

1856 First reports of silver
1896 Murder of Juan Jaacks
1906 Incorporation of Quien Sabe Mining Company
1925 Zara (La Rusa), living in Chapala, invested in gold mines
1928 Alex von Mauch bought lakefront property in Ajijic
1929 Parahamansa Yogananda visited Zara and Ajijic
1933? Paul and Liesel Heuer opened lakefront inn
1937 Nigel Millett and father arrive
1938? Posada Ajijic opened
1939 Arrival of Georgette and Herbert Johnson
1940 Zara, Holger and mother moved to Ajijic
1943 Neill James first arrived in Ajijic
1945 *Village in the Sun* (Dane Chandos) published
1946 *Dust on my Heart* (Neill James) published
1947 Helen Kirtland and children arrived from Mexico City
1947 Mexican Art Workshop first held in Ajijic
1948 Opening of La Galería, Ajijic's first art gallery
1948 Neill James moved into Quinta Tzintzuntzan
1949 Posada Ajijic operated by Peter Elstob and Arnold Eiolart
1950? Health spa opened in Quinta Mi Retiro
1950 Ajijic Hand Looms established
1950 Neill James started silk business
1953? First Children's Library opened
1954 Comité Pro-Defensa del Lago de Chapala established
1955 Lake Chapala Society founded (in Chapala)
1955 Lake Chapala fell to record low
1957 *Life* photo-article about Ajijic
1957 Ajijic finally had 24-hour electricity
1958 Start of Chula Vista subdivision
1962 Iona Kupiec settled in Ajijic
1965 Lakeside Little Theater formed
1966 Regional Handicrafts School opened
1969 Start of La Floresta subdivision
1972 Bulldozer driven through Ajijic cemetery
1978 Lake Chapala Auditorium inaugurated
1978 First Ajijic Chili Cookoff
1983 Lake Chapala Society moved to Ajijic
1988 Lakeside Little Theater moved to current location
1989 Death of Zara (La Rusa)
1990 Eager family opened La Nueva Posada

Bibliography

Anon. 1945. "Neill James in Mexico." *Modern Mexico* (New York: Mexican Chamber of Commerce of the US), Vol. 18 #5 (October 1945), 22, 28.

Anon. ca 1978. "Philanthropist Leads an Eventful Life in Mexico." Alumni magazine of Mississippi University for Women, 16-17.

Arroyo Alejandre, Jesús and David E Lorey (compilers). 1995. *Ajustes y desajustes regionales. El caso de Jalisco a fines del sexenio salinista.* Guadalajara: Universidad de Guadalajara.

Banks, Stephen. 2016. *Kokio: A novel based on the life of Neill James.* Valley, Washington: Tellectual Press.

Bárcena, Mariano. 1888. *Ensayo estadístico del Estado de Jalisco.* Second edition: Guadalajara: Gobierno de Jalisco, Secretaría General, Unidad Editorial, 1983.

Bashford, G M. 1954. *Tourist Guide to Mexico.* McGraw-Hill;.

Bassing, Eileen. 1963. *Where's Annie?* Random House, New York.

Bateman, Alexandra and Nancy Bollenbach (compilers). 2011. *Ajijic: 500 years of adventurers.* Mexico: Thomas Paine Chapter NSDAR.

Bedford, Sybille. 1953. *The Sudden View: A Mexican journey.* London: Victor Gollancz Ltd. Revised edition published as *A Visit to Don Otavio: A Traveller's Tale from Mexico,* (London: Collins, 1960).

Boehm Schoendube, Brigitte (coord.) 2002. "Cartografía Histórica del Lago de Chapala" (CD), El Colegio de Michoacán.

Burton, Tony. 1993. *Western Mexico: A Traveler's Treasury.* 4th edition, 2014. Canada: Sombrero Books.

———. 2009. *Lake Chapala through the ages; an anthology of travellers' tales.* Canada: Sombrero Books.

———. 2020. *If Walls Could Talk: Chapala's historic buildings and their former occupants.* Canada: Sombrero Books.

Bynner, Witter. 1951. *Journey with Genius: Recollection and Reflections Concerning The D.H. Lawrences.* New York: The John Day Company.

Carreño, Arturo. 2003. *Guad-alhajero.* Guadalajara: Editorial Ágata. (Reprinted as "Añoranzas de Guadalajara: Carrera y mortaja del cielo baja", *Gaceta Municipal,* Guadalajara, September 2013, 13-14.)

Chandos, Dane. 1945. *Village in the Sun*. New York: G P Putnam's Sons. London, UK: Michael Joseph (1948). Reissued in Mexico (Tlayacapan Press) in 1998.

———. 1949. *House in the Sun*. New York: G P Putnam's Sons. London, UK: Michael Joseph (1950). Reissued in Mexico (Tlayacapan Press) in 1999.

———. 1997. (Compiled by Moreen Chater, translation by Rosa María Casas). *Las recetas de Candelaria / Candelaria's cookbook*. San Antonio Tlayacapan, Jalisco: Ediciones Tlayacapan Press.

Charbonneau, Louis Henry. 1980. *The Lair*. New York : Fawcett Gold Meda; Ebook edition, 2014, Jabberwocky Literary Agency, Inc.

Compton, Barbara. 1964. *To The Isthmus*. New York: Simon & Schuster,

Cristina, Zaida (Cristina Zaida Reynoso Camacho). 2010. *El Chapala de Natalia*. Chapala: Editorial Clavileño.

———. 2015. *Chapala, Siglo XIX, Tomo II: Atotonilquillo, San Antonio y Hacienda del Cuije*. Ediciones Clavileño.

de Brundige, Frances (pseudonym of Eleanor Saenger aka Zara Alexeyewa). 1973. *Quilocho and the Dancing Stars*. Philadelphia: Dorrance & Co.

Dodge, David. 1969. *The Best of Mexico by Car*. Macmillan.

Dollero, Adolfo. 1911. *México al día*. (Impresiones y notas de viaje). Paris-Mexico: Librería de la Vda de C Bouret.

Dunlap, Jan. 2017. *Dilemma*. Canada: Sombrero Books.

Edwards, Henry F. 2008. *The Sweet Bird of Youth*. BookSurge Publishing.

Embree, Charles Fleming. 1900. *A Dream of a Throne, the Story of a Mexican Revolt*. Boston: Little, Brown and Company.

Farías, Ixca. 1963. *Casos y cosas de mis tiempos*. Guadalajara: Colegio Internacional.

Ford, Norman D. 1965. *Fabulous Mexico, where everything costs less*. New York: Harian Publications.

Gallop, Rodney. 1939. *Mexican Mosaic: Folklore and Tradition*. London: Faber and Faber.

Ganung, Arthur L. 1972. *A Cookbook with Color Reproductions by Artists from the Galería*. 1972. Ajijic, Mexico: La Galería del Lago de Chapala.

Gilbert, Jack. 1962. *Views of Jeopardy*. Connecticut: Yale University Press.

Gottlieb, Elaine. 1959. "Passage Through Stars", in *Noonday* #2, 80-93. New York: Noonday Press.

Grupo Acalli San Antonio Tlayacapan. 2019. *San Antonio Tlayacapan: Recorriendo su historia*. Grupo Acalli, 67-68.

Hargraves, Michael. 1992. *Lake Chapala: A literary survey*. (Los Angeles: Michael Hargraves).

Helm, MacKinley. 1948. *Journeying Through Mexico*. Boston: Little, Brown and Co.

Hughes, Edan. 1989. *Artists in California, 1786–1940*. Hughes Pub. Co.

Ingram, Katie Goodridge. 2020. *According to Soledad: memories of a Mexican childhood*. Canada: Sombrero Books.

Jackson, Everett Gee. 1985. *Burros and Paintbrushes, A Mexican Adventure*. Texas A&M University Press.

James, Neill. 1945. "I Live in Ajijic." *Modern Mexico* (New York: Mexican Chamber of Commerce of the US), Vol. 18 #5 (October 1945), 23-28.

———. 1946. *Dust on my Heart: Petticoat Vagabond in Mexico*. New York: Charles Scribner's. Reprinted 1997, The Lake Chapala Society.

———. 1948. "Mexican Story," Unpublished manuscript dated 26 October in Lake Chapala Society Neill James Archive (NJA).

———. 1967. "Ajijic Carrousel", *Guadalajara Reporter*, 11 March 1967, 8.

Kamstra, Jerry. 1974. *Weed: Adventures of a Dope Smuggler*. New York: Harper & Row.

Kaufman, Charles. 1939. *Fiesta in Manhattan*. New York: William Morrow & Co.

Kernick, Zoe. 1951. "Ajijic." *Mexican Life*, April 1951, 13-14, 58, 60, 62-63.

Kingsley, Rose Georgina. 1874. *South by west or winter in the Rocky Mountains and spring in Mexico*. London: W. Isibister & Co.

López Cotilla, Manuel. 1843. *Noticias Geográficas y Estadísticas del Departamento de Jalisco*. Guadalajara: Imprenta del Gobierno. 3rd edition 1983.

MacDonald, Ross (pen name of Kenneth Millar). 1962. *The Zebra-Striped Hearse*. New York: Alfred A. Knopf.

Marsh, Willard. 1960. "Mexican Hayride." *Esquire*, March 1960.

———. 1965. *Week with No Friday*. New York: Harper & Row. A limited edition private reprint was published in Mexico in about 2000.

Marsh, Willard. 1969. *Beachhead in Bohemia: Stories*. Baton Rouge: Louisiana State University.

Martínez Réding, Fernando. 1973. *Chapala*. Guadalajara: Jalisco Turista S.A.

McCombe, Leonard. 1957. "Yanks Who Don't Go Home. Expatriates Settle Down to Live and Loaf in Mexico." *Life*, 23 December 1957.

McDonald, Jack. 1969. "Horses, Hobby and Business For This Ajijic Man." *Guadalajara Reporter*, 8 March 1969, 18-19.

McGinnis, Ralph J. 1964. "Lotus Land." An open letter to friends, later published (in parts) in *El Ojo del Lago*, from June 1994 to February 1995 inclusive.

McLaughlin, Thomas. 1985. *The Greatest Escape, or How to Live in Paradise, in Luxury, for 250 Dollars Per Month*.

———. 1986. *How to Find Peace in the Mexican Alps Lake Chapala*. Bookman House.

Melby, Aileen Olsen. 1991. *Song for Mexico*. Guadalajara: Impre-Jal.

Menéndez Valdés, José. 1980. *Descripción y censo general de la Intendencia de Guadalajara, 1789-1793*. Guadalajara, Jalisco: Gobierno de Jalisco, Secretaría General, Unidad Editorial.

Miller, Carol. 1963. "Guadalajara balances the old with the new." *Mexican Life*, vol 39 #8 (August 1963), 14.

Morales López, Dionicio. 2010. *Santos Rico—Ánimas de Axixic*.

Netherton, Ruth. 1977. "More about the Way it Was." *Guadalajara Reporter*, 3 September 1977, 17-18.

Norman, James. 1959. *In Mexico. Where to Look, How to Buy Mexican Popular Arts and Crafts*. New York: William Morrow, 241-242.

Nottonson, Ira N. 1972. *Mexico My Home. Primitive Art and Modern Poetry With 50 easy to learn Spanish words and phrases. For all children from 8 to 80.* Guadalajara: Boutique d'Artes Graficas.

Parmenter, Ross. 1983. *Stages in a Journey.* New York: Profile Press.

Purdy, Al. 1980. *The D H Lawrence House at Chapala.* Sutton West, Ontario: The Paget Press. This was a limited edition of 44 copies.

Reynolds, Mack. 1963. *The Expatriates.* Regency Books.

Richman, Jan. 1994. "Ajijic." *Ploughshares*, Vol. 19, 4, (Winter, 1993/1994), 16.

——. 1995. *Because the Brain Can Be Talked into Anything: poems.* Louisiana State University Press.

Ross-Merrimer, Ruth. 2001. *Champagne & Tortillas.* Texas: We-Publish.com.

Schneebaum, Tobias. 1979. *Wild Man.* New York: Viking.

——. 2000. *Secret Places: My Life in New York and New Guinea.* Univ. of Wisconsin Press.

Scofield, Sandra. 1996. *A Chance to See Egypt.* New York: Cliff Street Books (Harper Collins).

Shekerjian, Regina. 1952. "You can Afford a Mexican Summer: Complete Details on how to Stretch your Dollars During an Art Trek South of the Border", *Design*, Volume 53, Issue 8, pp 182-197.

——. 1993. *Hoofbeats on the Door: Poems.* Kansas City, Missouri: Helicon Nine Editions.

Spicer, Bart. 1955. *The Day of The Dead.* New York: Dodd, Mead.

Stephens, Charles J. 1999. *Louis E. Stephens: His Life in Letters.* New York: Jay Street Publishers.

Talavera Salgado, Francisco. 1982. *Lago Chapala, turismo residencial y campesinado.* Mexico City: INAH.

Tello, Antonio. 1891. *Libro segundo de la Crónica Miscelánea.* Guadalajara: Impr. de la República Literia de C.L. de Guevara, 1891.

Terry, Thomas Philip. 1909. *Terry's Mexico Handbook for Travellers.* México City: Sonora News Company and Boston: Houghton Mifflin Co.

——. 1947. *Terry's Guide to Mexico*, Revised Edition. Printed in Boston.

Terry, Thomas Philip and James Norman. 1965. *Terry's Guide to Mexico.* New York: Doubleday.

Upton, John. 1950. "Ah-hee-heek: A Place to Loaf in Mexico." *San Francisco Chronicle*, 7 May 1950.

ruth weiss. 2011. *Can't stop the beat, the life and words of a Beat poet.* Studio City, California: Divine Arts.

Yogananda, Swami. 1929. "Ode to Lake Chapala." *East–West*, November–December, 1929 Vol. 4–3.

Young, Al. 1975. *Who is Angelina?* New York: Holt, Rinehart and Winston.

Index to creative writers and visual artists

More information about most of these artists and authors
is available at lakechapalaartists.com

Creative writers

Visual artists

General Index

Author

Tony Burton, born and educated in the UK, taught, researched, lectured and guided specialist cultural and ecological trips in Mexico for eighteen years. A three-time winner of ARETUR's travel-writing competition for articles about Mexico, he has written extensively about Mexico for more than thirty years, bringing its history, economics, tourism and geography to a wide audience.

His previous books on Mexico are *Western Mexico: A Traveler's Treasury* (fourth edition, 2014), *Lake Chapala Through the Ages, an Anthology of Travelers' Tales* (2008), *Mexican Kaleidoscope: myths, mysteries and mystique* (2016), *If Walls Could Talk: Chapala's historic buildings and their former occupants* (2020), and *A postcard history of Lake Chapala* (2022). He also coauthored, with Dr. Richard Rhoda, the landmark volume *Geo-Mexico, the Geography and Dynamics of Modern Mexico* (2010).

Tony's original articles and maps have appeared in numerous magazines, journals and books in Mexico, Canada, the US, Ireland and elsewhere.

Tony and his wife, Gwen, live on Vancouver Island in Canada and revisit Mexico as often as they can.

Cover artist

The watercolor of Ajijic plaza gracing the cover of this book is the work of Peter Shandera, who credits his seventh grade teacher, in 1957, with giving him permission to dabble in the arts. After studying at the California College of Arts and Crafts, he designed parks, playgrounds and theater sets, before heading up large teams of graphic designers for environmental engineering firms.

Peter feels strongly that being an artist is a way of life that is always seeking new ways of seeing. He continues to explore art and photography since retiring to Ajijic, and joined several like-minded enthusiasts to establish the very active art group, Urban Sketchers, Ajijic.

Other books by this author

Western Mexico: A Traveler's Treasury (4th edition, 2014)
The author departs from "the stock formula found in conventional guides. He adheres to a more organic approach, drawing on personal experience and meticulous research to divulge the virtues and peculiarities of every destination."
—Dale Palfrey, *The Guadalajara Reporter*

Lake Chapala Through the Ages, an Anthology of Travelers' Tales (2008)
"Intermingled with the firsthand accounts of the area in different eras, Burton provides snippets of background history to give some larger context.... Burton is a consummate scholar whose writing is also enjoyable to read."
—novelist Robert Richter

Geo-Mexico, the Geography and Dynamics of Modern Mexico (2010) (coauthored with Richard Rhoda, PhD)
"GeoMexico illustrates both the richness of geography as a field of study and the spectrum of cultural, economic, and environmental anomalies that make Mexico so eternally fascinating." —Felisa Rogers, *The People's Guide to Mexico*

Mexican Kaleidoscope: myths, mysteries and mystique (2016)
"In this lively interweaving of history, cuisine, culture, tradition and superstition, Tony Burton brings the reader refreshing and often startling insights into the forces that shaped Mexican culture." —author Dr. Michael Hogan

If Walls Could Talk: Chapala's historic buildings and their former occupants (2020)
"Tony Burton's thoroughly researched and utterly fascinating book takes us through the surprising and richly textured history of Chapala's past from the mid-eighteen hundreds onwards.... a wonderful historical gift to the people of the village." —Rita Pomade, *MexConnect.*

Lake Chapala: A Postcard History (2022)
A visual history of Lake Chapala, enthrallingly told via vintage postcards. Marvel at the diversity of sights, cultural experiences, architecture and scenery that so entranced early tourists—from rattling stagecoaches, religious festivals and old haciendas to railroad stations, quaint fishing boats, grand hotels and fine villas.

Made in the USA
Middletown, DE
28 November 2022

16224306R00210